The American Conception of Neutrality After 1941

The American Conception of Neutrality After 1941

Updated and Revised Edition

Jürg Martin Gabriel
Swiss Federal Institute of Technology
Zurich

Published by
PALGRAVE MACMILLAN
Houndmills, Basingstoke, Hampshire RG21 6XS and
175 Fifth Avenue, New York, N.Y. 10010
Companies and representatives throughout the world.

PALGRAVE MACMILLAN is the global academic imprint of the Palgrave
Macmillan division of St Martin's Press, LLC and of Palgrave Macmillan Ltd.
Macmillan® is a registered trademark in the United States, United Kingdom
and other countries. Palgrave is a registered trademark in the European
Union and other countries. 1 0 0 35 0 1 8 7 7

First edition 1988
Updated and Revised edition 2002

ISBN 0–333–76256–8 hardcover

This book is printed on paper suitable for recycling and
made from fully managed and sustained forest sources.

A catalogue record for this book is available
from the British Library.

Library of Congress Cataloging-in-Publication Data

Gabriel, Jürg Martin, 1940–
     The American conception of neutrality after 1941 / Jürg Martin Gabriel. –
Updated and rev. ed.
          p. cm.
Includes bibliographical references and index.
ISBN 0–333–76256–8
1. United States – Foreign relations – 1945–1989. 2. United States –
Foreign relations – 1933–1945. 3. Neutrality – History – 20th century.
4. World politics – 1945– I. Title.

E744.G23 2002
341.6′4′0973–dc21

                                                              2001058648

11 10 9 8 7 6 5 4 3 2
11 10 09 08 07 06 05 04 03 02

Printed and bound in Great Britain by
Antony Rowe Ltd, Chippenham and Eastbourne

To Orlando Dea Cadonau

Contents

Acknowledgements

The original version of this study was produced the old-fashioned way and my thanks, therefore, went to my secretary for the typing. Times have changed – no secretary was involved this time. My gratitude now goes to Thomas Fischer, my assistant, who scanned the old text, produced an electronic version, and helped with the search for documents and literature. I also want to thank my ETH colleague, Professor Andreas Wenger, and his assistant, Christof Münger, for critically reviewing the new chapter on Southeast Asia. Finally, it was Ellen Russon who did a superb job proofreading the manuscript and improving on my English.

List of Abbreviations

ACC	Allied Control Council
AJIL	American Journal of International Law
ASIL	American Society of International Law
CFM	Council of Foreign Ministers
Chincom	China Coordinating Committee
CIA	Central Intelligence Agency
CINCEUR	Commander in Chief, Europe
CINCFE	Commander in Chief, Far East
CMEA	Council of Mutual Economic Assistance
Cocom	Coordinating Committee
DOD	Department of Defense
DoSt	Department of State
DSB	Department of State Bulletin
ECA	Economic Cooperation Administration
EDC	European Defense Community
EEC	European Economic Community
ERP	European Recovery Programme
EU	European Union
FEA	Foreign Economic Administration
FRUS	Foreign Relations of the United States
GA	General Assembly
ICC	International Control Commission
ICRC	International Committee of the Red Cross
JCS	Joint Chiefs of Staff
MAAG	US Military Assistance Advisory Group
MAC	Military Armistice Commission
NARS	National Archives
NATO	North Atlantic Treaty Organisation
NLF	National Liberation Front
NNRC	Neutral Nations Repatriation Commission
NNSC	Neutral Nations Supervisory Commission
NSC	National Security Council
NVN	North Vietnam
OEEC	Organisation for European Economic Cooperation
OSD	Office of the Secretary of Defense

POW	Prisoner of War
PPS	Policy Planning Staff
SEATO	South East Asia Treaty Organisation
UfP	Uniting for Peace Resolution
UNC	United Nations Command
UNRRA	United Nations Relief and Rehabilitation Administration
UNCIO	United Nations Conference on International Organisation
WEU	Western European Union

Introduction

There are two reasons justifying a second edition of this study. Since 1988, when the book was originally published, new documents have become available on a number of neutrality-related topics, most importantly on Southeast Asia and the Vietnam War. This in itself would have been grounds enough for updating the original study. A second reason was the termination of the Cold War and the unification of Germany, two events that had a strong impact on neutrality. Both contributed to the continuing decline of neutrality, thereby confirming the central thesis of this book.

The United States was deeply involved in both the rise and the demise of neutrality. The country contributed in a major way to the formulation of classical neutrality in the eighteenth and nineteenth centuries, but it was equally active in weakening neutrality in the twentieth century. A first turning point was the year 1917. The United States entered the First World War, began to violate many of the neutral laws and principles it had stood for previously, and introduced the idea of collective security, a concept at odds with neutrality. A second turning point occured in 1941: on the one hand America participated in a war that was truly total in character and further undermined neutrality; on the other hand the United States was instrumental in setting up the United Nations. By outlawing war altogether the organisation challenged the very foundation of neutrality. The Cold War did not alter the pattern. As a superpower America pursued policies that – by and large – promoted neutrality's gradual decline.

The American conception of neutrality was not uniformly negative, however. In general the United States was ready to respect military neutrality when it suited its security interests but rejected a neutral's right to free trade. Economic warfare had become a major pillar of

American foreign policy, and its practice clashed head-on with traditional neutral rights. There were geopolitical nuances as well. Once the situation in Europe had stabilised and the Cold War front had been drawn, the United States accepted – at times only grudgingly – the neutrality of those European countries that were politically stable and democratic. The situation in Southeast Asia was different, however. Here both domestic and international politics were in constant flux, if not in turmoil. From an American perspective neutralisation meant the abandonment of a country to the communist side. Neutrality, therefore, was not a viable policy in that part of the world.

Although the documents newly available emphasise the continuity of American foreign policy, they reveal a number of interesting insights. Most striking is the role neutrality played during the *Vietnam War*. It was an issue relating to all three countries directly involved, to Cambodia, Laos, and Vietnam. As the papers published by the US Department of State show, neutrality was one of the more important topics the American government had to deal with during that war.[1] Over a ten-year period, three American administrations were confronted with a number of awkward and difficult situations. Chapter 11 is devoted exclusively to the Vietnam era and constitutes a new addition to the book.

There are also new documents relating to the dispute between the United States and Switzerland about the question of the restitution of *Jewish assets*. The issue surfaced at the end of the Cold War, but it has its origins in Swiss–American relations during and after the Second World War. To shed light on the situation then prevailing, both governments commissioned historical studies.[2] The documents confirm what had been known for a long time but the general public and governments had chosen to forget and to ignore: at the end of the Second World War, Swiss–American relations were at an all-time low, and most of the problems involved related to economics and neutrality. In 1946 the questions of monetary gold, of German and Jewish assets, were at the heart of the dispute. At a conceptual level it was a clash between two highly incompatible conceptions of neutrality and of world politics.[3]

The *Austrian State Treaty* of 1955 was examined in the first edition of this book. Unfortunately, the documents then in print only covered the period up to 1954. The 1955 documents became available later and are now included here.[4] They confirm what could be anticipated: Secretary of State John Foster Dulles, however reluctantly, approved of Austrian neutrality, while vehemently opposing German neutralisation. Interestingly enough, the issue of German neutrality surfaced again at the end of the Cold War during the negotiations on German unification. Unfortunately, the US documents covering the events between early November 1989 and the middle of 1990 have not yet been released, but German papers are available in print.[5] This was an additional reason for republishing this book because, as I will show in this introduction, that information rounds off the story told in Chapter 9.

The present study covers the period from 1941 to 1970, a time when the United States confronted a number of important neutrality-related issues. In the two decades up until the end of the Cold War, neutrality was less of an issue. The topic surfaced in only three areas: the European Conference on Security and Cooperation (ECSC), the conflict between the Sandinistas and the Contra in Central America, and the tightening of Cocom sanctions as part of renewed Cold War tensions after 1979. The ECSC then embraced the members of the two alliance systems, the North Atlantic Treaty Organizaion (NATO) and the Warsaw Pact, but it also included a number of neutral and non-aligned states, the so-called N+N group. At times the neutral and non-aligned states tried to mediate between the two blocs, and retrospectively it would be interesting to learn the American evaluation of their efforts.

During the Reagan years the United States actively supported the Contra in Central America. Because the Contra tried to operate from Costa Rican soil, that country announced a policy of neutrality. It was a move that found much support within Costa Rica but met with disapproval in Washington.[6] As part of the renewed East–West tensions, the Reagan Administration also tightened its economic sanctions against the Soviet Union, thereby creating a situation not dissimilar to that prevailing during the Korean War. In both instances the European neutrals came under pressure to conform to Cocom rules and to limit their trade with the East.[7] For anyone interested in the American conception of neutrality, these are important issues that merit closer scrutiny. The documents are not yet accessible, however, and will have to be studied at a later date.

Now that the Cold War is over, neutrality is hardly an issue in international politics. The general decline of the policy is plainly visible. It began with the outbreak of the First World War and continued thereafter. There may be isolated instances of neutrality in the future, but as far as Europe is concerned, neutrality is fading fast. It was intimately tied to classical European balance of power politics. However, with the advent of European integration, the consolidation of the European

Union after the unification of Germany, and the initiation of a common European security policy during the wars in former Yugoslavia, neutrality is becoming progressively irrelevant.[8]

The diplomacy surrounding *German unification* was a clear indication of this trend. The German documents now available show that while neutrality was mentioned at times, it remained a marginal issue at best. As a German historian recently commented, it was a strictly minor matter.[9] The idea of a united Germany outside of NATO found no support within Germany and was never seriously debated by the powers concerned. Even the Russians, who on some occasions broached the idea, did not want to see a reunited, armed, and neutralised Germany. As early as June 1989, when the Berlin Wall still stood but the changes in Poland and the German Democratic Republic became manifest, Gorbachev was of the opinion that a neutralised Germany would destabilise Europe and was not in the Russian interest.[10] There is some evidence that Foreign Minister Edward Shevardnaze at time lobbied for the idea and that he had the support of East Germany's Prime Minister Hans Modrow.[11] But the issue of Germany's continued NATO membership was settled definitely between George Bush and Mikhail Gorbachev at their summit in Washington D.C. on 31 May 1990.[12] During the course of the formal Two-plus-Four negotiations that lasted until September, neutrality may have been mentioned, but it was not a realistic option.

The *American position* was clear throughout: the Bush Administration opposed German neutralisation, as had Truman in 1952 and Dulles in 1954. George Bush and James Baker knew that their stance was firmly supported by Chancellor Kohl and his foreign minister, Hans-Dietrich Genscher, which allowed them to declare officially that the question of alliances was a matter for the reunited Germans to decide themselves. This most comfortable situation, especially after the Washington summit, was not put into question by any of the parties. On the part of the United States, it meant a continued commitment to Western Europe and to multilateral security. There would be no return to unilateralism, no re-nationalisation of security, and no resurgence of balance of power politics. The fundamental policy decisions inherent in the Atlantic Charter, the Truman Doctrine, and the North Atlantic Treaty were not reversed.

The US position was spelled out clearly before and after the fall of the Berlin Wall. It was presented at the February 1990 conference in Ottawa where the NATO countries met with the members of the Warsaw Pact and decided upon the Two-plus-Four formula.[13] The US position was expressed again the same month when George Bush met Helmut Kohl at Camp David.[14] And, as already mentioned, it was presented to Mikhail Gorbachev during the Washington summit in the summer. The *German stance* was equally firm. There is a great number of internal memoranda showing that despite some arguments over tactics between the Federal Chancery and the German Foreign Office, there was no disagreement on basics.[15] German policy was regularly co-ordinated with the White House; a number of telephone calls and notes were exchanged between Helmut Kohl, George Bush, and James Baker.[16] Kohl spoke frankly with Mikhail Gorbachev when he was in Moscow in February 1990,[17] but for him and Genscher it was the July summit in Moscow and the Northern Caucus that proved to be decisive. On this occasion Gorbachev repeated the wording he had agreed upon with George Bush: a reunited and sovereign Germany was free to decide on its alliance policy.

Although Washington never opposed German unification, there was some hesitation in Paris and London. While François Mitterrand quickly changed his mind, Margaret Thatcher never liked the idea. Mitterrand's reluctance was overcome when Kohl and Genscher promised to tie German unity to a further step towards European integration.[18] It is interesting to note, however, that neither the French nor the British or the Russians liked the idea of a neutralised Germany.[19]

The United States and neutrality

Let me now introduce the general thrust of this study. Neutrality has played an important role in American history. It was the policy recommended by George Washington in his Farewell Address, and it was the course most regularly pursued towards Europe between 1793 and 1941. Through this long period of time, the United States also contributed materially to the development of the international law of neutrality and the Hague Conventions of 1907, in which many of these laws were codified. Small wonder that much has been written about America and neutrality.[20] In particular, the specifically American conception of neutrality has received much attention.[21]

The same cannot be said about the period after 1941. There is no study of the American conception of neutrality covering the years of the Second World War or the Cold War.[22] Scholars seem to have lost interest in knowing what the United States thought about neutrality. Perhaps they have had good reasons for doing so, since, after Pearl

Harbor, America has itself no longer practised neutrality, and many people have been happy to forget a matter that divided the nation severely between 1914 and 1941.

Still, neutrality has remained an issue since 1941, and the United States has had to deal with it regularly. During the Second World War, economic and military warfare had to take into account the existence of a handful of neutrals, and in drafting the United Nations Charter, the State Department had to take a stand on neutrality. During the Cold War, America had to decide who was friend, foe, or neutral, and this decision influenced NATO membership. The Korean War began as an exercise in collective security, therefore excluding the idea of neutrality, but it ended as an exercise in conventional diplomacy, very much embracing the idea of neutrality. John Foster Dulles had to come to terms with Russian proposals for the neutralisation of Germany and Austria, John F. Kennedy, Lyndon B. Johnson, and Richard M. Nixon dealt with neutrality in the context of Southeast Asia, and – at the end of the Cold War – George Bush once again faced the question of German neutralisation. In these and in many other instances, the United States confronted the issue of neutrality.

There are other reasons why it is important to know what America has thought of neutrality. The success of neutrality has at all times depended on the attitude of the great powers. If they respect it, neutrality can be a constructive factor in world politics; if the major powers do not respect it, however, then the policy is in trouble. America was one of the leading powers in the twentieth century, and today it is the only remaining superpower. For the small countries practising neutrality it is important to know the United States' position. Neutrality may be a very marginal theme in American foreign policy, but it can still be a major issue for a number of other countries. [23]

The original version of this study covered the period between 1941 and 1955. This second and expanded version considers the American stance on neutrality up to 1970. There were several reasons why the first study chose the mid 1950s as a point of termination. To begin with, the State Department documents then available ended roughly with the year 1954. [24] To go further beyond that point was inadvisable, because secondary sources alone are not a sufficient basis on which to establish clearly the American conception of neutrality.

Furthermore, several events made the years 1955/56 a natural cut-off point. In 1955, Austria was neutralised, and the United States made a constructive contribution towards the definition of Austrian neutrality. Unfortunately, one year later, Eisenhower and Dulles made a number of public statements that left some doubt as to what the American conception of neutrality really was. The two occurrences taken together reveal much about the American attitude. However, the years 1955 and 1956 also saw the US Army and the Navy restate their views on neutrality. The US Army released a new field manual on the law of war and neutrality, and the US Naval War College even published a major scholarly investigation on the subject. The two publications had been stimulated by the Korean War, in which it became clear that the traditional law of war and neutrality could have some importance despite the existence of the modern law of the United Nations.[25]

By 1955–56, therefore, the post-1941 conception of neutrality had emerged. As will be shown, this was not a clear and coherent conception comparable to that prevailing in the eighteenth and nineteenth centuries. Too much had happened in the meantime. Wilson had departed from traditional neutrality in the early years of the First World War and later on sponsored the founding of the League of Nations, an organisation that did not tolerate the practice of classical neutrality. As a result, the United States never returned to its traditional conception of neutrality. Three competing views prevailed in the interwar period. Given this background, it could hardly be expected that a clear or even traditional conception would prevail in the Second World War or thereafter.

To this must be added the fact that, beginning with the First World War, there was a general decline in the observance and practice of the international law of war and neutrality. Modern warfare provided all kinds of reasons and excuses for the violation of well-established rules. In addition, the 'just war' doctrine re-emerged, and with it the legal definition of war and peace became ambiguous. The United Nations Charter did its share to promote this tendency, and during the Cold War, as well, the dividing line between war and peace became blurred.

An analysis of contemporary neutrality cannot, therefore, be a purely legal matter. In earlier days, neutrality was indeed primarily a legal phenomenon, but in this century it has become increasingly important to see it also as a political matter. Legal considerations still do play a role but, by and large, they have become secondary in importance, particularly from an American point of view. This investigation will consequently refer to legal questions whenever necessary and useful, but it is not intended to be a juridical treatise.

Nor is this a truly historical account. To be sure, the subject is treated chronologically, in the sense that I trace the development of the American conception of neutrality after 1941, but this in itself does not make for a fully-fledged historical study. Documentary evidence serves the purpose of tracing a conception and not of writing a step-by-step analysis of America's relations with neutral countries. This is not a history of American policy towards Sweden, Switzerland, Austria or any other neutral. Such investigations would have to be of an entirely different nature.

Documents must be used carefully, of course. They should not be employed merely as a means of justifying preconceived opinions. At the same time, the bulk of available evidence must be handled selectively, which introduces the risk of excessive selectivity. This problem arises, however, with the sifting of all data in the natural and the social sciences. The best protection against it is to select the evidence conscientiously and not to suppress untidy or unpleasant facts. This the author has tried to do.

The essence of this study is, therefore, neither legal nor historical – it is political. Raymond Aron has formulated a useful definition of international politics:

> Inter-state relations present one original feature which distinguishes them from other social relations: they take place within the shadow of war, or, to use a more rigorous expression, relations among states involve, in essence, the alternatives of war and peace.[26]

Neutrality is intimately related to the alternatives of war and peace. Without war there is no need for neutrality, since, in a state of total peace and harmony, there is no opportunity for anyone to play the role of indifferent bystander. The reverse, however, is also true. In a situation of total war, entailing complete polarisation and the involvement of all countries, there can be no third parties. Neutrality, for its very existence, presupposes 'the shadow of war'.

Actually, the existence of neutrality presupposes a very particular type of peace and of war. This is demonstrated by history. During the centuries of religious conflict in Europe, peace was precarious and war pervasive. Under these circumstances, neutrality could hardly develop. Later on, war became less generalised and was organised by only a few sovereigns. Limitations were placed on the actual conduct of hostilities, and in this climate neutrality could develop. In the twentieth century this changed. Nations began once more to fight total wars and to develop philosophies to match them. As a result, neutrality suffered. Of course, neutrality also suffers when nations integrate and establish permanent peace, as happened in Western Europe after the Second World War.

The United States, perhaps more than any other power, was dramatically involved in this transition. America developed its neutrality when wars were limited in character. Then, when war became total again, America made the transition from a small to a great power. This changeover was bound to be affected by its conception of neutrality. To be sure, the United States also contributed to the stability of the North Atlantic area and the integration of Europe. The purpose of this study is to trace these developments after 1941.

The book is divided into twelve chapters, the first of which summarises the American conception of neutrality before 1941. The subsequent nine chapters each deal with an event in United States foreign policy after 1941 when neutrality became an issue. The first part of each of these chapters investigates the circumstances under which neutrality became an issue and analyses the American reaction. In the last part of each chapter an effort is made to summarise and to draw conclusions. Chapter 10 deals with the legal questions as they arose from the Korean War. The results of all these reflections are summed up in Chapter 12.

Basic terms

The language used in this study is a blend of classical legal and modern political terminology. The classical legal terms are those used by international jurists in their handbooks and commentaries on the law of war and neutrality; the modern political terms are those suggested in recent years by political scientists dealing with neutrality. These terms are not too difficult to understand, but they can still create problems for the uninitiated. Neutrality, after all, is a rather remote subject for most scholars. It is advisable, therefore, to enumerate and define clearly some of the most important terms at the outset.

The review will have to be brief and general, and it may not satisfy the specialist. But it will lay the foundation for a more comprehensive treatment of the same questions later on and also pave the way for dealing with a multitude of historical, economic, political, and legal specifics that unavoidably combine to make up the story of America and its conception of neutrality.

One of the most important features of neutrality is the idea of *abstention*, of *distance* from conflict between two or more belligerents or, as the Swiss used to say, 'sitting still'. Daniel Frei, in a theoretical analysis of neutrality, speaks of *indifference* when referring to abstention and distance, and he distinguishes two kinds: spatial (*räumliche*) and substantive (*sachliche*) indifference. The former refers mainly to geography, the latter to the substance of the quarrel or the issues involved.[27] Examples of both exist in American and European history.

Indifference played a central role in early American foreign policy. The United States wanted to profit from the great physical distance that separated it from Europe, and it exhibited a marked disinterest in European quarrels. For too long the colonists had been too closely tied to the European powers and their wars. They developed the conviction that these were none of their business, that they had a right not to care, a right to be indifferent.

It came less naturally to the Swiss, who, as mercenaries for the European powers during the late Middle Ages, made a lucrative business of going to war. They only reluctantly distanced themselves from wars when internal dissent over some of the negative side-effects threatened to split the Confederation. Furthermore, unlike the Americans, the Swiss never had a great physical distance between themselves and their neighbours. On the contrary, their mountain passes linking north and south formed a natural focus of European geography and tended to funnel problems into the country. The Swiss, therefore, had to learn to practise great mental indifference and to put an especially great *political* distance between themselves and their neighbours.

Another important feature of neutrality is the *intermediate position* (*Zwischenstellung*) that a neutral occupies between two belligerents.[28] This position can be either *symmetrical* or *asymmetrical*. A symmetrical intermediate position exists when military, economic, diplomatic, or legal relations to the two belligerents are the same; an asymmetrical situation exists when the neutral tends more to one side or the other. In terms of sheer military *power*, Frei distinguishes a number of possible intermediate positions, ranging from neutral impotence (*Ohnmacht*) to neutral preponderance (*Vormacht*). The first can entail division and absorption of a neutral, the other can make it an arbitrator of international affairs. The typical neutral tries to steer a middle course between the two extremes, such that its own military power is great enough to deter a potential aggressor but not important enough to play an excessively ambitious role. This shortens the distance between itself and the belligerents thereby reducing the threat of involvement.

In the eighteenth and nineteenth centuries, when the United States was regularly neutral, it did not have any military power to speak of. The danger of absorption would have been great were it not for the

British Navy, which, except in 1812, put a protective shield between Europe and America. When America did acquire power, however, it was tempted to drift to the other end of the neutral power spectrum and to practise the role of an arbitrator. Wilson did so when he offered to act as an 'armed mediator' in Europe in 1916. At that moment, America came close to sacrificing its distance and indifference.

Tied to the idea of symmetry and asymmetry is that of *impartiality* and *partiality*. This differentiation does not relate to power alone but to the general treatment a neutral affords the two warring parties. In 1793, when war broke out between England and France, George Washington counselled Americans to treat the two sides impartially, and Congress passed legislation to enforce this posture. Impartiality became a central component of the original American conception of neutrality and, later on, of international neutrality law in general.

As wars became more total, however, impartiality became increasingly difficult to practise, particularly for a strong neutral power like the United States, whose position in the First World War meant the difference between victory and defeat. Wilson was tempted to give up impartiality, and whether or not he did so was an important question in the debate over the Neutrality Legislation of the interwar period. What is beyond dispute is that Wilson gave up indifference when he acted as an 'armed mediator' in 1916.

The relation between indifference and impartiality is an intricate one. A state can, for instance, be impartial *and* indifferent when it abstains from supplying either belligerent party with troops. The same state would still be impartial but *no longer* indifferent if it supplied both sides with troops, as the Swiss did at times. And the state would be *neither* impartial *nor* indifferent if it supplied one side with troops to the detriment of the other, as Franco did, for instance, in the Second World War.[29]

Indifference, power, and impartiality are instrumental; they are useful means to achieve certain ends. But what are these ends? According to Frei, these can be found in the national *identity* of a country or, perhaps more usefully, in its *values*.[30] When Franco practised neutrality his aim was to preserve Spanish fascism; when the nineteenth-century Tsars declared themselves neutral they wanted to defend their semi-feudal form of authoritarianism; Switzerland and Sweden are neutral in order to protect their respective conceptions of justice and democracy.

The Americans, too, pursued a definite set of values when they declared themselves neutral in the early days. As will be shown in more detail, these values related strongly to certain freedoms, mainly to the freedom of trade and to the freedom of the seas. Unfortunately, these very freedoms often clashed head-on with the ideas of impartiality or indifference. The interrelation among values, indifference, and power is thus a complex one that will have to be looked at closely in this investigation. It will be especially interesting to trace developments during the crucial years immediately before and after 1941.

Other basic terms are *occasional neutrality* and *permanent neutrality*. A nation is occasionally neutral when it declares neutrality in a particular war and only for the duration of that war. A nation is permanently neutral, however, when it commits itself to remain neutral in all future wars.[31] America, in the past, practised occasional neutrality. George Washington declared neutrality for the first time in 1793 and only for the duration of that war. Wilson did so in 1914, and Roosevelt again in 1939. Since the Second World War, states have become very reluctant to declare occasional neutrality.

Permanent neutrality is still alive but also suffering. As the term implies, this type of neutrality is not limited to a single conflict but has continuous validity. It is, therefore, also called 'perpetual' or 'everlasting'. Such neutrality implies that a state will never start a war and never enter into one unless it itself is attacked. Formally at least, Switzerland, Sweden, Austria, and Finland still adhere to this kind of neutrality.

Neutrality has a legal and a political dimension. *Neutral law* is a body of rights and duties codified, to a considerable extent, in the Hague Conventions of 1907.[32] The United States, as will be shown, contributed materially to the shaping of neutral law and the drafting of the Hague Conventions. *Neutral politics*,[33] on the other hand, has no foundation in law. It comprises all measures intended to strengthen and protect the law of neutrality. For an occasional neutral country, this embraces actions to prevent being drawn into a particular ongoing conflict. For a permanent neutral power, the implications are broader: it should do nothing to undermine the practicability and, equally important, the credibility of its neutrality in a future war. A permanent neutral, therefore, should not enter into peacetime alliances or permit the establishment of foreign military bases on its soil. This is why most permanent neutrals rely on their own armed strength, why they practice *armed neutrality*. If permanent neutrality and neutral politics imply a policy of peace, they should not be mistaken for appeasement. Most permanent neutrals are not disarmed. They impose upon themselves the duty of defending their neutral rights.[34]

America has never practised permanent neutrality; it believed in extensive freedom of action, including, if necessary, the freedom to go to war. Isolationism did not mean permanent neutrality, since it meant non-participation in certain types of conflicts only – those of the European powers.[35] It did not imply permanent non-involvement in other regions, for example in the Western hemisphere or the Pacific. Also, isolationism is a much broader term than neutrality. Neutrality was but one aspect of American isolation, although a fairly important one.

Some Americans believed in *armed neutrality*. It is well known that George Washington, in his Farewell Address, called upon Americans to avoid getting involved in European wars. It is often forgotten that he also looked forward to the day when America would be militarily powerful enough to defend its neutrality.

The record of American armed neutrality is a mixed one, however. A few years after George Washington delivered his address, America fought rather successfully an undeclared war against France in order, among other things, to defend its conception of neutrality. When it tried the same strategy a dozen years later against Great Britain, the results were very different. The disastrous military campaigns of the War of 1812 did not amount in any way to a policy of credible armed neutrality. In the First World War, on the other hand, when the country did have the military potential to back up its foreign policy, it chose to use it not for the defence of neutrality but for the establishment of a new international order that would have abolished neutrality once and for all.

Neutralisation is another important term. It refers to the way in which permanent neutrality comes about. It can be voluntary or involuntary, and it can be based on international agreement or simple unilateral declaration and practice. There are also cases where permanent neutrality has been guaranteed by other states. Belgian neutrality, for example, was involuntary in the sense that the European powers in 1831 imposed it upon the country. Swiss neutrality was voluntarily agreed upon by all parties at the end of the Napoleonic wars. Sweden declared its neutrality unilaterally, whereas the neutrality of Austria is based both on unilateral declaration and international recognition. In contrast to Switzerland, Austrian neutrality is not internationally guaranteed.[36]

Two other important terms are *integral* and *qualified neutrality*.[37] Integral neutrality refers to a wide range of neutral rights and duties in military and economic matters and embraces most importantly extensive freedom of private trade with all belligerents. This latter right is implied in the Hague Conventions of 1907, and the United States was one of its most fervent proponents. This very comprehensive conception of neutrality became known, at least in the United States, as *traditionalist neutrality*. In the interwar period, it was severely criticised by the neo-isolationists, who favoured a more restricted view of neutrality, one that did not permit neutral merchants to trade freely. This was a *qualified* notion of neutrality, and it became popular because business 'interests' were widely seen as having drawn the United States into the First World War.

Given the relatively isolated geographic location of the United States 'beyond the oceans', the economic aspects of neutrality were more important to Americans than the military ones. As a typical *sea neutral,* the United States, at least in the eighteenth and nineteenth centuries, was more worried about its merchant ships than about its own security – this is in contrast to a *land neutral* such as Switzerland. Threatened on all sides by potential enemies, the Swiss placed more importance on the military aspects of neutrality. From 1776 on, therefore, the American preoccupation with neutrality revolved mainly around neutral trading rights. Commercial questions formed a constant bone of contention between the then small country, often neutral and eager to trade, and the large powers of the day, often at war and worried lest neutral trade help their enemies.

The development of integral neutrality at sea, therefore, was characterised by the constant struggle between the small powers (including Holland, Denmark, and the Hanseatic towns) interested in wide commercial rights in times of war and the large powers (chiefly Britain) interested in restricting these rights. As this study will show, the modern American conception of neutrality that developed after 1941 still reflects this preoccupation with neutral trading rights. However, the United States has changed its position: it now argues in favour of restricting those rights, while the small neutrals like Sweden and Switzerland argue in favour of stretching them. Nowadays it is the United States that takes the British stand and pursues a qualified conception of neutrality.

Throughout modern history, qualified neutrality has been very common. As a result, it manifests itself in many forms. *Involuntary* qualified neutrality is practised under military pressure in times of war. In the eighteenth and nineteenth centuries, the United States regularly had to put up with British restrictions on neutral trade, and in two World Wars the European neutrals, too, had to live with many restrictions on their trading rights.

There are several kinds of *voluntary* qualified neutrality. In order to avoid military entanglement, a neutral may decide unilaterally to restrict its commerce or even to cease trading altogether. The latter is usually referred to as a *neutral embargo*. George Washington briefly considered an embargo in 1794 but decided against it. Thomas Jefferson put a fully-fledged embargo into force, although with mixed results. Many neutralists favoured an embargo in the First World War, and the Neutrality Acts of 1935, 1936, and 1937 also represented embargo legislation. The advocates of this interwar legislation were called *neo-isolationist* neutrals.

Neutral embargoes can also be justified as a *sanctioning instrument* against actual or potential aggressors in the name of a just cause. As a member of the League of Nations, Switzerland was willing to qualify its neutrality (to give up some trading rights) and to participate in the League's economic sanctions if necessary. It chose to call this *differential neutrality*.[38] During these years many influential Americans called for the same type of neutrality. They wanted the country, although not a member of the League, to co-operate indirectly in the implementation of sanctions. The United States actually did so during the Ethiopian War. Proponents of this policy were called *internationalist neutrals*.

Much will have to be said about qualified neutrality, voluntary and involuntary. In the post-1941 American conception of neutrality, the idea of a neutral embargo plays an important role. Seeing the Second World War and also the Cold War as a just cause, Americans put pressure on the European neutrals in order to gain economic co-operation in the struggle against fascism and communism.

In *benevolent neutrality,* as the term implies, the neutral looks with favour upon the cause of one belligerent and does all it can to help short of entering the war. In contrast to qualified neutrality, benevolence includes the provision of military support. Franco practised this when he sent a brigade to help Hitler in the war against Stalin, and the United States did the same when, in 1940, it supplied the British with destroyers. Since actions of this sort border closely on belligerence, benevolent neutrality is often also referred to as *non-belligerence*.[39]

In legal history, benevolent neutrality was justified by Grotius, the famous Dutch legal scholar of the early modern period. Grotius maintained that there were two types of wars – those that could be morally justified and those that could not. In the case where moral judgement was impossible, where the cause was neither just nor unjust but obscure, third states should not take sides and should remain truly impartial. In the case where a good or evil cause could be determined, sides should be taken in the sense that a neutral should do nothing to further the cause of the party in the wrong and nothing to hinder the cause of the party in the right. A neutral's attitude towards the 'good' belligerent is thus benevolent, while his attitude towards the 'evil' belligerent is malevolent.

In the early days, the United States adhered closely to Grotius' philosophy of indifferent war and therefore stressed the need for strict impartiality. In the course of the First World War, however, this belief was shaken. Seeing the results of total warfare (especially of unrestricted submarine warfare), many Americans began to perceive the European struggle as an issue between good and evil. They turned increasingly from being impartial to become partial neutrals and finally joined the struggle on the side of the just cause.

Finally, there is *neutralism*.[40] The term is of recent origin, having emerged in the context of decolonisation and the Cold War. Many newly independent states refused to align themselves with one or the other of the two contending superpowers. The term is, consequently, not legal in nature, is not based on any neutral rights and duties, and has no relation to either integral or qualified neutrality. Nor is it related to permanent neutrality, since neutralist states have gone to war when it served their national interest (India, Egypt, Ethiopia, Libya, Vietnam, and so on). At heart, then, neutralism is non-alignment or, as it is termed in German, *Blockfreiheit*.

As mentioned earlier, in the era of isolationism the United States also practised something like neutralism when it tried to avoid 'foreign entanglements' with the dominant European powers. This non-alignment was combined with the active espousal of integral neutrality, something the neutralists of the later twentieth century failed to do.

Neutralism emerged in the course of the Korean War, when India tried to mediate actively between the United States, on the one hand, and the Russians and Chinese, on the other. From the very beginning, the United States had difficulty coping with the concept, and particularly during the Eisenhower Administration some high officials confused it with neutrality, thereby creating considerable international embarrassment.

1
Neutrality Before 1941

Three competing conceptions

When the United States entered the war in 1941, it did not possess one single, coherent conception of neutrality. Too much had changed since the outbreak of the First World War, when America had expected to practise integral neutrality but discovered that this had become difficult. Between 1914 and 1917, there was a furious debate over the meaning and practice of neutrality, a dispute that revealed that there was no longer any consensus on neutrality. The withdrawal into neo-isolation after the First World War did nothing to settle the question. On the contrary, as Congress and the nation began to define the new neutrality in the mid 1930s, the divisions were as deep as ever. The debates over the Neutrality Acts of 1935, 1936, and 1937 showed how unsure America had become about its role in the world. This was plainly a time of transition, and the country did not yet know which way to go.

In the course of the Congressional debates, three types of neutrals emerged: the *traditionalist neutrals,* rooted in over a century and a half of American history and emphasising extensive trading rights in times of war; the *neo-isolationist neutrals,* aiming at a reduction of these rights (and favouring an embargo) to prevent another First World War experience; and the *internationalist neutrals,* who also favoured an embargo but with the intention of using it as a sanctioning instrument against aggressors.[1]

Initially, the neo-isolationists triumphed. The three Neutrality Acts were largely the product of those political forces in the country that wanted to isolate the United States radically from international affairs, even at the cost of lost trade. Supporting this movement were important senators and representatives from all parts of the country. The neo-isolationist victory was short-lived, however. After the outbreak of war in

17

Europe, and particularly after the fall of France, international events made total abstention difficult. Once more, the United States became the chief supplier to the European states fighting Germany and, consequently, abolished the Neutrality Acts. Roosevelt was only too happy to do so because, at heart, he had always been an internationalist neutral. He favoured the Neutrality Acts only in so far as they could be turned into instruments to 'quarantine' aggressors and thereby to (indirectly) support the League.

Since the Neutrality Acts were mainly shaped by the neo-isolationists, they could hardly be used as international sanctioning instruments. In the short run, therefore, the internationalist neutrals had a difficult stand. But time was on their side. Internationalism was to become the dominant force in American foreign policy from 1940 onwards and, as this study will show, it shaped the American conception of neutrality decisively after 1941.

The biggest losers were the traditionalist neutrals. They won neither in the short nor in the long run. In the twentieth century, theirs was a story of constant decline and frustration. They took a first beating in the First World War, when Wilson, in their view, failed to enforce neutral trading rights vis-à-vis the British and the Germans. They experienced a second setback when the Neutrality Legislation of the 1930s firmly abolished most neutral trading rights, and finally, they lost out once more when Roosevelt instituted Lend-Lease to use American economic power as a sanctioning instrument against Germany.

Beginning in 1940, Roosevelt began systematically to eliminate neo-isolationist politicians from positions of power. He engaged in a thorough campaign to eradicate isolationism from the American body politic. Neo-isolationist neutrality was thus wiped out consciously.[2] Not so traditionalist neutrality – after their many defeats, the traditionalists simply became unimportant and finally died out. When the United States emerged from the Second World War, there were no serious proponents of the old school of neutrality left. Not even scholars of international law showed much enthusiasm for integral neutrality. It was an indication of the general decline of neutrality and had direct consequences for the American neutrality conception that emerged after 1941. Before turning to that question, let us take a closer look at the three competing conceptions of neutrality.

Traditionalist neutrality

In the 1930s, the traditionalists were still an impressive group. They included many important senators and congress members who enjoyed strong support in the business community, particularly among export oriented business people along the Eastern seaboard; there were powerful 'interests' behind the idea of free wartime trade. The group also included eminent scholars. John Bassett Moore, Professor of International Law at Columbia University and the dean of international jurists, was perhaps the most prestigious figure among the traditionalist lawyers. Other well-known figures like Manley O. Hudson of Harvard and Edwin Borchard of Yale also belonged. It is fair to say that the overwhelming majority of established scholars in international law favoured the traditionalist position. Dissenters belonged mainly to the younger generation of lawyers.

The traditionalists had the full weight of history and of precedence in their favour. The Founding Fathers had established the policy of integral neutrality, which for over a century had served the country exceedingly well. To be sure, America did enter the First World War, but from the traditionalist point of view that was because Wilson was not neutral, as he favoured the British from the start, yielded too quickly to British violations of trading rights, and failed to defend integral neutrality. With truly impartial and armed neutrality, the traditionalists argued, America would have had a much better chance of staying out of the war.[3]

They could point to George Washington and his first declaration of neutrality in 1793. War had broken out between France and England, and the United States found itself in a very difficult position due to its treaty of alliance with France, signed during the War of Independence and honoured by the French in subsequent years. The most obvious policy for the United States would have been to live up to its treaty commitments, but this would have meant war with England, for which America was ill equipped. With a huge merchant fleet and practically no navy to protect it, war with the largest sea power was a foolhardy idea. Although some sections of the country supported war, opposition in New England was vehement. A decision to go to war could have split the newly founded republic. A declaration of war was consequently out of the question.

A more realistic option was to practise benevolent neutrality (nonbelligerence), which would have amounted to honouring the French alliance in an indirect manner by providing any means of assistance short of war. This is what the French had in mind. They sent a new consul to America, Citizen Genêt, who landed at Charleston and began to collect money, enlist troops, and commission ships in support of the French cause on his way up to Philadelphia. Genêt's drive for support provoked the hostility of the pro-British segment of the population, and by the time he met Washington his mission had become highly controversial. He got a cool reception and learned that America was about to embark on a policy of impartial, not benevolent, neutrality. The president proclaimed impartial neutrality on 22 April 1793.[4] To make the provision binding, Congress later passed the Neutrality Act of 1794.[5]

This act was innovative in a number of ways. It outlawed the outfitting of ships and troops on neutral soil, called for strict impartiality, made both of these neutral duties explicit, and wrote the provisions into domestic law. None of this was demanded by the prevailing notion of neutrality, since, in those days, it was still the Grotian rule that was usually followed, permitting states to be partial if they considered a war to be just.[6]

The Neutrality Act of 1794 was only the first of a long list of such acts. Three more were enacted during the French Revolutionary Wars,[7] and five were passed between the Civil War[8] and the outbreak of the First World War. Three more Neutrality Acts came about during the Great War and a number of others in the interwar period, including the Acts of 1935, 1936, and 1937.[9]

The early acts dealt mainly with military matters, but they also outlawed privateering for American citizens (Act of 1797) or the provision of coal for foreign ships of war (Act of 1898). All of them served the purpose of promoting *impartiality* and of increasing the *distance* between a neutral and the belligerents. It should come as no surprise that Americans were eager to put great distance between themselves and Europe. After all, this was what independence stood for. It meant terminating one-sided dependence and permanent alignment with one of the world's greatest powers, a power constantly at war. Americans had had enough of being a pawn on the European chessboard.[10]

Indifference combined neatly with impartiality in the American experience. It was important for the young nation not to care too much about European quarrels and especially not to worry about whose cause was just or unjust. Quincy Wright described this combination of indifference and impartiality many years later with the following words:

> We had little political interest in the results of European wars. We were far off and had no alliances. It meant nothing to us which side won, at least it meant nothing to the Government and though there might be pro-English and pro-French parties during the revolutionary period ... it was wise for the Government to be neutral so that hyphenization should not be encouraged.[11]

In the eighteenth and nineteenth centuries the United States made a constant effort to promote the idea of neutral duties, and it launched a number of initiatives to have nations write them into their domestic laws.[12] This was but one manifestation of traditionalist neutrality, however. A more important American preoccupation was with the promotion of *neutral rights*.

A first effort was undertaken in 1776, when the Continental Congress drafted a model plan for negotiating treaties of amity and commerce with foreign powers, a plan that was to guide American foreign policy for over a century. It became known as the 'Plan of 1776', and it contained, among other things, a number of ideas about neutrality, particularly *neutral trading rights*.[13] 'Free ships, free goods' was one of these ideas. It meant that a belligerent ship, when stopping and searching neutral vessels (called 'search and seizure'), could not confiscate (and take to prize courts) non-contraband goods destined for the port of an enemy. It was the ship that determined the nature of the cargo and not vice versa. A 'free' or neutral ship by definition carried 'free' or neutral goods. This was in contrast to the custom up to that time of emphasising ownership of goods and not of ships.[14]

Another provision of the 'Plan of 1776' claimed the neutral right to trade freely in non-contraband between the unblockaded ports of belligerents, even beyond peacetime levels. This could mean that a neutral could not only pick up the trade formerly carried on between the belligerents themselves, but in addition, trade between their overseas possessions and the mother country as well. In a war between France and England, for example, superior British naval power usually managed to blockade all trade between France and the French West Indies. The American trader was then allowed by France to do what was forbidden in peacetime – to take over the carrying trade between the colonies and the mother country. The British (and the prevailing international law) were not entirely opposed to neutral trade in war, but they favoured what is called 'courant normal', or an amount of business not exceeding peacetime levels. They incorporated this view in what became known as the 'Rule of 1756' – a ruling that greatly angered Americans before and after independence.[15]

A third provision called for short lists of contraband excluding foodstuffs and naval stores. As exporters of raw materials, it was in the American interest not to have these goods included as contraband. The large naval powers, however, had the opposite interest. They wanted contraband lists to be long and detailed in order to prevent the enemy from obtaining essential war materials. In later times, a distinction was introduced between 'absolute' and 'conditional' contraband.[16]

Shortly after the Peace of Paris (1783), the Americans drafted another model treaty called the 'Plan of 1784'.[17] It went further than the earlier one in that it called for the total abolition of all contraband, absolute immunity of private trade in war, abolition of privateering, and the outlawing of 'paper' blockades. Privateering was a menace to trade for obvious reasons, and the Americans, with a small navy and a huge merchant fleet, had a clear interest in prohibiting it.[18] Blockades too were harmful to American traders when carried on at 'long distance', that is, when checking United State's ships in the West Indies (and on 'paper') instead of at the blockaded port of destination. For the belligerent, of course, the exact opposite applied. Effective blockades demanded a great number of naval ships, while paper blockades required only a few.

In 1823, Secretary of State John Quincy Adams issued the so-called 'Project of 1823', which embraced both of the earlier plans but went well beyond them. Adams called for the total immunity of all private property in war and even declared 'search and seizure' a relict of a barbarous age. The plan included, in the words of a historian of the Department of State, 'possibly the most far-reaching propositions regarding commerce in war ever by a Secretary of State of the United States'.[19]

As this brief survey shows, the neutral trading rights claimed by America were extensive, far beyond what international law or custom at that time provided for. Obtaining these rights was a different matter, however. The French approved of them twice, once in the Alliance Treaty of 1778 and again in the Paris Agreements of 1800.[20] But the British resisted; neither the Jay Treaty of 1795[21] nor the Treaty of Ghent (1814) even mentioned neutral rights. For a long while Great Britain either ignored the whole matter, openly violated 'American' neutral rights, or even ruled against them.[22]

During these years, two conceptions of neutrality clashed with each other. The *integral American conception* emphasised extensive neutral rights and duties, while the *qualified British conception* denied the existence of broad commercial rights. Since the British had the power to enforce their conception, the Americans had to tolerate it, however grudgingly.[23] Not surprisingly, in those days it was said that the British had a 'big navy' and the Americans a 'small navy' conception of neutrality.[24] This reflected the fact that the United States had indeed failed to systematically maintain a strong national defence. The country remembered only part of George Washington's Farewell Address. He certainly emphasised that America should be committed primarily 'to extending our commercial relations' and to 'having as little political connection as possible.' But he also added the following:

> If we remain one people, under an efficient government, the period is not far off, when we may defy material injury from external annoyance; when we may take such an attitude as will cause the neutrality, we may at any time resolve upon, to be scrupulously respected; when belligerent nations, under the impossibility of making acquisitions upon us, will not lightly hazard the giving us provocation; *when we may choose peace or war*, as our interest, guided by justice, shall counsel. [Emphasis added][25]

This was a plea for integral neutrality, but also for *armed neutrality*. As the Hague Conventions stated over a century later, a neutral not only had the obligation to prevent belligerents from violating its territory or its ships, but it also had the right to do so with force, if necessary. Since the United States failed to maintain adequate military power, the traditionalist conception of neutrality lacked an important dimension; it emphasised *indifference* and *impartiality*, but it neglected *power*.[26]

The conception may have been weak in terms of power, but it was highly developed in terms of *values*. Free wartime trade to Americans meant free private trade carried on by independent companies. It was not mercantilist trade handled by para-governmental bodies, such as in England, France, or Spain. Not only was mercantilist trade considered inefficient in maximising benefits, as Adam Smith argued in those very years, but it was also political and war-oriented trade, because it constituted an instrument of colonial rule and imperial expansion.[27] Liberal trade, in contrast, meant greater wealth for all nations and *greater peace* among them. Underlying the philosophy of free neutral trade was thus a philosophy of peace.[28]

These convictions were grounded in a relatively optimistic vision of man and, correspondingly, a relatively critical view of the state. They were also tied to a belief that a free society could be built and that it would be based on the rule of law. These were fundamental *values*, and they formed part of the early *identity* of the country. They gave Americans a national purpose, and neutrality was meant to promote it. Neutrality was not an end in itself; it was a means to achieve a higher end.

Economic motives of self-interest were certainly part of this conception. To do business with belligerents in times of war and to engage in lucrative war profiteering were major goals of Southern planters and New England Yankee traders.[29] However, from an American point of view, these motives were in harmony with liberal goals and values; they were nothing but the concrete expression of an expanding and peaceful 'universal trading republic'.

If universalist values were part of the traditionalist conception of neutrality, it would be wrong to assume that these were matched with a universalist view of power. There was at that time hardly a conception of national power, let alone one of universal or imperial power. No American leader at that time propounded a universal organisation to match universal values, as Wilson did later on.

This is reflected in the traditionalist American attitude towards international law. Like any newly independent state, the country was extremely conscious and protective of its sovereignty. It would simply not have tolerated an international organ imposing any rule of law, however justifiable in terms of universalist values this might have been. 'Freedom of the seas', for instance, was to be achieved through the spread of interstate agreements on neutrality and not through any kind of supranational authority. As a result, traditional neutrality was in part contradictory: a nationalist (or particularist) conception of power contrasted with an internationalist (or universalist) conception of values. In the twentieth century, critics of traditionalism would often point to this weakness.

There was another contradiction. Extensive neutral trading rights may have been in harmony with universal liberal values, but they were at times in sharp conflict with the need for *indifference*. After all, integral neutrality meant economic involvement coupled with military abstention, and the two at times clashed sharply. For geopolitical reasons, this was especially true of a sea neutral such as the United States.

Contiguous frontiers often permit a *land neutral* to trade directly with both sides in a conflict or, when surrounded by one belligerent, to trade with one side only. The latter case may raise questions of partiality, but it does not entail the risk of military involvement, since there is no reason to fear attacks on neutral trucks or trains crossing common frontiers. Furthermore, the relative proximity of large hostile armies deters a land neutral from letting commercial considerations overly interfere with military ones. Security is a central preoccupation.

This was roughly the experience of Sweden and Switzerland in past wars.[30] It was never the experience of the United States. For the *sea neutral* there is constant opportunity and temptation on the high seas to move back and forth between the belligerents and to try to trade with all of them. There are no clear frontiers, and ships constitute highly vulnerable floating pieces of sovereignty likely to get into trouble at any time. The chances of being drawn into war through the exercise of trading rights are, therefore, much greater for the sea neutral than for the land neutral. In addition, it is more likely to neglect security concerns, because the oceans afford a good amount of 'natural' protection.[31]

As a result, Americans ran the constant risk of 'neutral entanglement', or getting involved in war by trading freely or, put differently, by undermining their neutrality while practising it. This danger existed in the French Revolutionary Wars and again during the First World War. Critics of the traditionalist school could, therefore, point to a basic contradiction inherent in integral neutrality: a policy meant to keep the country out of war regularly threatened to draw it into war.

Embargoes were suggested as a cure, as a means of de-emphasising neutral rights and of re-emphasising neutral duties. The results were not encouraging, however. As the Jeffersonian embargo of 1807 demonstrated, more economic distance between neutral and belligerents did not eliminate the difficulties, because the effects of not trading were very uneven. Britain was affected a great deal more than the continental powers with their self-imposed blockade. The American measure was consequently seen as a highly *impartial* step chiefly directed against the British. An embargo could also contribute towards sliding into war. America was damned if it did engage in trade and damned if it did not.[32]

This dilemma became particularly evident in the First World War. By trading extensively with both sides, American trade would inevitably have helped the Germans more than the British, but the result of not trading at all would have been the same. Since Wilson sympathised more with the British than the German cause, he avoided both options, that is, he neither enforced neutral trading rights nor did he initiate an embargo. He chose to send long notes to London protesting British trade restrictions, but in essence he gave up integral neutrality and conformed to the British conception of qualified neutrality. As a result, trade with the belligerents became totally one-sided. When America finally entered the conflict in 1917, critics of the administration argued that the country was now paying the 'wages of unneutrality':

the American people, in pointing an accusing finger at the submarine, were prone to overlook their own responsibility for what befell them. Their large-scale assistance to the Allies in munitions and other contraband, coupled with Washington's acquiescence in the British blockade, drove the Germans to desperate expedients that ultimately involved the United States. A more even-handed neutrality might have averted a clash.[33]

What upset the traditionalists even more, however, was the fact that when Wilson entered the war in 1917, he did so to transcend neutrality once and for all. His plans for collective security were meant to usher in a kind of international order that would make neutrality redundant. In other words, Wilson was willing to match universalist values with a universalist conception of power, thereby making the existence of bystanders in times of war impossible and even illegal. In traditionalist eyes Wilson initiated a veritable 'cult of unneutrality'.[34]

It was between 1914 and 1917, therefore, that America abandoned its long tradition of integral neutrality and entered an era of transition that was to last until 1941.[35] In this period no one conception of neutrality prevailed. To be sure, the *traditionalist* position was still the most prestigious, but the *neo-isolationist* (embargo) argument became very popular after the unhappy involvement in Europe and after the outbreak of the Great Depression.

Neo-isolationist neutrality

Neo-isolationism was a reaction to the Wilsonian policy of international involvement and to the confusion created between 1914 and 1917 over the exact meaning of traditional neutrality. Neo-isolationism, therefore, called for an abridgement of neutral trading rights, or a strict policy of embargo. Samuel Flagg Bemis, renowned diplomatic historian and ardent neo-isolationist, saw it as a withdrawal to what he called the 'continental position':

> The continental position has always been the strength of the United States in the world. American successes in diplomacy have been based on a continental policy. The interests of the United States today rest on the same support. It is a safe ground on which to watch and wait for a better world. A continental policy was instinctive with the Fathers. Its pursuit has been most constant with the genius and the welfare of the American people.[36]

Traditionalist neutrals would not have basically disagreed with Bemis since they too believed in taking advantage of America's geographic isolation. For them, however, extensive foreign trade, guaranteed by international law, was also important. The freedom to trade and the freedom to travel unmolested on the seas were, in their view, as instinctive with the Founding Fathers as the desire to avoid foreign entanglements. The two did not exclude each other.

Who was the true interpreter of American history and values? The question became highly controversial once concrete efforts were undertaken to introduce embargo legislation in the mid 1930s. Various attempts had been made between 1927 and 1933 but without success.[37] It was only after the Chaco War and the Manchurian incursion that public attention was alerted to the possibility of another war.[38]

An article written by Charles Warren and published in the April 1934 issue of *Foreign Affairs* did much to rouse public debate and trigger political action. Warren had been Assistant Attorney General of the United States, and in this capacity he was in charge of enforcing neutrality laws from 1914 to 1917. He consequently spoke with authority, and his counsel carried much weight.[39]

His argument was simple: if the United States intended to stay out of a future war, it had to define more clearly a wide range of neutral duties, and it had to get ready to enforce them strictly. He enumerated twelve such neutral obligations, ranging from the use of neutral radio stations to the non-acceptance of prize in American harbours.[40]

His main point, however, was that America had to abandon totally the notion of neutral trading rights:

> If, in the future, we intend to insist on the alleged rights for which we persistently contended from 1914 to 1917, then there is little likelihood that we can avoid entering a war, on the one side or the other. For these alleged rights, at the present time, are 'rights' only in name. They are a legal fiction … in view of our past experience, discontinuance of the use of the inflammable words 'rights of trade' in diplomatic correspondence will be one of the chief factors in helping a neutral to remain neutral.[41]

This was strong language, and it came from a source that could not easily be dismissed. Furthermore, the article appeared at a time when Congress was getting ready to investigate the connection between war profiteering and American entry into the First World War. Under the chairmanship of Senator Nye, a committee of Congress conducted extensive hearings and concentrated particularly on munitions makers and bankers. Although it was impossible to prove that these 'interests' had conspired to draw the United States into war, the general impression remained that free trade and free financing had contributed greatly to the partial American policy and to eventual entry on the side of Great Britain.[42] It must also be remembered that this was the time of the Great Depression and the New Deal, when charges against Big Business and Big Money fell on particularly fertile soil.

In these circumstances it was relatively easy for Congress to pass the first Neutrality Act in August of 1935.[43] It provided for a mandatory embargo on arms, munitions, and implements of war, and it created a National Munitions Control Board to regulate and supervise the export of such materials. Furthermore, in future wars American citizens were to take passage on belligerent vessels at their own risk, and American ports were not to be used for supplying men and cargo to any belligerent warship at sea.[44] The act, limited to a duration of one year, was renewed in 1936. At that time, a prohibition on loans to belligerents was added.[45]

Realising the need to compromise, the traditionalists did not overly object to the two bills, even though the measures considerably abridged neutral trading rights as granted by international law. The Hague Conventions permitted complete freedom of trade by private individuals and merely prohibited the provision of arms and loans by neutral governments. The traditionalists only opposed the attempts by the more radical neo-isolationists to go beyond absolute contraband and to put an embargo on raw materials. In this they succeeded in 1935 and 1936.[46] A year later, however, the traditionalists failed when the new Act granted the President a certain amount of discretionary power to shape the embargo according to his will. The bill also included the cash-and-carry clause. Under this provision, title to any commodity exported from the United States had to be transferred to a foreigner before it went to sea.[47] This went too far for the traditionalists, but the political tide had turned against them. This was also shown by the fact that the Act of 1937 was no longer limited to a duration of one year. The defeat of neutral trading rights was painful for the proponents.

With this act, the traditional American conception of integral neutrality had been twisted beyond recognition. Instead, a highly qualified conception had been adopted that even went beyond the British 'big-navy' conception of earlier years. After all, the British had never disputed a neutral's basic right to trade; they had merely insisted on 'courant normal' and a number of other qualifications, such as the abandonment of the 'broken voyage'.

What the Americans now introduced was, in effect, the notion of *neutral economic duties:* a duty not to permit the private export of armaments, a duty to prohibit the granting of private loans, and a duty not to let ships and goods become entangled in war.[48] This was new in the history of neutrality, but from the viewpoint of the sea neutral it had a certain logic. After all, neutral trading rights regularly came into conflict with the neutral military duty of abstention. Why not establish, then, a parallel neutral duty of economic abstention? It would have made sense in that it gave more weight to the important dimension of *indifference.*

Another question was whether this conception of neutrality was in line with American *values.* The United States, for all its political isolation from Europe, had never been an economically autarchic nation. From the very start, it had been assumed that a liberal economy at home would be tied to liberal foreign trade. How would the country react to a severely restricted wartime economy? And, even more painful, would the public be ready to tighten its belt in times of war?

Bemis thought this possible: 'American foreign policy is now settling back into the tradition of the Fathers adapted to the circumstances of a satiated continental nation ... . It is a safe ground from which to watch and wait for a better world.'[49] Many people wondered in 1937 whether a nation built on free trade was so easily satiated and whether a nation surrounded by total war was a safe ground from which to watch and wait. One must not forget that the Neutrality Acts were not accompanied by armaments acts calling for a strong navy to practise *armed neutrality.* On the contrary, the neo-isolationists were the very people who also wanted to keep the military question at arm's length. They assumed that America was still the unimportant nation of a century ago, able to remain indifferent to the outcome of the next war.

From 1937 to 1939, the neo-isolationist neutrals were at the height of their power. They celebrated another success in January 1939, when Roosevelt tried in vain to soften some aspects of the neutrality legislation. But it was to be their last victory. Once the war in Europe had started, Congress passed the fourth and last Neutrality Act, which no longer contained the arms embargo provisions. The debate was stormy, but the administration won. From then on, Great Britain and France could buy arms in the United States, although still at their own risk. As Wayne Cole stated in his study of Roosevelt and the isolationists, this was to be 'the first in an uninterrupted succession of Roosevelt Administration triumphs over isolationists in legislative contests on neutrality and aid-short-or-war.'[50]

After the fall of France came a large defence appropriation bill and the institution of compulsory recruitment (draft). In September 1940, Roosevelt, relying solely on executive power, turned fifty American destroyers over to the British in exchange for bases on Newfoundland and in the Bermudas, which was a gross violation of neutrality. After winning this third term, Roosevelt won the Congressional battle over Lend-Lease in early 1941, and, beginning in April, American naval ships convoyed British Lend-Lease vessels across the Atlantic. In July, the United States took over bases in Iceland to assure its convoy traffic, and in August, Roosevelt met Churchill in Newfoundland to issue the Atlantic Charter. In October, Roosevelt finally requested the repeal of the 1939 Neutrality Act and won a handsome victory exactly one month before the attack on Pearl Harbor. Neither the neo-isolationist nor the traditionalist neutrals ever recovered from these blows.[51]

Internationalist neutrality

In contrast to the traditionalist and neo-isolationist neutrals, the internationalists favoured American involvement in world politics and co-operation with other nations in the pursuit of a just cause, particularly in opposition to aggression. They saw the neutral embargo as a useful weapon to this end, especially when practised in tandem with League of Nations sanctions. Internationalists, therefore, were for a flexible and selective embargo directed exclusively against actual or potential aggressors. They feared that a general embargo directed against both belligerents would punish the victim as well as the aggressor and undermine League action. In contrast to the traditionalists and neo-isolationists, who favoured an impartial embargo, the internationalists wanted a partial one. Internationalist neutrals were thus also referred to as 'discriminatory', 'sanctionist', or 'co-operationist' neutrals.

Internationalist neutrals also favoured a discretionary embargo, which meant that the President would be given extensive freedom to determine what country was to be embargoed and with what means when a situation of crisis or war existed. Here again the other two schools disagreed. As a rule, both traditionalists and neo-isolationists favoured a mandatory embargo, giving the President as little discretionary power as possible, that is, making the embargo practically automatic. Furthermore, the internationalist neutrals favoured the embargo of a wide range of commodities, particularly raw materials essential to the conduct of war. On this issue the other schools were divided. As a rule, the neo-isolationists supported the embargo, while the tradition-alists, as we have seen, opposed it.

The internationalist neutrals did not have a large following. They were a small group of scholars and politicians but – and this made all the difference – they managed to get into very important positions. Henry L. Stimson, for example, was Secretary of State under Herbert Hoover and Secretary of War under Franklin D. Roosevelt.[52] Cordell Hull was Roosevelt's Secretary of State for eleven years. Most impor-tant, Roosevelt himself was at heart an internationalist.[53]

The international jurists favouring the cause were generally of the younger generation. Most prominent among them were Quincy Wright of the University of Chicago, Clyde Eagleton of New York University and Charles Fenwick of Bryn Mawr College. They had all been trained in the 'classical' school of traditionalist international law but began to question and even reject it. They belonged to the Wilson tradition, and that made them highly suspect to the other neutrals.

Both the traditionalist and the neo-isolationist neutrals feared that the internationalists regarded neutrality as a mere back door to full involvement in world politics and that, at a given moment, they would shed their neutral pretence altogether. In many quarters inter-nationalist neutrality was seen as nothing but a disguise for a return to full fledged Wilsonianism and to the complete elimination of neutral-ity from world politics.

These apprehensions were in part justified. Roosevelt, Hull, and Stimson did indeed draw America back into complete international involvement and thereby turn their backs on neutrality as a policy for the United States. But they did not completely abandon neutrality as such. As this study will show, some internationalists would in fact try to outlaw neutrality altogether in years to come, but this was not typical for the majority of internationalists, and it would never really become official United States foreign policy.

Internationalist neutrals began pushing for a discriminatory embargo as early as 1927, at a time when the Kellogg–Briand Pact was in the air. While preliminary negotiations for this treaty were going on, Representative Burton of Ohio introduced a resolution calling for an embargo prohibiting the export of arms, munitions and war materials to any country engaged in a war of aggression against another, in violation of a treaty, convention, or any other arrangement providing recourse to peaceful means for the settlement of international differences.[54]

The use of terms like 'war of aggression' or 'violation of a treaty' indi-cates that this proposal was internationalist and discriminatory in spirit. It was vehemently opposed for its partiality by the traditionalists but warmly embraced by Quincy Wright. In an article published at about the same time, he called for a new status in international law located halfway between war and traditional neutrality:

> This status might be denominated 'partiality' and would be recognized only in case one or more states had resorted to war in violation of treaties to which they were parties. In such circumstances other states might be 'partial' which would entitle them, without going to war, to discriminate against the guilty state and to assist in shutting off its commerce even by maritime blockade.[55]

Once the Kellogg–Briand Pact had been signed and ratified by the United States, disagreement arose among scholars of international law on its interpretation. Traditionalists saw it as having absolutely no impact on neutrality, but internationalists disagreed. Clyde Eagleton wrote that 'no signatory of the Pact could complain, if we went to war against him, or if we deprived him of the benefits of neutrality. Indeed, the state which asserted its rights as a neutral in such circumstances would surely be in a positive violation of the Pact.'[56]

The tug-of-war went on for several years.[57] In 1929, Senator Capper introduced a bill calling for an embargo against any country that the President declared to have violated the Kellogg Pact, but once more the traditionalists managed to block the proposal.[58] Internationalists scored a minor victory, however, when, on 7 January 1932, Secretary of State Henry L. Stimson declared that the United States (in the spirit of the Kellogg Pact) would not recognise any territorial conquest by violence. The Stimson Doctrine, as it came to be called, was issued in the context of the Japanese conquest of Manchuria.[59]

In early 1933, Senator Borah made another attempt to get discriminatory embargo legislation. He introduced a bill consistent with the Burton and Capper resolutions. The traditionalists once more opposed it. John Bassett Moore, as adviser to the House committee handling the bill, used all his academic prestige to defeat the attempt. The internationalists almost won, however. The bill passed both houses of Congress and died only in conference. It was an indication that the idea of an embargo was gaining ground.

The year 1935 was notable for the Warren article and the Nye investigations. These were moves in the direction of neo-isolationist neutrality and led to a bill that called for a mandatory embargo. The Neutrality Act of 1935, therefore, can not really be regarded as an internationalist success. When Roosevelt signed it into law, he criticised it for its inflexible provisions that gave him no discretion in applying it in concert with similarly minded governments. The internationalists would have to try harder next time round. After all, the bill was limited to one year.

During the Ethiopian crisis, the United States had an opportunity to implement the new embargo policy.[60] Roosevelt promptly declared an impartial embargo on both Italian and Ethiopian trade. Since Ethiopia did hardly any business with the United States, the impact was largely one sided and, in effect, amounted to discriminatory action very much in the internationalist spirit. The United States had finally done what the internationalists had advocated for years – it had co-operated indirectly with the League of Nations in pursuit of a just cause.[61]

For the internationalists, the Neutrality Act of 1936 was only a minor improvement over the earlier one. It was again a mandatory and impartial embargo bill, but it did provide the President with some discretion in the export of lethal weapons. A more significant discriminatory provision was contained in the 1937 Act, however. Once the President had implemented the automatic features of the embargo, he could decide at his own discretion on the cash-and-carry plan.[62]

Looking at the three Neutrality Acts together, the internationalist neutrals could not rejoice. These were partly traditionalist but mostly neo-isolationist bills. The internationalists had tried hard, however. They had the President on their side as well as the Department of State, but they lacked strong public and congressional support. Internationalism was, after all, not the mood of the 1930s.

Of greater interest was the battle that the internationalists fought on the *academic front*. In countless publications, they analysed and criticised the other schools of neutrality, the traditionalists in particular. The latter represented more of a challenge to the internationalists, because behind traditionalist neutrality stood an intellectual framework with which internationalists fundamentally disagreed. The exchanges between internationalists and traditionalists are, therefore, worth a closer look. They go to the very heart of the theory of international politics and reveal much about American *values* and identity.

At first glance, there was no difference between internationalist and traditionalist values. Indeed, both schools adhered to self-determination, democracy, human rights, the rule of law, the promotion of international law, freedom of trade, freedom of the sea, progressive elimination of war, and promotion of peace. This is what the Founding Fathers stood for, and this is what the internationalists stood for, too.

Seen from this very general perspective, there is perfect harmony between traditionalist and internationalist aims. On further inspection, though, there are important differences. When Washington and Jefferson spoke of international law, they were thinking of engagements whose execution was left up to each individual state. A state might enter into any number of international obligations, but in the end it remained the sole and best judge of its actions, in peace and in war. No other state had the right to enforce any kind of law against the will of any other state.

When Wilson and the internationalists spoke of international law, for instance of the League Covenant or the Kellogg Pact, they meant something very different. They saw a binding kind of international law, the interpretation and execution of which was up to a larger body of states. Such law had much in common with domestic law in that it was backed by authoritative power. From the internationalist point of view, the voluntaristic philosophy of international law was dying.[63] They were ready to match *universalist values* with *universalist power*.[64]

Combined with these divergent views of law and power were different *conceptions of war*. For the traditionalists, nothing much had changed in the way of warfare. To be sure, there were now new techniques of destruction, but the central, age-old effort to subjugate the enemy by force persisted. The internationalists disagreed. They were convinced that the moderate international system of the nineteenth century had come to an end and that the world was about to enter a revolutionary age. Because of new ideologies and technologies, the planet was shrinking and becoming a vastly more dangerous place. As the First World War had shown, warfare was becoming total.[65]

Under such circumstances, the internationalists argued, war was increasingly the business of all states and had to be discussed and managed collectively. Most of all, the very outbreak of hostilities, and not merely the conduct of hostilities, had to be regulated by international law. The causes of war would have to be investigated, and it was vital to distinguish between just and unjust causes, legal and illegal conflicts, victims and aggressors.

In the 1930s, the debate between the two schools was also carried on in terms of 'realism' and 'idealism'. When Borchard denounced Fenwick or Wright for their 'idealism', he meant their inherently false philosophy of law. In his opinion, it was based on the untenable assumption that politics could be shaped by ethical standards. From the 'realist' point of view the opposite was true: 'Law follows life, it does not lead it .... Any attempt to impose a rule which does not grow

out of previous experience is almost sure to fail .... Only after politics
has done its work does law enter the field.'[66] Schemes like the League
or the Kellogg Pact were bound to fail, since law could never preserve
peace and prevent war – at best it could moderate war.

From the 'realist' point of view, traditional law of war had performed
this function well, and by doing so it had had a moderating and civilis-
ing effect on warfare. The same applied to neutrality, part and parcel of
the law of war. The existence of every neutral and of every regulation
respecting neutral trade was a contribution to the humanisation of
warfare. Law could not do more. The prevention of war was the job of
the diplomat and the soldier.

By gradually eliminating neutrality, the 'realists' contended, international politics were brutalised. Making war the business of all meant
spreading conflict instead of containing it. Collective security, therefore, did not bring security at all but merely collectivised brutality. At
heart, 'idealism', for all its moral pretensions, was a return to the
Crusades and the Middle Ages, when barbarous wars were fought in
the name of a just and universal cause. The truly 'peace-loving' nations
were, consequently, not those promoting unworkable collective
security, but those adhering to the workable traditional law of war and
of neutrality.

The 'idealists', needless to say, saw things very differently. Quincy
Wright pointed to the fundamental contradiction inherent in the
'realist' conception of law. A system of law, to mean anything at all,
must at the very least be premissed on the right of a state to exist, to
possess its domain, to protect its nationals, to govern within its juris-
diction, to enjoy its status and whatever additional benefits it may
have acquired through the legal exercise of its powers. War to Quincy
Wright is a denial of all these rights:

> If each state is free to institute a state of war by unilateral action,
> and by that act to relieve itself of most of the obligations of interna-
> tional law toward its enemy and of many of those obligations
> toward third states, it is clear that international law takes away with
> one hand what it gives with the other. It both asserts and denies the
> right of states to exist.[67]

Quincy Wright concludes that a system of law embracing war as a
means of conflict resolution is a contradiction in terms: a 'system of
war' and a 'system of law' cannot coexist.

From the 'idealist' point of view, this contradiction becomes evident
in the situation of a neutral country that, as America experienced a

number of times, is forced to go to war in order to protect its rights.[68] Is it not, as Charles Fenwick asked, 'the supreme folly to go to war to maintain your right to stay out of war?' And he put his finger on the ultimate cause of it all, the international state of anarchy: 'The story of American neutrality is the story of a nation trying to live its own life in peace in the midst of lawlessness and anarchy.'[69]

For the 'idealists' the conclusion was simple: if Americans wanted to live up to some of their basic *values*, such as enjoying certain rights protected by law, then voluntaristic international law would no longer do. It would have to be a new type of law, one that would outlaw *indifference* in the face of calamity and that would no longer permit dealings with belligerents on a footing of *impartiality*. Combined with this, of course, would have to be the determination to use American *power* to bring about international respect for law.

These arguments reveal that the internationalist neutrals were anything but interested in preserving neutrality. Their arguments, pursued logically, led not only to the 'outlawry of war' but also to the 'outlawry of neutrality'. Not all scholars were willing to go all the way, however. Efforts were made to define a middle ground between fully-fledged internationalism and classical neutrality. During the interwar period, this school was not perceived to be a separate one because of its affinity with internationalism. Retrospectively, it merits separate treatment. For the sake of differentiation, let us call it moderate or qualified internationalism and contrast it with radical or strict internationalism.

Qualified internationalism

Among the many neutral concepts that surfaced in the 1930s, two could be classified as qualified internationalist, as standing somewhere between true traditionalism and true internationalism. One was the *Argentine Anti-War Pact*, launched by Argentine Foreign Minister Saavedra Lamas in 1932 and signed by many countries, including the United States. The other was a project commissioned by Harvard Law School in 1939 to elaborate *Draft Conventions* regulating neutrality in modern war.

Philip C. Jessup, Professor of Law at Columbia University, was identified with both these schemes. He took a great interest in the Argentine Pact and became one of its most prominent supporters, but he also chaired the working party that elaborated the Harvard conventions. The two plans are not identical, since one leans somewhat more to the internationalist side than the other, and it is also difficult to know how much Jessup identified (as chairman) with the conclusions of the Harvard conventions. Still, both schemes share a concern for the maintenance of peace without total indifference and impartiality, and both foresee the use of a certain amount of neutral power to contribute to the maintenance of international law and order. In a qualified way, both are internationalist.

Jessup dealt with neutrality as early as 1932. In an article entitled 'The Birth, Death and Reincarnation of Neutrality' he argued that neutrality, although declared dead a number of times, was still a concept to be reckoned with. In commenting on an anti-neutral remark by Secretary of State Stimson, Jessup concluded that 'this is not the first requiem for the late but not lamented Law of War and his vacillating sister Law of Neutrality.'[70] The Hague Conventions, he continued, were still in force, and it could be expected that even members of the League would again declare neutrality: 'It is clear that neutrality may peep in through the famous "gap" in the Covenant and that the lack of power to define a covenant breaker leaves it open to member states legally to hold aloof from a conflict.'[71]

Next, Jessup wrote two articles about the Argentine Anti-War Pact.[72] What this document amounted to was a revival of the old idea of *neutral leagues,* or the proposition that neutrals should act together in times of war to defend their rights. Neutral leagues had in the past come about mostly among sea neutrals in defence of trading rights.[73]

The Argentine Anti-War Pact had in mind the formation of such a neutral league, but it also went further – it aimed at the prevention of war. As Nils Ørvik put it succinctly, the aim of the pact 'was to coordinate the system of neutrality with the sanctions system ... and attempt to incorporate parts of the Covenant, the Kellogg Pact, and the Stimson Doctrine, and to combine these into a new version of neutrality.'[74] The central provisions of the treaty make this clear:

> The contracting states undertake to make every effort in their power for the maintenance of peace. To that end, and in their character of neutrals, they shall adopt a common and solidary attitude; they shall exercise the political, juridical or economic means authorized by international law: they shall bring the influence of public opinion to bear; but in no case shall they resort to intervention either diplomatic or armed.[75]

The treaty must have inspired Jessup to study neutral co-operation more closely. This he did in a part of his massive four-volume publication entitled *Neutrality: Its History, Economics and Law.* It is the most comprehensive investigation of American neutrality ever undertaken, and in the last volume Jessup addresses the question of revising neutrality and achieving 'peace through neutrality'.[76]

In reviewing the record of neutral leagues, he concludes that 'where the neutrals have been able to rally sufficient naval or military power, they have succeeded in persuading the belligerents to come to terms.'[77] However, the United States missed a chance in Jessup's view when, from 1914 to 1917, it systematically disregarded suggestions by other neutral governments for co-operation. This should not happen again. Signature of the Argentine Anti-War Pact was a step in the right direction. By organising an international neutral embargo, America might in a future war be able to 'deter belligerents from violating neutral rights and thus reduce the usual points of friction between belligerents and neutrals.'[78]

Jessup's plan had traditionalist and internationalist aspects. Although abandoning some neutral trading rights in opting for an embargo, Jessup defended the idea of neutrality as such. As the title 'peace through neutrality' indicates, he was convinced by the traditionalist argument that neutrality was a policy of peace and not war.[79] Military abstention was still of great importance to him.

The internationalist traits of the plan showed in the belief that neutrals ought to use their economic power to sanction an aggressor and thereby promote peace. Jessup's words indicate this clearly:

> The success of such cooperation would naturally depend on the power – political, economic and armed – of the neutral group. In the second place, in some respects analogous to the theory of economic sanctions under Article 16 [of the League Covenant], neutral cooperation would tend to shorten the war by cutting off the sources of supplies essential to the belligerents. It may also be suggested that assurance in advance that essential supplies would be embargoed, either through League action under Article 16 or through neutral cooperation, might serve to deter states from resorting to war.[80]

In Jessup's scheme, two leagues, the League of Nations proper and a League of Neutral Nations, would in effect maintain world peace. The second would be an unofficial arm of the first, aiding it in the field of economic sanctions. The difference between the two would, therefore, lie mainly in the military field and in the form of organisation: the neutral league would have no formal structure, and it would refrain from military sanctions. But it, too, would make a definite contribution towards deterring and, if necessary, containing aggression. It was meant to help in the pursuit of a just cause and consequently did not entirely live up to traditionalist standards of indifference and impartiality.

As mentioned above, in 1939 Harvard Law School commissioned a study on neutrality that had to deal with such up-to-date questions as air-war and collective security. Over twenty of the most distinguished scholars in international law were on the panel, among them Edwin Borchard, Clyde Eagleton, Charles Fenwick, Charles Warren, and Quincy Wright. Chairman and reporter was Philip C. Jessup.

In view of the composition of the group it should come as no surprise that it could not agree on one document; the divisions were too deep. Two documents were consequently elaborated 'based on the assumption that a distinction in law is to be drawn between war on the one hand and, on the other hand, certain forceful acts determined to constitute a violation of a particular type of legal obligation.'[81] While the traditionalists obviously addressed neutrality in the context of 'war', the internationalists dealt with it in the context of 'certain forceful acts determined to constitute a violation of a particular type of legal obligation.' The two conventions were labelled accordingly. One carried the title 'Draft Convention on Rights and Duties of Neutral States in Naval and Aerial War', the other 'Draft Convention on Rights and Duties of States in Case of Aggression'.[82]

The convention dealing with 'war' mentions neutrality in its classical shape and deals extensively with rights and duties in naval and aerial war. The chapter on aerial war is particularly innovative, since this type of war had never before been dealt with in international agreements. The Hague Conventions do not mention it at all.

The convention on 'forceful acts' does not mention neutrality. Article 1 defines aggression as 'a resort to armed force by a State when such resort has been duly determined, by a means which that State is bound to accept, to constitute a violation of an obligation.' Article 1 also enumerates four different parties to the conflict: an 'aggressor', a state that commits aggression; a 'defending state', the victim or object of aggression; a 'co-defending state', which assists a defending state with armed force; a 'supporting state', which assists a defending state without armed force.[83]

In Article 10 the 'supporting state' is defined as follows:

> By becoming a supporting State, a State acquires the right to discriminate against the aggressor, but it may not do any act to the

detriment of States other than the aggressor unless such act would be lawful if done by defending or co-defending State. Against an aggressor, a supporting State has the rights which, if it were neutral, it would have against a belligerent.[84]

The difference between a 'co-defending' and a 'supporting' state boils down to a differentiation between military and economic sanctions. The distinction was also made by the League of Nations. Switzerland, for instance, was granted the right to participate in economic sanctions only. In the language of the Harvard Draft Convention, Switzerland would have been a 'supporting state' of the League. For the Swiss themselves it was a qualified form of neutrality, since they voluntarily gave up some neutral trading rights. Obviously, the drafters of this convention would have liked to see the United States become a 'supporting state' in a future conflict. This would have constituted another step in the direction of internationalism, but it would have stopped short of joining the League of Nations. Under this convention, America would have played the same role outside that the Swiss were willing to play inside the League.

This scheme is more explicitly internationalist than the Argentine Anti-War Pact or Jessup's League of Neutral Nations. In assuming that aggression can be defined and determined, it regulates the recourse to war and thereby establishes what is a just cause. States are called upon to take sides clearly and to associate themselves openly with the party in the right, the defending state. There is a more clear-cut commitment in this convention to the use of national *power* in pursuit of collective *values*. On the other hand, there is less emphasis on the virtues of *indifference* and *impartiality*.

The Argentine Anti-War Pact, the idea of a League of Neutral Nations, and the Harvard notion of the 'supporting state' had no impact on American foreign policy in those years. In 1939, it was too late to submit the Harvard Conventions to an international conference, and once the war in Europe had broken out, Roosevelt was in no mood to set up a neutral league.[85]

There was a lame attempt in February 1940 to get in touch with neutral governments elsewhere. Under Secretary of State Sumner Welles proposed to Roosevelt and Hull in January that over forty neutral governments be approached to determine their willingness to discuss closer co-operation in war and in the organisation of peace. The telegrams that went out, however, made no mention of wartime co-operation, but merely referred to 'the future maintenance of a lasting world peace, namely, limitation and reduction of armaments, and the establishment of a sound international economic system.'[86] This was not the kind of initiative that would lead to a league of neutral nations. From what we know today, Roosevelt never wanted such a league.[87]

What Roosevelt really intended was to give the Allies all the support he possibly could. With the passage of the Neutrality Act of 1939, the British and the French could obtain American private aid on a cash-and-carry basis. With the base-destroyer deal in 1940 the British got semi-official American military supplies, and with the passage of Lend-Lease legislation, military and economic aid became official.[88] In the eyes of legal experts, America became a benevolent neutral with the base-destroyer deal, although the country itself may not have seen it that way in 1940.[89] What was becoming increasingly evident was that America felt more and more like a 'supporting state' helping the Allies in pursuit of a just cause.[90]

The administration did not bother to send long telegrams to London protesting about infringements of neutral trading rights, as Wilson had done between 1914 and 1917. The government now co-operated intimately and voluntarily in the organisation of the British blockade. There was no question of observing any indifference or impartiality in matters of trade. Furthermore, the fact that this was a just cause fought for definite American values was made plain in the Atlantic Charter. That document established beyond any doubt that America perceived itself in the spirit of a 'supporting state'.[91]

It was only a matter of time until America itself would enter the war and become a belligerent. The country could then choose between one of three options: first, to act in the spirit of traditionalism and to support integral neutrality. Second, and in line with moderate internationalism, to expect the remaining neutrals in Europe to become 'supporting states'. Third, to act in the spirit of radical internationalism thereby expecting all neutrals to join militarily in the conflict and to become 'co-defending states'. The purpose of the following chapters is to determine which option was chosen.

2
Second World War, 1941–1945

Military warfare

Between 1941 and 1945, the United States dealt with neutrality in the actual conduct of war and in the preparation of peace. As is well known, America handled the two questions separately: the conduct of hostilities was not related to concrete plans for peace, and, conversely, the Charter of the United Nations was not drafted against the background of military realities.[1] A similar division prevailed with respect to neutrality. The United States adopted one conception of neutrality in the conduct of war and quite another in the writing of the UN Charter. It is useful, therefore, to deal with the question in two separate chapters, in this and the next.

In the war itself, America confronted neutrality in the areas of good offices, military warfare, and economic warfare. The acceptance of neutral good offices was largely unproblematic,[2] while a number of difficulties arose in the pursuit of military and economic war. American planes regularly violated neutral air space or bombed neutral territory, and American officials were busy organising an economic blockade directly affecting the neutrals. Let us look at military warfare first.

Neutrality was violated massively in the Second World War. Early in the war, the Germans conquered Holland, Denmark, and Norway, all of which had declared neutrality. The Japanese record was no better, and both Fascist powers were unwilling to co-operate fully with the neutral International Committee of the Red Cross (ICRC). The Russians, too, forced the Baltic states to abandon their neutrality and to align with the Soviet Union.

In contrast, the American record was nearly perfect. At least from a military point of view, the United States respected the neutrality of

42

Ireland, Portugal, Spain, Turkey, Sweden, and Switzerland.[3] As Cordell Hull stated in 1944, 'we have scrupulously respected the sovereignty of these nations; and we have not coerced, nor shall we coerce, any nation to join us in the fight.'[4] Germany asked Spain to send troops to the eastern front; America never made such demands on any neutral. Germany requested and obtained rights of military passage from Sweden; America did not make such requests.

There was an attempt to violate Portuguese neutrality in 1943. George F. Kennan, at that time stationed in Lisbon, received orders to present to Salazar a list of demands for installing naval and air facilities on the Azores, demands that would have completely eliminated Portuguese neutrality. Horrified, he refused to obey orders and flew to Washington to argue against the strategy. Only by talking to Roosevelt himself did he manage to change the plan. Since the Portuguese had a long-standing military alliance with the British, who had just succeeded in obtaining extensive rights on the islands, Kennan's idea was to work through the British. He was successful:

> I was soon able to report that he [Salazar] was not only prepared to permit us to make liberal use of the facilities granted to the British in the Azores, if appearances were kept up in certain respects, but that he was even not disinclined to permit Pan American Airways to construct – albeit for the account of the Portuguese government – a second airport there, which we could eventually use on favorable terms.[5]

Since international law of neutrality permits a neutral to honour alliance obligations signed in times of peace, no crass violation was committed. It was most questionable whether the Americans, as the allies of the British, were allowed to use these facilities. Perhaps this constituted a breach of international law, but it was a minor one by the standards of the Second World War.

De facto violations did take place. American planes flying against Germany and Japan at times passed over neutral air space, crash-landed on neutral soil, and in a few instances bombed neutral cities by mistake. At the end of the war there were compensation claims for damages suffered by Switzerland, Portugal, San Marino, and the Vatican. In 1945, American planes had bombed the Portuguese island of Macao off the coast of China. In reconquering Italy, the Americans bombed San Marino, and when the town of Albano was taken in February 1944 the Vatican was partially damaged.[6]

The most extensive damage by far was suffered by Switzerland. One hundred and sixty-seven planes either crash-landed or were forced down. Mistaken bombings were frequent, and one case was serious. On 1 April 1944, thirty American planes appeared over the city of Schaffhausen, dropping all their bombs and causing extensive damage, including hundreds of injured and forty killed. The Department of State immediately put one million dollars at the disposal of the Swiss government to finance repairs and promised full compensation.[7]

At the end of the war, compensation for neutrality violations from the air was forthcoming without any problems. After careful inspection of the various claims, the Department of State and the White House drafted a bill that was sent to Congress in December 1947.[8] A legal memorandum written by the State Department's Office of the Legal Adviser accompanied the bill. For an understanding of the American conception of neutrality, the reasoning in this paper is of some interest.

Since the Hague Conventions did not deal with air war and since the United States had not signed any other international convention dealing with the matter, the Legal Adviser had to base his case on precedent and on legal opinion. Various British compensation cases were cited, as were the writings of two American scholars in international law. One scholar mentioned was Charles Cheney Hyde. The Department of State chose to quote a paragraph from his writings in which he took a very firm stand in favour of neutrality.

> A belligerent State must be deemed to be responsible for all injuries inflicted by its aircraft upon subjacent neutral territory, regardless of the circumstances which may in fact serve to cause flights over that territory ... the sharpest penalties need by some process to be visited upon the belligerent whose aircraft unintentionally or otherwise are heedless of the general prohibition and cause injury within the domain of the neutral.[9]

The cases cited dated back to the First World War but concentrated mainly on instances occurring in the early years of the Second World War. The British had mistakenly bombed towns in Denmark, Sweden, Switzerland, Ireland, Spain, and Turkey. In all cases, the British government assumed responsibility and made payments of compensation.[10]

The most interesting reference in the Department's opinion, however, is to the Harvard Draft Convention on Neutrality in Naval and Aerial War of 1939. This convention, as noted earlier, occupies a very interesting place in the history of American neutrality during the interwar period and was to have further influence. The passage quoted by the Legal Adviser reads as follows:

Combat in the air raises another problem of great importance to neutrals whose land frontiers coincide with those of a belligerent. A belligerent is, in principle, justified in engaging in hostile operations over the territory of its adversary. If, however, the result of such operations is to cause missiles to fall upon neutral territory, the belligerent may expose itself to neutral claims for damages.[11]

As will be remembered, this was the convention dealing with 'war' and not with 'forceful acts' and 'aggression'. It was drafted by the traditionalists and was a conscious effort to promote the classical rights of a neutral. In military matters, therefore, America continued to remember its long and proud past and to act in accordance with it. A neutral was still seen to have definite military rights, and a belligerent had the duty to respect them. Would this also apply to economic matters?

Economic warfare

By the standards of the times, military warfare was total in the Second World War. So was economic warfare. As one American official put it, 'the effort to cut off economic aid to the Axis has been one phase of total war.'[12] The aim was to damage the economy of the enemy by all means available, and these included (i) destroying infrastructure and industry from the air, (ii) blockading visible and invisible foreign trade (commerce and finance), and (iii) preventing the acquisition of raw materials abroad through pre-emptive buying.

For the pursuit of the first aim the neutrals were irrelevant. For the other two goals, however, their co-operation was vital. Many neutral countries, especially in Latin America, were major suppliers of raw materials, and in Europe a handful of neutrals had common borders with Germany or territories occupied by it and, thereby, constituted potential loopholes in the blockade. In 1939, Great Britain began with the establishment of an effective blockade of commodities, but it did not have the means to pursue the other two aims successfully. That changed when America entered the war. It did have the means to bomb enemy territory, and it also had the money to engage in world-wide pre-emptive buying. Although there was much co-operation in all areas of economic warfare, a natural division of labour developed. The British remained chiefly in charge of managing the blockade of commodities, while the Americans took the lead in the other fields.

The naval blockade was no great problem to the British. They had plenty of experience in this business and enjoyed an immense strategic advantage. In the North Atlantic and in many other places around the globe, they managed to control the traffic of friends, neutrals, and enemies alike.

The land blockade was difficult, however. Germany had common borders with friendly countries and with neutrals: the Soviet Union (before 1941), Turkey, Spain, Portugal, Sweden, and Switzerland. Basically, these frontiers could not be controlled, but there were possibilities none the less. Many of these countries were not economically self-sufficient but were dependent on overseas markets for imports and exports. Since the British controlled a number of these markets directly (colonies) or indirectly (friendly governments), they had the capability to put pressure on the neutrals. And since the neutrals knew from their experience in the First World War that the British were willing and able to exert such pressures, they decided for the most part to co-operate voluntarily in the blockade. The result was a 'Blockade by Agreement'.[13]

From 1939 to 1941, the British entered into blockading agreements with many of the sea neutrals (Latin American states and the United States) and with all the land neutrals (European neutrals).[14] At the core of these arrangements was the 'navicert' system. British consulates around the world issued export and import navigation certificates based on a quota system set up by the government in London. A ship in possession of such certificates passed British control points freely; others were visited, searched, and possibly seized. Since the arrangement was mainly based on paperwork, it freed the British navy from much of the duty of world-wide checking and patrolling, thereby making ships available for other purposes. As a result, the physical blockade was minimal.[15]

The blockade had many features well known from past wars. It was what used to be called a 'paper blockade' or 'long-distance blockade'. It included such features as 'continuous voyage' and 'ultimate destination', since it was the British who decided whether a commodity headed for a neutral country was ultimately destined for Germany or not. By this decision the British prevented phoney 'broken voyages'. Needless to say, there were long contraband lists, and the principle of 'free ships free goods' was non-existent.[16]

The system was in direct violation of international law, but neutrals had long ago stopped protesting. The United States, the most prominent neutral up to December 1941, co-operated fully. This was no longer the First World War; no long and tortuous legal messages were dispatched to London. When the United States finally entered the war, this earlier co-operation provided an additional benefit: the necessary paperwork merely had to be transferred from the British consulates to the appropriate American agencies. For the exporters and importers nothing much changed. As far as they were concerned, America had been at war all along!

From the viewpoint of economic warfare, the American entry into the war at first brought no fundamental changes. It was initially a question of carrying on what the British had started. Joint organisations were set up to co-ordinate matters, and co-operation was, on the whole, successful. But it was not always smooth. The British, particularly in regard to 'their' blockade, often saw the Americans sent to London as inexperienced and overly zealous intruders hampering the functioning of a well-running machine.[17] It did not help that for quite some time administrative matters in Washington were in the hands of too many different agencies. It was, in the words of one British official, 'a real Klondike of economic warfare'.[18]

The Americans, as part of the division of labour, stepped up preemptive buying in Latin America, Africa, and Asia enormously[19] and, after some time, greatly intensified air war. Of more interest to us, however, is their attitude and contribution to the blockade. Here they came in direct contact with the issue of neutrality.

From the very beginning, the Americans wanted to put more pressure on the European neutrals than the British had. In 1942 and 1943, this was easier said than done, because the military situation was so unfavourable that the Allies lacked the necessary leverage. On the contrary, as long as the Germans completely dominated the Continent, the neutrals were clear assets. It was perhaps unfortunate that they all traded with Germany, but this was preferable to having them, as occupied territories, become fully integrated parts of the German war economy. In economic warfare, too, it was better to have a neutral than another enemy.

There were other advantages as well. Spain, although more nonbelligerent than neutral, co-operated quietly with the Allies in the reconquest of North Africa. Portugal, as shown, permitted the Allies the use of the Azores for air and naval operations, and Turkey was an invaluable partner for British undertakings in the Eastern Mediterranean.[20] Switzerland constituted a useful channel to the enemy, for both overt and covert schemes. Sweden finally, was home for many Danish and Norwegian expatriates, and it would be a reliable partner in any future attempt to deal with Finland, either against Germany or Russia.[21]

This relatively favourable assessment of the European neutrals to the Allied cause prevailed throughout 1942 and 1943. In preparation for the Teheran Conference of late November 1943, the United States Chiefs of Staff drafted a memorandum that reflected this positive line of thinking. Sweden was seen as a country 'determined to maintain her neutrality and ... taking a firm attitude in her relations with Germany.' Switzerland, despite its isolation, 'succeeded in maintaining a firmly neutral attitude', although it depended heavily upon trade with Germany and continued 'to make economic contributions of value to that country'. Spanish policy had been progressively readjusted away from non-belligerent adherence to the Axis to one of 'vigilant neutrality'. The government of Portugal desired 'above all to remain neutral on the Continent'.[22]

This assessment changed as the fortunes of war turned. With the gradual advance of Russian troops in the East and the Anglo-American forces in the Mediterranean, the value of the neutrals to the Allied cause diminished and, correspondingly, the possibilities for applying pressure grew. As Secretary Hull stated in his memoirs: 'Our greater strength and brighter prospects opened up new avenues for the development of our foreign policy. It enabled us to proceed more resolutely toward the neutrals, such as Spain, Portugal, Sweden, Turkey, Switzerland.'[23]

On 9 April 1944, Hull delivered a major speech on foreign policy. It was first going to be 'a dissertation on the benefits of unhampered international trade and the true road to it through agreements reducing tariffs'. But Dean Acheson changed that: 'I had long waited for an opportunity to push economic warfare a stage further ahead.'[24] He rewrote the speech to concentrate heavily on the problems of economic warfare and neutrals.[25]

Hull felt that the United States could no longer acquiesce to the neutrals' drawing upon the resources of the Allied nations 'when they at the same time contribute to the death of troops whose sacrifice contributes to their salvation.' He also told the neutrals that it was no longer necessary for them 'to purchase protection against aggression by furnishing aid to our enemy.'[26]

This was new language. Earlier on, America had appreciated the existence of any country that did not fall under the full sway of the enemy; neutrals had been seen largely as an asset. Now they began to be perceived as a liability. Actually, they were accused of collaborating with the enemy, and they were morally stigmatised. Words like 'purchasing protection' clearly went in that direction. Within six months, high State Department officials delivered two more speeches on the topic and repeated Hull's plea that the neutrals should 'cease aiding our enemy'.[27]

In one of the addresses, Livingston T. Merchant discussed the difference between the British and the American approach to economic warfare. The British, he said, believed that 'the neutrals possessed a right to maintain normal trade relations with the enemy.' The Americans disagreed. 'The economic and growing military force which followed the entry of the United States into the war ... enabled the adoption of steadily intensified economic operations and increasing pressure on the neutrals to gain the avowed objective of the total withdrawal of their economic support to the enemy.'[28]

As we have shown earlier, the British had a long-standing tradition of permitting 'courant normal'. Of course, the exact interpretation of this varied from war to war. In the eighteenth century, courant normal was subject to the 'Rule of 1756', and in the First World War 'normality' was something very different. Still, the British adhered to the principle; the Americans did not. In the eighteenth century, the latter advocated total freedom of trade, permitting unlimited war profiteering, and now that they were involved in a major war, they sought the objective of 'total withdrawal'. In economic warfare, the Americans were not willing to follow the British pattern. This was in sharp contrast to the example cited earlier regarding violations of air warfare. Needless to say, the European neutrals preferred the British conception of economic warfare!

The neutrals were bound to resist American pressures. Resistance varied, however. Turkey, Spain, and Portugal, more non-belligerent than neutral anyway, were not the most difficult to deal with.[29] It was the more genuine neutrals like Sweden and Switzerland that offered the most resistance. As Acheson stated, 'both Swedes and Swiss are among the most independent-minded, not to say stubborn, people in the world ... . If the Swedes were stubborn, the Swiss were the cube of stubbornness.'[30] This did not bode well for America's relations with the neutrals towards the end of the war. Policies of 'total withdrawal' on the one hand and neutral stubbornness on the other were bound to make things difficult.

'Total withdrawal'

From the Allied viewpoint, Sweden aided the enemy in various ways: it provided Germany with iron ore, sold ball-bearings of high quality, permitted a limited transfer of German troops across Swedish territory, and also tolerated German use of Swedish territorial waters.[31] The American aim was to stop this collaboration progressively and, although at times involuntarily, the Swedes complied. As the Russian troops advanced westward and the possibility of a German invasion of Sweden became less likely, the Swedish government gained more bargaining leverage over the Germans and used it in the interest of the Allied cause. In 1943, the transit arrangement was cancelled and trade was substantially reduced. 'The British Ministry of Economic Warfare was in fact so pleased with Sweden's policy after the summer of 1943 that its chief spokesman declared that Sweden had gone further to meet the Allied requests than any other neutral state.'[32]

The British could not foresee, however, that much more would be demanded of the neutrals. Throughout 1944, the Americans put the Swedes under great pressure and ultimately succeeded in their aim to obtain a promise for the total cessation of trade with Germany.[33] The ban was to become effective on 1 January 1945. On 2 January, the American ambassador to Sweden could proudly report that 'all exports of Swedish goods to Germany were terminated January first'.[34] There were two problems, however: continued trade with Norway and Denmark, still under German control, and the question of the so-called 'Göteborg safe conduct traffic'.

Throughout the war, the Germans, controlling the Baltic and access to it, had permitted regular traffic between the Allies and Sweden. As part of this arrangement, they granted Allied ships safe conduct to the Swedish port of Göteborg. Until 1945, the Germans got something in return, but with the total cessation of German–Swedish trade this was no longer the case. The danger was, therefore, that if the Germans found out too quickly about the ban, they would end the Göteborg traffic and seal Sweden off from the West entirely. The Americans were willing to run this risk.

The Americans were also intent upon ending all Swedish trade with Denmark and Norway, still occupied territories. Unfortunately, the agreement with Sweden was not entirely clear on that point. In the American view, the term 'Germany' was meant to cover the country itself and all its occupied territories, whereas the Swedes interpreted it more narrowly. In their eyes, it was not in the Allied interest to have the economies of Denmark and Norway suffer needlessly.

The British shared this view. As early as 2 January, the First Secretary of the British Embassy in Washington telephoned the Department of State to argue in favour of 'token shipments from Sweden to Germany in order that the Göteborg safe conduct traffic may remain open.' Furthermore, the Secretary 'could not understand why we [US government] were opposed to Sweden's exporting goods to Norway and Denmark.'[35]

The United States felt betrayed and began to look for ways to coerce the Swedes. Unfortunately, two ships with goods destined for Sweden could no longer be withheld, because they had just left Allied harbours as part of the deal. Other means were necessary. On 4 January, the Secretary of State alluded to one possibility in a terse telegram to Stockholm: 'This Government's dissatisfaction over failure of Swedes to observe their commitment to terminate exports to Norway and Denmark is such that no guarantee can be given that matter can be withheld from the press.'[36]

If the secret American–Swedish agreement had been leaked to the press, the Germans would most likely have terminated the Göteborg traffic at once, and Sweden would have been punished before the Germans ever got to feel the consequences of the trade ban. But it did not come to that. On 5 January, the American ambassador in Stockholm cabled Washington that 'present situation not deliberate attempt on the part of the Swedes to mislead us.'[37] And the day after, in a more conciliatory mood, Stettinius cabled back that there was 'possible room for honest misunderstanding'.[38] The State Department finally gave in, stating on 13 January that 'the agreement proposed by the Swedish Government regarding exports to Denmark and Norway ... is acceptable to this Government.'[39]

The American aim with regard to Switzerland was also that of total withdrawal, although circumstances were different. The Department of State knew that Switzerland was more dependent than Sweden on trade with the Axis powers. The country had absolutely no raw materials of its own and had to rely on a complicated arrangement of wartime trade, coupled with a well-managed system of storage inside the country and out. As it was totally surrounded by the Axis, it had to get its raw materials either from Germany itself or through German occupied territories (France and Italy). If the Swiss economy was to function at all, the country simply had to deal with the Fascist powers. In the early part of the war, this negated American efforts to get real concessions from the Swiss.[40]

There was also the matter of valuable Swiss channels with the enemy. Too much pressure could endanger these contacts. Therefore, the Americans and the British agreed, as Hull stated in his memoirs, that their approach to Switzerland, while strong, should not be such as to destroy their only channel of representation to the Axis.[41]

Still, by 1944, the aim was to stop all trade between Germany and Switzerland. This was the goal of the Foreign Economic Administration (FEA) and its head, Leo T. Crowley. The agency began to gain increasing influence and managed progressively to impose its views on the

Department of State. In the opinion of the FEA, it was especially vital for the Swiss had to stop all rail transit traffic between Germany and Italy through the St Gotthard tunnel, even though the Swiss had been very careful not to permit the trans-shipment of arms.

By August 1944, the Department of State had adopted the FEA line of thinking. In a message to the American ambassador in Switzerland, Hull declared that 'military developments will soon justify our making a formal demand, jointly with the British, that the Swiss suspend all exports to the enemy and prohibit all enemy transit traffic through Switzerland.' Should Switzerland ask what the Allies would do in return, 'you may reply that upon cessation of Swiss exports to Germany and German transit traffic through Switzerland we will be glad to enter into immediate negotiations with the Swiss.'[42]

As in the case of Sweden, the British tried to moderate the policy. Within days after Hull's stern message to Berne, the British made it clear that they were prepared to follow the American course 'provided these demands are not of such a nature as to force Swiss breaking off political and diplomatic relations with Germany or endangering its position as protecting power.' The British felt that 'we should be willing to accept, if necessary, something less than complete stoppage of all Swiss exports ... to the Axis.'[43] The plea came too late.

Although the Swiss did make concessions and, among other things, stopped all armaments-related exports to Germany as of 1 October 1944, the Americans were not satisfied.[44] With American troops now close to the western borders of Switzerland, matters were no longer solely in the hands of the diplomats. At the beginning of November 1944, SHAFE (Supreme Headquarters American Forces Europe) suspended all traffic between France and Switzerland. For the first time in the war, Switzerland was totally cut off from overseas trade and, perhaps more importantly, from large supplies stored in Lisbon and brought by rail and road through Spain and France.

When the Swiss inquired in Washington about the nature of this blockade, the Department of State was evasive. Woodruff Wallner, the officer who talked to the Swiss representative, made the following record of the conversation:

> I said that in a general way we were interested, insofar as operational requirements permitted it, in having traffic resumed with Switzerland but that we generally were reluctant to make suggestions to SHAFE based on political or economic considerations. I added that in view of the present indeterminate state of our negoti-

ations with the Swiss Government on the question of transit traffic, we were hardly in a position now to make any suggestions of any sort regarding General Gray's order. It was my intention to create by innuendo a grave doubt in Dr Freer's mind as to whether or not we had really been behind the order prohibiting Swiss traffic in France. I believe I succeeded in this.[45]

From these lines it is difficult to determine whether the Department of State was indeed behind the order. Whatever the exact facts, Wallner's words make it amply clear that the blockade served the general intentions of the Department, which had no real interest in opposing it. The intentions of SHAFE, FEA, and the State Department coincided. This put enormous weight behind the policy of total withdrawal.[46]

Although under great pressure to compromise, the Swiss did not act in haste. Crowley was displeased and suggested towards the end of December that pressures be increased. He submitted a four-point plan for further action to Edward R. Stettinius, now Secretary of State. It included specific reference to an indefinite extension of the blockade. The Swiss 'should be put definitely on notice that transit facilities across France cannot be made available, at the expense of Allied transportation needs, for a country which continues to work with our enemy.'[47] The content of Crowley's memorandum was leaked to the press, and at a press conference on 3 January Stettinius was asked about the possibility of applying further pressure on the Swiss. He answered that the whole policy towards Switzerland was under review.[48]

For the moment, the Swiss were alarmed, for it was not clear what Stettinius meant by 'review'. It soon became apparent, however, that the pressure would not mount further. SHAFE was reconsidering the military necessity of the blockade and even envisaged placing orders in Switzerland for electrical equipment needed immediately for infrastructure repairs in France.[49] At the Department of State as well, matters were again looked at differently. The British ambassador had called on Under Secretary Joseph C. Grew and made it clear that 'since stern tactics had failed to achieve results', it would be advisable now to change course.[50] In answering Crowley's letter, Grew therefore felt that Switzerland's neutral position was still of value and that the same was true of its 'future potential usefulness in the economy of Europe'. In short, it was 'inadvisable to place too great pressure upon the Swiss government at this time.'[51]

Grew also told Crowley that the Swiss had suggested sending an Allied delegation to Berne in order to consider all economic warfare questions now in dispute, and that the Department of State favoured such a step. He asked Crowley to submit names of persons whom he wished to be represented in such a delegation. The mission ultimately sent to Berne was headed by Lauchlin Currie, Assistant to the President and former Deputy Foreign Economic Administrator.

The negotiations lasted from 12 February until 8 March, and the US government was very pleased with the results. On 7 March, the American delegation could report to Washington that 'the Swiss delegation capitulated today'.[52] The results of the capitulation were published in the Department of State Bulletin of April 1945: (i) complete stoppage of shipments of coal from Germany to northern Italy across Switzerland, (ii) reduction of Swiss exports to Germany to a small fraction of the former amount, (iii) termination of all electricity exports to Germany. In return, the Allied governments would again allow the import of various quantities of foodstuffs and industrial raw materials into Switzerland.[53]

The aim of total withdrawal had practically been achieved.[54] Neither Sweden nor Switzerland carried on economic relations with Germany in any meaningful way. Although the stoppage came late in the war, it constituted a great success in American eyes. Total military warfare had been matched with total economic warfare.

But in the Second World War total economic warfare had an additional dimension. Beyond bombing and blockading visible assets, the goal was to control and stop the flow of invisible assets as well. In other words, the Second World War saw the conduct of intensive financial warfare. To a large extent this was an American concern, and the agency responsible in Washington was mainly the Treasury Department.

Tracing visible goods is relatively easy; tracing invisible goods is extremely difficult. To penetrate the jungles of international finance, entirely new strategies and methods of economic warfare had to be developed, and in the process a new and unconventional type of warfare emerged. As one commentator remarked, financial warfare ultimately became a kind of economic guerrilla warfare.[55] And, once again, the neutrals were the main battlefields.

'Safehaven'

Like most conquerors, the Nazis looted extensively. They stripped Europe of gold, foreign exchange, securities, jewels, art, and anything else of particular value. Much of it they stowed away in Germany proper, but some they transferred abroad, often via neutral countries.

The Allies had an interest in returning this loot to the proper owners after the war (mostly the treasuries of conquered countries), but they also worried that assets transferred abroad might be used to finance a resurgence of fascism at a later date. American authorities were particularly concerned with the latter aspect of the problem. For them, the question of Germany finding a 'safe haven abroad to provide the Nazis of the next generation with resources for a new try at world domination, was one which went far beyond the mere restitution of loot; it involved fundamental considerations of post-war peace and security.'[56] It was, in contrast to conventional economic warfare, not only a question of winning a war but also of winning the peace that followed. Economic warfare was to be carried on in times of peace as well. As a result, the traditional separation between war and peace disappeared. This new situation in international politics was to become rather common in the postwar era.[57]

The beginnings of a systematic US policy in this area can be traced back to a declaration issued by the Secretary of the Treasury on 22 February 1944. It related to the question of gold and stated unambiguously that the United States would not recognise transfer of title to looted gold that the Axis powers had disposed of abroad.[58] In the spring of the same year, the government defined the problem more generally and gave it the code name of 'Safehaven'.[59]

At the Bretton Woods Conference in July 1944, the United States submitted a strongly worded draft resolution that was adopted by all participants as Resolution VI of the conference. The resolution was addressed explicitly to all neutral countries and called upon them to take immediate steps to prevent the disposition or transfer of any assets belonging to governments and individuals of occupied territories, including gold, currency, art, securities, or any other evidence of ownership in financial or business enterprises. In addition, the neutral countries were asked to uncover and segregate these assets and to hold them at the disposal of the post-liberation authorities.[60]

Resolution VI of the Bretton Woods Conference became the official American and Allied policy. And, since the same conference established the World Bank and the International Monetary Fund, Resolution VI also became identified with the newly emerging international institutions and the United Nations in general. Safehaven was an intimate part of the plan for a better postwar world and, as it turned out, was also an instrument to assist in reconstruction and to help stateless refugees and Holocaust survivors.

Since Switzerland served as the main channel for getting invisibles out of Germany, it was selected as the first target, the assumption being that once the Swiss succumbed, the other neutrals would quickly follow. Sweden, the second most important neutral, was also suspected of holding gold and assets, but on the whole the country was more important as a supplier of iron ores and ball bearings.[61]

The negotiations held in Bern in February and early March of 1945 provided a welcome opportunity to discuss the problem. Actually, Lauchlin Currie's mission had two broad aims: to handle matters of trade and to deal with the question of invisibles, the Safehaven programme. In his 'capitulation' cable at the end of the conference, the American ambassador, therefore, also reported major progress on the financial front. He listed the concessions made by the Swiss and added that 'if this is approved by [the Federal] Council, bringing Sweden, Spain, and Portugal in line should prove easy, and the second battle of Safehaven (Resolution VI being the first) will have been won.'[62] Switzerland agreed to the following: to block assets of all European countries and Japan, to prevent cloaking of enemy assets, to interrupt gold purchases from Germany, to assist in the restoration of looted property, and to conduct a census of German assets. They were also willing to consult with the governments concerned before removing controls and, finally, to further discuss matters with the four Allied powers. [63]

The Swiss assumed that they had gone a long way toward meeting American wishes, but Washington was disappointed. The Currie Agreement indicated some Swiss flexibility, but the result was a far cry from the goal set in the Bretton Woods resolution. The Swiss had not agreed to segregate assets, and they hesitated to return them to their proper owners, be it private individuals, governments, or Allied authorities. Worse yet, intelligence sources soon reported that the Swiss National Bank was continuing to accept German gold. The Americans had been lied to.[64]

In the meantime the war had ended, and the forthcoming Potsdam Conference offered another opportunity for the Allies to discuss the issue. In preparation for the conference, basic strategy was discussed. Two options presented themselves: to claim Allied ownership of all German property abroad and to let the Allied Control Council (ACC) handle practical matters, including redistribution to the various individuals and governments; or to let the neutrals handle the job based on exact instructions given by the Allied governments. Both methods had their drawbacks and advantages. The former might be administratively the most efficient, but it was bound to raise questions of international law. The latter method would get round these issues, but it permitted the neutrals to create endless practical difficulties.

The question of German external assets was dealt with at the Potsdam Conference, and a solution was agreed upon that favoured the supranational approach.[65] The Big Three agreed on the following resolution: 'Appropriate steps shall be taken by the Control Council to exercise control and the power of disposition over German-owned external assets not already under the control of the United Nations which have taken part in the war against Germany.' They also decided to restore looted monetary gold and to use external German assets for reparations and for compensating non-repatriables. It is also worth mentioning that the Soviets waived all claims to external assets.[66]

The Western Allies then moved to assert their claim. The Allied Control Council issued a decree claiming ownership of all German assets abroad on 30 October 1945. It became ACC Law No. 5. The British had objected up to the last minute on legal grounds, but the Americans prevailed.[67] At the Paris Reparations Conference of January 1946 further steps were taken. The decision was made to restore looted monetary gold, to set up a Gold Pool, and to establish a \$25 million fund to assist non-repatriables and Holocaust victims. The fund would be financed out of the proceeds of liquidated German assets held by neutrals.[68]

The machinery was thus set up, but neutral compliance would not be easy to obtain. The Swiss, once again, were expected to offer the most resistance, but the United States held a number of trump cards. For one, Swiss imports still had to pass through territory controlled by the Allies. The blockade of late 1944 had been lifted early in 1945, but it was relatively simple to cut off supplies once again. In view of the general shortage of many commodities, such threats were doubly credible. The British, however, considered sanctions 'unnecessary and impractical'. And, as already indicated, they also had doubts about the legality of the entire matter.[69]

Despite British reluctance, the Americans were able to pressure the Swiss. In 1941 they had put a freeze on neutral assets in the United States, and the Swiss money had still not been released in 1946.[70] The so-called 'blacklists', containing the names of neutral companies suspected of dealing with the enemy, were also continued. Both measures hurt Swiss companies doing business in the United States.[71]

The United States also had the power of public opinion working on its side. As early as July 1945, the Department of State decided to go public. It published a lengthy article written by Assistant Secretary Clayton on the topic of 'Security Against Renewed German

Aggression'. It dealt extensively with the Safehaven programme and emphasised that there was a real danger of a resurgence of German power. The ultimate Allied objective was to 'deny Germany the economic bases of future aggression'.[72] The neutrals were to play a vital part in this effort. Another article was released in November 1945 and contained a full 'Survey of Economic Policy Toward the European Neutrals'.[73] The press, both national and international, was supportive of the American position and also gave broad coverage to congressional investigations of neutral collaboration with the former enemies.

It must be added that the neutrals were not invited to participate in the founding of the United Nations in San Francisco. As a result they began to feel rather isolated on the international scene.[74] In addition, Swiss companies were eager to resume normal business with their American partners and began to put pressure on their government. Locked in from all sides, the Swiss agreed to a conference in Washington D.C.. Talks began in March 1946.[75]

The negotiations were difficult, long, and unpleasant. As Under Secretary of Commerce Stuart Eizenstat wrote in his 1998 report, 'The Swiss team were obdurate negotiators, using legalistic positions to defend their every interest, regardless of the moral issues also at stake.'[76] The negotiations went so badly that during the second part of April they had to be interrupted, to be resumed only in early May.[77] An accord was finally signed on 26 May. The Swiss agreed to pay $58 million into the Gold Pool and to liquidate German assets in cooperation with a commission set up for that particular purpose. The returns of liquidated assets were to be split evenly between Switzerland and the Allies, and German owners would be compensated in German currency by their own authorities. In return the Allies agreed to release frozen Swiss funds and to discontinue the blacklisting of Swiss firms.[78]

The Swiss yielded on a number of points but never abandoned their legal position. On the gold issue, they maintained that the Nazis had an internationally guaranteed right to war booty; as a consequence the Swiss government had a legal right to acquire such gold. On the issue of assets, they argued that as occupying powers the Allies (and the ACC) had no legal claims to assets outside Germany. The Swiss were so sure of their position that at various times they proposed international arbitration.[79] Within six weeks, an agreement was reached with the Swedish government. The Swedes were much more co-operative than the Swiss, and the negotiations had none of the bitterness of the Swiss talks. However, the Swedes held to the same legal arguments.[80] In 1947 and 1948 agreements were signed with Portugal and Spain.[81]

In June 1947, the Swiss turned over 51.5 metric tons of gold to the Tripartite Gold Commission, the equivalent of the agreed upon $58 million. The liquidation of German assets, however, dragged on for years. It was not until 1952 that the matter was finally settled.[82] This confirmed US suspicions that the Swiss had not acted in good faith and had no intention of implementing that part of the agreement.[83] It was also evident that the Swiss had not been telling the truth about the gold they had acquired. Not only did they at first deny having accepted any looted gold,[84] but they also cited a much lower amount than US intelligence reported. In 1946, the Americans estimated the total flow to be between $185 and $289 million, much of it looted. Recent figures published by the Swiss themselves show that $440 million is closer to the truth.[85]

Small wonder that Senator Harley Kilgore, Chairman of the War Mobilization Subcommittee, was unhappy with the settlement: 'Justice, decency, and plain horse sense require that the Allies hold Switzerland responsible for all of the $300,000,000 of looted gold which they accepted from the Nazis and reject their proposition of settling for 20 cents on the dollar.'[86]

Predictably, members of the Swiss parliament were equally unhappy,[87] and representatives of the Swiss business and banking community thought that the accords represented a clear violation of neutral sovereignty, private property rights, and banking secrecy. It was, as most observers would agree, the lowest point in the history of Swiss–American relations.[88]

The contrast between 1919 and 1946 was marked. At the end of the First World War, the Swiss felt that the American government had a keen understanding of their special neutral position. In no small part was this due to President Wilson himself, who was 'one of the greatest friends Switzerland has ever had in America.'[89] No such friendship and understanding prevailed at the end of the Second World War. No one would have argued then that the man sitting in the White House was Switzerland's greatest American friend! In Swiss eyes, the Americans were now exhibiting a very peculiar understanding of neutrality.

As already indicated, the Swiss were in no hurry to liquidate German assets and, as we know today, the question of heirless assets of Holocaust victims was never addressed honestly at all.[90] The Swiss procrastinated on both fronts and profited from the changing climate created by the oncoming Cold War. Only when the Cold War was over did the issue resurface, which again proved to be extremely painful. Once more Swiss–American relations suffered badly.

Looking back over the entire Second World War, it is quite obvious that total economic warfare had succeeded in some areas but had failed in others. In the area of visible commodities, the aim of 'total withdrawal' was practically achieved, although the Swiss maintained token trade and transit traffic in order to uphold their principles of neutrality. In the area of visible goods, the policy was only partially successful. The Americans got less than half of what they had aimed for – only indirect recognition of their extensive interpretation of rights of occupation and only a portion of the gold and of the assets involved. Conventional warfare was easier to practise than 'economic guerrilla warfare'. In the complex labyrinth of invisible goods, the neutrals were vulnerable, but less so than on the open battlefield of conventional war.

The making of 'supporting states'

The record is clear: America respected neutral rights and duties in military matters, but it paid no respect to neutral rights in matters of economics. It did not adhere to a conception of integral neutrality, nor did it have a totally negative view and call for its abandonment. The United States was neither traditionalist nor extremely internationalist; it pursued a middle course of moderate internationalism. Or, as seen from the side of the neutrals, America imposed upon them a qualified conception of neutrality.

Expressed in the language of the Harvard Draft Convention on Aggression, America expected the neutrals to become 'supporting states' and did all it could to attain that goal. Having acquired the necessary power, it had considerable success. 'Total withdrawal' and 'safe-haven' were the concrete expressions of this. Neutrals were supposed to wield the embargo weapon in favour of a just cause, in support of the 'United Nations at War against Fascism'. In pursuit of this cause, neutral trading rights had to be sacrificed.

The idea of neutral economic sanctions had deep roots in the inter-war period. As shown, there were several efforts to pass discriminatory embargo legislation, and a success of sorts was achieved in the 1937 Neutrality Act. President Roosevelt called for economic sanctions in the Chaco War and again in the Ethiopian War. He alluded to sanctions in his controversial 'quarantine speech' in Chicago in 1937.[91] America signed the Argentine Anti-War Pact and finally became a 'supporting state' itself between 1939 and 1941.

The idea can be traced back to Wilson and to his followers in the years after 1920. They were disappointed by the American failure to join the League of Nations and tried hard to obtain at least indirect co-operation through discriminatory economic sanctions. Viewed from this perspective, the Wilsonians felt that the neutrals of the Second World War owed the United Nations alliance the kind of support that, in their eyes, America had owed the defunct League. Sweden and Switzerland saw things differently. This was not collective action organised by the League of Nations. They had been members of the League, but the organisation had failed. Actually, Switzerland had been formally released from its duties to co-operate in economic sanctions after the Ethiopian crisis. Sweden and Switzerland felt once more that they were integral neutrals whose rights should be respected. In defending these, they resembled America in the eighteenth and nineteenth centuries, when it struggled to defend its integral conception of neutrality against the qualified British conception. Times had changed. Now it was the United States that had a big navy and a conception of neutrality to match!

Power had its obvious influence on the American conception of neutrality in the Second World War, especially economic power. Not that it alone determined the entire conception; on the contrary, as we have shown, the conception itself had deeper roots. But power led American officials to overestimate the effects of economic warfare, particularly the effects of the blockade. The British regularly warned Americans not to expect too much, predicting that there would be no strangulation effect and no German Achilles' heel. The British doubted whether 'total withdrawal' and 'safehaven' would have the desired results.[92]

Exhortations were in vain. From the President on down, there were people who believed that the instrument of economic warfare could be used in the future as a means of policing the world without recourse to war.[93] One wonders whether the existence of a large and strong neutral power in 1945 would not have dampened some of these hopes. American officials were far too motivated by a feeling of omnipotence, which, of course, was an integral part of the nascent American hegemony. Once the United States abandoned isolationism, it emerged as the leading power, as the nation that would determine the shape of international relations for the rest of the twentieth century.

The Roosevelt administration, as was typical of New Dealers, also had a tendency to project its domestic experience onto the world scene. This showed in its attitude toward economic warfare but more lastingly in the conception of international institutions. At home, the

New Deal aimed at overcoming the Great Depression and at promoting well being among the lower income groups with the help of interventionist institutions. In the war, the same Keynesian approach was pursued abroad. At Bretton Woods a set of universal economic institutions meant to lay the groundwork for a global New Deal was created. These institutions reflected the typically American combination of power and values.[94]

America continued to believe in free trade, but henceforth it would be carried on within a framework of globally enforceable rules. After the Great Depression, few people in Washington expected that free trade alone would make for world peace. It was not the values as such that had changed, but the belief that they would spontaneously make for a harmonious world. In this respect the spirit of the Founding Fathers had been altered.

Other ideas were also projected abroad. The New Dealers saw the causes of the Depression in the excesses of *laissez-faire* capitalism, in the concentration of too much economic and political power in too few hands. Consequently, they were suspicious of 'Big Business' and 'Big Money', at home and abroad. During the Nye Committee hearings, for instance, large corporations and banks were accused of having drawn America into the First World War by engaging in excessive war profiteering. To be an international financier was tantamount to being a criminal. Many New Dealers accepted William Jennings Bryan's famous dictum that money was the worst kind of contraband.

Small wonder that some members of the Roosevelt administration looked forward eagerly to dissolving the large German conglomerates and to keeping a sharp eye on German financial dealings. Safehaven was in this spirit. Anyone still doing business with Germany was suspect – Swiss financiers in particular. They were well known for their expertise in money lending and money dealing. They could not be trusted until New Deal experts investigated their books.

Neutral financiers became indistinguishable from the enemy: they *were* the enemy. That this was in fact the working assumption is demonstrated in the documents now available. Dean Acheson, on behalf of the Secretary of State, wrote a memorandum concerning Safehaven to the American diplomatic representatives in Latin America on 6 December 1944. In it he stated explicitly that

> for the purpose of this instruction the term 'enemies' should be defined as persons or entities in any of the Axis countries, or countries which have or are allied with the Axis, and *nationals of any*

country who in your discretion could be considered a present or potential threat to the effective execution of Allied control plans. [Emphasis added][95]

The reference to 'nationals of any country' goes to show that esteem for the neutral businessman, held so high in 1776, had suffered badly. This was not the classical liberalism of former centuries.

Some State Department officials were more outspoken than Dean Acheson. This was true of Thomas K. Finletter, Head of the Division of Defense Materials and member of the Board of Economic Operations. In an introduction to a study of American economic warfare, he dealt at some length with the question of neutrality. He felt that

> a non-belligerent may not have a right to traffic with a criminal if the exercise of that right would interfere with the efforts of law-abiding states to suppress the crime. We must, I think, regard Nuremberg as striking down finally the premise of international law that the trade of neutrals with aggressor nations is a right. We may perhaps go even further and assert that now that aggressive war is a crime, it is the positive duty of nations not to be neutral, but to do their share in suppressing the criminality.[96]

This statement shows that with respect to economic warfare, classical international law no longer applied, and neutrals were expected to become 'supporting states'. Finletter spoke and acted in the spirit of the Harvard Convention on Aggression. His ideas were also in line with the arguments of Quincy Wright and Charles G. Fenwick, both of whom made no bones about the inherently negative and even amoral qualities of neutrality.

The same spirit underlies the United Nations Charter. As I will show in the next chapter, this document outlaws war and instead distinguishes between unjust and just conflict, between aggression and enforcement measures. The Nazis, from this perspective, are seen as 'aggressors', the Allies as the 'enforcers'. Classical international law no longer applies, because it conceived of war as a normal, rational, and legal instrument of sovereign states. To Americans especially, the Second World War, although formally not yet covered by the UN Charter, was not just another balance-of-power conflict but a total and unjust war unleashed by criminals. The Allies, on the other hand, fought for a universally just cause and the establishment of a new world order.

As a consequence, the clash between Sweden, Switzerland, and the United States over gold and assets went beyond sheer economic interest; it had deeply normative roots. What is so surprising is that fifty years later the disagreement has not yet disappeared. In 1997 the Swiss were still convinced that the Americans 'misunderstand' neutrality, and Under Secretary Eizenstat was equally convinced that the Swiss needed a lecture in ethics:

The international community's standards of morality and proper conduct have evolved since the end of World War II. The searing experience of the War itself, the Holocaust which it wrought, the Nuremberg trials, and the adoption of the Universal Declaration of Human Rights together injected a new moral content into accepted international norms of conduct.[97]

Of course, the neutrals think that morality is on their side – just as the Americans did when in former centuries they defended neutral rights against the dominant British. This is indeed a conflict between two different conceptions of morality and, correspondingly, two different conceptions of law. In the interwar period the difference was referred to as that between traditionalism and internationalism.[98]

The United Nations was the most obvious pillar of the new internationalism, but it now also embraced the Nuremberg Trials, the Bretton Woods Institutions and Resolution VI, the Safehaven programme, and the Allied Control Council. In the Swiss worldview, these had no place. The difference showed most concretely in the interpretation of the concept of war booty. While the Americans considered looting a criminal act, the classical law of war saw it as a legitimate right of sovereign states. It followed that if Germany possessed the right to loot, the neutrals had a right to acquire booty.

With all due respect for the classical position to which the neutrals adhered, it is indeed a good question as to whether the Second World War was just another European war. It was a total war and proved to be a watershed in the history of international relations. The United States prevailed and succeeded, albeit in small steps and only over a longer period of time, to change some of the rules by which world politics had traditionally been played. However, the new era was visible in 1945 and 1946, and a greater sensitivity for changing times would have helped the neutrals to moderate their position, to accept many of the American demands, and to make a serious effort in favour of the victims. It would have been much wiser for the neutrals to become 'supporting states' out of their own free will.

As I will show, the Swedes proved to be adaptable in the years to come. The Swiss, however, continued to steer their traditionalist course. It was only in 1993 that the government officially modified its position.[99] The change came far too late, but let us not forget that the American changeover was also tortuous and lasted from 1917 to 1941. Furthermore, the United States was rather pragmatic in its attitude toward neutrality after 1941, since there was no complete switch from traditionalism to internationalism. The American government respected neutral rights and duties in military matters; it was only with respect to economics that these rights were no longer accepted. As mentioned earlier, in effect the United States practised a moderate type of internationalism.

3
United Nations, 1945–1946

The Charter and neutrality

The UN Charter is no mere copy of the League Covenant. The differences are important. This has much to do with the fact that different American presidents stood behind them: the League Covenant was Wilsonian in spirit, while the UN Charter has a strong Rooseveltian bent. The two men, while agreeing on many questions of international politics, had different perceptions of a number of issues, among them the role and usefulness of small countries, particularly small neutral countries.[1]

Compared with the League, the United Nations is more *hierarchical* and *centralised,* and it is based on a different conception of *international law.* The UN is more hierarchical in that it makes a distinction between large and small powers (veto and non-veto powers), and it is more centralised because the Security Council has the power to decide questions of war and peace authoritatively. It breaks more sweepingly with established international law, because it embraces the outlawry of war. All three aspects affect neutrality.[2]

From what we know today, Roosevelt aimed at *hierarchy* from the very beginning. He wanted 'Four Policemen' to stand at the centre of the future international organisation.[3] Cordell Hull put it as follows: 'The President favored a four-power establishment that would police the world with the forces of the United States, Britain, Russia and China. All other nations, including France, were to be disarmed.'[4]

There is much evidence of this intention. When Molotov visited the White House for the first time during the war, in May 1942, Roosevelt indicated that the Big Four ought to impose peace, and 'if any nation menaced the peace, it could be blockaded and then if still recalcitrant, bombed.'[5] At the Teheran conference, FDR spoke to Stalin directly about the same ideas.[6] Sumner Welles, who was in charge of drafting initial plans for the future organisation and who conferred with Roosevelt most frequently on such matters, confirms these reports. Although the president had a number of different plans in those initial years, he adhered faithfully to the idea of the Four Policemen.[7]

Roosevelt felt strongly that a future international organisation could function only if the four great powers acted in concert. In his view, nothing could operate without them. A great power could make or break world peace. This was not the case with smaller powers: singly and even in larger groupings, they could not draw the world into another major war, certainly not against the combined will of the Great Powers. Roosevelt was also convinced that, as recent history had shown amply, small nations under conditions of modern warfare were incapable of defending themselves against powerful aggressors.[8]

Welles reports that Roosevelt had a condescending attitude towards smaller nations: 'I often felt during these years that in his attitude to the smaller countries outside the Western Hemisphere the President was unduly impatient.'[9] Nothing of the sort is known about Woodrow Wilson. On the contrary, he was impatient with the Great Powers and very understanding of the small powers, particularly those in Europe. His popularity in the small successor states of Eastern Europe was legion. For the neutrals this had very favourable consequences.

Roosevelt enjoyed dealing with the representatives of the larger powers and was eager to meet them at various summit meetings during the war. The Yalta conference also shows that he did not hesitate to enter into secret understandings with them. Wilson, on the other hand, disliked the 'wheeling and dealing' in Paris and truly believed in open covenants openly agreed upon. The results of both approaches were in part questionable, but the difference is marked.

Roosevelt was convinced that Wilson had made a mistake in his handling of the Great Powers, in not granting them special privileges in the League. Opposition to American membership had actually arisen in part from the erroneous assumption that the Covenant would permit an agency of the League to give orders to the American government. Had the veto existed then, this fear might never have arisen. This would be different under the UN Charter. The veto, Hull told a group of concerned Senators in May 1944,

is in the document primarily on account of the United States. It is a necessary safeguard in dealing with a new and untried world arrangement ... the main focus of the veto would be military and other means of exercising force, such as economic sanctions, and not the numerous other issues that were certain to come before the Council.[10]

Hull's words reveal a surprising amount of scepticism about the United Nations and contrast sharply with the official optimism propagated publicly. The stark 'realism' of Hull's view also contrasts with Woodrow Wilson's famous 'idealism'. One wonders whether Woodrow Wilson would ever have used such words, even in private, about the potentialities of collective security.

The *centralised* character of the United Nations is evidenced in the Security Council's competence to determine authoritatively a breach of the peace (and with it the existence of aggression), to decide on whether or not to act and, ultimately, to take direct charge of enforcement action. These powers go considerably beyond those of the League Council. While the League Council did have the authority to determine aggression, it did not have the authority to decide on unified action and certainly could not take charge of enforcement. The League Council and the League Assembly could only appeal to the duty of all member states to participate individually in collective action. This made enforcement decentralised and more voluntary. It left more room for sovereignty and, with it, more leeway for neutrality.

The UN Charter severely limits these degrees of freedom. In Art. 2, 5, members pledge to give the organisation 'every assistance in any action it takes in accordance with the present Charter', and since the Charter makes centralised decisions for unified action possible, it become virtually impossible to remain aloof. Assuming unanimous support of the Great Powers in such a decision, the pressure for small states, neutral or not, to align themselves becomes overwhelming.

Given the functioning of the Security Council, there are only two ways a neutral might still be able to salvage some of its status. A first possibility is provided in Art. 48, which states that the action required to carry out Security Council decisions shall be taken by all the members 'or by some of them, as the Security Council may determine'. This gives the Security Council the freedom to release members from the obligation to participate, but it is the Council that decides and not the individual state.[11] It is, therefore, questionable whether such a state would be neutral in the traditional sense of the word or whether it would assume the status of non-participation.[12]

A second possibility is provided in Art. 43. It stipulates that states have to conclude special arrangements with the Security Council to make available armed forces assistance and facilities, including rights of passage, necessary for the purpose of maintaining international peace and security. A neutral could possibly refuse to negotiate such additional agreements and thereby practise *de facto* abstention. It would be an act of bad faith, however, not in the spirit of the Charter.[13]

Because Art. 43 applies to military sanctions only, a neutral would still have to participate in economic sanctions. Under these circumstances, a neutral would practise qualified neutrality, or what the Swiss under the League called differential neutrality. There still remains an important difference: while the League formally recognised this status, the United Nations never has. For a small neutral nation intent on getting international recognition for its special position, this is a highly unsatisfactory situation.[14] It demonstrates how hostile the UN Charter is to the very principle of neutrality. It is a clear expression of radical internationalism.[15]

Neutrality can gain no legal recognition under the United Nations Charter; it can only be obtained under the traditional law of war. For the UN there is no war as such. The Charter speaks instead of 'breaches of the peace', 'aggression', or 'enforcement actions'.[16] This was different under the League of Nations. The Covenant uses the term 'war' throughout and in its traditional meaning. Art. 16, representing the core of collective security, explicitly stated that treaty violations by one member constituted an act of war against all other members. League action, therefore, brought about a traditional state of war in which the classical law of war would presumably still have its validity.

One of the basic features of the traditional law of war is the legal equality of the belligerents; both sides in a conflict have rights and duties. The neutral, too, has to deal with both belligerents on an equal footing. The Covenant does not appear to challenge this view, but the UN Charter does. Under the Charter an authoritative determination of aggression is possible; based on that there is no more room for the equal and impartial treatment of the two sides.

Today we know that the UN Charter is interpreted less strictly. In the Korean War, for instance, the United Nations recognised the legal equality of the aggressors when it sat down with them at the negotiating table and concluded an armistice. It also recognised the impartiality of neutrals when two neutral commissions were set up to deal with various ceasefire matters. And in the context of peace-keeping missions, the UN regularly operates on the principle of impartiality. But such actions were not the intent of those who framed the Charter. They manifestly had in mind the elimination of the ideas of impartiality and neutrality from the future organisation. The framers were predominantly Americans sitting in the Department of State. Their conception of neutrality will have to be analysed later on.

San Francisco and Potsdam

After what has been said, it should not come as a surprise that the neutrals were not invited to San Francisco. There were some interesting reasons for this. In order to be present and to become a founding member of the United Nations, participants had to fulfil certain conditions. Either a country had to be a signatory of the United Nations Declaration of 1 January 1942 (which in fact set up the wartime alliance), or it had to have declared war on Japan or Germany before 1 March 1945. Since the neutrals could meet neither of these requirements, they could not participate.

Turkey was an exception. It had remained neutral throughout the war, but towards the end of February 1945, mainly in response to British pressure, it declared war on Germany. Several other non-European states did the same. It was rather ironic that countries that had remained at peace now had to declare war in order to join an organisation intent upon abolishing war and preserving peace! The Swedes and the Swiss were not about to play this questionable game.

As a result, they became, in the new language of the United Nations, countries that were 'not peace-loving'. Apparently, the argument that neutrality was a policy of war and not of peace had taken hold in the new organisation. Of course, it did not take long for the UN to change its mind. Already by 1953, the Swiss and the Swedes were called upon to assist in the termination of an awkward conflict, the Korean 'war'. As neutrals, the UN then argued, they were particularly fit to make a contribution to peace.

In his opening address at the first plenary session in San Francisco, the new Secretary of State, Edward R. Stettinius, condemned neutrality explicitly. He argued that for the successful maintenance of peace and security, all countries of the world had to unite: 'Tyranny and barbarism have never recognised neutrality and they never will. We do not intend to build a world organization that will overlook this cardinal fact.'[17] If the neutrals had not known so before, they now had it directly from the mouth of the American Secretary of State. This was not 1919, when at the Paris Conference Woodrow Wilson tried to accommodate the neutrals and to find a solution for their participation in the exercise of collective security.

In 1945, the neutrals felt that they were being punished for their role in the war.[18] Stettinius, in his opening address, denied this. He thought that writing the constitution of the new world organisation was 'a task wholly separate from the punishment of the international gangsters who started this war.' The conference 'should not, therefore, be entangled with the many and the complex political and economic issues involved in the defeat of Germany and Japan.'[19]

To the neutrals, the Allies had not succeeded in fully practising this separation. In their eyes, they were now being punished for having collaborated with 'the international gangsters' who had started the war. After all, in the immediately preceding months both Sweden and Switzerland had been put under a great deal of pressure to stop trading with Germany. Furthermore, the enforcement of the Safehaven programme, set up in the name of the emerging United Nations, was about to begin. This was definitely no time to face the neutrals at San Francisco. It would have created an entirely false impression. Some agencies in Washington would have strongly objected.

The Russians also had reasons for not wanting to see the neutrals in San Francisco. Stalin could not forget fighting Franco in the Spanish Civil War and having Spanish troops support Hitler during the Great Patriotic War. His dislike of Portugal's Salazar was no less intense, although for somewhat different reasons.

There were a number of reasons why Stalin disliked Sweden, but the main factor was its relationship with Finland. The Swedes have traditionally had close contacts with the Finnish, and when the Russians attacked the Finns in the winter of 1939, the Swedes gave them all the diplomatic and economic support that they could. This was in accordance with international law, but it did nothing to endear them to the Russians.[20]

The hostility towards Switzerland had deeper roots. It went back to the years immediately after the First World War, when the Swiss expelled the entire Bolshevik diplomatic contingent for having engaged in subversive activities. Diplomatic relations between the two countries then remained suspended throughout the interwar period and during the Second World War.[21] They were only resumed in 1946.[22]

The French pursued the most openly anti-neutral course in San Francisco. Since they had not been invited to the preparatory conference at Dumbarton Oaks, they were now eager to submit some particularly new proposals. One concerned neutrality. The provisions for membership, the French argued, should be amended with the following words: 'Participation in the organization implies obligations which are incompatible with the status of neutrality.'[23] The French delegate explained that 'status of neutrality' referred to permanent neutrality.[24] The proposal ran into opposition, however. Not only were some of the smaller powers unhappy, but the United States disliked it, too. The question came up twice in internal discussions among the American delegates. Two objections were raised:

(a)   such a provision was unnecessary, since the fact was already clear,
(b)   a discussion of this matter would precipitate the committee into a discussion of the seat of the Organisation.[25]

The position shows that for the Americans it was already an established fact that neutrality was incompatible with the letter and the spirit of the UN Charter; no additional emphasis was needed. United States opposition to the French proposal was, therefore, not motivated by a desire to defend neutrality but, rather, by practical considerations. Bringing Switzerland into the discussion would have raised the question of the seat of the League of Nations. Was it a wise decision to locate the headquarters of an international organisation on neutral territory? In 1920, a number of countries thought so, and perhaps some still did in 1945. But now the United States wanted to have the future organisation on its own soil – so why raise the awkward question of neutrality?[26] Furthermore, by declaring Switzerland an international outlaw, the United Nations might unnecessarily complicate future discussions with that country. After all, the League buildings were part of the UN heritage, and their use would have to be renegotiated with the Swiss.[27]

The Americans, therefore, decided to talk the French out of the idea. In deliberations with the French delegation, they came up with a face-saving strategy. It was agreed that the proposed amendment would be supported by one of the other four veto powers 'whereupon the French would "gracefully withdraw" their amendment'. It was also agreed that the proposed words would be written into the protocol and be given the weight of an official interpretation of the Charter. The proposal would then be sanctioned when voting took place on Articles 5 and 6 of Chapter II on Membership. In this manner an explicit condemnation of permanent neutrality was avoided, and the 'outlawry of neutrality' had found its limits.[28]

The incident shows that the Americans were not the most anti-neutral among the veto powers in San Francisco. Russia was the most hostile, but France tried to give its hostility the most clear-cut expression. Despite Stettinius' harsh words at the beginning of the conference, there were limits to American anti-neutrality. It was one thing to be anti-neutral in principle but quite another to turn this attitude into a specific policy aimed against a particular country.[29]

Still, the American position on neutrality in 1945 stood in marked contrast to the position taken by Woodrow Wilson in 1919. During the Paris Peace talks, the Swiss had managed to convince Wilson that, as a permanently neutral state, they deserved a special status in the coming international organisation. Their aim was to obtain the status of a differential neutral, taking part in economic sanctions but abstaining from military sanctions. Wilson declared himself to be in full agreement with military neutrality and thought that the neutrals could join the League with reservations. Article XXI, which specifically excepted the Monroe Doctrine from being affected by the covenant, could be constructed to include also other 'international engagements', such as the perpetual neutrality of Switzerland.[30]

The Swiss also managed to convince Wilson that the new international organisation ought to be situated on neutral territory, in Geneva. The Europeans were divided on this question (the French and Belgians pressed for Brussels), but the Swiss finally won, 'thanks to the favorable disposition of President Wilson toward Switzerland.'[31] No such favourable disposition prevailed in 1945.[32] America was no longer willing to admit that placing an international organisation on neutral ground might have its advantages. On the contrary, the organisation had to be placed squarely on the ground of one of the great powers. This was symbolic of the shift in American thinking. The new virtue was partiality and not impartiality.

Within three weeks after the closing of the San Francisco Conference, the Big Three met in Potsdam and paved the way for the admission of neutral countries. The final communiqué stated that 'the Three Governments, so far as they are concerned, will support applications for membership from those States which have remained neutral during the war and which fulfil the qualifications set out above.' These were the qualifications contained in the UN Charter. A state had to be 'peace-loving' and had to accept the obligations of the organisation. Only Spain was excluded *per se*. Because 'of its origins, its nature, its record and its close association with the aggressor States', Spain did not possess the necessary qualifications.[33]

The United States and Great Britain supported such a solution from the start of the negotiations; only Russia tried for a while to make things difficult. Molotov tied the question of the neutrals to that of former belligerents like Romania, Bulgaria, and Hungary, now also potential candidates for admission. His aim was to get countries now under Russian control into the UN before the neutrals or, if that did not succeed, to get them in together and to obtain recognition for their governments, which had so far been refused by both England and America.

On 20 July, during the third session of the foreign ministers, the question of admissions was broached for the first time, and Britain's Eden mentioned Sweden, Portugal, and Switzerland as potential neutral candidates. Molotov did not enter into a discussion about the three countries but talked about Italy.[34] Only during the seventh session of the foreign ministers, on 24 July, did the discussion concentrate fully on the actual candidates. Molotov, after steering the discussion his way, concluded that 'the choice between Switzerland and Portugal on the one hand and Rumania and Bulgaria on the other hand should be resolved in favour of those who helped us to win the war.' That would have excluded Switzerland and Portugal but included Romania and Bulgaria, because the latter had turned against the Fascist powers at the end of the war.

Eden rejected this proposal. He stated flatly that the UK did not consider these two East European governments as representative and therefore refused to recognise them. Realising the deadlock, Byrnes, the new US Secretary of State, suggested a formula that ultimately brought about a solution:

> The three Governments also hope that the Council of Foreign Ministers may without undue delay prepare peace treaties with Rumania, Bulgaria, Hungary and Finland. It is also their desire on the conclusion of these peace treaties with responsible democratic governments of these countries to support their application for membership in the United Nations Organization.[35]

Thus the barrier to admission of neutrals to the UN was removed. It remained to be seen how the Security Council would interpret the term 'peace-loving' and the further condition that, as stated in Article 4 of Chapter II, candidates had to be 'able and willing' to carry out UN obligations. Would Switzerland and Sweden, in view of their record of long-standing permanent neutrality, be regarded as 'able and willing' to give their full support to UN enforcement actions? Would the

French, in view of their intervention in San Francisco and the commentary written into the official record, use their veto to block the admission of a permanent neutral? The test came quickly. Sweden had been ready to join the UN from the beginning. The government had proclaimed its interest openly on various occasions, but also let it be known that Sweden would return to a policy of strict neutrality should collective security fail because of a quarrel among the veto powers.[36] Despite such candour, Swedish admission proved to be no problem. The country was admitted on 19 November 1946, together with a number of other nations. No awkward questions were raised by any delegation.[37]

On the contrary, the American delegate on the Security Council made some very flattering remarks about Sweden. These may have reflected personal opinion more than official policy, but they show that some American diplomats must have had a very favourable impression of some neutral countries during the war:

> I associate myself with enthusiasm with the remarks made by my colleagues (Holland, France, China) on the application of Sweden. Sweden is a country where I had the honour to live during nearly five years at the time when my country was at war, and I learned to have for the people of that country the greatest admiration and respect. I know of no country in the world which could make and will make, if admitted to the United Nations, a richer and more constructive contribution to its labours.[38]

The case of Switzerland was different. Although it was clear after 1946 that, in principle, Switzerland would be welcome in the United Nations, the Swiss government did not intend to join unless the country's perpetual neutrality, recognised and guaranteed since the Congress of Vienna, would once again be acknowledged. As the Swiss were aware, however, the prospects of gaining such recognition were unrealistic in the years immediately after the war. They consequently postponed the question of joining the United Nations, and they have not joined to this day.

Two kinds of internationalism

It is evident that in the drafting of the UN Charter, the radical internationalists within the American government prevailed, those who were committed to the 'outlawry of war and of neutrality'. What the traditionalists had feared all along finally happened – many of the internationalist neutrals were neutral in name only and simply waited for an opportunity to transcend neutrality once and for all. Their espousal of neutrality had been purely opportunistic. They saw that during the interwar period a return to Wilsonian policies was out of the question, and as a result they opted for the best alternative they could get under the circumstances – the discriminatory embargo in the name of neutrality. In this strategy, neutrality played a useful but temporary role.

Obviously, the traditionalists were not happy. Already in 1944, when the outlines of the United Nations Charter became visible, the traditionalist Edwin Borchard vehemently attacked the idea of collective security and of enforcing peace. He deplored that apparently

> the punitive theory of 'peace enforcement' will again be tried, as against the more profound effort to deal with war as a disease having causes and symptoms which must be treated with psychological understanding by a concert of nations looking not for 'criminal' nations but for that physical distress which evokes demands for change.[39]

The United Nations would, in Borchard's view, not be able to handle the many profound changes that the world was constantly undergoing. Instead, it would tend, very much like the League of Nations, to sanction the status quo. Furthermore, the UN would suffer from the inequality on which it was built: 'the centralized agency whose supposed impartial decisions are to be "enforced" by the theoretical community, is in fact replaced by the few ruling states whose decisions are to be "enforced" by themselves upon the others.'[40]

In a book published in 1946, Borchard pursued the same theme. The new system, he argued, 'is consistent only with a theory of subordination, not legal equality ... it necessarily plays havoc with the rules concerning non-intervention, recognition, neutrality, and the relation of States to each other; it substitutes the whim and caprice of certain hegemonial Powers for law.' Borchard doubted whether the United Nations would ever be able to enforce peace, and therefore he recommended that 'it would be better not to attempt what they cannot achieve and to remain consultative, recommendatory, advisory, administrative.'[41]

The UN Charter did not have to be so rigorously anti-neutral. The men drafting the document could have opted for solutions affording neutrality a more comfortable place. Some of these options were widely discussed in the interwar period, and one was even suggested by Roosevelt himself during the war. The President made it a habit, almost a pastime, to discuss questions of postwar organisation freely and informally. His approach indicated that he was 'less interested in systematically developing a detailed plan of post-war organization than in testing reactions to various ideas and in launching "trial balloons" without committing himself.'[42] His idea about building a 'neutral watchdog commission' into the future organisation was one of these trial balloons. It would be a commission

> which would report to the four major states any violations of the armaments prohibition or any impending threat of aggression. The policing powers could then threaten to quarantine the offending state and, if that did not work, to bomb some part of it.[43]

Not much more is known about the scheme, but the meaning is fairly clear. The permanently neutral states, presumably Sweden and Switzerland, would be full members of the United Nations having the role of investigating and reporting, on behalf of the Security Council, actual and potential breaches of the peace. If the Council played the part of the fire department fighting the fire, then the neutrals would constitute the alarm mechanism. The arrangement would give them an important role in fact finding, and presumably they would be suited for this task because of their greater impartiality. In order not to impair this advantage, it would be logical to exempt them from participating in military sanctions. The watchdogs would maintain differential neutrality.

The idea is attractive, because it serves both sides. The Council benefits from the impartial character of the investigation, and the permanent neutrals have an active and constructive role to play without abandoning all their cherished assets. They yield some of their indifference for the benefit of the collectivity but preserve the right not to take sides militarily. That the neutrals were willing to play such a role became evident some years later during the Korean War.

Another option favourable to neutrality would have been to structure the United Nations more along the lines of the Harvard Draft Convention on Aggression. It referred to 'forceful acts constituting a violation of legal obligations' and embraced the concept of 'supporting state'. The language would have served both the neutrals and the United States. For the neutrals the situation would have been similar to that under the League, for the United States the conception would have coincided with the policy adopted in the conduct of hostilities and in the pursuit of military and economic warfare. The same moderate internationalism would then have prevailed inside the United Nations and out. Actually, the United Nations Charter could have been used in these circumstances to legally sanction a policy that in the war had been established as a fact.

Whether the State Department task force drafting the Charter discussed these questions is uncertain. It is a fact, however, that the option existed and that it was not pursued. Instead, two tendencies regarding neutrality emerged during the war: one clearly hostile to neutrality and the other willing to tolerate supporting states. The radical position prevailed among officials assigned to draft a new world organisation, while the more moderate stance predominated among officials charged with the actual conduct of war. Both attitudes were internationalist, that is, both assumed that wars were to be fought for a just cause and that consequently total indifference and impartiality were unjustifiable. The difference between the two tendencies was merely one of degree.

From what we know, no one within the American government argued in favour of integral or traditional neutrality during the Second World War. At best, that concept had some academic supporters, but America had, *de facto,* abandoned integral neutrality during the First World War. From 1914 to 1917 it did so under pressure, but from 1917 to 1918, when the country itself became a belligerent, it abandoned integral neutrality voluntarily.[44] After this reversal and after all the confusion about neutrality in the interwar period, a commitment to integral neutrality could hardly be expected during the Second World War. America was now irrevocably on an internationalist course, but, unfortunately, *two kinds of internationalism prevailed.*

This raised some interesting questions for the postwar period. Would the two tendencies continue to coexist, and if so, how? Would they be in constant conflict with each other? Or would one simply prevail over the other? All these developments were possible. If the United Nations became a truly universal organisation and functioned as anticipated, then the concept of 'supporting state' would most likely die. If, however, the opposite should be true, if conflicts could not be settled within the new world organisation, then it was conceivable that the United States might return to the concept of 'supporting state'.

It was also conceivable that the two tendencies would simply coexist. This would be the case if the UN Charter had some impact on conflict resolution after 1945 but not enough to prevent some conflicts from being settled along traditional lines. If that were to be the case, then America would have to live with its dualistic neutrality conception for a long time to come, and it would have to try to manage the two conflicting tendencies in a very pragmatic fashion.

Hallward Library - Issue Receipt

Customer name: Dinesia, Inke Hilarie

Title: East-West conflict and European
neutrality / Harto Hakovirta.
ID: 6003350583
Due: 28/05/2008 23:59

Total items: 1
02/04/2008 15:32

All items must be returned before the due date
and time.
The Loan period may be shortened if the item is
requested.

4
UN Law versus Geneva Law, 1946–1949

Humanitarian law of war

In the eighteenth and nineteenth centuries, America actively promoted the development of the law of neutrality, but it also did much to further the development of the humanitarian law of war. Americans abhorred impressment and the cruel treatment of sailors and soldiers at the hands of the British.[1] The American campaign against privateering was also in part motivated by humanitarian concerns. Finally, the Civil War taught Americans a great deal about the problems of the wounded in battle, prisoners of war and civilian refugees. The universalist liberal values so intimately related to neutrality and free trade also extended to humanitarian concerns in war.

The idea of the Red Cross, therefore, found great sympathy in the United States. It had originated among a few Swiss, centring around Henri Dunant, and it spread rapidly to many parts of the world. It was the International Committee of the Red Cross (ICRC) that took special charge of promoting the idea abroad. Made up entirely of Swiss citizens, the ICRC made an effort to be neutral and not to get involved in national politics. It was particularly successful in getting a large number of nations to sign various conventions on humanitarian law of war.

The ICRC was very active in the Second World War, and towards the end of the conflict it was the ICRC's intention, as it had been at the end of the First World War, to evaluate the various conventions after six years of gruelling war. In February 1945, before hostilities had ceased, the ICRC therefore informed all governments and national Red Cross societies of its intention to undertake a revision of the various conventions. The American government, of course, was also approached.

In the eyes of the ICRC, three former conventions would have to be revised: the Xth Hague Convention of 1907, covering the victims of maritime war, the 1929 Geneva Convention on the victims of land war, and the 1929 Geneva Convention on prisoners of war. In addition, the ICRC envisaged setting up a new convention for the protection of civilians in war.[2]

The relation of humanitarian law of war to traditional law of war is very close. The Hague Conventions of 1899 and 1907 both dealt with humanitarian law of war, but, as we know, they also dealt with matters of war in general, including neutrality.[3] As a result, Geneva Law has always been considered to be part and parcel of the kind of international law that the United Nations Charter was meant to abolish. What would the American reaction be? The ICRC request came at a time when the United States was about to put its signature on the Charter and when public support for the new organisation was overwhelming.

It was also a time when neutrality was not highly regarded in the United States. The neutrals were not welcome in San Francisco, and the Swiss, in particular, were practically regarded as international outlaws. But it was the neutrals that stood behind the ICRC effort to revise the various conventions. Evidence that the United States was fully aware of this connection is contained in a 1950 Department of State Policy Paper on Switzerland:

> The role of the International Committee of the Red Cross (ICRC) is closely related to Swiss neutrality. As the Swiss frequently point out, neutrality enables the ICRC to function effectively, while Switzerland in turn is strengthened in its resolve to remain neutral in order that such indispensable services to humanity in time of war may be rendered. The importance which the Swiss attach to the ICRC was well illustrated by their official sponsorship of the international diplomatic conference which met at Geneva last year to adopt the convention for the protection of civilian war victims. The Swiss Foreign Minister was chairman of this conference, and the Confederation contributed some $200,000 toward financing it.[4]

In the Second World War, the interrelation became even more intimate because Switzerland, being one of the few countries not involved in the war, assumed in a great number of cases the role of a protecting power. As such, it was charged by the various conventions with the duty of taking care of victims of war. Large numbers of American POWs came under the purview of either the ICRC or the Swiss. The roles of the two were often indistinguishable.

The same intimacy characterised the ICRC initiative of February 1945. While it was true that the ICRC wanted governments the world over to consider the state of the Geneva Conventions, it was equally true that for the Swiss government this was a welcome opportunity to remind the world of the usefulness of neutrality. After all, it was precisely at this time that the neutrals were coming under severe pressure, as we have seen. They felt the squeeze of Allied economic warfare, and they were cold-shouldered by the United Nations. It hurt not to be considered a 'peace-loving' state; the ICRC initiative was thus, for the Swiss foreign ministry, a means of easing diplomatic and moral isolation.

Some proponents of the United Nations were anything but happy with the ICRC proposal. Geneva and Hague Law, in their eyes, was something the United Nations should do away with once and for all. Responding favourably to the ICRC initiative would show an appreciation of all that was wrong with the traditional international system, including neutrality, and it would indicate a definite lack of faith in the system of the United Nations.

Such thoughts were voiced at the first postwar conference of the International Law Association, the professional organisation of international jurists. It met in 1946 in Cambridge, England, and the agenda included, among other items, the following: 'The Effects of the United Nations Charter on the Development of International Law with Special Reference to the Status of Neutrality and the Hague and Geneva Conventions'. Quite obviously, the title went straight to the heart of the matter. The problem, in its essence, could hardly be expressed more clearly.[5]

The main speaker on the subject was C. G. Dehn of the United Kingdom. After a lengthy introduction dealing with the general development of international law, Dehn came to the central issue. The Hague and Geneva Conventions, he argued, 'were based on the legality of war. That basis has disappeared. A revolution in international law has taken place and international law must now concern itself with the consequences of that revolution.'[6]

There would, in the future, be no need for neutral states and, in regard to the Geneva Conventions, no need for Protecting Powers, a function often assumed by neutrals. Said Dehn:

> There would seem to be no valid reason why hereafter any state should play the part of a protecting power – and unless some countries are granted special privileges that Switzerland is understood to be seeking – there will be no neutral states from amongst whom a

protecting power could be chosen. The United Nations will need no Protecting Power.[7]

Of the nine speakers addressing the question after Dehn, only one was in favour of maintaining the traditional laws of war and of neutrality.[8] This was the Swiss delegate, Paul Guggenheim of the Institut Universitaire des Hautes Etudes Internationales at Geneva. He suggested that the organisation created in San Francisco was not perfect enough to guarantee that collective security would function. If the Security Council should be paralysed by the use of the great power veto, there would again arise conflicts that had to be settled outside the organisation. In that case, there might be two kinds of conflicts in the future, just and indifferent ones.

Guggenheim made specific reference to the two Harvard Conventions of 1939: 'Les experts de la Harvard Law School ont établi deux projets de conventions spéciales pour tenir compte de ces deux situations différentes.'[9] States should follow this example and get used to the possibility of two kinds of conflicts. The Hague and Geneva Conventions would then still have a reason for existing.[10]

The road to Geneva

In the United States, the issue was debated at the annual meetings of the American Society of International Law. At the 1949 conference, the agenda included the topic of the 'Revision of the Rules of Warfare', and the main speaker was Major William G. Downey, Jr, Chief of the International Law Branch of the Judge Advocate General's Office, Department of the Army. He represented that part of government that had to deal directly with the law of war, and he had seen its advantages when it came to protecting American soldiers, sailors, and airmen. Needless to say, Downey spoke in favour of taking the road to Geneva.

Downey had already spoken briefly at the annual meeting of 1948, and he was well aware that his task was a difficult one. 'I am here', he said in his short remarks in 1948, 'to plead what I am sure a lot of you are going to regard as an unpopular cause. That cause is simply a plea for some constructive thought concerning the development of the international law of war.'[11]

At the 1949 meeting, Downey began with a quote from the Bible: 'Do unto others as you would have others do unto you.' And he continued: 'In 1907 at the time of the Hague Conference of International Peace, this standard guided those wise men of many nations who gave us the Hague Conventions.' He then proceeded to enumerate the various insufficiencies of the Hague Conventions in view of the technological developments in warfare. Next, he spoke of the need to review parts of the Geneva Conventions, the Prisoners of War Convention in particular. Downey closed with the hope that he had been able to demonstrate that there existed an urgent need for a complete revision of the rules of warfare.[12]

Charles G. Fenwick was the first to enter the discussion. To say that he disagreed is to put it mildly. He was outraged. His words are important enough to be quoted at some length:

> First I must apologize to our speaker who has proposed a revision of the laws of war. I think the whole thing is as fantastic as anything I have heard of since 1923 when a great and distinguished jurist ... Mr. John Bassett Moore, proposed, after the First World War, that we have a revision of the laws of war. You all know that a commission was appointed which met at The Hague. We had a meeting of the American Society of International Law to discuss the revision of the laws of war and I remember ... that we protested with all our energy against the fantastic conception of revising the laws of war. Thank God, in spite of very bitter opposition, the proposal was abandoned.[13]

Major Downey was upset and responded in equally clear language:

> I dislike saying that Dr. Fenwick does not know whereof he speaks, but the successful application of the Prisoners of War Convention, the Sick and Wounded Convention, as well as many items of the customary law of war which I don't have time to enumerate, prove beyond a shadow of a doubt that the rules of warfare do exist, that they were used successfully during the past war, and that they did protect our American personnel from the treatment Dr. Fenwick knows they would have received if the rules had not existed to protect them.[14]

Downey concluded with a few remarks that related directly to the Geneva Conventions: 'Today at Geneva the Prisoners of War Convention is being revised. Recently, we received word that the Russians had arrived with a delegation of twenty-nine men. This fact may not seem at all important to you, but in the prior conferences, held at Geneva two years ago and at Stockholm last year, the Russians and their satellites refused to attend.'[15]

The division between Downey and Fenwick has a number of dimensions. Besides showing the well-known differences between 'realism' and 'idealism', it highlights the clash between the people at the Pentagon who had to deal with actual victims of war and scholar–diplomats occasionally working for the Department of State. For officers like Downey it was a professional duty to think about the next war, and he had little patience with people like Fenwick, who propounded abstract ideas while on assignment in peaceful Latin America. Divisions ran deep and had personal and professional overtones.[16]

Within the government, the 'realist' line prevailed. When approached by the ICRC in 1945, the United States reacted favourably and immediately set about preparing administratively for the task. This was facilitated because, for a long time, the American government had made it a habit to co-ordinate matters of humanitarian law of war with the American Red Cross. Actually, members of this organisation had often assumed a leading role on behalf of the US government and were to do so again this time.[17]

In preparation for the actual conference of 1949, the ICRC advanced on three levels, that is, the field experts, the various national Red Cross Societies, and governments. The United States co-operated fully on all levels. It sent experts to Geneva in the autumn of 1945. The American Red Cross attended the 1946 meeting of the national societies, and the government itself participated in the 1947 conference of governmental experts.[18]

To prepare for the various conferences, the Department of State, early in 1946, set up an interdepartmental committee to co-ordinate matters. Various departments and agencies were represented, including the American Red Cross. From this group a list of suggestions emerged that was submitted to the two large governmental conferences held in 1948 and 1949. The first was held in Stockholm and the second, final conference, in Geneva. A governmental delegation and the American Red Cross represented the United States at both conferences.

Four conventions emerged from these conferences, all of which were signed by the United States and confirmed by the Senate in 1951:

1.   Geneva Convention for the Amelioration of the Condition of the Wounded and Sick of Armed Forces in the Field;
2.   Geneva Convention for the Amelioration of the Condition of Wounded, Sick and Shipwrecked Members of Armed Forces at Sea;
3.   Geneva Convention Relative to the Treatment of Prisoners of War;

4. Geneva Convention Relative to the Protection of Civilian Persons in Time of War.

The American government was happy with the results.[19] As Dean Acheson could report to the Senate, 'substantial portions of the United States position on all four of the conventions were accepted by the Conference as presented.' The United States had made half a dozen major suggestions, almost all of which found their way into the new conventions. Acheson was not boasting, therefore, when he told the Senate that the United States had 'played an active and prominent role in furthering the efforts to revise and extend these humanitarian conventions.'[20]

Once the Senate had ratified the conventions, Raymund T. Yingling, vice-chairman of the American delegation in Geneva, explained their contents to a wider public in the *American Journal of International Law*.[21] He placed special emphasis on the first eleven articles, which are of a general nature and common to all conventions. The articles are important, because they deal with the organisational questions of applying the conventions. Article 2 stipulates that the conventions apply to 'declared war or any other armed conflict' arising between the signatories; Article 4 provides that they apply to 'Neutral Powers' as well. The concepts of 'war' and of 'neutrality' are thus an intimate part of the conventions.

Yingling calls Article 8 the keystone of the agreements. It provides that the conventions 'shall be applied with the cooperation and under the scrutiny of the Protecting Powers whose duty it is to safeguard the interests of the Parties to the conflict.' As it happens, neutral states have often been chosen to play the role of protecting powers. Once more neutrality is emphasised.

Article 10 provides for substitutes for protecting powers. This can be any 'organization which offers all guarantees of impartiality and efficacy' to take over the duties. Special reference is made to the International Committee of the Red Cross, which, after all, is the organisation most often charged with such duties. Article 11, finally, provides for the settlement of disputes between the parties to the conflict. The protecting power, so it is suggested, should lend its good offices to find a meeting place, 'possibly on neutral territory suitably chosen', and it may propose 'a person belonging to a neutral Power or delegated by the International Committee of the Red Cross, who shall be invited to take part in such a meeting.'[22]

These few references show that the Geneva Conventions do indeed accord the traditional notions of war and neutrality an important place. Opponents of the Law of Geneva were therefore entirely justified in regarding it as a concession to the traditional philosophy of international law, and, conversely, as an expression of little faith in the law of the United Nations. The fact that the US government supported this effort so soon after the signing of the UN Charter raises some interesting questions about the conceptions of collective security and neutrality in the postwar era.

Pragmatic humanitarianism

Earlier, I came to the conclusion that America had two conceptions of neutrality at the end of the Second World War. On the one hand, there was a tendency to outlaw neutrality within the framework of the United Nations and, on the other hand, a propensity to tolerate qualified neutrality in the conduct of military and economic warfare. What did the signing of the Geneva Conventions mean in this context?

It was obviously a move that strengthened the 'realist' tendency, or the conviction that conflicts outside the framework of the United Nations might still be possible and that qualified neutrality might still be useful for the United States. In this sense, the signing of the Geneva Conventions constituted a victory for moderate internationalism and a defeat for radical internationalism.

It would be a mistake, however, to interpret it as a success for integral or traditionalist neutrality. The United States did not take the road to Geneva in order to return to the Hague spirit and the comprehensive espousal of the traditional laws of war. If Major Downey meant to start such a process, he must have been disappointed. As Fenwick sensed correctly, such a venture would have had even fewer chances of success in 1949 than in 1923. Too much had changed in the meantime; the United Nations was a manifest fact of international life.

It would have been entirely wrong, therefore, for the traditionalists to celebrate. They had always insisted on a classical and integral interpretation of neutrality embracing wide neutral trading rights. To see the Geneva Convention as a step in this direction would have been an illusion. But there were hardly any traditionalists left in 1949. John Bassett Moore had died in 1947 at the age of 80, and Edwin Borchard was 67 when he died in 1951. Manley Hudson was 63 when the Geneva Conventions were signed. The Old Guard of traditionalist jurists was on its way out.[23]

Such illusions possibly prevailed abroad, within the ICRC and the Swiss government. Not that either of them wanted to restore all the traditional law of war by launching the renegotiations of the Red Cross Conventions, but there were hopes that the Swiss would thereby escape their isolation and that their conception of permanent and integral neutrality would gain renewed acceptance and even formal recognition.[24] These hopes were in vain.

While it is true that the renegotiating of the Geneva Conventions indeed helped the Swiss out of their isolation, it did not help them to regain recognition for their conception of neutrality. This was no longer 1920, when in London the League members paid their respects to the 'unique situation' of Switzerland and thereby renewed the recognition given to Swiss neutrality at the Congress of Vienna. In 1949, there was no hope that the members of the United Nations would do the same, either collectively or individually. As a result, the Swiss also had to learn that the ICRC Conventions were not a useful backdoor for obtaining recognition of traditionalist neutrality.

It follows that the signing of the Geneva Conventions cannot be interpreted as a victory for any one conception of neutrality. From the American point of view in particular, it must be seen against the background of the two competing views about neutrality. The United States (and most other countries as well) now stood with one leg inside the United Nations and with the other somewhat outside it.

This dualism has some interesting dimensions. At the level of *values* it is hardly noticeable, because, after all, there is a strongly humanitarian spirit behind both the Law of the United Nations and the Law of Geneva. In the preamble of the UN Charter, the People of the United Nations express their determination 'to save succeeding generations from the scourge of war ... to reaffirm faith in the fundamental human rights, in the dignity and worth of the human person.' The same spirit pervades the Red Cross principles. The first of these, entitled 'humanity', is a commitment 'to prevent and alleviate human suffering wherever it may be found. Its [the Red Cross's] purpose is to protect life and health and to ensure respect for the human being. It promotes mutual understanding, friendship, cooperation and lasting peace amongst all people.'[25]

These are the values that the United States subscribed to from the beginning of its existence. The liberal enlightenment ideas behind the 'Plan of 1776' and John Quincy Adams' 'Project of 1823' are virtually the same. American efforts against impressment and privateering also go in this direction. From a purely humanitarian point of view, the strict and moderate internationalists could only agree with the goals of both systems of law.

Neither was there any disagreement over *indifference,* since both the United Nations and the ICRC stressed the need to get actively involved in order to better the lot of this world. Difficulties set in, however, over the meaning of *impartiality.* Although both the United Nations and the ICRC are dedicated to solving problems in a spirit of impartiality, this means two very different things to them. The ICRC is devoted to impartiality in the classical sense of standing as a mediator between two conflicting parties. The United Nations, however, sees itself more as a referee standing over the two conflicting parties, as an arbiter empowered to enforce a body of mutually binding law.

This brings us to the core of the problem: it is a disagreement not over ends, but over means, or, more precisely, over the appropriate *type of law.* Should peace and human dignity be pursued on the basis of vol- untaristic law backed by national power, or should they be pursued on the basis of binding law backed by universalist power? At this point, the discussion boils down once more to the well-known debate between 'realism' and 'idealism'. As shown, this debate raged as furi- ously after the Second World War as it had before.[26]

For true internationalists like Charles Fenwick and Quincy Wright, peace and the dignity of man could never be guaranteed by a 'system of war', and the Geneva Conventions were to them an expression of exactly that. To the more moderate internationalists, the opposite was true. In their eyes, peace and the dignity of man could best be pro- moted not by advanced legal schemes unlikely to be implemented, but by more primitive legal efforts having a good chance for success. Downey, in his heated exchange with Fenwick, expressed this differ- ence very lucidly:

> It is not fantastic to reconsider the rules of war. If Dr. Fenwick thinks that we are going to enter into a long period of Utopia when no wars are going to be fought, let me call to his attention the periods of peace from 1919 to 1940, during which time, to my knowledge, this Society never discussed the rules of war. We were not interested; we were only interested in the laws of peace. But what happened when the law of peace collapsed? We are all inter- ested in peace, we all want peace but we must prepare for the time when peace no longer is with us.[27]

These are sentences full of meaning for the postwar era. What if the 'law of peace' collapsed once more? What would the United States do in such a case? By signing the Geneva Conventions the United States was better prepared for the time when there would no longer be peace, but would it stand by the ICRC? What if a conflict developed between the Law of the United Nations and the Law of Geneva? America's dualism could lead to a number of possible complications. The country might have to steer a highly pragmatic course in regard to humanitarian matters in a future war.

5
Alliance Building, 1948–1949

No Scandinavian bloc of neutrals

When the United States put its signature to the Geneva Red Cross Conventions of 1949, the Cold War was already on, and NATO had been created. For the first time in its history, the United States had entered into a peacetime alliance that tied it irrevocably to permanent international involvement. It was the kind of 'entangling alliance' that the Founding Fathers had warned of and that the isolationists of the interwar period had hoped would never come about.

The founding of NATO also meant that the UN system was not functioning. It was a return to traditional alliances in an anarchistic and hostile international setting – something that should have been overcome through the existence of the United Nations. But the Security Council was paralysed by the use of the great power veto, and the United States came to the conclusion that conflicts must be settled outside the organisation. The existence of NATO symbolised the fact that the idea of security by universal power had been replaced by the idea of security by blocs of power. It was a blow to universalism that reflected the emergence of more traditional concepts. Would it also lead to a greater appreciation of neutrality?

Since the question of neutrality arose in the context of membership, the first test came with the building of the alliance itself. Sweden, also feeling the growing tensions between East and West, made a serious attempt to organise a Scandinavian Neutral Bloc consisting of Sweden, Norway, and Denmark.[1] How would America react? Would it appreciate such a buffer zone between the Cold War fronts, or would it rather woo the Scandinavians away from their plans and into NATO membership? This was the question that America had to deal with in 1948 and early 1949.

Much would depend on strategic realities and on political perceptions. Of what military value were these countries to US defence? What
strength would they have as armed neutrals? How could the Russians
be expected to react? Would the next war, like the Second World War,
be a total war, or would it be more limited? Would America face
another Hitler? Such considerations were bound to influence the
American attitude towards Scandinavian neutrality.

If one perceived Russia as a true military imperialist with an aggressive worldwide strategy, then there was not much room for neutrals,
since they would be a liability in a totally polarised international
setting. Neutrality thrives in a multipolar world characterised by a
diffuse configuration of power. If, however, one saw Russia primarily as
a power seeking to dominate its western and southern borders and to
prevent hostile regimes along these flanks, then there was room for a
zone of militarily independent states that lessened rather than heightened the confrontation along these sensitive border areas.

What emerged in early 1949 was a large NATO that had many points
of direct contact with the Russian sphere – in the Eastern
Mediterranean, in Central Europe, and in Northern Europe. There was
no Scandinavian Bloc of Neutrals – Norway and Denmark decided to
abandon Sweden and to join with the other North Atlantic states. The
more sceptical assessment of strategic and political questions prevailed
on both sides of the North Atlantic.

Immediately, questions were raised about the American role in the
Danish and Norwegian decision to join NATO, and they have given
cause to much scholarly analysis ever since. Did America exert pressure
on the Scandinavians to abandon their plan, or did the Scandinavians
disagree among themselves so that a natural convergence of interest
drew Norway and Denmark into the Atlantic region? Revisionist historians of the Cold War have tended to emphasise the 'pressure' thesis:
the United States, in true Cold War fashion, practically forced Norway
into the Atlantic Alliance, and Denmark had no choice but to follow
suit. According to this view, America again overreacted to the Russian
challenge and contributed to the escalation and the worsening of the
tension.[2]

The countries that participated in the negotiations have, from the
beginning, tended to lean towards the 'convergence' thesis, or the
argument that Norway in particular, from the very outset, cared little
for the Swedish plan, felt the Russian threat more keenly than Sweden,
and could not resist the natural pull towards the Atlantic. The
Americans did not have to apply any pressure.[3] Traditionalist historians

have repeated this contention, and more recent analysts with access to the published State Department documents have tended to confirm this view, although with many qualifications. Geir Lundestad has undertaken the most exhaustive study of the question and concludes that 'in this period the influence of the United States on the foreign policy choices of the Scandinavian states, although certainly important, was not decisive.' And he adds that 'regardless of the policies of the Western Powers, Norway and in part Denmark simply felt much closer to the West than did Sweden.'[4] Grethe Vaerno, who also examined the records closely, comes to the conclusion that 'a fascinating convergence emerges from the *Foreign Relations* (FRUS) documents.'[5]

All kinds of reasons have been offered to account for this convergence.[6] It is not the purpose of this study to look at all of them and to delve into the details and intricacies of the actual decision-making process. Instead, I will concentrate on the perceptions of war and of neutrality as they emerge from the available documents. Since these are State Department records, the viewpoint is mainly the civilian one, but the military perception also shines through at times. It is also fair to assume that George C. Marshall, Secretary of State until early 1949 and an important military figure in the Second World War, expressed a point of view that was not totally devoid of military considerations.

The record shows that, for all the governments involved, the years from 1947 to 1949 were a time of transition: 'There were a variety of ideas in the air in those years, little was certain, and foreign policies of nearly all countries were being reappraised.'[7] This was also true of the United States, where a number of ideas prevailed about the nature of the future alliance and its potential membership. With regard to Scandinavia, two views emerged: a majority opinion opposing the idea of a neutral bloc and even taking issue with traditional Swedish neutrality, and a minority opinion that was not necessarily enthusiastic about a neutral bloc, but saw merits in neutrality and certainly opposed any attempt to put pressure on Sweden.

The debate between the two sides was carried on throughout 1948 and well into 1949. A final American decision emerged only on 11 February 1949, when the Norwegian foreign minister visited Washington. This was almost seven weeks after the principal participants had agreed upon the text of the treaty. The Scandinavian option remained open for a long while. This had to do not only with the uncertainties among the Scandinavians themselves but also with the divisions within the Department of State. Decisions were also delayed because of the presidential election of November 1948 and the change at the head of the Department of State in early 1949, when Dean Acheson took the place of General Marshall. It is also true that the Americans believed in letting the Europeans take the initiative. This had worked well in the case of the European Recovery Programme (Marshall Plan), and it was a strategy that again bore fruit in the case of the North Atlantic Alliance. It was the British Foreign Secretary, Ernest Bevin, who first raised publicly the idea of an alliance in January 1948 after another fruitless meeting of the Council of Foreign Ministers. American reaction was non-committal; further steps were expected of the Europeans. These were forthcoming when the Europeans set up the Western Union (Brussels Treaty), a core alliance of five states. Only then were exploratory talks about an extension of this alliance held at the Pentagon among the United States, Great Britain, and Canada (March–April 1948). In June, Congress passed the Vandenberg Resolution, giving the green light for further talks. A working party of seven powers met again in July, and formal alliance proposals went to the various governments in early September. It was only after the US election, however, that the Department of State stood fully behind the proposal and gave its approval to the final version of a treaty. It was published on 18 March 1949 and signed on 4 April.

It was also in the final phase of January and early February 1949 that the Swedes made their concentrated effort to bring about a Nordic Pact. Although Undén, the Swedish foreign secretary, had mentioned the idea on a trip to Oslo in May 1948, no decisive efforts were undertaken until early 1949, when it became apparent that the United States stood fully behind the NATO proposal. Within three weeks, the Scandinavian foreign ministers met three times (at Karlsbad, Copenhagen, and Oslo), but they failed to reach agreement. When the Norwegian foreign minister, Lange, travelled to Washington in February and signalled his definitive support of NATO, he did not do so behind the backs of his Scandinavian colleagues or pursuant to a prior deal with the Americans. It is true that Lange had favoured a Western orientation all along, but it is equally true that regular talks were held among the Scandinavians and that the Americans only reached their final decision, as mentioned, during the visit of the Norwegian foreign minister.

Within the Department of State there were various positions on the Scandinavian question. The common denominator was that no one wanted to see a fully neutral Scandinavian Bloc, as proposed by Sweden. Walter Lippmann advanced such ideas as early as 1943, and he reiterated them later on, but he was not a member of the government.[8] George Kennan also spoke of the neutralisation of Scandinavia, but that was in his memoirs, and there is no record that he fought for it in 1948 and 1949 as Director of the Policy Planning Staff.[9]

The majority position within the government favoured full NATO membership for Norway and Denmark and, as the results were to show, it won the day. The proponents were divided into two groups, however. A more moderate wing was satisfied with the membership of Norway and Denmark alone, whereas a more radical wing strove unsuccessfully for Swedish membership as well. The minority position, represented by Kennan and others, revolved around the idea of a loose membership for Norway and Denmark and, obviously, for the full maintenance of Swedish neutrality. As Norway and Denmark became full members, this position was also defeated. In the end the winners were the moderate proponents of the majority position.

The majority position

Although the officials associated with the majority opinion agreed that close Norwegian and Danish membership was desirable, they split over the question of Swedish neutrality. This division was not clear in all cases. Since Sweden was the driving force behind the idea of a Scandinavian Bloc, it cannot be expected that everyone always drew the rather fine distinction between all-Scandinavian neutrality and mere Swedish neutrality. Still, there were those who were actively engaged in an effort to persuade the Swedes to abandon their own neutrality, and there were others who did not worry about Sweden as long as Norway and Denmark joined the alliance.

Under Secretary Robert Lovett belonged to the latter group. As of July 1948, he was the chief American negotiator, and he strove hard to gain full membership for Norway and Denmark and to prevent the Scandinavian scheme. But his thinking must have been mainly strategic. He thought in terms of the North Atlantic as a vital defence area, which for him included Denmark (Greenland), Iceland, Ireland, Norway, and Portugal (the Azores).[10] In a conversation with Swedish Ambassador Erik C. Boheman in October 1948, he also concentrated on questions of strategy and avoided the topic of Swedish neutrality, although Boheman talked about it in detail.[11] Others would seize such opportunities to lecture the Swedes intensively about the demerits of neutrality.

The Joint Chiefs of Staff (JCS) thought along similar lines. One of their aims was to deny the Russians air and naval bases in Norway, something that could have been achieved by Norwegian neutrality.

But they feared that like Finland, a neutral Norway would be unable to resist Russian pressures. They also wanted to be able to fly over Norwegian territory, something that neutrality excluded. In addition, they had an interest in using Norwegian air and naval bases themselves in times of actual war, and they wanted to make sure that Spitsbergen (controlling the area between the Barents Sea and the North Atlantic) would not fall into Russian hands. Similar apprehensions existed about Denmark's ability to control access to the Baltic Sea. As a result, the JCS strongly favoured the inclusion of these two countries in the Alliance. Sweden, to them, simply did not have the same strategic importance.[12]

The more assertive orientation among the officials of the majority position was represented by John Hickerson, Chief of the Office of European Affairs, the person most actively involved in shaping NATO. He wanted the most comprehensive membership possible. At the Pentagon talks in March 1948, where he was mainly in charge, Sweden and Switzerland were both mentioned for potential membership, and he is on record again in July, at the outset of the seven power discussions, as favouring the inclusion of both these neutrals.[13] As late as November 1948, Hickerson felt that 'Sweden and Germany were natural members of the Atlantic community.'[14]

Hickerson also favoured the idea of double membership: as many European countries as possible should join the Western Union, which, in turn, would enter into a pact with the United States and Canada. The five members of the Brussels Treaty were opposed to the idea, however, and most of them liked the thought of including the neutrals even less. Hickerson thus ran into opposition abroad, but he had some important allies at home. Both Theodore Achilles, Chief of the Division of Western European Affairs, and Benjamin Hulley, Chief of the Division of Northern European Affairs, supported his position.

They had an invaluable ally in Freeman Matthews, the American ambassador to Sweden. Matthews had himself been in Hickerson's position before he was sent to Stockholm in July 1947.[15] There is plenty of evidence that the two men saw eye to eye on the Swedish question.[16] Consequently Matthews must have felt that he had strong backing at the Department, and he proceeded to act accordingly. He mounted a crusade to manoeuvre the Swedes away from neutrality and into NATO membership. He pursued his effort relentlessly for three years, even after the treaty had been signed. Matthews failed thoroughly and left Stockholm a disappointed man, but his efforts are worth studying in more detail, because they offer a number of insights into American perceptions of neutrality at that time. Upon his arrival in Sweden, Matthews embarked on a programme to inform the State Department of the Swedish point of view. On 16 February 1948, he sent the Department a most comprehensive statement: 'I have now drawn up a twelve-point summary of "basic fallacies of Swedish thinking" which may be useful to Department in appraising Swedish reaction to ERP, Western Union and any future international crises.'[17] The twelve fallacies, as Matthews saw them, were the following:

1. Sweden may well keep out of a third war if it comes. Both sides may find Sweden's neutrality advantageous.
2. Therefore, Sweden must take no step now that might lessen its chances of avoiding future war.
3. Any steps toward west in political or military field now will incur future Soviet ire and suspicion and therefore lessen Sweden's chances of avoiding involvement in war. Present political 'neutrality' may keep Sweden out.
4. If there is no war and great powers compose their future differences Sweden will be left in isolation to incur Soviet reprisals for any present leaning to west. (Look what great power 'deals' did to Czechoslovakia and Poland in 1939.)
5. In last weeks before war Sweden will have ample opportunity to determine policy, that is, to side with the west or neutrality. Therefore, time is not ripe to choose now.
6. Sweden's association with the west now may bring disastrous Soviet occupation of kindred buffer state Finland.
7. Any possible moral obligation to join other free nations to use moral influence to oppose Soviet expansion is subordinate to Swedish self-preservation through neutrality.
8. Moral influence of world opinion does not change Soviet policies anyway.
9. There is no danger that the west will resent Swedish neutrality and therefore leave Sweden to her fate. It is the devil (Russia) that must be appeased.
10. Because of its geographical position Sweden is more vulnerable than west Europe, that is, a Maginot line psychology in reverse without conception of modern warfare.
11. Even if 'neutrality' is not the wisest policy, there must be no agitation against it, for this would split the Swedish nation, and internal unity in these times must be preserved at all cost.

12. The east bloc stands for communism; the west bloc may be dom-
     inated by 'capitalist reaction'. Sweden (Social Democratic major-
     ity) must pursue a middle course.

While the pressure of events may modify some of the above, Swedish
evolution will at best be slow. I am of course doing my best to hasten
the process of education.[18]

The twelve points reflect Cold War thinking at its purest. According to
Matthews, the international system is totally polarised between the forces
of good and evil; Russia is about to copy the policies of Hitler; an intermediate position becomes impossible, because it underestimates the forces of
the devil and is either naive or hypocritical in its unwillingness to recognise the true enemy; it amounts to appeasement and loses credibility
('neutrality'), and it will ultimately be modified by the pressure of events.
The duty of an ambassador consists in promoting the inevitable process
by engaging the misguided nation in a programme of re-education.[19]

Re-education was to be mainly achieved by pressure, both psychological and material. The Swedes were to be told squarely and clearly that
America disapproved of neutrality. They were also to be driven into
mental isolation by giving them the feeling that all the free world was
against them and that they risked becoming an international pariah.[20]
The Swedes were not impressed, however. After a strongly pro-neutral
speech in parliament by Swedish Foreign Minister Undén, Matthews'
cable to Washington expressed much frustration: 'it shows that events
of the past months have taught him nothing and confirms as I have
reported that any Swedish departure from neutrality must be over
Undén's dead body.'[21]

Expecting resistance, Matthews had from the start suggested applying material pressures. In the military field especially, the Swedes were
to be told that they could not count on American supplies, while, at
the same time, the Danes and Norwegians were to receive opposite
signals. It was the usual carrot-and-stick approach, and it also failed.
Unlike the other Scandinavians, the Swedes emerged from the Second
World War with their economic and military position intact. Sweden
simply did not need American assistance. In addition, it was Britain
that mainly supplied its military needs. Above all, Sweden possessed
deposits of uranium in which the Americans at that time were highly
interested. As Matthews was to find out, Washington simply could not
follow his recommendations.[22]

He did not give up easily, however. One year after the signing of the
North Atlantic Treaty, Matthews was still attempting to re-educate.

Sweden was interested in buying twenty Bendix ground control radar sets in the United States and applied for export licences. The ambassador suspected that Washington was favourably disposed and feared that his entire effort would be torpedoed once and for all. He decided to make this the touchstone of his endeavours. In a long telegram he asked some fundamental questions:

> I respectfully request information as to whether it is the policy of the US Government to seek Sweden's eventual adherence to the North Atlantic Treaty or whether we consider it preferable that Sweden remain outside the Pact while retaining, of course, friendly and as close relations as are possible under Swedish Government's rigid concept of neutrality.
>
> If we desire Sweden's adherence to NAT on important policy objectives, I feel strongly that we should refuse radar export application.[23]

The answer was not long in coming. Only ten days later, Dean Acheson, now Secretary of State, informed Matthews of the official policy. In polite but unmistakable language, he was told that Washington disagreed with him. 'We recognize that material change in Sweden's subjective neutrality attitude is long range goal and do not therefore attach same importance as you appear to do to current decisions on mil supplies ... we are therefore inclined to approve present application.'[24] The re-education programme had come to an end. Matthews was transferred out of Stockholm a few months later; he had outlived his usefulness. Perhaps the ambassador had been unaware that a policy shift had occurred in Washington. A top secret NSC position paper on Scandinavia, dated 3 September 1948, still recommended a fairly harsh course. It stated that the United States should endeavour by all appropriate measures 'to influence Sweden to abandon this attitude of subjective neutrality'.[25] A departmental Policy Statement issued in 15 August 1949, suggested a softer line: 'while we recognize the importance of Sweden for our own security and that of our allies, it is against our policy to exert pressure on Sweden to join the North Atlantic Pact.'[26] Matthews might not have known about the change or might simply have decided to ignore it.

The minority position

The person who disagreed most strongly with the Hickerson/Matthews line was George F. Kennan, at that time Director of the Policy Planning

Staff. In 1946, when he wrote his 'long telegram' from Moscow, Kennan was more sensitive to the Russian threat than most officials at the Department; he was ahead of them, so to speak. In 1948 and 1949, when the question of establishing NATO was discussed, the situation had changed: Kennan seemed less sensitive to the Russian threat, and to many he appeared to lag behind. Kennan thus had a conception of NATO (and of Scandinavian membership) that was shared by few others and remained a definite minority position.

Kennan believed that the Russian challenge was mainly political and economic but not military. What was needed, therefore, was a demonstration of American determination to come to the aid of Western Europe if the need arose. Demonstration of this intent was for the moment more important than intensive military preparation. In Kennan's view, Washington had already overreacted to the Czech coup of February 1948 and was now overreacting again to the Berlin blockade.[27] The US government was thinking too much in military terms and not enough in political terms:

> I was well aware that we had demobilized and the Russians had not. This I considered unfortunate but not fatal or even very important. The Russians had no idea of using regular military strength against us. Why then should we direct attention to an area where we were weak and they were strong?[28]

Initially, Kennan advocated the 'dumbbell' concept for the shaping of the alliance. In North America, the United States and Canada would sign a mutual pact, and in Europe as many countries as desired would join the Western Union. The North American states would then assume a unilateral guarantee of the security of those West European states.[29]

Discussions with the Canadians and Europeans in March and July 1948 revealed, however, that a closer association was intended. The Vandenberg Resolution also spoke of 'the association of the United States by constitutional Process with such regional and other collective arrangements as are based on continuous and effective self-help and mutual aid.'[30] Kennan consequently had to adapt to new realities; he came up with the idea of 'gradated' membership in an alliance built around the American–Canadian–Western Union core. Among the members loosely affiliated with the core were states such as Iceland, Ireland, Norway, Denmark, Portugal, and Italy. This, to Kennan, constituted the ideal form of a North Atlantic alliance.

In moving away from the 'dumbbell' concept, Kennan took a step in the direction of the majority position, but differences remained. Everyone in the majority group felt that Norway and Denmark should become full members, and Hickerson even argued for 'double membership'. Furthermore, Hickerson and Matthews lobbied for the inclusion of Sweden, and on this point the differences became sharp. Early in the July talks, Kennan stated that the United States 'doubted the advisability of pressing certain countries close to the Soviet Union into making military engagements when their neutrality might in certain circumstances be more desirable.'[31] He gave Sweden as an example but must also have been thinking of Finland.

As a specialist on Russian affairs with a number of years of first-hand experience in Moscow, Kennan must have been keenly aware of the link between Swedish and Finnish neutrality. As he stated later in his memoirs, inclusion of Sweden in NATO would have jeopardised the possibilities that the Finns possessed 'of continuing to pursue an independent political life in a neutralised status, and it could easily have led in this way to an actual expansion of the real limits of Soviet power.'[32] Fortunately, others at the Department of State and the Pentagon saw this danger, too. It must have been one of the major reasons why the Hickerson–Matthews policy had to be dropped.[33]

Kennan must have been in a fairly isolated position in those days. Inside the government hardly anyone agreed with him, and those expressions of sympathy that can be traced point to a very occasional form of support. Charles Bohlen, for instance, shared many of Kennan's views. He was absent from Washington, however, for a good deal of the time when NATO was being discussed and only returned to a position of influence under Acheson at a time when the treaty was practically completed.[34] But, as we will see, he was to use that opportunity as best as he could.

Republican foreign policy spokesman John Foster Dulles must also have had some doubts about the wisdom of including Norway. In a book he published in 1950, he suggested that Norwegian membership could possibly be viewed as an unnecessary provocation of the Soviet Union because of the border that the two countries shared.[35] Dulles must have kept this opinion to himself, since there is no evidence that he spoke out for the exclusion of Norway. Only the French were clearly in favour of a loose association of Norway and Denmark, but they could not convince the British and the Americans.[36] Another occasional ally was Secretary Marshall, although it is more accurate to say that his views were not consistent.[37] More than any other person at the Department of State, he symbolised the American government's desire to remain uncommitted for as long as possible. General Marshall's views, however ambivalent, are, therefore, of particular interest.

Marshall showed some sympathy for Kennan's viewpoint in conversations he held with the Norwegian and Danish foreign ministers while in Paris for the UN General Assembly meeting in September and early October 1948. Although he remained non-committal throughout, he told Lange (Norway) on 29 September that if the Scandinavian countries managed to defend the southwest coast of Norway credibly, such a grouping might have real merit.[38] According to his own memorandum, he told Rasmussen (Denmark) on 5 October that he could see 'the possibility of a neutral group, provided such a group could ensure that the straits leading from the Baltic to the Atlantic could, and would be, closed in the event of trouble.'[39]

These statements show that Marshall thought at times along the same lines as Kennan. He was possibly willing to go even further by accepting the existence of a neutral Scandinavian bloc – something no one dared argue for back home in Washington. That he remained undecided and merely played with these ideas becomes evident, however, in a further talk he had with Lange in November. To the inquiry about the likely American response to a truly neutral grouping with no ties to the Atlantic alliance, Marshall answered in generalities, saying that this was something he would have to think about further.[40]

His attitude towards Swedish neutrality was equally ambivalent, or so it must have appeared to his subordinates. At times, he condemned the Swedish policy in outspoken terms and, at others, he treated the country rather gently. In June 1948, when Prince Bertil of Sweden visited Washington and was received by President Truman, Marshall sent the President a memo opening with the following words: 'Sweden has followed stubbornly a policy of neutrality which since the end of the war has been of more benefit to the Soviet Union than to the Western countries.' He added that Sweden's true interest lay with the West and that 'a neutrality policy which reveals a division among the free nations of the world can only serve to invite aggression.' The short memo informed the President that the American ambassador in Stockholm 'during recent months has explained the American position fully to officials of the Swedish Government.'[41] Small wonder that Hickerson and Matthews felt they could go ahead with the programme of re-education.

When Hickerson did what Marshall recommended, however, he was reprimanded. On 12 October, the Director of the Office of European Affairs told Swedish Ambassador Designate Boheman that the United States was 'worried, distressed and shocked by the adherence of Sweden to the policy of neutrality, a word which was really offensive to us.' Learning about this conversation while in Paris, Marshall himself was shocked. He felt that Hickerson had gone too far. In a cable to Washington he told Lovett that 'it seems to me that such obvious pressure at present time does more harm than good' and that in future Department officials should abstain from 'such outspoken pressure tactics with Sweden'.[42]

Only two days later, on 14 October, Marshall himself had an opportunity to talk at some length with Swedish Foreign Minister Undén. The memorandum sent back to Washington is rather long and detailed. It is a fascinating document, because it records one of those rare moments in international politics when two important figures sit down to discuss their different viewpoints of neutrality.

Undén spoke first and opened the conversation by stating rather apologetically 'that he realized that his well-known views on neutrality were unpopular in America'. He then explained that Swedish neutrality was as traditional as that of Switzerland and that it had brought the country one hundred and thirty-five years of peace. Undén admitted that in the event of another general war it would most likely be impossible for Sweden to remain neutral for any extended period of time, but that a change now would cause a similar change in Russian policy towards Sweden. He also spoke of the adverse effect that such a move would have on Finland and defended the idea of a neutral Scandinavian bloc.

Marshall then presented his own ideas about neutrality: 'I mentioned that there had also been traditionally a strong feeling of neutrality in the United States, especially in the Middle West. I inquired what the effect would have been in the world if President Wilson and President Roosevelt had maintained such a policy.' Undén felt that this would have been tragic but the difference was that 'the United States is a great power'.

Marshall could not agree and argued that 'the United States, among almost all of the other countries of the world, could best afford from its own selfish security point of view to be neutral.' He then went on to state that the world was now 'confronted by a state which appeared to be utterly ruthless and devoid of all the human decencies of modern civilization', and that, if this force was not opposed, there might be a possibility of the gradual establishment of police states across the world, an idea abhorrent to America. He added that 'the United States was against the imposition on free peoples anywhere, against their will, of the police state.'

The Secretary went on to explain American plans to contain Russia, the European Recovery Programme, rearmament, and the possibility of military co-operation. 'Towards the end of our conversation, Foreign Minister Undén made the comment that the problem of Swedish neutrality was his problem. I agreed that it was, but indicated that as he had spoken frankly to me, I wanted to give him my frank views on the question.'[43]

The two men obviously disagreed, but this was a truly diplomatic exchange of views lacking the harsh tone that was characteristic of Hickerson and Matthews. Marshall made no bones about his dislike of Swedish neutrality but tried to reason rather than to threaten. It is perhaps best to say that the two men agreed to disagree, which is an entirely civilised approach in diplomacy.

The Secretary's overall stand on Sweden and the neutral bloc remained ambivalent. After all, it was during his same stay in Paris that he spoke to Lange and Rasmussen and gave them the impression that neutrality might have its merits. If he really intended to block the Scandinavian scheme, then his approach was counterproductive, since it could have driven the Norwegians and Danes into Swedish arms. The only explanation is again that the administration consciously did not want to commit itself in the autumn of 1948. The intensive Swedish drive was still months away, and there was room for manoeuvre on all sides.

This was revealed in early 1949, when Dean Acheson became Secretary of State. He made Charles Bohlen his primary adviser on security questions and not, as some expected, John Hickerson. Since Acheson had not been involved in the NATO question and James Webb, who had little to do with the final phase of the treaty, replaced Robert Lovell, Bohlen's role became potentially crucial. Given his preference for the Kennan position on Scandinavia, would the minority stand win out after all?

Time was pressing. The Swedes now pushed hard; they had three meetings in January with the Norwegians and the Danes. In early February, Norwegian Foreign Minister Lange came to Washington to get a final answer, while at the same time the Seven Power Exploratory Talks (United States, Canada, Western Union) entered into their final phase as well. An American decision on the Scandinavian question could not be postponed much longer.

Negotiations with Lange began on 7 February. Acheson attended the first session, but Lange did most of the talking. He made the Norwegian stand very clear: 'He said that Norway was not willing to go along with Sweden and Denmark in presenting to the western democracies a joint Scandinavian security plan along the lines of what might be called Swedish neutrality.'[44] The ball was thus in the American court, but the United States remained uncommitted for a few days longer.

Bohlen was in charge of the American delegation when the talks continued the following day. He thanked Lange for his frank statement, saying that this was the first definite information America had had on the subject. Bohlen emphasised once more that 'we expect adherence to the Atlantic Pact to be purely voluntary. We do not want to persuade any country which feels doubtful.' Bohlen admitted that from a military point of view the inclusion of Norway and Denmark was of great importance, but he also stressed the fact that America was not going to rush into this treaty; that there was no deadline and no take-it-or-leave-it offer.[45] Was Bohlen trying to gain time? He had good reason: Acheson had ordered a total review of the American position regarding Scandinavia. And this after Lange's arrival in Washington!

On the same day, Acheson himself attended a session of the ongoing Exploratory Talks. From what he said it appears that he too wanted to leave all options open. He discussed the various aspects of the Scandinavian question at some length, listened to the viewpoints of other representatives, and finally concluded that

> looking at it from all points of view, it might be that a certain kind of Scandinavian agreement involving arrangements between some Scandinavian countries and the Atlantic Pact countries, and staff conversations and the supply of arms, would add up to something more valuable than the alternative of having Norway alone in the North Atlantic Pact.[46]

This was the Kennan position – a type of loose association limited to staff conversations and arms supplies. The problem, however, was Sweden. The Swedes wanted a truly neutral bloc without links of any kind, however informal, to NATO. This Ambassador Boheman told Acheson clearly the following day.[47]

By 10 January, Acheson had before him the information he wanted for a final decision. He knew the Norwegian and the Swedish position, he received a memo from Bohlen once more supporting Kennan,[48] and he had a letter from Secretary of Defense Forrestal transmitting a memorandum of the Joint Chiefs of Staff. They supported the majority position of full Norwegian and Danish membership.[49]

As did Acheson when he reached his decision. Perhaps he had wanted the full inclusion of the two countries all along and never believed in the minority position. In that case, the Kennan–Bohlen line never had a realistic chance. But the final review called by Acheson corresponded with his style of work, and those around him took it seriously. What hurt the minority position, therefore, was not so much the rivalries and divisions of opinion within the government, but the fact that the Swedes insisted on a truly neutral bloc and that neither the Norwegians nor any of the Americans involved wanted that solution.

Strong and weak neutrals

However reluctantly, America ended up respecting Swedish neutrality, and it also respected Swiss neutrality. But there was an important difference in the way the United States perceived and treated the two neutrals in 1948 and 1949. The Swiss strategic position, from the American point of view, was stronger than that of Sweden, and as a result Swiss neutrality was considered more credible. This had important consequences for the treatment the Swiss received. While Sweden was discussed at great length and pressure was brought to bear on the country, the Swiss were mentioned only briefly during the Pentagon exploratory talks in the spring of 1948 and no pressure was ever applied.[50] The different handling of Switzerland at this crucial juncture is illustrative of the American conception of neutrality that began to take shape during those early Cold War years.

Evidence for the different perception of the Swiss emerges from the conversation that Marshall held with Undén in Paris, in October 1948.[51] As will be recalled, there was a short exchange about the neutrality America itself had practised in the past and about the fact that, for entirely selfish reasons, the United States could still do so at present. The transcript of the conversation then continues with the following words: 'I [Marshall] also pointed out that it seemed to me there was a considerable difference geographically in this respect between the position of Sweden and that of Switzerland. I mentioned the vulnerability of Denmark, and the importance in a defense way to the West of Denmark, as well as Norway.'[52] When Marshall met Lange in Paris later on, he told him virtually the same thing.[53]

By 'geography' a soldier like Marshall must have meant the geopolitical situation of a country and possibly its topography. In this respect, the difference between Sweden and Switzerland is indeed significant. Geopolitically, Sweden occupies a sensitive intermediate position, with Finland and the Soviet Union on one side and two NATO countries on the other. Should the Russians ever occupy Sweden, American security interests would be affected along a very long frontier. The United States had assumed all along that Russian occupation was possible. The Swedes, like the Finns, would not be able to withstand a prolonged Russian drive. Among other things, such a drive would be facilitated by topography.[54]

The case of Switzerland was different.[55] In those years, the Russians would have had to approach Switzerland via territory occupied by American forces (southern Germany, western Austria, northern Italy), and the topography of the region would have been a real problem for troops trained to fight on very different ground. Furthermore, the Swiss were expected to resist resolutely, a factor that the Americans greatly appreciated. Evidence of this is contained in a State Department Policy Statement on Switzerland drafted in March 1949:

> Despite its tenacious attachment to neutrality, Switzerland has a number of attributes in terms of major United States foreign policy aims .... While traditional neutrality precludes their political or military alignment with the west, the Swiss can nevertheless be relied upon to defend their territory resolutely against any aggressor. As such Switzerland constitutes a deterrent to the expansion of Soviet influence in western Europe and a strategic asset, even though a passive one, within the frame of United States objectives.[56]

The policy statement then draws the inevitable conclusions: 'We have accepted the fact that Switzerland ... cannot be considered a potential member of any of the existing political and military alliance systems .... We have equally accepted the inadvisability of attempting to exert direct pressure on the Swiss to join in these organizations.'[57]

The contrast with the assessment of Sweden is marked. There is not a word about the selfishness, naïveté, or immorality of neutrality; there are no suggestions of re-educating the Swiss or putting them under pressure. On the contrary, neutrality at once becomes an asset, a positive and calculable factor,[58] and this for mainly *strategic reasons*. The conclusions for the American conception of neutrality are evident: in the case of Sweden, the military factor weighed against a favourable assessment of neutrality, in the case of Switzerland, the same factor weighed in favour of it. America preferred strong neutrals to weak ones, and, in that sense, it respected the very essence of neutrality. A neutral, after all, wants to stay out of war, and it can do so only if, among other things, it can credibly deter aggression. A weak neutral is a liability for potential belligerents, and the United States preferred to turn weak neutrals into allies.[59]

It is important to note that this assessment is decidedly not a political one. It matters little whether a neutral has a long tradition of freedom and democracy, a free-market economy, a healthy political pluralism, no communist party to speak of, a record of successfully surviving two World Wars. All this applied to both Sweden and Switzerland, and yet the United States saw the two countries with very different eyes.

Had these political considerations prevailed, the American reaction to Swedish neutrality, and possibly also to a Nordic Neutral Bloc, could have been very different. As Barbara Haskel shows, it might then have sounded something like this: 'We will not only supply you arms on favourable conditions and with priority, but we will consider that in taking care of the stability of your corner of the world you are making a contribution to the common weal.'[60] A response like this could not be expected, of course, once strategic considerations were given top priority.

Thinking in mostly military terms also meant that the administration was ready to accept the division of Europe into rigid blocs of allies and enemies. Kennan, as we have seen, resisted this tendency somewhat. As he notes with some disappointment in his memoirs, 'everyone else seemed content to accept the split of the continent as it then existed.' In contrast, he wanted 'to hold the door open to permit the eventual emergence of large areas (a united, demilitarized Germany, a united Europe, a demilitarized Japan) that would be in the military sense uncommitted, as between the two worlds.'[61] The emergence of non-aligned Yugoslavia fitted neatly into this scheme.

Much more will have to be said later on about the chances of a neutralised Central Europe. It is very doubtful, though, whether the idea ever had a realistic chance, given the continuous tensions and constant prodding from the East. After all, such large-scale neutralisations would have presupposed broad agreement between Russia and the United States. The United States alone could never have brought it about. But the United States could have been a decisive force in bringing about a Northern Neutral Bloc – and this is where Kennan himself failed, as well. He was never in favour of such a scheme and, consequently, it is somewhat surprising that later on he should become a proponent of more far-reaching neutralisation plans.

If anyone lobbied for neutralisation in those days, it was not George F. Kennan, but General Douglas MacArthur. Throughout 1949 and well into 1950, he advocated the neutralisation of Japan. The Joint Chiefs of Staff were opposed to his ideas. They wanted to keep a number of American bases in Japan, even after the signing of a peace treaty. MacArthur argued that Okinawa would suffice and that any further presence would harm Japanese–American relations in the long run.[62]

In MacArthur's opinion, Japan should have been neutralised by an international agreement that would have included the Soviets. This was possible, in his view, because the Russians were as much interested in keeping the Americans out of Japan as were the Americans in keeping out the Russians. He told Ambassador Jessup that Japan could be 'a neutral spot to the advantage of the United States and of the Soviet Union as well. We should be able to convince the Russians that here at least their interests and ours were parallel.'[63] Secretary of State Acheson disagreed. He was convinced that

> neutrality is illusory in the context of East–West tensions. Thus, while Western Powers honored their obligations to observe Japan's neutrality, the Soviets would continue to pursue infiltration tactics, permitting them ultimately to turn Japan into an aggressive military threat.[64]

MacArthur did not give up easily. He continued to oppose the Joint Chiefs of Staff and the Secretary of State right up to the outbreak of the Korean War. His last report favouring Japanese neutrality was written on 14 June 1950![65] It must also be remembered that much of this happened after Mao's conquest of China, an event that in many quarters had been interpreted as a victory for Moscow. Why should the next move not be in the direction of Korea or Japan? In view of MacArthur's opinion about the Chinese and the Russians during the Korean War, it is rather interesting to note that he had held a much more relaxed view of their aims only a few months earlier. Small wonder that his superiors back home began to doubt his political wisdom.

In the early Cold War years, Washington was highly sceptical of Russian designs and, consequently, military considerations had priority. The available evidence suggests that the American conception of neutrality fitted into this picture: better to have an ally than a neutral, and better to have a strong neutral than a weak one. It is impossible, however, to draw final conclusions about the conception of neutrality until the question of economic warfare has been analysed.

6
Cold War Economic Warfare, 1949–1951

Embargoing Russia and China

The Cold War was also fought with economic means. Under American leadership the Western countries began to embargo Russia and, once the Korean War began, China as well. As in any such effort, the neutrals presented a problem, because as potential loopholes, they could undermine the arrangement. Sweden and Switzerland, therefore, had to be dealt with. As will be shown, the United States exerted considerable pressure to make the two neutrals part of its economic warfare strategy.

At first, the American government was reluctant to fight the Cold War with economic means. Once the Second World War ended, it committed itself to a programme of world-wide trade liberalisation and to the gradual abolition of wartime controls. If Russia were now to be embargoed, this trend would have to be reversed. It should thus come as no surprise that some sections of the country and some branches of government did not welcome new controls. Nevertheless, the question of embargoing Russia arose in late 1947, when it became clear that Marshall Aid would soon flow to Europe in large quantities and with important consequences for East–West relations and, more precisely, for the war-making potential of Eastern Europe and the Soviet Union. A new policy was needed.

There were two schools of thought within the government. At the Department of State the dominant opinion was that liberalisation should be continued, especially since there seemed to be no immediate need for concern. Trade with the USSR and Eastern Europe was extremely limited and decreasing. The recovery of Europe would at first accentuate this trend, since it would make those commodities that were already in short supply and that the Eastern countries needed most even scarcer. Through this natural process, a limitation of East–West trade would be accomplished 'by means which could not raise any question of the propriety of our action in the light of the principles of non-discrimination and trade freedom which we have stood for in our international trade policies.'[1]

A different opinion emerged at the Department of Commerce and the National Security Council. These agencies demanded the screening of all exports to Europe, or what amounted to laying the foundation for a potential American embargo. This view prevailed when the government decided on a new course late in the year. The NSC decision of 17 December 1947 stated that all Europe, including the USSR, would be declared a recovery zone for which all American exports had to be controlled. Licences were to be issued according to the following criteria: (a) importing countries had to show adequate need, (b) the European Recovery Program (ERP) and world peace had to be served, and (c) the position of the United States ought not to be adversely affected.[2]

An additional instrument for controlling East–West trade was written into the Foreign Assistance Act of 1948 (Marshall Aid). Labelled the 'Mundt Amendment' after the Congressman who sponsored it, a section of the act directed the Administrator of Marshall Aid to refuse to participants delivery of such American goods 'which go into the production of any commodity for delivery to any non-participating European country which commodity would be refused export licences to those countries by the United States in the interest of national security.'[3] The amendment went a good deal further than the NSC decision. If the first control action focused on American trade and aimed at all of Europe, this second action was aimed specifically at aid-receiving countries. It made them instruments of American foreign policy. As one commentator put it, 'this provision throws part of the United States export control system around the Marshall Plan countries.'[4]

The administration was not too happy about the provision. For one thing it constituted a propaganda victory for the Russians, who had argued for some time that Marshall Aid was nothing but another aspect of American imperialism. Also, it disregarded the fact that the success of the Marshall Plan depended to a large extent on supplies from Eastern Europe. An obvious American attempt to organise the Western European countries into a formal blockade might give the Russians a welcome excuse to do the same. Needless to say, the Western Europeans themselves were not too happy about the provision either.[5]

As a result, the government was in no hurry to put pressure on the Europeans. Top priority was given to implementing the unilateral

American export licensing system, and only slowly were steps taken to discuss matters with ERP recipients. Instructions to begin negotiations were sent to Paris in August 1948. Averell Harriman was told to pursue a moderate course: 'primary object of these negotiations must be export control program for which voluntary agreement of ERP countries based on recognition of a common purpose may be secured.' No ERP recipient should be asked to terminate existing commercial commitments to Eastern Europe 'if such action will seriously jeopardise their political or economic relations with Eastern European countries.' Harriman was also warned that negotiations might be difficult, and that the multilateral approach, through OEEC, should be avoided if possible. Informal bilateral discussions, starting with the British, would be the most advisable avenue.[6]

For most of 1948, Washington carried on with these informal contacts. As in the case of NATO, the administration did not want to commit itself to any truly new policies in a presidential election year. Further steps were taken only in February 1949, and the initiative lay mainly with Congress. To substitute the wartime legislation upon which the first control measures were based, the Export Control Act was passed. It allowed the Executive to control the flow of exports selectively and efficiently.[7] Although preparations for economic warfare had been under way for some time, the act symbolised a turning point, since plans for a completely liberal and non-discriminatory international trade policy were in part shelved. Trade could henceforth be used openly as another weapon in the ongoing East–West struggle. This instrument took its place alongside the military and political weapons – all of them created in early 1949.

In the following months, efforts to gain European co-operation were intensified. By July, the Department of State could report that considerable success had already been achieved in securing similar controls over exports to Eastern Europe of commodities on which the United States had placed an embargo. Also emphasised was the fact that the United States would continue to seek informal co-operation 'because of the necessity of registering agreements with the UN.'[8]

As the talks continued, it became evident that some form of co-ordination was necessary. The government concluded that Paris would be an ideal location for regular contacts with a select group of ERP recipient countries and managed, in November 1949, to set up a Consultative Group composed originally of the United States, Great Britain, France, Belgium, the Netherlands, and Italy. In January 1950, the group was joined by Canada and Denmark, and it was decided to set up a permanent Coordinating Committee to handle day-to-day matters.[9]

Cocom, as it was later called, was an informal body co-ordinating trade controls throughout the Cold War. Originally it was kept totally secret. Officially its existence was acknowledged only toward the end of the Cold War. According to congressional sources, Cocom engaged in three kinds of activities: the development of lists of technologies and products to be embargoed, controlled, or monitored; weekly consultations on exceptions to these lists; and consultation on enforcement.[10]

Cocom lists covered (i) munitions, (ii) atomic energy items, and (iii) industrial/commercial commodities. These goods were contained in three different lists: International List I covered embargoed items of a truly strategic nature, International List II named quantitatively controlled items of a semi-strategic nature, and International List III specified items under surveillance. The multilateral Cocom lists were largely identical to the unilateral American lists set up under the Export Control Act of 1949.[11]

When the Korean War broke out in June 1950, the number of items on the various lists increased sharply, and the Cocom embargo was extended to cover the Peoples Republic of China (Chincom). This effort was paralleled by a resolution of the General Assembly on 28 May 1951, calling on all nations to apply embargo sanctions on strategic goods against China. Once the Korean War was over, the lists were shortened again, and Chincom was slowly phased out.[12]

Gaining neutral co-operation

The United States began to contact the neutrals in late 1948 and early 1949.[13] The talks were highly confidential and, as Washington soon discovered, both Sweden and Switzerland insisted on absolute secrecy. When Ambassador Matthews approached the Swedes in January 1949, he was told by Secretary General Baron Beck Friis that the preservation of Swedish autonomy was a vital consideration and that the government could not commit itself in writing. Matthews promised that this was unnecessary and that 'Swedish cooperation in this matter would not be made public in the hearings before Congress.'[14]

The Swiss were approached at about the same time. Alfred Zehnder, speaking for the Foreign Ministry, told Ambassador Vincent that Switzerland could not adopt a programme that exposed the government to charges of permitting the United States to intervene in Swiss trade policy. According to Vincent's report, the following exchange also took place:

> Zehnder raised questions [of] secrecy [in] these discussions, specifically inquiring whether there would be congressional presentation of status discussions. After I assured him that there would be no public reference in US to these discussions, he remarked that public knowledge thereof would force Swiss government to deny flatly any intention [of] cooperating.[15]

These statements show that neither the Swiss nor the Swedes could afford to admit publicly that they were co-operating with the United States in limiting trade with the Soviets. The credibility of their permanent neutrality was at stake. To be sure, this was not a time of actual war and, consequently, the international law of neutrality did not formally apply. Neither Beck Friis nor Zehnder could argue in legal terms. For the Swiss it was strictly a matter of neutral politics. Nonetheless, had participation become public knowledge the Soviets would have protested and the domestic reaction would also have been negative. Although liberal and democratic in their tradition, the overwhelming majority of people in Sweden and Switzerland were convinced of the usefulness of neutrality – even in the Cold War.

For the same reasons, Sweden and Switzerland could not officially join Cocom. As in the case of NATO, they would have been welcome to do so, but they preferred to stay out, much to the displeasure of some Americans. Representative Laurie C. Battle of Alabama, sponsor of the 1951 Mutual Defense Assistance Control Act (Battle Act), toured Europe in early 1953 to check on the progress of the embargo. In a report to Congress he listed some of the accomplishments but regretted that neutrals like Sweden and Switzerland 'still refuse to join in agreements with this international coordinating committee.'[16] However, Battle adhered to the agreement not to publicise any details about informal neutral co-operation. Neither Sweden nor Switzerland was mentioned in a list of over sixty countries that he surveyed. The same practice was adopted in the annual reports that followed and that continue to appear for many years.[17]

In approaching the neutrals, the United States could choose between bilateral and multilateral channels. Before Cocom existed, contacts were mostly bilateral. Once the committee was set up, the approach varied. Initially, bilateral discussions were carried on permanently and Cocom was used only occasionally and for limited ends. As will be shown, the bilateral approach was also more successful. During the Korean War, however, and especially in the long run, multilateral contacts became routine. It appears that both countries assigned some of their diplomats stationed in Paris the task of keeping in touch with Cocom.[18]

Throughout 1949 bilateral negotiations were carried on, but they achieved very little. Reports from Stockholm and Berne were a mixture of optimism and disappointment. A report of the Atomic Energy Commission summing up the results of 1949 reflects the situation well. While some progress had been made with the Swedes, the Swiss seemed to procrastinate. Misunderstanding had occurred and 'at the close of the year the Legation was disposed to make a formal approach at the highest level of the Swiss Government.'[19] Regular contacts had obviously failed.

It was only natural that in such circumstances multilateral contacts would also be tried. At a meeting of the Consultative Group of Cocom in late May 1950, it was decided that the chairman, Hervé Alphand of France, should present Lists I and II to Sweden and Switzerland and should inquire about the possibility of their adopting similar controls. Alphand was also to inform the two countries of Cocom progress.[20] Alphand got in touch with neutral representatives stationed in Paris, but he had to report to Cocom in September that he had received no definitive response.[21] He tried again in December, but an American report characterised the progress made as inconsequential and recommended abandonment of the effort.[22]

In the meantime, the Korean War had broken out, and the administration began to act unilaterally and with determination. Against the background of a general shortage in raw materials, the National Security Council decided on 24 August 1950 that export of strategic items to a Western European country should be denied if that country shipped identical items or equivalent amounts thereof to Eastern Europe.[23] The neutrals immediately felt the results.

By September, the Commerce Department was beginning to suspend export licences to Sweden for commodities such as petroleum coke, molybdenum, lubrication oils, and special steels.[24] The Swedes felt the pinch. When Undén met Acheson at the United Nations on 3 October, he was concerned about the increased difficulty his country encountered in obtaining American export licences. Acheson's reply was not reassuring. He explained that America had no intention of setting up a general embargo, but that 'the tightening up of export controls on certain items to the Soviet Union was a matter of serious concern to the United States.'[25]

The Swiss also felt the pressure. In a conversation with the American ambassador, Zehnder of the Foreign Office wondered 'whether this was policy directed solely against Switzerland or whether it was general measure.'[26] Evidently, the Swiss suspected that they might have been singled out for special treatment. To show some good will, Zehnder informed the ambassador that the Swiss were now prepared to see to it that imported strategic materials would not be re-exported.[27] At about the same time, the Swedes also showed more co-operation. And, finally, the news came in from Paris that the Swedish and Swiss ambassadors had informed the French Foreign Minister of their willingness to co-operate informally with Cocom.[28]

In view of the good news, Cocom decided to work out a detailed approach to the two governments. A Trilateral Group was set up, consisting of representatives of the United States, Great Britain, and France. Together with the American ambassadors in Berne and Stockholm, it was given the task of making another try. Secretary Acheson outlined the strategy in a long cable to Paris. Admitting that the Alphand mission had been a failure, Acheson believed that another effort was of great urgency, because, among other things, the Swedes were about to embark on trade negotiations with the Soviet Union and Czechoslovakia. They were to be told that America hoped the whole question could be discussed in detail before the end of January. As far as the Swiss were concerned, more information should be obtained about Swiss plans to breathe new life into a Parliamentary Act of 1939 permitting extensive export control.[29]

The tripartite discussion took place in January. In a report to Washington, the Paris embassy reported on 6 February that both France and Britain were satisfied with the results. The French in particular 'felt Swiss reply tripartite démarche completely satisfactory and nothing further should be done because Swiss neutrality and results exceeded those expected.' Great Britain agreed and 'questioned whether pressure should be exerted against Swiss, saying best tactics this time would probably be to await expected Swiss parliamentary action on 1939 legislature.' The French and British reactions to Swedish answers were equally positive.[30]

Washington disagreed. On 9 February, Acheson told Paris that 'US cannot concur in Tri response to S/S or Tri report to COCOM which implies that progress thus far achieved is sufficient.' Much remained to be done. The Swiss response in particular was unsatisfactory; additional efforts should be undertaken to get more satisfactory agreements with both countries.[31] The bilateral road had to be taken again. By May, progress could be reported on the Swedish front. A report to the National Security Council mentions that the Swedes, in their negotiations with Russia and Czechoslovakia, had shown a determination to cut exports of strategic goods. Furthermore, SKF had agreed to reduce considerably exports of ball-bearings to the East.[32]

However, the Swiss still would not move. Apparently, they were unwilling to handle questions through regular channels. On 11 June, the Swiss ambassador in Washington proposed to the Department of State that the United States send a delegation to Berne 'with the necessary qualifications and authority to deal with Switzerland's situation as a whole, in particular the larger political aspects of its problem.' Bruggmann indicated that the Swiss had no use for 'traffic policemen' and technicians concerned with the problem of 'which way materials go'; they wanted to talk about neutrality and maintaining their international credibility. The ambassador also added a few remarks that deserve full citation:

> The Swiss are afraid of radical changes in US foreign policy in the future as a result of possible development on the American domestic political scene such as a Republican Administration in 1953.... . If Switzerland now incurs increased Soviet and Satellite hostility by cutting off certain exports to those areas at US insistence it may later find itself holding the bag should US foreign policy change along the above lines.[33]

This was plain talk, but the Swiss got what they wanted: bilateral negotiations at a higher level.[34] On 22 June, Acheson informed the embassy in Berne about the department's plans to send a sizeable delegation headed by Deputy Assistant Secretary for Economic Affairs Harold Linder. Talks were to begin in early July, and the expectation was that Swiss resistance might very likely only be overcome by increased American pressure.[35]

After an opening meeting on 3 July, serious talks began the following day. Linder demanded full Swiss compliance with the Cocom lists, but, to his great surprise, the Swiss claimed that as they were not in possession of the complete lists and were thus in no position to talk about them. The Americans were incredulous; after all, both Alphand and the tripartite group had contacted the Swiss.[36] Was this once more part of a strategy of procrastination?

The Swiss also kept repeating their well-known arguments: exports to the East were minimal; existing commitments represented counterpart of earlier imports; an imports certificate system was now in place and prevented undesirable re-exports; neutrality required 'courant normal'. The Americans had heard it all before. They decided to argue from a position of strength, suspending American export licences for Swiss commodities: 'Linder replied that we could not possibly recommend to US Govt that these exports be licensed under existing circumstances. Mtg adjourned to enable Swiss think matter over.' The report to Washington ends with the following words: 'Entire del including Leg reps convinced Swiss were shaken by firmness of our position.' [37]

So they were. Harold Linder left Berne for almost three weeks while two of his delegation members sat down with the Swiss to work on details. When Acheson was informed of the progress, he was pleased and felt that Linder, upon his return to Berne, should express gratification that the Swiss were ready to take action.[38] This Linder did when the final round of talks opened on 24 July. Although he expressed some disappointment that the Swiss did not go along fully with the embargo, he could point to the following list of achievements:

1. Swiss agree full embargo AEC items.
2. Swiss agree embargo all but 18 items of IL I.
3. Swiss agree maintain shipments of IL II items at 1949–50 level, or approximately 65 million Swiss francs.
4. Swiss agree give Western European countries unwritten priority in execution of orders.
5. Swiss to administer quotas on company and country basis.[39]

In Switzerland the arrangement became known as the Hotz–Linder Agreement of 23 July 1951. No written communication was exchanged, and no formal paper signed. The State Department did not want to give the appearance of having entered into a 'deal', and the Swiss wanted to preserve total secrecy anyway. For the third time within six years, they had come under considerable American economic pressure, and although they tried hard to resist each time, they had to make some concessions.[40]

Cold war 'supporting states'

The investigation of the military question in the previous chapter and the analysis of economic issues in this chapter now permit us to draw final conclusions about the American conception of neutrality in the early years of the Cold War.

Up until the outbreak of the Korean War, the Cold War knew no open hostilities. No state declared war or neutrality in this situation of neither peace nor war. As a result, the international law of neutrality did not directly apply to any of the military or economic questions discussed.[41] In contrast to the Second World War, therefore, the United States did not have to respond to questions of neutral law, but to questions of neutral politics. What stood in the foreground in those years was what in German is called *Neutralitätspolitik* and not *Neutralitätsrecht*.[42]

The distinction was very important to the neutrals with which the United States had to deal. Sweden and Switzerland are neutral not only in times of war but also in times of peace. They are *permanent neutrals*. To them, as to an occasional neutral, *Neutralitätsrecht* is what comes into play in times of war. But, and this distinguishes them from occasional neutrals, *Neutralitätspolitik* is what extends into times of peace, when the permanent neutral is trying to preserve its neutrality in anticipation of a future war.[43] This is what the Swiss and the Swedes endeavoured during the Cold War years, and the challenge for the United States was to develop a counter-policy, a kind of American *Neutralitätspolitik*.

The United States had hardly ever confronted such a situation. While a minor power in the nineteenth century, the United States was too unimportant and too remote a nation to worry about the permanent neutrals of Europe and their specific problems. At the Paris Peace Conference of 1919, Woodrow Wilson, for a very brief period, had to deal with the question, but during the interwar period the United States again consciously kept out of such issues. It did have to deal with the European neutrals in two World Wars, but since these were situations of open conflict, there was no distinction between a permanent and an occasional neutral. The typical questions of permanent neutrality and of *Neutralitätspolitik* simply did not arise. Now, in the post-1945 era, the questions were highly relevant.

What is it that a permanent neutral is trying to achieve in times of peace; what is the core of *Neutralitätspolitik?* While it is difficult to provide an answer that does justice to all permanent neutrals at all times, it is fairly simple to define the Swedish and Swiss viewpoint in those years: they aimed at avoiding any step that would have compromised respect for their neutrality in the next war. This meant that political, economic, and military policies were unacceptable if they undermined the credibility of neutrality in Russian or American eyes.

Because both Sweden and Switzerland practised *armed neutrality*, military questions were of great importance. The Hague Conventions require that a neutral prevent belligerents from using its territory, its harbours, and its air space. To live up to these obligations, a neutral has to be armed, and the two European neutrals have made it a long-standing tradition to maintain large military establishments in times of peace in anticipation of this duty.[44] By acknowledging the military independence of Sweden and Switzerland and by permitting, however reluctantly, the sale of military hardware, the United States took an important step in developing a *Neutralitätspolitik* in line with Swiss and Swedish wishes. As shown, this did not prevent the United States from regarding the armed neutrality of the Swiss as more credible than that of the Swedish. Furthermore, by not coercing the Swedes into NATO membership more directly, the United States also ended up respecting a permanent neutral's desire to stay clear of *peacetime alliances*.[45] This was despite the fact that a majority of State Department officials would have preferred an allied to a neutral Sweden.

When it came to *economic matters*, the United States showed less understanding. The Hague Conventions are written in a liberal spirit that grants neutrals extensive freedom of trade. As noted earlier, the United States did much to promote this free trade in the eighteenth and nineteenth centuries. The Swedes and the Swiss, being liberal traders, were used to putting up with major restrictions in times of war (as, for instance, in the Second World War), but the United States was now forcing them to accept important restrictions *in times of peace,* and from the viewpoint of *Neutralitätspolitik*, this was problematic. It forced the neutrals to participate in economic sanctions before a war had even started, and thereby to take sides. This prejudiced the credibility of neutrality in a future war.

The United States showed little understanding for this problem. Particularly once the Korean War began, the Swedish and the Swiss came under a great deal of pressure to participate in the American sanctions against the Eastern bloc countries. The Swiss resisted more successfully than the Swedes, but indirectly both became involved in Cocom. This was not necessarily a violation of international law, but it was certainly bad neutral politics.[46]

The United States, at the very least, could have granted the neutrals the right to carry on 'courant normal', as demanded by the Swiss in their negotiations with Linder. But there was no sympathy for the argument; the Americans must have regarded it as a selfish request. Given their own history, they should have known better. The British, at various times in the eighteenth century, were willing to grant the neutral Americans the right to trade at peacetime levels (or 'normally') with British enemies. But the Americans refused – they demanded absolutely free trade in non-contraband goods, and the contraband list was extremely short!

The permanent neutrals of the Cold War did not raise such far-reaching demands. They knew that times had changed, that America had long ago abandoned an appreciation for traditional neutrality. But they did expect, particularly in times of quasi-war, that the dominating Anglo-Saxon power of the twentieth century would do what the dominating Anglo-Saxon power of the eighteenth and nineteenth century had done: settle for a compromise with like-minded states. In this they were mistaken. If the British held what Americans in those days disrespectfully called a Big Navy conception of neutrality, then the Americans now held a Super Navy conception.

Seen as a whole, the American conception of neutrality, as it developed in the Cold War, strongly resembled that which had emerged in the course of the Second World War. In both cases, the United States ended up respecting the military aspects of neutrality but showed great disregard for the economic questions. It expected the neutrals to sanction its enemies economically; the Fascist states in the Second World War, and the Communist states in the Cold War.

This was a continuation of the position taken by the more moderate internationalist neutrals during the interwar period. They demanded at that time that the United States should take sides with the states fighting a just cause and support them with a discriminatory embargo policy. In the 1939 Harvard study such a nation was labelled a 'supporting state'. Now, more than a decade later and under very different circumstances, the United States expected the European neutrals to do the same, to become supporting states in the conduct of the Cold War.

As a result, the United States continued to adhere to a *qualified conception of neutrality*, something it had done since the early days of the First World War, when Wilson abandoned integral neutrality by not defending neutral trading rights effectively and impartially. The two European neutrals, of course, still adhered to an integral view, and their problems with the United States, therefore, can largely be reduced to the differences between the two conceptions. Let us look at this question more closely.

In terms of *values*, the American conception did not differ from that of the two permanent European neutrals. Universalist values such as free international trade, human rights, and democratic government were subscribed to by all of them. Sweden and Switzerland were not mercantilist, fascist, or communist states. Neutrality was to them not merely a policy for selfish national survival under any circumstances; it was a policy that tied national survival to virtually the same values that had guided Americans since the eighteenth and nineteenth centuries. The differences lay at the level of *power*. For the European neutrals, these values went hand in hand with national power or, more precisely, with a traditional conception of international order. For the United States, however, power had to be organised multinationally, and it had to be used actively to defend these values. A nationalist philosophy of power thus contrasted with a universalist one. The two views were bound to clash, and the danger in such confrontations was that disagreements over power might become so severe that the mutuality of values might be forgotten in the process. Ideological friends might become enemies! Some examples will illustrate this.

The United States insisted on calling NATO a 'collective security' arrangement, a term used to characterise the United Nations. In fact, NATO became necessary because true collective security within the framework of the United Nations had failed.[47] To give NATO this label was evidence of the American urge to match universalist values with universalist concepts of power. And it was not without its dangers, since it could lead American officials to actually believe that NATO had to fulfil a universal mission.[48]

Ambassador Matthews held this opinion. For him, NATO was indeed more than an alliance meant to promote American security; it was a substitute for true collective security and, as such, engaged in a struggle for a just cause. Under such circumstances, there was no room for *indifference* and *impartiality*. Nations had to take sides and become engaged. The Swedes, by refusing to become allies, chose to ignore the merits of the universal cause and therefore became enemies. It did not mean anything to him that in actual fact the Swedes were ideological friends. It will be recalled that Secretary Marshall held similar views. In his conversation with Undén, he practically accused the Swedes of selfishness and completely forgot that they, too, stood up against fascist and communist regimes. Was it really worth making enemies with countries that shared the same values?

This intimate identification of universalist values and universalist power also occurred in the area of economic warfare. The NSC decision that called for the creation of a European recovery zone and for the control of commodities going into it set up criteria that goods had to meet in order to be admitted to the zone. One of these criteria was that goods had to serve 'world peace'.[49] The language in many Cocom documents was similar, and what it meant, of course, was that a commodity was not supposed to serve Soviet aims or, worse, get into Soviet hands. But, once again, such language was likely to make Americans believe that the Swiss and the Swedes were actually against world peace and were, consequently, ideological enemies.

These examples show that excessive identification of universalist values with universalist power could, at least in regard to the European neutrals, be counterproductive. A more moderate position would have been advantageous. Such a position would have weighed carefully the advantages of ideological friends against the disadvantages of reduced military power. After all, the Cold War was not only a military struggle but also an eminently political and ideological one. Soviet policy in Europe was aimed at undermining liberal and democratic institutions, and in this struggle the Swedes and the Swiss were pillars of strength. By placing too much emphasis on the virtues of 'collective' power, the United States at times failed to take full advantage of this factor.

In *economic* terms, a moderate stance would have meant weighing more carefully the advantages of two strong liberal democracies against the disadvantages of a certain amount of neutral trade with the East.[50] Given the difficulties of implementing economic sanctions and of assessing their effect on the Soviet economy, it was not wise to arouse ill will and to promote unnecessary anti-Americanism in countries that were doing so well in the struggle against communism. The Russians must at times have been pleased by the heavy-handed American measures. And, who knows, perhaps free international trade was, after all, a force working for peace as the Founding Fathers once believed. Was that contention totally without merit?

In military matters, the Americans did bend their 'collective' power philosophy. They came to accept the fact that the two permanent neutrals refused to be part of a joint defence arrangement and preferred to stand alone. In the case of Sweden, this admission did not come easily because of the perceived military weakness. The military strength of Switzerland made the decision a good deal less painful. Although the Americans continued to assign the acquisition of allies a high priority, they were willing to settle for second best when it came to the armed neutrals of Europe. Quite clearly, the next best thing to alliance power was the independent power of an ideological friend. This all fitted in with the moderate type of internationalism that had evolved since the Second World War. Once more, however, the inherent tensions of this policy became apparent: universalist components lay side by side with traditionalist ones. It did not necessarily make for a coherent American version of *Neutralitätspolitik*.

7
Korean War, 1950–1953

Neutrality, non-participation, neutralism

The Korean conflict was an exercise in United Nations enforcement; it was not meant to be a traditional war. The initiation, the conduct, and the termination of hostilities were supposed to be different. This implied that under ideal conditions the Security Council would take decisions based on great power unanimity, its military forces would defeat the forces of aggression, and, finally, the vanquished would have to accept a settlement imposed by the enforcers of world law. The reality was different: the Korean conflict opened in a legally question-able manner, the conduct of hostilities was militarily inconclusive, and in the end the two sides negotiated a ceasefire as in old times.[1] What had begun as an effort to implement the modern law of the United Nations ended very much as an exercise in the traditional law of war. As a part of this development, neutrality resurfaced once again.[2]

It was not the traditional conception, of course, that re-emerged, because the Korean War, if anything, added confusion to the definition of neutrality.[3] There were some states that claimed to be *traditionally neutral,* but the majority assumed a posture of *non-participation,* a concept related to the United Nations and defined in various ways in the course of the war.[4] Furthermore, some states began to assume the positions of mediators between the blocs of the General Assembly, thus pursuing a policy that came to be known as non-alignment or, more confusingly, *neutralism.* Neutrality, non-participation, and neutralism – all these played a vital role in the Korean War, and the result was one of great confusion.

The purpose of this chapter is to describe the American attitude towards these three concepts and to highlight some of the most obvious difficulties that arose. This is not an attempt to deal with neutralism and non-participation in detail but, once more, to trace the American view of neutrality. As will be shown, the Korean War did nothing to clarify that view. To a considerable extent, American problems with respect to these concepts were self-inflicted, because Washington was the driving force behind the effort to put the Korean question before the United Nations and in getting the Security Council to act.[5] Above all, the United States provided most of the troops that did the fighting. There would certainly have been no collective action without US leadership. This meant that a number of problems America faced during the war had their origins in American initiatives.

This was true of the two Security Council resolutions of 25 and 27 June 1950 that laid the groundwork for collective enforcement.[6] These were sponsored by the United States, but their very nature opened the door for non-participation, neutrality, and neutralism.

The 25 June resolution 'determined' that North Korea had committed a breach of the peace; it 'called for' an immediate cessation of hostilities and 'requested' the United Nations Commission on Korea to take various steps. The 27 June resolution 'recommended' that UN members furnish South Korea with such assistance as may be necessary to restore international peace and security in the area. It also 'recommended' that all military forces and other assistance be made available to a unified command under the United States.

The Security Council 'determined', 'called for', and 'recommended', but it never 'decided'. The reasons for this are well known: Russia, protesting at the presence of Taiwan on the Security Council, was absent from the crucial meetings, and, consequently, some council members were reluctant to pass binding decisions on an issue that Russia was bound to veto.[7] Such action could have provoked the Soviets into leaving the United Nations. A softer wording might prevent this.[8]

As a consequence, UN members were not legally bound to live up to their obligations under Articles 2 and 25 of the Charter. Art. 2 requires them to 'give the United Nations every assistance in any action it takes in accordance with the present Charter and [to] refrain from giving assistance to any state against which the United Nations is taking preventive or enforcement action.' Art. 25, however, specifies that this only applies to Security Council *decisions:* 'The Members of the United Nations agree to accept and carry out the decisions of the Security Council in accordance with the present Charter.' This meant that a UN member was not forced to participate in the Korean sanctions and that it could not be compelled to stop supporting the aggressor state. It follows that the Security Council actions were no more than a moral appeal, leaving the ultimate decision to participate or not up to the individual member state.[9] This marked a return to the situation under the League of Nations Covenant, where the ultimate decision to act collectively lay explicitly with the individual member states.[10] The same applies to the Uniting for Peace Resolution (UfP), passed by the General Assembly at a later stage in the war in order to circumvent the Security Council, in case it should again be prevented from acting. The resolution itself, as all General Assembly action, is recommendatory in nature. Any resolution under UfP, therefore, is also voluntaristic in nature.[11]

Given this legal situation, a policy of *non-participation* became entirely justifiable. It was to be hoped that not too many states would opt for it, but, from the viewpoint of the Charter, there was no argument against it. The United States, in agreeing to the wording of the two initial resolutions, had to anticipate such a possibility and, consequently, ran a calculated risk.[12] The two resolutions also opened the door for a course of *neutrality*. After all, if a state was not bound to participate in sanctions and not required to desist from giving assistance to a state against which the UN was taking enforcement action, what would prevent such a state from declaring itself neutral? Under these circumstances the application of the traditional law of neutrality should not provoke a conflict with the law of the United Nations.[13]

The policies of non-participation and neutrality could thus be justified with reference to the wording of the two UN resolutions. This was not the case, however, with the policy of *neutralism*. Neutralism has no legal foundation but is an entirely political concept. It is not tied to any set of rights and obligations relating to abstention from war. Actually, many neutralist states have regularly participated in war. Neutralism merely signifies the refusal to align with one or the other of the two great powers in the Cold War. The core of neutralism, therefore, is non-alignment. Still, the fact that non-participation and neutrality became legally justifiable policies meant that the General Assembly members could refuse to vote with either the East or the West and so remain outside the feuding blocs. The emergence of neutralism was definitely facilitated by the two June resolutions.[14] The consequence for the United Nations was bewildering. While some members decided on a policy of participation, others preferred non-participation. Among the latter, some opted for neutrality and others for neutralism. Members choosing to participate showed a wide spectrum of forms of participation, ranging from mere psychological and political support in the General Assembly to fully-fledged military support in the field.

The UN Secretariat kept a careful record of the various types of participation and non-participation.[15] The result was five categories of participating (or non-participating) member states and, surprisingly enough, another four categories of participating (or non-participating) non-member states!

Members

1. Member states participating actively with military forces: Australia, Belgium, Canada, Columbia, Ethiopia, France, Greece, Great Britain, Luxembourg, Netherlands, New Zealand, Philippines, South Africa, Thailand, Turkey, United States.

2. Member states granting economic and (or) financial support: Argentina, Brazil, Costa Rica, Cuba, Denmark, Ecuador, Iceland, India, Israel, Lebanon, Liberia, Mexico, Nicaragua, Norway, Pakistan, Panama, Paraguay, Peru, Sweden, Uruguay, Venezuela.

3. Member states giving political and moral support: Afghanistan, Bolivia, Burma, Chile, El Salvador, Guatemala, Haiti, Iran, Nationalist China.

4. Member states not participating in any of the UN measures: Dominican Republic, Egypt, Honduras, Indonesia, Iraq, Saudi Arabia, Syria, Yemen, Yugoslavia.

5. Member states questioning the legality of the UN action, rejecting any action, and granting the aggressors direct and (or) indirect support: Czechoslovakia, Poland, Soviet Union.

Non-Members

1. States granting economic and (or) financial support: Austria, Cambodia, German Federal Republic, Italy, Japan, Switzerland, Vietnam.

2. States supporting the UN politically and morally: Spain.

3. States showing no support: Portugal.

4. States questioning the legality of the UN action, rejecting any action, and granting the aggressors direct and (or) indirect support: Albania, Hungary, People's Republic of China, Rumania.[16]

The consequence was that, during the Korean War, a state had a wide range of options if it decided to remain aloof. It could choose any one of the foregoing versions of participation or non-participation, but it could also decide to declare neutrality according to traditional international law. In addition, a state could opt for a policy of neutralism. Given these various possibilities, problems were bound to arise. These had to do mostly with the inherent vagueness of some of the concepts and with the overlap among them.

As will be shown, the difficulties arose in the *conduct of hostilities*, when some states, participating or not, claimed to be neutral while providing large-scale military assistance to the aggressors. But uncertainties also arose in the *termination of hostilities* when creating two commissions required the recruitment of neutrals from among the various kinds of participating and non-participating states. In all these cases, the United States faced some very awkward choices.

The conduct of hostilities

Although Korea is a country surrounded by water on three sides, the war was fought overwhelmingly on land. Naval matters, therefore, never entered too much into consideration. However, many problems were raised by the fact that Korea at its northern end had a common land frontier with China and Russia and that massive assistance was pouring south from these two neighbouring countries. For the questions of neutrality that arose during the hostilities, these strategic facts were of basic importance. It meant that issues of sea neutrality played only a minor role. United Nations naval forces imposed a traditional 'close', or 'effective' blockade on North Korea, which was respected by all states that were ostensibly neutral in the conflict, particularly China and the Soviet Union. Because of the common land frontier, the Russians and the Chinese had no need to test the blockade.[17]

Potentially more significant would have been a blockade imposed against the People's Republic of China. According to Patrick M. Norton, such a blockade was discussed in Washington:

> In particular, it was believed that any such blockade would have to exclude Dairen and Port Arthur, which were still under Soviet control. As neutral ports, those two cities were thought immune to blockade, but vessels entering them were thought to be subject to checks for contraband ultimately destined for Chinese or North Korean forces.[18]

This comment shows that, as in earlier times, the US military was discussing blockades in terms of the traditional law of war and neutrality.[19] It did not seem to matter to them that, in the language of the United Nations, this was no longer war at all, but enforcement action. The idea of a conventional blockade was ultimately dropped, not for legal reasons, but because Washington could find no friends to participate.[20] The United States then decided to turn to the United Nations and to request that the General Assembly, under the Uniting for Peace (UfP) provision, recommend the imposition of a wide-ranging embargo against China and North Korea. An American draft resolution was submitted on 7 May 1951, and it was adopted with broad support on 18 May.

The embargo was breached frequently by both participating and non-participating states. Since action under UfP was only recommendatory, these states did not violate the Charter. It would have been entirely possible for any of them to explain their action with reference to the international law of neutrality. This was unnecessary, because no issue was ever made over any of the breaches.[21] Naval matters were simply secondary for most of the war. Of much greater importance were the issues of neutrality along the northern frontiers of Korea. Here, there were ample opportunities for belligerent interests to clash with neutral rights and duties. Problems of this nature arose when American aeroplanes downed Russian fighters or strafed air-bases over Russian and Chinese territory or, more importantly, when the Chinese permitted their territory in Manchuria to be used as a sanctuary for attacks against the UN forces. The greatest problem arose when China sent huge numbers of 'volunteers' to assist the North Koreans.

In a number of these instances, the Chinese and the Russians made use of the law of neutrality to defend their interests, but in a number of other instances they failed to do so. Both types of cases are of interest, because they reveal a good deal about the American conception of neutrality at the time.

On 4 September 1950, the US Air Force downed a Russian aeroplane over the west coast of Korea. The following day, 5 September, the United States informed the Security Council of the incident, giving its version of the accident. On 6 September, the American ambassador to the Soviet Union was called into the Russian foreign office and handed a note protesting the incident. The Russians rejected the American version and demanded an investigation, immediate full indemnification, and punishment of those responsible. The note also made reference to violations of 'accepted norms of international law'.[22] It did not specify what type of international law had been violated.

The American ambassador refused to accept the note, arguing that the United States was acting on behalf of the United Nations and that, consequently, the note should be addressed to the Security Council.[23] The Soviets submitted the note to the Security Council the same day. The decision of the council went against the Russians.

A month later, on 8 October, American planes mistakenly attacked a Russian airfield 100 kilometres inside the Soviet Union. Again Moscow protested, and again the Americans told them to turn to the United Nations. Once more, there was no mention of neutrality. The Russians could have easily phrased both these protests in terms of the Hague Law. For some unknown reason, they chose not to do so at this time in the war.[24]

The Chinese did the same. On 28 and 30 August 1951, they submitted complaints to the Security Council about airspace violations by American planes. Neutrality was not mentioned. The same applied to a charge dated 24 September. On this occasion, the Chinese claimed that 'military aircraft of the United States had flown over Chinese territory and dropped bombs on the city of Antung, causing damage to property and wounding a number of people.'[25] Again, there was no reference to neutrality. China merely demanded that it be seated on the Security Council and that the Council take effective measures to condemn the aggressive crimes of the United States. The language was rather propagandistic.[26]

Two days later, the United States admitted to the violation of Chinese territory and the dropping of bombs on Antung. The United States deeply regretted the incident and was willing 'to assume responsibility and pay compensation through the United Nations for any damages which an impartial investigation on the spot might show to have been caused by United States planes.'[27]

This all took place two weeks after the spectacularly successful Inchon landing and only shortly before the crossing of the 38th parallel became an issue in the General Assembly. At this time Indian diplomats repeatedly warned the United States that Peking was seriously contemplating intervention. To allay Indian fears, the Department of State was willing to send Nehru a conciliatory message through the British Foreign Secretary, Bevin, a message that sheds some light on the American conception of an 'impartial' commission. This is what Bevin was to tell Nehru:

> the Americans would be the first to regret such unintentional damage and continue to be agreeable to having the matter investigated and any damage assessed by competent *neutral* judgment

[added emphasis]. Mr Acheson has authorized me to inform you that the Americans are quite willing to have a representative of India and of Sweden look into the charges and assess any damages which it would be found the Americans should pay. They do not insist upon UN machinery and would accept an informal arrangement on the side.[28]

There was to be no need for such an investigative body, because the Russians vetoed the American proposal when it was made on 12 September in the Security Council.[29] But the mere fact that the proposal was forthcoming in this manner is of some interest. It shows that early on in the Korean War, the United States was entirely willing to let neutrality play a role. In a highly pragmatic fashion, the 'competent neutral judgment' of India and Sweden was combined with an exercise in 'collective enforcement' in order to permit an 'informal arrangement', thus avoiding the cumbersome UN machinery! Communist China, at least in this incident, had avoided making use of neutrality. The United States had not. The roles were soon to change, however.

In November, the Chinese intervened massively in the war, and in early December the General Assembly, still in session, decided to debate the issue.[30] Since China could not speak at the meeting, the Russian representative presented its case. Vyshinsky's argument was that, as a neutral state, the People's Republic was not legally bound to prevent volunteers from crossing the border and assisting a belligerent state:

I must again draw your attention, as I did yesterday in the General Committee, to two conventions concluded at The Hague, namely, conventions V and XIII which were signed by the same countries which are now raising the question of the intervention of the Central People's Government of the People's Republic of China in Korea ... . Those conventions have a direct bearing on the question we are discussing.[31]

The Russian representative then quoted Articles 6 and 7 of Convention V, signed at The Hague, and Article 7 of Convention XIII. These regulate the questions of armaments and of volunteers in land and naval warfare. As regards armaments, a neutral power is not required to stop private shipments to the belligerents, but it must abstain from official assistance. The conventions, in other words, distinguish between the private and the public economic sphere, something that had made sense in the 'liberal' nineteenth century. To argue that private shipments were crossing the border between two countries with state-controlled economies made no sense at all.

As regards volunteers, the conventions state that a neutral power 'is not engaged by the fact of persons crossing the frontier separately to offer their services to one of the belligerents.' 'Separately' had always been interpreted as meaning singly and in small numbers. In view of the massive Chinese drive south, none of these terms seemed to apply. Vyshinsky's conclusions were, therefore, less than credible: 'it is clear beyond any doubt that these articles settle conclusively the question of the legal ... right of neutral governments not to hinder individual members of their peoples from helping another country in its fight against its enemies, if they so desire.'[32]

Vyshinky's remarks provoked a lengthy debate. On 8, 9, and 11 December, the representatives of Uruguay, Ecuador, Peru, Cuba, and China (Taiwan) answered the Russian delegate. Two main arguments emerged from practically all the responses: (i) it was impossible to maintain that the Chinese forces had come across the frontier separately and, in view of their organisation, strength, and supplies, that they were volunteers; (ii) the Hague Conventions were no longer applicable, since they had been superseded by the signature and ratification of the United Nations Charter. The latter point was strongly emphasised by the Peruvian representative, who thought that the Hague Conventions 'should be placed in their historical and doctrinal context; it should be remembered that in the years which had since elapsed there had been a radical change in the legal principles accepted by mankind.' And he added: 'The innovation introduced was that the principle of unlimited sovereignty and the legitimacy of war would be relegated to the museum of antiquities. Yet those prehistoric monsters were now being resurrected.'[33]

The United States preferred to remain silent. It was one thing for minor states to stand up uncompromisingly for the law of the United Nations and to denounce roundly the traditional law of war. It was quite another for one of the veto powers to do so. As is well known from the words of the Secretary of State, Cordell Hull, the veto was introduced in the UN Charter precisely because the United States was unwilling to relegate unlimited sovereignty to 'the museum of antiquity'.[34] The very presence of veto powers on the Security Council was a constant reminder of those 'prehistoric monsters'.

Vyshinsky knew that remaining silent was a conscious strategy on the part of the Americans, and he could not help but make reference to it:

> in replying to the arguments drawn by the delegation of the USSR from The Hague Conventions of 1907 on the laws of war, the representative of the United States of America and the United Kingdom had preferred to remain silent and use the good offices of Peru (410th meeting), Cuba (411th meeting), and Uruguay (410th meeting) rather than to state clearly whether or not they regarded themselves as bound by those Conventions.[35]

The United States was indeed not eager to take a clear stand on the Hague Conventions at this time. The International Law Commission of the UN had dealt with the issue in 1949 and concluded that the traditional law of war and of neutrality had no place within the framework of the United Nations.[36] Now the Russians claimed that it did have a place, and – who knows? – possibly some of the American military would also have been willing to make use of it under certain circumstances. It was better to remain silent.

In their internal correspondence, the Department of State, the Joint Chiefs of Staff, and the Far Eastern Headquarters also avoided making reference to neutrality wherever they could. As the published documents show, the entire question of 'hot pursuit' (briefly raised in August and September 1951)[37] and the question over the bombing of Rashin (near the Russian border)[38] were discussed in purely military and diplomatic terms. No questions of neutral law were ever alluded to.

The Russian and Chinese handling of neutrality actually served to help this policy of silence. At no time did these two countries pursue a consistent course in this matter. They used neutrality very selectively, mostly as a tool to achieve various foreign policy aims of a propagandistic nature, or so it seems. As a result, there were a number of occasions when they felt it was useful to argue in terms of neutrality, and a number of occasions when they decided it was not. If they had systematically adhered to neutral legal arguments, it would have been a great deal more difficult for the United States to dodge the issue.[39]

The supervision of the truce

The Korean War may have begun as an exercise in collective enforcement, but it ended very much as a conventional war. Ceasefire negotiations were carried out by the commanders of both sides; the aggressors were granted *de facto* recognition as equal and sovereign belligerents; a truce was signed that placed equal burdens on both parties; a demilitarised buffer zone was created, demanding equal strategic sacrifices from both armies; a mutually agreed upon inspection commission was set up to supervise the implementation of the truce provisions; and, finally, another commission was brought to life to repatriate the prisoners of both sides. All these measures had more in common with a traditional settlement of war than with the imposition of a collective decision over the misguided will of an international law-breaker. There was no call for 'unconditional surrender'.

Under such circumstances, it was only natural that neutrality came to play an important role in terminating the war or, more specifically, in the negotiations that began in July 1951 at Kaesong and continued at Panmunjom for almost two years.[40] Two very important issues on the agenda were the supervision of the truce and the repatriation of POWs. Neutral commissions were established to address these issues. A Neutral Nations Supervisory Commission (NNSC) was created to keep an eye on the flow of arms in the demilitarised zone and on some strategically important locations in North and South Korea; a Neutral Nations Repatriation Commission (NNRC) was set up to handle the difficult question of either freeing or repatriating the prisoners of war of both sides.

Although both commissions were called neutral, they were very different. They differed in origin, composition, assigned tasks, and ultimate success. The NNSC had its origins in the Panmunjom negotiations of December 1951 and was proposed by the Communist side. The NNRC was mentioned for the first time a full year later during the 1952 session of the General Assembly and as a result of an Indian initiative. The NNSC was composed of Sweden, Switzerland, Poland, and Czechoslovakia; the NNRC embraced the same four states, but also included India as 'umpire'. The NNSC was practically stillborn, because it had been given an almost impossible task and was split down the middle on most issues. In contrast, the NNRC was capable of reaching decisions, and it accomplished its goal in a short while. Ironically, the NNSC exists to this day in its paralysed form; the NNRC was dissolved soon after the prisoners had been freed or repatriated.

For the United States, too, the two commissions posed different problems, particularly when it came to settling the membership of each. For the NNSC, it was a question of deciding generally what countries could pass as neutral and serve American interests. The choice of Sweden and Switzerland was not a very difficult one. But in regard to the NNRC, the question was whether India could be trusted as an 'umpire', as a kind of 'neutral above the neutrals' destined to cast the deciding vote on a commission of five. That decision, as will be shown, was not an easy one. Let us first look at the question of NNSC membership. On 30 June 1951, General Ridgway broadcast his famous radio message that led to the first negotiations with the enemy. The same day, he received a message from the Joint Chiefs of Staff containing American armistice proposals. It mentioned a Military Armistice Commission (MAC) of mixed and equal membership and designated by the Commanders in Chief of the two sides.[41] The idea of a truce supervisory body was thus part of American thinking from the very start of the negotiations. But there was no reference to neutrality whatsoever. General Ridgway was the first American to make any mention of neutrality in this context. In one of his messages to the other side (meant to clear the way for a first meeting of liaison officers at Kaesong), he offered that 'the area within a 5 mile radius from the center of Kaesong will be observed by me as a neutral zone from the time of arrival of your delegates in Kaesong.'[42] In the termination of hostilities, it was the Americans who first made reference to neutrality![43]

The neutral zone proved problematic, because the two sides could not guarantee freedom of movement in and around Kaesong,[44] and ultimately negotiations were moved to Panmunjom, at the eastern limits of the zone. But the many messages that went back and forth made extensive reference to neutrality.[45] Small wonder, therefore, that some time later the Communist side should come up with the idea of setting up a 'neutral nations supervisory organ'. This was in early December 1951.[46]

For quite some time, it was not clear what the relation would be between MAC and the neutral supervisory organ. MAC, composed of the belligerents, was at times assumed to be the overall co-ordinating body, while the neutral organ, composed of non-belligerents, would have the subordinate role of inspection north and south of the armistice line.[47] While these uncertainties persisted, the Communists began to mention specific countries to serve as neutrals. On 5 December, they spoke of Czechoslovakia, Poland, Switzerland, Sweden, and Denmark.[48]

Back in Washington, the government thereupon began to ponder the question of whether or not to agree to a neutral inspection body. At a joint meeting of representatives of the Department of State and the Joint Chiefs of Staff on 12 December, it was decided that 'the extent and nature of inspection was not of major importance',[49] because other items on the negotiating agenda carried more weight, among them the prisoners of war. Against that background, the consensus was that Washington could go along with the idea and start preliminary consultations with Switzerland, Sweden, and Norway.[50]

Talks began with Switzerland[51] and Norway on the very next day and with Sweden on 14 December. The first contacts in this matter were awkward, because the nature of the inspection body was largely unclear. Furthermore, American officials were rather reluctant to talk about 'neutrals'. This is best reflected in the exchange between Assistant Secretary of State Hickerson and the Swedish and Norwegian ambassadors. The following words are taken from Hickerson's memorandum on his talk with Ambassador Boheman of Sweden: 'I then told him that as he knew there had been discussions in the truce talks of the setting up of a truce inspection commission of neutrals or as I preferred to describe it of non-belligerents or non-combatants.'[52]

Hickerson had good reason to feel ill at ease about using the term 'neutral'. Only a few years before, he had been one of the staunchest critics of Swedish neutrality. He was, it will be remembered, the man at the Department of State who forcefully backed Ambassador Matthews in his drive to re-educate the Swedes when NATO was set up. To refer now to neutrality as a constructive force would have required Hickerson to radically alter his personal conception of neutrality. He preferred, instead, to talk about 'non-belligerent' and 'non-combatant' states. But what exactly did these terms mean? What was their relation to 'non-participation', for instance? No one really knew.

The meaning of neutrality became even more tenuous in the conversation held with Ambassador Morgenstierne of Norway, because that country had been a NATO ally since 1949 and was thus anything but neutral. The following are again Hickerson's words:

I then told him that, as he knew, there had been discussion at Panmunjom of setting up a truce inspection commission of 'neutrals' to operate behind the lines. He [Morgenstierne] interjected that Norway was not a 'neutral'. I quickly agreed, and said we were using the term 'non-belligerent' or 'non-combatant'.[53]

As these conversations reveal, the meaning of neutrality suffered badly in those days. There were manifest neutrals, such as Sweden and Switzerland, which were referred to as 'non-belligerents' or 'non-combatants' (or, in the case of Sweden, 'partial participant'), and there were manifest allies such as Norway, Czechoslovakia, and Poland, which were, at least verbally, referred to as 'neutrals'. But the real challenge for the meaning of neutrality came when, in February of 1952, the Soviet Union claimed to be neutral and demanded a seat on the inspection body. Needless to say, the United States could not tolerate this. It was one thing to accept Norwegians, Czechs, and Poles as neutrals, but quite another to regard the Russians as such. The limit had been reached.[54] The Russian move did not catch the United States entirely by surprise. There had already been talk earlier that the Russians might want to sit on the NNSC, and there was agreement that such a move would have to be forestalled.[55] When it occurred, however, there was some disagreement on how to counter it. Differences of opinion existed between General Ridgway in Korea and the Washington co-ordinating body made up of representatives from the Joint Chiefs of Staff and the Department of State. On 27 February this group authorised Ridgway 'to make it entirely clear to Commies that UNC refusal to accept Soviet Union as a member of Neutral Supervisory Commission is absolutely firm and irrevocable.' However, the Washington group did not object to the Soviet Union serving on a commission that was no longer called neutral, provided the United States was also represented.[56]

In a message to Ridgway dated 15 March, this position was spelled out clearly:

> In event Commies select USSR (or Communist China) as mbr it would then be mandatory that mbrs from our side include United States. View here is that while Soviet Union (or Communist China) entirely unacceptable in position of 'neutral' there is no objection to Soviet Union as mbr of supervisory commission that is not identified as 'neutral' provided United States is also mbr. Commission would then be composed of United States along with, for example, Sweden and Switzerland on our side, while on Communist side Poland, Czechoslovakia and USSR would be acceptable.[57]

General Ridgway disagreed. He felt that Russia should not be allowed to serve on any commission, neutral or not. To have Russian inspectors below the 38th Parallel represented, to him, an unacceptable risk.[58] A number of messages went back and forth between Ridgway's headquarters and Washington, and for a while the question remained unsettled. In the end, Ridgway won; the American official position was, henceforth, that a neutral commission without superpower representation was preferable to any other solution. In the end, this was the version adopted at Panmunjom.[59]

The reason Washington would have liked to see Russia represented on the supervisory commission was spelled out in one of the telegrams to Ridgway: 'Considered here there would be definite advantages to having Soviet Union publicly associated with and forming part of armistice mechanism in position clearly identifying Soviets with Commie aggressors'.[60] Associating the Russians with the forces of aggression was an intimate concern of American diplomacy in those days. But it was not easy, because Russia, as so many other states, enjoyed the comfortable legal position of a non-participating state, whatever that might mean in detail.[61]

It was a frustrating spectacle for Washington: here was the instigator of aggression and major supplier of armaments passing as a non-participating state. Russia could not be accused of violating the UN Charter, because the June 1950 resolutions made non-participation possible and because the term was also part of the terminology developed at Panmunjom. Getting the Soviets to serve on a truce supervisory commission made up of 'both sides' would finally have associated them openly with the side of aggression. Obviously, the Russians wanted none of it, and Washington failed in this respect. But, by keeping the Russians off a neutral supervisory body, the United States prevented the situation from getting worse. A neutral Russia would have been infinitely less desirable than a non-participating one.

The repatriation of prisoners

The POW question was deadlocked for a long while.[62] It was not until the Indians undertook a major initiative during the autumn 1952 UN General Assembly session that some progress began to be made. Krishna Menon, Indian Foreign Minister, submitted a draft resolution that, after much discussion and many amendments, demanded the shipment of all POWs to a demilitarised zone and the creation of a commission composed of Sweden, Switzerland, Poland, and Czechoslovakia or any other combination of states not participating militarily. To help settle disputes the commission was called upon to appoint an umpire who might also act as chairman. Should the commission fail to name an umpire within three weeks, the General Assembly would do so on its behalf. Together with other provisions about the repatriation of POWs, the resolution became known as the 'Menon Plan'.[63]

The final agreement reached at Panmunjom on 8 June 1953 strongly resembled the 'Menon Plan', although there were some modifications.[64] India was mentioned as a full fifth member of the Commission, along with Sweden, Switzerland, Poland, and Czechoslovakia. But it was yet another modification that gave more weight to the Indian position:

Sufficient armed forces and any other operating personnel required to assist the neutral nations repatriation commission in carrying out its functions and responsibilities shall be provided exclusively by India, whose representatives shall be the umpire in accordance with the provisions of Article 132 of the Geneva Convention, and shall also be chairman and executive agent of the neutral nations repatriation commission.[65]

This was a major victory for Indian diplomacy. Not only had Menon initiated the plan that was ultimately adopted at Panmunjom, but he had also succeeded in having India play the decisive role in the entire matter of repatriation. After all, India was the only neutral on the commission that had the trust of both sides; it was the only truly impartial member and, as such, was bound to play the pivotal role on the commission. As a sign of its power, it was granted the chairmanship and the authority to use its own armed forces. Not everyone in Washington was happy with this outcome.

To understand the American position, it is important to know that the question of membership was closely intertwined with a number of more substantive issues: was repatriation to be forced or voluntary; who would take charge of the POWs and who would interview them; would they remain in their present location or would they be transported elsewhere; what were the proper criteria for liberation and repatriation? These and other questions stood in the foreground, and the question of membership was often a mere consequence of these considerations. It is, therefore, wrong to assume that friendship or hostility towards any one potential member alone determined the American position. Things were more complicated than that.

The State Department had early information about Menon's plan. On 29 October 1952, Selwyn Lloyd, British Foreign Secretary, informed Acheson in general terms of India's intentions,[66] and on 8 November Acheson was in possession of a detailed 11-Point Programme containing the essential features.[67] At a joint meeting of Indian, British, Canadian, and American UN representatives, the programme was discussed for the first time. In subsequent discussions with Menon, US Ambassador Gross had an opportunity to state American priorities concerning membership very clearly:

I told him ... our 'overwhelmingly strong preference' was for GA designation of an impartial comm, composed of one or more states not Communist-controlled ... . Menon repeated arguments previously made that Chi Commies would not admit that any other states were 'impartial', including India ... . I said that as very poor second alternative we might consider possibility of GA designating a bilateral comm of the Pole–Czech–Swede–Swiss variety, plus an umpire fixed simultaneously by the GA, for example Norway, Brazil or India ... . I mentioned, as a third possibility, that the GA res might call upon the negotiators to set up a mixed POW comm which should agree upon an umpire within a fixed period at the end of which the GA would designate an umpire if agreement had not been reached.[68]

This discussion took place during the presidential election, and there followed a period of diplomatic inactivity while the new Eisenhower Administration was getting ready to assume power. Once in charge, its preferences were the same, however. Dulles continued to favour an 'impartial' commission made up of Sweden and Switzerland over one composed like the NNSC and presided over by an Indian umpire. It took Washington several months to accept the fact that the choice of India was the only possible solution acceptable to both sides.

Under the new administration, therefore, the distrust of India showed initially as much as it had under the Democrats. On 2 April 1953, U. Alexis Johnson of the Department of State briefed a member of the British embassy on the American position regarding the choice of commission members. Johnson explained that Washington 'would not be happy over such a choice as India, as India all too often seemed to consider it necessary to be "more neutral" toward the Chinese Communists than toward the UN.'[69]

There was Congressional opposition too. Senator Knowland, in close contact with the Department of State, proposed to the new administration that because of the unpopularity of India on Capitol Hill, Indonesia should be considered as an alternative.[70] But neither the Department of State nor the Joint Chiefs of Staff was happy with this proposal. Indonesia had an unstable government and lacked the troops to take physical charge of the POWs, if that became necessary.[71]

South Korea also distrusted India. Of course, Korean opposition had deeper roots. Syrigman Rhee was against any kind of armistice at all, and he aimed for the re-conquest of the entire North. What he particularly disliked, however, was that any 'Asian neutral' should play any part at all in the war.[72] His views had little impact on Washington, and they were more than offset by the pro-Indian views of Great Britain, Canada, and France. In line with this critical view of India, the new administration made preparations for the resumption of negotiations on 26 April at Panmunjom. The Joint Chiefs of Staff, General Clark, now Commander in Chief for the Far East, and John Foster Dulles continued to prefer a commission headed by either Sweden or Switzerland.[73]

A shift in this position only came about on 22 April, after President Eisenhower himself had had his say. At that time, the Army Chief of Staff sent General Clark final negotiating instructions stating unambiguously that 'neither the USSR nor a Soviet Satellite nor India is acceptable as the "neutral state"'.[74] Officials at the Department of State and the Joint Chiefs of Staff objected to this wording, and they took the matter directly to Eisenhower, who backed a more moderate stand. He believed 'that the negotiations could not be allowed to fail if the selection narrowed to India.'[75] From here on, India's chances improved, as was evident in one of the regular meetings between representatives of the Department of State and the Joint Chiefs of Staff on 8 May. The drift of the discussion was so typical of the thinking at that time that it is worth quoting in some detail:

> *Mr Nitze*: Personally I think it would be better to have the Indians act as a single neutral rather than to accept the 5 Power proposal at all.
> *General Bradley*: Would the Commies accept that?
> *Mr Nitze*: I don't know why not.
> *General Vandenberg*: The President has said that it was politically impossible for him to accept India alone.
> *Mr Nitze*: I agree that we would have real initial difficulties with the Hill, but the eventual difficulties that we would run into from having Communists on the Commission or particularly from having Communist troops would be considerably greater.
> *General Hull*: Have the Swiss and Swedes said they would provide forces?
> *Mr Matthews*: The Swedes have reserved their position and the Swiss are very much worried about their ability to provide forces of the magnitude required.
> *General Hull*: It certainly would be better to have all the troops come from just one country.
> *General Bradley*: I think it would be better to accept the Indians if we are going to end up with the Indians anyway.[76]

The gist of the conversation was summarised in a memorandum written the same day by the Assistant Secretary of State, Robertson, to John Foster Dulles. There was no merit, said Robertson, in further temporising on the Communist proposal to have India as a full fifth member. India was the only neutral capable of providing the necessary forces, and, furthermore, it seemed very probable that India would end up on the Commission even under different agreements. Then, however, 'India will enter its duties on the commission more or less offended by us and probably less subject to our influence than if we had accepted India.'[77]

The decision was made: India's candidacy received American backing. But it had been a difficult decision, as it meant acceptance of what Acheson in November had classified as a 'very poor second choice' and the abandonment of an 'overwhelmingly strong preference'. How strong that preference was is shown by some of the words chosen to characterise Swiss or Swedish neutrality. On a number of occasions in the spring of 1953, Switzerland in particular was said to be the 'obvious' choice;[78] that there was 'no reason for considering any country other than Switzerland whose neutrality was proverbial';[79] that the country had 'outstanding qualifications to play the role of the neutral state to take custody of the POWs.'[80] For the delicate job of handling its own nationals, the United States trusted the European neutrals a great deal more than neutralist India.

For India, on the other hand, it was a moment of triumph. For almost three years, Nehru had continuously mediated between the two sides and, in the process, had experienced all the humiliations and setbacks typically associated with this thankless task. His good offices were not always appreciated and, at times, led the belligerents to question Indian integrity and motives.[81] Now they ended up trusting India and regarded it not merely as a 'UNC neutral'[82] like Sweden or Switzerland or a 'Communist neutral'[83] like Poland or Czechoslovakia. India became the true neutral on the NNRC or, as one legal expert called it, a kind of 'super neutral'.[84]

Avoidance and confusion

Let us now look at the Korean War as a whole and summarise how it affected the American conception of neutrality. Initially, the United States intended the conflict to be an exercise in collective enforcement, but it soon realised that it had become a regular war. Especially when it came to finding ways to terminate the conflict, traditional diplomacy was used, and the re-emergence of neutrality was one aspect of this development.

The United States, therefore, did not overly resist the reappearance of neutrality as such – it merely tried to prevent the Communist powers from becoming neutrals. More particularly, the United States tried to separate the concept of neutrality from that of non-participation, because the Communist states, despite their massive assistance to the North Koreans, were regarded as non-participants. From the American point of view, it was one thing to tolerate the aggressors as passing as non-participants, but it was quite another to permit them to carry the still rather respectable title of a neutral.

As part of this strategy of separation, the United States tried to *avoid* the concept of neutrality whenever possible. The purpose was not to hurt such permanent neutrals as Sweden and Switzerland, but to counter shrewd Communist tactics. This effort met with some success in the conduct of hostilities, but it failed in their termination. The United States ultimately had to agree to the formation of two commissions on which 'non-participating' Communist states were sitting as 'neutrals'. Separation thus failed, and neutrality resurfaced in a highly complicated context. Not only was the exact difference between non-participation and neutrality no longer evident, but the prominent position of India also raised the question of the relation of these terms to neutralism. The result was a good deal of *confusion,* which did nothing to sharpen the American conception of neutrality as it had developed since 1941.[85]

In the *conduct of hostilities,* the United States managed to separate non-participation from neutrality on several occasions. It twice refused to accept Russian protests directly and in so doing avoided possible claims under the Hague Conventions. More importantly, however, it avoided the possibility of having to recognise Russia as a neutral. It was bad enough to see a nominal non-participant provide massive military assistance to the aggressor states, something that would have been illegal under the Hague Conventions, of course.

By not accepting the Russian protests directly, however, the United States departed from its policy, still pursued in the Second World War, of assuming direct responsibility for damages done by its armed forces to third parties not involved in the war.[86] This implied a weakening of the American conception of neutrality that, as I have shown earlier, had been rather traditional in the military sphere. It is likely, of course, that the United States would still have assumed these responsibilities towards a truly neutral neighbour of Korea, such as an 'Asian Switzerland'. If so, the change in policy was due solely to the special circumstances of the Korean War. Still, the refusal to accept direct responsibility was new.

A similar policy of avoidance was applied to China. In the case of the accidental bombings, the United States proposed to keep the matter outside the sphere of international law, and it even suggested keeping it outside the United Nations. Acheson, as will be recalled, suggested that 'an informal agreement on the side' be reached. This too was a departure from established rule.

The United States also managed to keep neutrality and non-participation apart when the question of Chinese 'volunteers' was raised in the United Nations. The Russians, speaking on behalf of the Chinese, claimed that the troops pouring south were covered by the Hague Conventions. The claim was so blatantly false that it would have been easy for the United States to refute it, but it was wiser to avoid the issue. Defending the Hague Conventions had its dangers. In another accidental shooting down of a Russian plane, the Soviets might very well have argued their case in terms of the international law of neutrality. Had the United States stood up earlier and publicly in defence of the Hague Conventions, it would have faced a real predicament. Non-participating Russia would then have received its recognition as a neutral.

The policy of separation and avoidance no longer worked in the *termination of hostilities*. The inconclusive outcome of the war made the United States eager to settle, and, consequently, the attitude towards neutrality changed. After offering relatively little resistance, America accepted the idea of neutral good offices. Since these services were not regulated by the Hague Conventions, acceptance was legally unproblematic.[87] Politically, however, the matter was very awkward. The Communists insisted that the definition of neutrality be based on the concept of non-participation and thereby completely undercut the American position. It was now possible for almost all the Communist states, Russia included, to become neutrals. The aggressors had at last succeeded in putting the mantle of neutral respectability around their shoulders.

The United States succeeded in limiting the damage: only Poland and Czechoslovakia were accepted as 'neutrals'. Because 'each side' was allowed to appoint its own neutrals, the Poles and Czechs became, in effect, the 'aggressors' neutrals'. But the case of Sweden and Switzerland was no less strange; by virtue of the arrangement, they became the 'UNC neutrals'. In other words, these two permanent neutrals were appointed to be the representatives of the very organisation that in 1945 had declared permanent neutrality to be incompatible with its charter. Furthermore, Sweden was a member of the United Nations, while Switzerland was not. How could Switzerland, then, be a

'UNC neutral'? It must be added that Sweden was a partially participating state, because it put a medical unit at the disposal of the UN.[88] India did the same, and it passed as the 'neutral above the neutrals'. But India was the only state that 'both sides' really regarded as impartial, not by virtue of its permanent neutrality, but because it had followed a course of neutralism.[89]

The United States had good practical reasons for agreeing to this confused arrangement. It saw the usefulness of neutral good offices in settling a number of questions, primarily the issue of American POWs. In his election campaign, Eisenhower had promised the nation to bring the boys home in due course, and he must have been willing to accept any good offices, neutral or not. How could he now refuse to lend his support to a solution that was conceptually murky but had, at least in the case of the NNRC, a good chance of succeeding? The public would not have understood.

The various members of the two commissions were equally opportunistic. It must have pleased the Communist states to embarrass the United Nations and to rob it of some of its enthusiasm for collective action. India relished the important role it was playing only a few years after reaching independence. Menon managed to push the country right to the forefront of world politics and to promote powerfully the cause of non-alignment and neutralism.[90] The Swedes and the Swiss were eager to see neutrality regain a place of respectability after what they had experienced in the Second World War. It pleased them that the very organisation that had condemned neutrality in San Francisco was now in need of it, and they were also happy that they obtained an opportunity to prove to the United States that neutrality could still be a constructive force. The Swedes, in particular, had come under heavy moral pressure when NATO was established.

The sum total of all these particular national interests permitted resolution of a pressing international problem, but it did nothing to clarify the concept of neutrality. If anything, neutrality was now a more confusing notion than ever. This was certainly true from an American point of view. Did America still adhere to its qualified conception of neutrality, to the idea of the 'supporting state'? In a general way, the answer is yes. From the military viewpoint, the United States continued to respect abstention. No pressure was put on either Sweden or Switzerland to commit themselves with armed forces. But the status of abstention became confusing once it was identified with non-participation.

In economic warfare, too, the established line was continued. The United States expected all states, neutrals included, to embargo the aggressors. Cocom was used to this effect, and the United Nations was also made part of the effort.[91] After China had been condemned as an aggressor, the General Assembly passed a resolution calling on 'every state' to embargo the shipment of arms, ammunition, implements of war, atomic energy materials, and petroleum.[92] This action was, once again, not binding on members and certainly not on states outside the organisation, but it helped legitimise the general American embargo measures, particularly those of Cocom.

As a result, the Korean War had not altered the American conception of neutrality significantly. The acceptance of neutral good offices showed that there was continued appreciation for the merits of *Neutralitätspolitik*, and the disregard for neutral international law marked decreasing appreciation for *Neutralitätsrecht*. This should come as no surprise. In the early years of the Cold War, the United States learned to see neutrality more as a political than a legal phenomenon. The Korean War confirmed this trend. This did not bode well for the future application of the international law of neutrality.

8
Geneva Conference, 1954

The choice of participants

Article 60 of the Panmunjom agreements provided for the convening of a political conference to discuss the future of Korea. Preparatory discussions were held at Panmunjom throughout 1953 and into 1954, but they led nowhere. Only at the Berlin Foreign Minister Conference in early 1954 was agreement reached. The political conference was to be held in Geneva in the spring of the same year, and it was to have two parts: one relating to the future of Korea and another to the situation in Indochina.

One of the many issues complicating the preliminary talks in Panmunjom was the issue of participants. The wording of the ceasefire documents, that stated that 'both sides' would be represented at the conference, left some questions open. Would this include the Russians, and if so, in what capacity? Could this also include the neutrals, India in particular? These questions were not settled until the foreign ministers met in Berlin in January 1954, yet they dominated the negotiations in Panmunjom throughout the autumn. During the course of the exchanges on the topic, a number of interesting references to neutrality were made. These are revealing with regard to the attitudes that prevailed in Washington and the views of the new administration in particular.

John Foster Dulles regularly dealt with the matter. On 13 August 1953, he sent the American chief delegate at the United Nations, Henry Cabot Lodge, a brief set of instructions on the conference. It contained eight points, the first of which dealt with participation: 'The Korean Political Conference should represent the two belligerent sides, as contemplated by Article 60 of the Armistice Agreement. It is *not* to be a "roundtable" conference with the participation of neutrals.'[1] The neutral uppermost in Dulles' mind was India. This became clear when Lodge talked to Krishna Menon a day later. Lodge thought that it would be a great embarrassment for the United States to have India at the conference 'because of the well-known attitude of the President of Korea',[2] whose participation would be essential. To soften the impact of his words, Lodge then added the following comment:

> I said that we had the greatest respect and admiration for India and were delighted that India was Chairman of the Neutral Nations Repatriation Commission. We felt grateful to India for having accepted this difficult post, thereby contributing to the ending of the hostilities.[3]

The Indians got the message. As soon as 26 August, the American ambassador to India cabled Washington that Nehru did not seem to insist on participation, and a few days later Menon asked the UN General Assembly to withdraw a resolution calling for Indian participation.[4]

The Communists, however, kept insisting on some form of neutral participation, and the Indians once more began to show some interest. In the course of a lengthy exchange between Dulles and Menon on 13 October, it became clear that, in some form or other, the Indians might be willing to serve as intermediaries once more.[5] As a result, Dulles began to reconsider his position. Only a week later, he expressed the view that it might be possible to have India present as a reporter on the progress of the NNRC and that

> if the Indians were there in some such capacity it might be possible for the Communists to use them as messenger boys with the other side.... . India might be used as an intermediary under such circumstances without there being official Indian participation in the conference.[6]

Dulles reiterated his position in a message to the special American Representative for the Korean Political Conference, Arthur H. Dean, thereby making neutral participation official policy. But the United States left Moscow out of its calculations.[7] In early December, the Communist negotiators demanded that Russia, too, be permitted to attend the conference as a neutral! This was a reminder of the Russian move in 1952, when they had claimed neutrality in order to get a seat on the NNSC. Was this an attempt to frustrate a political conference or, as in 1952, merely a move to procrastinate? Whatever the reasons, neutral participation was once more a wide open question. The question of Russian participation had been in the air for some time. The American view was that the political future of Korea had to be discussed in the presence of the Soviets, but that they should not be permitted to participate as representatives of the United Nations[8] or, worse, as 'neutrals'. In view of these decisions, progress at Panmunjom became difficult. By the middle of January 1954, the American negotiating team concluded that the negotiations in Korea had come to a standstill. In a cable to Washington, they suggested that 'some other forum or avenue might be more practical'. Perhaps the Soviet problem 'can only be handled directly with the Russians in appropriate place – perhaps at UNGA, perhaps inside at Berlin, or through diplomatic channels.'[9] This was what happened. In Berlin, Dulles and Molotov issued a communiqué on 18 February announcing that a political conference on Korea was scheduled to begin on 26 April 1954, in Geneva. The Russians would be present, but their precise role was not immediately explained. Later on, it became known that the Soviet Union would attend as one of the sponsoring powers.[10]

There was no reference to neutrals whatsoever, which indicated that the two great powers had tacitly agreed to simply drop the issue.[11] It also meant that Russia had made two concessions: it no longer claimed neutrality for itself, and it abandoned the demand for other neutrals at the conference. India, in other words, had been excluded. Dulles was happy; he reported to Washington that 'the composition of the Korean conference will be precisely as we sought it. The agreement excludes the participation of "neutrals" in the projected conference.'[12]

Two people were unhappy, however – Krishna Menon and Syngman Rhee. The Indian diplomat would have liked very much to be present at the conference, and he continued to lobby for the good offices of his country. Syngman Rhee was generally unhappy with the conference. He would have preferred no conference at all, did not want to attend, resented facing the Communists at the negotiating table, and disliked Menon's efforts to take part. On 8 April, Syngman Rhee voiced his disappointment in a personal letter to President Eisenhower:

> Regarding Geneva conference, we were told Russia would not be admitted as neutral. Now we find Russia is one of sponsors of conference, sending out invitations. Again we were told positively India would not be allowed attend conference, but we hear Indian delegates are already in Geneva.[13]

Nothing came of Rhee's fears. India was not admitted as a participant, and Russia was not present as a neutral. But the Koreans did have to attend the conference under American pressure, and they had to face the instigators of aggression at the negotiating table.

The Korean phase

The Korean phase of the 1954 Geneva Conference, which lasted from 16 April to 15 June, was a failure. Ending in deadlock, it passed into oblivion mainly because the Indochina phase of the conference succeeded. Still, the Korean phase is of some interest, since the question of neutrality surfaced, first, before the conference ever opened and, second, when it came to setting up a commission to supervise all-Korean elections. Furthermore, the eventual neutralisation of a unified Korea was part of the American strategy in those days.

For a while it appeared that the conference could not even have its first meeting without bringing in a neutral state. The question was that of *chairmanship*. To rotate the chair among the five permanent Security Council members (all present) was impossible from the American point of view, because the United States did not recognise the Chinese People's Republic.[14] To choose the Secretary General of the United Nations was equally impossible, because the UN had been one of the 'two sides' in the Korean War and, from the Communist point of view, could not be trusted with an impartial task.[15] Would a neutral country be useful at the conference after all?

It was Dulles who suggested the idea in a meeting with the French and English foreign ministers. He thought that a Swiss chairman could be found, and he submitted the names of four diplomats. Two were deigned undesirable, but two others were found acceptable.[16] Some days later, Dulles defined the American position more precisely. He still rejected rotation among the 'Big Five' but saw three other options: (1) a chairman from among the minor powers, excluding the Koreans; (ii) a neutral chairman of either Swiss or Swedish nationality, or (iii) a provisional chairman whose first duty would be the selection of a permanent one.[17] None of these options materialised, however, because in the end agreement was reached to rotate the chair among the two sponsoring powers (USSR and UK) and Thailand.[18] This arrangement was valid for the Indochina phase as well.

The next time the question of neutrality arose was in the context of organising *all-Korean elections* as a first step towards unification. The elections, it was agreed by all sides, would have to be supervised, and the Communists suggested a neutral body. Once more, they did not want the UN to become involved, because it had been a 'belligerent'. On 22 May Chou En-lai proposed that the neutral commission should be composed of nations that had not participated in the war.[19] Nam Il of North Korea and Molotov of Russia shared his view.[20]

On 5 June, Chou suggested more precisely the creation of a commission similar to the NNSC, as that body had been very effective.[21] The Americans disagreed. In their view, the NNSC had been an almost complete failure and no longer served any useful purpose. For some time already the United States had wanted to dissolve the commission. Now that the Communists were suggesting the formation of a second NNSC, they felt that the time had come to end the farce. Arthur H. Dean submitted the following plan to Washington:

> We should endeavor to persuade the Swiss and the Swedes to withdraw from the NNSC, and give wide publicity to the futility of the NNSC, thus undercutting the Communist hints that some such allegedly neutral body, rather than the UN, might be acceptable for working out all-Korean election laws, overseeing all-Korean elections, etc.[22]

Dean's suggestions were part of a wider strategy to end the Korean phase of the conference altogether. The United States had become convinced that the Communist powers had no interest in arriving at a political settlement of the Korean question. Dissolving the NNSC would have been a useful expression of disenchantment. It was unnecessary, however, because the Korean phase ended on 15 June without any results whatsoever.

It is interesting to note that neither side suggested the formation of a commission along the lines of the NNRC. That body, after all, had functioned because the Indians served as an umpire among the 'neutrals'. Why not let a second NNRC handle the elections? Apparently, both sides had lost confidence in an all-Korean solution. The gulf between North and South Koreans was as great as ever, and nobody believed that it could be bridged. It was better to end the conference on Korea.

Seen as a whole, neutrality was rather unimportant in this phase of the conference. The problem of the chairmanship was resolved in other ways, and because the conference failed, no election commission was ever set up. Were it for these two events only, neutrality would hardly be worth mentioning. However, neutrality was potentially an important issue, because the United States had, for some time, made preparations for the *neutralisation of a unified Korea*. Whether Dulles was ready to make an important issue of this in Geneva is not certain, but the administration was certainly prepared for it.

The NSC Report 81/1 of 9 September 1950 contains the first available evidence that the neutralisation of Korea was envisaged. The report is a comprehensive study of the various courses of action that the United States was preparing with respect to Korea. In the final passages, the National Security Council suggests that

> the U.S. should recommend that the U.N. Commission [in Korea] should consider the desirability of permanent neutralization of Korea accompanied by political understandings by the R.O.K. and by other states separately, including the USSR, to refrain from any aggression.[23]

On 19 October 1950, the Acting Assistant Legal Adviser for Far Eastern Affairs submitted an analysis of the legal implications of neutralisation. He dealt with the meaning of permanent neutralisation, gave some examples of neutralised states, and discussed the objectives and effectiveness of such a step. Of special importance were his conclusions about the 'compatibility of neutralization with the principle of the United Nations'.

The case of Switzerland under the League of Nations was discussed first. In the eyes of the Legal Adviser, the Covenant had in principle established the incompatibility of neutrality and collective action, but a resolution of the League Council of 20 February 1920 had recognised that Switzerland was in a special position based on a tradition of several centuries: 'Accordingly it was found that the perpetual neutralization of Switzerland was justified in the interest of general peace and compatible with the Covenant.'[24]

The Legal Adviser was of the opinion that the same principle of incompatibility prevailed under the United Nations Charter but that no exception was tolerable:

> The neutralization of a single potential member of the United Nations adds nothing to the security of that State against wanton aggression, which is already guaranteed by the United Nations, but subtracts from the power of the United Nations to enforce its guarantee. It not only removes the neutralized State from the roll of the

United Nations that stand ready to oppose and punish an aggressor (unless the aggression happens to be directed against the neutralized state itself), but it may also hamper action against an aggressor State by preventing access to the aggressor across the territory and territorial waters, and the air above them, of the neutralized State. This would be potentially true of any proposition, for instance, to remove Belgium from the Atlantic Union and transform her again into a neutralized State. It may be equally obvious should the Soviet Union or China become an aggressor, and the United Nations desire to project their defensive action across Korea.[25]

This was the most curious argument for a Legal Adviser of the Department of State. His concern was overwhelmingly political and strategic rather than legal. He did not deal with the various Charter articles relating to neutrality, and he did not make reference to scholarly opinions on the subject. His main concern was the security of a neutralised state or the war-making potential of the United Nations, matters that statesmen and soldiers were more concerned with. Small wonder that his advice carried little weight.

Philip Jessup, for one, was not impressed. As Ambassador-at-Large, he was at times involved in the delicate process of dealing directly with the Russians. In that capacity, he had learned to be flexible. While neutralisation might not be the way to preserve peace and security in the long-run, it might 'still be possible that a gesture along these lines would be helpful in the short-run.'[26]

As a consequence, Korean neutralisation remained a short-run goal under the Truman Administration. This changed when the Republicans came to power. For Dulles, a military alliance with South Korea had a higher priority than neutralisation. He offered Syngman Rhee a mutual security pact in June 1953 at the time the Panmunjom agreements were signed. Negotiations began soon afterward, and as early as 8 August, Dulles was able to initial the finished treaty in Seoul.[27] Neutrality had been pushed into the background.

There were some very practical reasons for the alliance. It helped overcome Rhee's resistance against the armistice, and it was a useful instrument in getting him to abide by it. The treaty also helped to get Rhee to come to Geneva and to participate in the political conference. With all these advantages and with Korean unification far off in the distant future, it was not unnatural that neutralisation should become a long-range goal. The eagerness and speed with which the alliance was signed was an indication that Dulles gave extremely high priority to such arrangements.

The new Republican strategy emerged formally in November 1953.[28] Evidence is contained in a draft report to the National Security Council of 9 November (NSC 170)[29] and again in the final report of 20 November (NSC 170/1).[30] In both papers, the United States is committed to seek 'a unified and neutral Korea' while, at the same time, to 'ratify the Mutual Defense Treaty with the Republic of Korea'.[31] In a progress report written one year later, the very same goals are listed, although the Senate had ratified the treaty in the meantime.[32]

Given these priorities, it is not overly surprising that the State Department papers drafted for the Korean conference make no mention of neutralisation.[33] The United States was ready to discuss three different plans for unification, and none referred to neutrality. Plan A envisaged the administrative incorporation of North Korea into the existing Republic of South Korea; Plan B provided for elections in both parts of Korea and for the establishment of a Korean National Government within the ROK constitutional structures; Plan C foresaw all-Korean elections for a Constitutional Assembly and a New National Government.[34] Of course, these plans did not exclude neutralisation, and had the Communists advanced the idea it is quite possible that Dulles would have approved of it. But the fact that neutralisation no longer appeared in the American position papers shows that priorities had changed.

The Indochina phase

The Indochina phase of the conference was successful. Nowadays, in fact, the Geneva Conference of 1954 is often identified simply as the Indochina Conference. In a general historical sense, this part of the conference was much more important than the Korean phase. The American viewpoint, however, was different. The United States was directly involved in the war and in the fate of Korea, whereas it had only an indirect interest in Indochina at that time. This Southeast Asian war was then a French affair from which the United States consciously remained at some distance. The Indochina phase of the conference was thus of less concern to the Americans, at least in the short run.

This was evident in a statement that Eisenhower issued at the end of the Indochina conference, on 21 July 1954. He expressed gratitude that the bloodshed had been stopped and emphasised that 'the primary responsibility for the settlement in Indochina rested with those nations which participated in the fighting.' The American role in Geneva, he declared, had at all times been to try to be helpful in obtaining a just and honourable settlement, but no more. Eisenhower concluded that the United States 'has not itself been a party to or bound by the decisions taken by the conference.'[35] It is only natural, therefore, that American diplomats did not play a very active role in this phase of the conference.

This was true, for instance, in the discussion of a *ceasefire supervisory control commission*, which again raised the question of neutrality. The matter was on the agenda during the entire span of the Indochina phase, from early May until 21 July. Opinions about the nature of the commission and its composition varied widely, and agreement was not easy. Once more, the Communist negotiators saw the issue in part as a convenient tool for procrastination.

The Russians and the Chinese once again proposed a commission similar to the NNSC. It had to be called neutral and be composed of four states. Only this time they suggested India, Pakistan, Poland, and Czechoslovakia. This was entirely unacceptable to the Western states. The Americans had already made it clear during the Korean phase that, based on the experience of the NNSC, they considered such a body to be unworkable. The French and British agreed.[36] Various proposals and counter-proposals were made, the details of which are not very interesting. In the end a commission was established that was neither identified as neutral nor similar to the NNSC in its composition. The two sides agreed that

> an International Commission shall be set up for the control and supervision over the application of the provisions of the agreement on the cessation of hostilities in Viet-Nam. It shall be composed of representatives of the following States: Canada, India and Poland. It shall be presided over by the Representative of India.[37]

India was again entrusted with the role of umpire, but this time its position was no longer identified as neutral. This was a more forthright solution that avoided a number of conceptual and legal problems. It also spared Canada from being both a NATO member and a neutral. The Poles, of course, would have been accustomed to the travesty.

As Eisenhower implied in his statement at the conference end, these short-term questions did not overly interest the United States. America thought more in the long term about the situation after the independence of Laos, Cambodia, and the two Vietnams. In this respect, the question of a possible *neutralisation of Indochina* was of some concern. The American government took the issue seriously and prepared for it before the conference began. Edmund A. Gullion, of the State Department's Policy Planning Staff, wrote a memorandum about 'Negotiations on Far Eastern Questions at Geneva', discussing the pros and cons of a possible neutralisation of Southeast Asia. He came to the conclusion that it would very likely not be a viable alternative:

> It seems to me most unlikely that the Communists would accept such a proposal. They have never yet agreed to pull back their zone of control beyond the line occupied by Communist forces. Even if they did accept such a proposal, we could expect the Viet Minh Communists eventually to take over control. The example of a Red Indochina would have a powerful impact on Southeast Asia.[38]

Eisenhower and Dulles agreed with this analysis. They did not want to see neutrals in that part of the world. On the contrary, they aimed at having allies. Eisenhower's above statement welcoming the end of the Indochina conference made it very clear that the United States was 'actively pursuing discussions with other free nations with a view to the rapid organisation of a collective defense in southeast Asia in order to prevent further direct or indirect Communist aggression in that general area.'[39]

In secret, the United States had already made important commitments towards this end. In an understanding signed with the French Premier, Mendès-France, on 14 July, the goal of collective defence was mentioned prominently. As its fourth point, the document stated that 'the United States is prepared to seek, with other interested nations, a collective defense association designed to preserve, against direct and indirect aggression, the integrity of the non-Communist areas of Southeast Asia following any settlement.'[40] The same ideas were contained in the basic instructions sent to the American delegates in Geneva both at the beginning of the conference and again towards the end.[41]

Given this situation, there were worries during the negotiations that the Communists might propose the neutralisation of some parts or all of Indochina.[42] The South Vietnamese, for instance, feared that China might suggest the neutralisation of Laos and Cambodia and that the two countries would accept. One of the South Vietnamese delegates told the Americans 'that China was a large cat which was suggesting that two mice, Laos and Cambodia, be neutralised. But who would ensure the neutrality of the cat?'[43]

The Cambodians also reported that neutralisation talk was in the air. Before leaving Geneva on 12 July, the Cambodian ambassador let the

Americans know that his government would continue to maintain a firm position against Communist efforts to demilitarise or neutralise his country. Dulles responded by saying that the United States was working towards a collective security pact and hoped that Cambodia would be party to such an arrangement.[44]

The worries were mostly unnecessary. Neutralisation never became an official topic of the conference. Actually, the agreements signed did not even rule out membership in future alliances for Laos and Cambodia.[45] Only South Vietnam, interestingly enough, was prevented from doing so because, in the accord, the two sides had agreed that 'the zones assigned to them do not adhere to any military alliance and are not used for the resumption of hostilities or to further an aggressive policy.'[46] All this was to change, of course. Once independent, Laos and Cambodia pursued a policy of neutrality, and South Vietnam became a member of SEATO.

Irrespective of the eventual outcome, American policy in Geneva was based on avoiding neutrals and gaining allies.[47] As in the case of Korea, Dulles favoured allies to neutrals. Whether he would continue in the same vein would remain to be seen. In Europe, the neutralisation of Germany and Austria was in the air, and Dulles would have to deal with these questions, too.

9
Germany and Austria, 1953–1955

Neutralising Germany?

The North Korean attack in the summer of 1950 shocked Europe. It was widely feared that the Russians might encourage similar adventures in other parts of the world and that Europe in particular was threatened. As a result, the countries of Western Europe moved closer together. Several concrete steps were taken towards integration: the European Coal and Steel Community was set up, and negotiations began on the establishment of a European Defence Community (EDC). Western Germany was to be included in all of these organisations.

Such developments were not in the Soviet interest. The Soviets have at all times preferred a weak and divided Europe to a strong and united one. They especially did not want to see Western Germany become part of a militarily united Europe. To forestall that possibility they made various attempts to divide the Europeans. From 1952 to 1955 their favourite strategy was to suggest German unification coupled with disarmed neutralisation.[1]

Four major efforts by the Soviets can be identified: (i) in 1952, a number of diplomatic notes were dispatched to the three Western Allies; (ii) in early 1954, the question was raised at the Berlin Conference of Foreign Ministers; (iii) in the summer of the same year unification and neutralisation were propagated when the French National Assembly was debating the EDC treaty; (iv) a further attempt was made in 1955 when the West German Bundestag was debating the Paris Accords, making the Federal Republic a full member of NATO.

Possibly the Russians raised the question of neutralisation once more at the Geneva summit of 1955, but so far there is no documentary evidence for this. It would be rather surprising if they had done so, however, because by that time the question of German unification had become academic: once the Federal Republic was in the Western military camp, there was little likelihood that it could be dislodged.

Let us now turn first to the *four notes* sent in the spring and summer of 1952. They are dated 10 March, 9 April, 24 May, and 23 August; all were addressed to the three Western Powers jointly.[2] Roughly similar in content, they all dealt with German unification in a very aggressive tone. They denounced 'Fascist' military circles in Washington and Bonn repeatedly for attempting to remilitarise Germany under the guise of a European Defence Community. The notes were also aimed specifically at the negotiations then going on in Bonn between the Federal Republic and the Western Allies on 'contractual matters'. The purpose of the talks was to move the Federal Republic further along the road towards full sovereignty and eventual membership in either EDC or NATO.[3]

Some of the notes contained precise proposals for a treaty with Germany. One of the clauses obligated the future state not to enter into 'any kind of coalition or military alliance directed against any power which took part with its armed forces in war against Germany',[4] and one of the provisions also called for the creation of a German army. The Russians thus aimed at armed neutrality, although they avoided the term itself. Not so the Department of State; in commenting on the Russian notes Dean Acheson mentions neutrality regularly. The following passage from a memorandum to the US High Commissioner in Germany is typical:

> Sov Govt seeks to create impression that it offers Ger an independent 'neutral' position. But one of two things wld result. Either Eastern Ger wld continue to be occupied by Sov troops as at present, which wld permit neither independence nor freedom nor neutrality, or else all troops wld be withdrawn by all powers, leaving Sov troops poised on Oder-Neisse line and Western troops holding an uncertain bridgehead in Fr or US troops even withdrawn from Europe altogether. Such a vacuum wld invite aggression and domination from the East and wld permit neither independence nor neutrality. As long as Sov Union holds its present view on world situation, neutrality for Ger is impossible.[5]

These lines show that Washington saw the notes as clearly aiming at neutralisation, and they also indicate that the United States government was opposed to it. In internal memos the opposition was justified mostly on military grounds: neutralisation would weaken the Western position while strengthening that of the East. In public pronouncements it was a legal argument that counted most: neutralisation would deprive a unified Germany of its freedom in international affairs and thus limit its sovereignty. This was also the point that was put forward by the Western Powers in their formal replies to the Soviet Union: they felt that the future state should not be denied 'the basic right of a free and equal nation to associate itself with other nations for peaceful purposes.'[6]

For the Western Powers neutralisation was not an important issue, however. In their various replies to the Soviet Union they concentrated on the problem of free elections and the establishment of a truly democratic all-German government. It would consequently be wrong to assume that in 1952 neutrality was of major importance in East–West relations. It was at most a marginal issue.[7]

For the remainder of the year 1952, and for the rest of Stalin's regime, there was no more talk of neutralisation. The topic was only broached again when the dictator had died and international tensions lessened, especially against the background of the successful armistice negotiations at Panmunjom. On 15 August 1953, the Russian government sent another note to the Western Powers, suggesting a German settlement and a conference of foreign ministers to deal with it. This initiative eventually led to the Berlin Conference of early 1954. On this occasion the neutralisation of Germany was discussed again, and in anticipation of the event the United States government commissioned a study on the issue by the National Security Council. It became known as NSC 160/1. Before turning to the Berlin Conference, we must cast a brief glance at this important document. It outlines the ideas that were to guide American policy on this matter.

NSC 160/1 is very clear on the American objectives. These were (i) the restoration by peaceful means of Germany as a united state, with freedom of action in internal and external affairs, and (ii) its firm association with the West, preferably through an integrated European Community.[8] Such objectives obviously make true neutrality impossible. As the following paragraph shows, neutrality was merely regarded as a *transitional phase:*

> A Soviet proposal for a neutralized Germany would almost certainly require withdrawal of all foreign armed forces from German soil. Under a Western plan for a Germany with full freedom of action in external affairs, such withdrawal might be necessary temporarily, until Germany invited their return pursuant to her right to make alliances, and permanently if she failed to do so.[9]

It was with this conception of temporary neutrality that the United States went to Berlin. It entailed a certain amount of risk, because the view was based entirely on the hope that a truly democratic all-German government would automatically side with the West. The strategy was never tested, however, because the Russians were unwilling to yield on the more important issue of free elections.

The agenda of the *Berlin Conference* contained only three items: (i) convocation of a five-power conference (to include China), (ii) Germany and European security, (iii) the Austrian State Treaty. Agreement was reached only on the first point; a five-power conference was arranged to deal with the political questions arising from the Korean armistice (to be held later that year at Geneva). No agreement was forthcoming on the German and Austrian questions. The final conference document on Germany reflects the usual disagreement: while the Soviets stressed the need for a united state not part of 'any coalition or military alliance', the Western Powers emphasised the need for truly free elections.[10] Still, the discussions at Berlin are of interest, particularly in regard to German unification and neutrality.

At the sixth plenary session on 30 January, Secretary of State Dulles made a lengthy statement on the German and European questions. He felt that the issue had two aspects. First, there was the task of uniting Germany, and second, there was the task of ensuring that a united Germany would be a peaceful Germany.[11] As to the first task, he associated himself fully with the plan submitted by the British (the 'Eden Plan'), but he pointed out that that plan hinged entirely on free elections. In regard to the second task, he felt that much could be learned from history:

> It teaches us that a stable peace cannot be achieved by some countries imposing upon other countries discriminatory restrictions. These methods fall by their very nature ... . The very provisions which are designed to create controls, in themselves breed international lawlessness and violence.[12]

Dulles was, of course, referring to the Versailles treaty in which, once before, restrictions had been placed on German sovereignty. But he was also referring to neutralisation. Although he did not use the word, it must have been plain to all that that was what he had in mind.

The issue arose once more in a personal conversation between Dulles and Molotov on 6 February. Molotov argued that a Germany free of coalitions and military alliances would be allowed to have a limited army. Dulles' answer was predictable: such an arrangement would require a high degree of control, which all experience had shown to be unreliable.[13] Here was another reference to Versailles, and once again neutrality was not mentioned explicitly. As we shall see later on, in Berlin the concept of neutrality was used explicitly only with reference to Austria.

At the Berlin Conference the Russians had failed in their effort to make German unification and neutralisation palatable to the Western Powers, but they did not relax their efforts. They saw another chance when, six months later, in August 1954, the French National Assembly was debating the EDC treaty. The moment seemed opportune because France was in a very difficult situation: the painful negotiations in Geneva and the humiliating withdrawal from Southeast Asia had weakened the French government and with it the entire structure of the Fourth Republic. The Americans in particular saw the French as militarily and politically weak and began to lose faith. This was not helped when the Socialist, Pierre Mendès-France, assumed the premiership in an atmosphere of crisis and made some rapid and drastic decisions. When the EDC debate in the National Assembly dragged on for too long in August 1954, Dulles became suspicious.

Had Mendès-France made a deal with the Russians? He voiced his concern in a message to the American Ambassador in Paris, C. Douglas Dillon:

> His [Mendès-France's] position seems to me to amount to this: That France is prepared to abandon EDC if Soviets will agree to unify Germany by free elections. This can only mean that France is prepared to agree to neutralize Germany as basis for unification. A neutralized Germany will completely destroy NATO defense plans. Military experts agree that no effective defense strategy can be based on a Europe from which Germany has been excluded ... . You also know our firm conviction that an attempt to neutralize unified Germany will be illusory and seriously menace European stability and security. This thesis has been keystone of Western policy. The Mendès-France proposal would split basic Western position and solidarity, thereby providing Soviets with opportunity they have sought for years.[14]

Dillon immediately spoke to the Premier and was able to reassure Dulles in a message the following day, 13 August. As reported by Dillon, Mendès-France could not understand how the Department of

State had arrived at such conclusions: 'He said he is not in favor of a neutralised Germany. He also said that he had always felt, and still feels that Germany, whether united or not, must be politically and militarily tied to the West.'[15]

On 30 August, the French National Assembly tabled the bill calling for the ratification of the EDC indefinitely, thereby confirming at least part of Dulles' doubts. The idea of rearming the Federal Republic as part of a movement towards European integration was dead. The Russians had won the first battle. If in fact a deal had been made, it had more to do with Indochina than with German neutralisation. It is sometimes argued that Mendès-France got Russian support for a graceful withdrawal from Indochina in return for some foot-dragging on the EDC. In the context of the French predicament at that time, this theory seems plausible.

Dulles reacted forcefully to the EDC defeat. On 31 August, he issued a press release in which he said that the French action had not changed certain basic and stubborn facts:

(a)   the effective defense of Continental Europe calls for a substantial military contribution from the Germans
(b)   Germany cannot be subjected indefinitely to neutrality or otherwise be discriminated against in terms of her sovereignty including the inherent right of individual and collective self-defense.[16]

This was plain talk. In one and the same statement, Dulles demanded German rearmament, rejected neutralisation, and implied participation in Western defence. Dulles rarely made such explicit comments in public about Germany, but the defeat of the EDC seemed to justify exceptional candour.

The plans for an integrated Western European defence establishment having been defeated, new ways had to be found to rearm the Federal Republic of Germany and to tie it firmly to the West. Eisenhower submitted some proposals on 3 September:

(a)   through the revision of the EDC idea by the nations concerned.
(b)   through a meeting of the entire NATO group, with a view of including Germany as an equal partner therein.
(c)   through unilateral agreements with Germany – to which agreements we would, of course, have to get the concurrences of a sizeable number of Western and Atlantic nations.[17]

It soon became evident that the second option was the most promising. It was contained in a 15 September statement of policy drafted by the National Security Council[18] and discussed at a full meeting on 24 September. Dulles explained that the Germans would never rearm on the basis of a bilateral alliance with the United States alone. They wanted the French to be part of any arrangement, and whether the French would go along with the NATO option was very doubtful: 'The Soviets successfully used Mendès-France to kill, or at least to maim, EDC. Will they now try to use him to destroy NATO?'[19] All depended on the French, and who could trust them?

The decisions of the Council were summarised in an NSC Policy Statement issued the next day, 25 September (NSC 5433/1).[20] It anticipated the restoration of full German sovereignty, including the right to participate in the defence of Western Europe. Also envisaged was admission to full membership in NATO 'without precluding German participation also in the Brussels Pact or other European defense arrangements.' Political and economic strength should be promoted in order to 'enhance the European capacity and will to resist Communist subversion and neutralism.' Finally, the NSC Policy Statement also expected reunification of Germany on the basis 'of freedom and the maximum possibility of association with the West'.[21]

NSC 5433/1 also contained a cautious note. It prepared for possible failure of the programme and, therefore, listed in a final part seven questions about the basic objectives. These were addressed to the various departments concerned with the defence of Europe and were to be returned to the Council in due course. Question 6 referred to neutrality: 'If Germany were unified and neutralised with restricted armed forces, what would be the probable course of its policy, and the effect on its vulnerability in the cold war and on the stability of Western Europe?'[22]

The answers never came to the Council, because a decision was made on 28 October that in the light of events, the requirements of this final passage were redundant.[23] The events alluded to were two successful conferences in London and Paris leading up to the Paris Accords of 23 October 1954, in which Germany was restored to full sovereignty and made a member of the Brussels Pact and of NATO. Dulles' worries about the French had been unfounded. The French failed to support the EDC but did not prevent the expansion of NATO. Mendès-France was neither a Russian puppet nor a neutralist. American concern about a neutralisation of Germany could be put aside. With the inclusion of the Federal Republic in NATO, there was virtually no chance that neutralisation would ever again become a realistic option.

But the Russians did not see it that way. To be sure, the remilitarisation of Germany and the strengthening of NATO were for them a serious defeat, but they were not willing to give up easily. While the German Bundestag was preparing to debate the ratification of the Paris Accords, Moscow once more tried to promote the idea of unification and neutralisation. In February 1955, the governmental newspaper *Isvestija* contained an article urging the Germans to stay clear of any military alignments.[24]

At this time, the target was no longer the French but mainly the German Social Democrats who were opposed to ratification.[25] As State Department reports from Bonn and from specialists in Washington showed, however, the large majority of Social Democrats were not for neutrality and were not even against rearmament. What they felt was that 1955 was a good time to negotiate with the Russians, and that, in the meantime, nothing should be done to make unification more difficult.[26] Ratification of the Paris Accords was an admission, of course, that the reunification of Germany was a remote prospect.

In March, the German Bundestag ratified the accords, and in May, the Federal Republic joined the Western European Union and NATO. It was an important success for the West and a humiliating defeat for the East. As we shall see later on, the Soviets had to rethink their strategy – and they did. They decided to redefine some of their policies in regard to Western Europe. Among other things, they were willing to agree to a neutral and united Austria. Furthermore, there was to be a summit that summer in Geneva, and the German question was once more on the agenda. In anticipation of that event the German Chancellor visited Washington in June and talked to Eisenhower and Dulles. Their common press communiqué was brief, but it showed that the idea of neutrality for Germany was still haunting them:

> They agreed that one of the objectives of the forthcoming four-power meeting will be to pave the way for early German reunification. It was confirmed that in their combined opinion the concept of neutrality is in no way applicable to Germany and that only in collective security arrangements can Germany assure its independence.[27]

Perhaps this statement was meant to strengthen Adenauer's hand in his forthcoming visit to Moscow.[28] It was to be his first visit to the Russian capital, and one never knew what the new leadership was up to. Khrushchev's dynamism began to make itself felt in foreign affairs, and the concept of neutrality became part of his various diplomatic initiatives around the globe. The term was beginning to acquire new meaning with regard to Tito and the emerging neutralist movement. Perhaps it was better to be on the safe side.

Neutrality for Austria

The negotiations leading up to the Austrian State Treaty lasted from 1947 to 1955. In this long and tortuous process,[29] neutrality was not a central topic; it became an issue of negotiation only in 1954. This is not to say that the Austrians themselves did not at times think about a possible neutralisation of their country,[30] but the four victors of the Second World War did not talk about it formally until the Berlin Foreign Ministers' Conference. Even then, the issue remained vague and was only clarified in April 1955, in Moscow. It was Molotov who then broached the idea clearly and explicitly to a delegation from Vienna, thus making Austrian neutrality, in the final phase, mostly a Russian initiative.[31] At any rate, it was not an American idea; the United States merely reacted in this matter, but, as we shall see, favourably and constructively.

The American attitude towards Austrian neutrality was relatively constant from 1949 to 1955. Both Acheson and Dulles would have preferred to turn Austria into a Western ally, and often said so clearly, but they never opposed the idea fundamentally. From an American point of view Austrian neutrality was, therefore, always a possible option, but it was not a favourite one and definitely not one that the United States would wish to promote actively. This attitude manifested itself at four different stages: (i) before the Berlin Conference, (ii) during the conference, (iii) while the State Treaty was being finalised, and (iv) after its signature. Let us examine these various phases.

Although the Department of State was aware of Austrian ideas about neutrality as early as 1947, and although the question was even addressed by Dean Acheson himself in 1949,[32] the matter only became important with the lessening of international tensions in the summer and autumn of 1953.[33] NSC papers dealing with Austria reflect this. While NSC 38/4 of 17 November 1949[34] does not mention neutrality, NSC 164/1 of 14 October 1953 deals with it explicitly:

> Vigorously resist the neutralization of Austria as contrary to U.S. interest. However, should the Austrians, British and French press strongly for accepting some degree of neutralization, the United States may be required to make some concession to avoid the onus of unilaterally blocking a Treaty.[35]

This statement was the result of discussions between various agencies. It was a compromise formula between a harder line adopted by the Department of Defense and a softer line pursued by the Department of State. Admiral Radford, Head of the Joint Chiefs of Staff, felt that a neutralised Austria would greatly weaken the United States' military position in Europe.[36] Secretary of State Dulles did not disagree, but he argued that while the United States should oppose neutralisation 'the decision in the long run would depend on the Austrians themselves ... we can, of course, explain our position to the Austrians, but we could not impose our will upon them, nor could we carry the British and the French along if they agreed with the Austrian viewpoint.'[37]

The Department of State thereupon began to define its negotiating position. The Policy Planning Staff recommended that while the United States should go along with a unilateral Austrian declaration of neutrality, it ought to oppose multilateral neutralisation as part of the State Treaty. And if the Russians should make reference to German neutralisation, the United States should say quite frankly that 'Germany's neutralization neither fits the facts of history nor the realities of the European situation.'[38] The opposition to multilateral neutralisation was based on the fear that the Soviets, as guarantors of an international treaty, might one day decide to intervene in Austria unilaterally. It was a position that the United States defended successfully to the very end.

The *Berlin Foreign Ministers' Conference* met from 25 January to 18 February 1954. The Austrian question was the last item on the agenda. Discussions on the question began on 10 February, first among the three Western Powers, then together with Austrian representatives, and finally also with the Russians. In all of these discussions Foreign Minister Figl (formerly Chancellor) stated unambiguously that Austria wanted 'to abstain from military alliances'.[39] He did not use the word 'neutrality' although that was what he meant, and he had good reason for not doing so because the Russians did not use the term either.[40] Why offend the Russians needlessly? The Austrian intent was clear, but the language was cautious and diplomatic.

On 12 February, the Austrian question was discussed for the first time at a plenary session. Molotov proposed the creation of an independent Austrian state 'free from military alliances', but added that military occupation should be continued until a peace treaty with Germany had been signed.[41] At the next plenary session, on 13 February, Dulles vigorously opposed this idea. He was in favour of neutrality but rejected the various strings that the Russians attached to this status:

A neutral status is an honorable status if it is voluntarily chosen by a nation. Switzerland has chosen to be neutral, and as a neutral she has achieved an honorable place in the family of nations. Under the Austrian state treaty as heretofore drafted, Austria would be free to choose for itself to be a neutral state like Switzerland. Certainly the United States would fully respect its choice in this respect, as it fully respects the comparable choice of the Swiss nation.[42]

But, Dulles added, the Russian proposal did not permit such a solution; Austria would not become a sovereign, independent, and democratic state, as was the intention of the Four Powers. To break out of the impasse, Dulles made a proposal the next day that contained a number of economic concessions but remained firm on neutrality. He also suggested that a treaty be signed within four days.[43] But Molotov did not budge. He insisted once again that Austrian neutrality be linked to a German peace treaty and the stationing of troops.[44] That ended any hopes of signing the State Treaty in Berlin.[45] For the rest of 1954, the Austrian question was shelved.[46] What preoccupied Washington and Moscow was the Geneva Conference on Korea and Indochina, then the battle over the EDC and, later, the negotiations leading to the Paris Accords. Only when the Russians realised that their attempt to neutralise Germany had failed did they again turn to the question of Austria.[47]

These events in foreign affairs coincided with a transition of leadership in the Kremlin, as a result of which Malenkov was ousted from the inner circle on 8 February 1955.[48] The same day, Molotov, still surviving as foreign minister, gave a lengthy speech to the Supreme Soviet in which he suggested that an Austrian State Treaty could possibly be signed without keeping occupying troops in the country and without waiting for the conclusion of a German peace treaty.[49] The Russians became more flexible; Khrushchev was on the rise.

Two weeks later, the Russians moved. Molotov called the Austrian ambassador into the Foreign Office, first on 25 February, and again on 2 March, to reiterate his ideas contained in the speech to the Supreme Soviet and to request a speedy Austrian reply. It arrived on 14 March, and, among other things, stated that Austria would not enter into any coalitions or military alliances, but it avoided the term neutrality. On 24 March, Molotov gave the Austrians a written answer and suggested that a high-ranking delegation visit Moscow for serious talks.

In anticipation of the talks the US Embassy in Moscow expressed its concern to the Department of State that Moscow might link neutrality to some kind of Four Power guarantee giving the Soviets the opportunity 'to interfere in Austrian internal affairs or to dictate Austrian relationships with other countries...'.[50] The worries were not entirely unfounded, because the question of guarantees did indeed arise and turned out to be more difficult than neutrality itself.

Chancellor Raab, Foreign Minister Figl and, again, Kreisky, arrived in Moscow on 11 April. In their talks with Molotov, the three used the term *Bündnisfreiheit*, or 'non-alignment'; it was Molotov who insisted on neutrality.[51] He even suggested that it be modelled along Swiss lines. The Austrians did not object, and agreement was reached that, *after* the signing of the State Treaty, the Austrian government would issue a declaration 'which would commit Austria internationally to practice perpetual neutrality as handled by Switzerland'.[52]

After each negotiating session the Austrian delegation met with the three Western ambassadors, and in its telegrams to Washington the US Embassy was pleased to report that the neutrality declaration would be 'outside the treaty'. The same applied to guarantees, yet the Soviets 'gave no indication of exact form of this guarantee but cited guarantee of Switzerland as example.'[53] The question remained open, and it had to be settled at an Ambassadorial Conference held in Vienna in early May. As it turned out, the Soviets now preferred a separate Four Power Declaration guaranteeing the 'integrity and inviolability of Austrian state territory', but no Western Power approved of the plan. France and Great Britain now objected more strenuously than the United States did. Dulles was actually ready to meet the Soviets half way.[54] In the end it was decided that the Austrians should include the relevant passage in their unilateral neutrality declaration.[55] The State Treaty was signed in Vienna on 15 May, and the Austrian *Nationalrat* passed a neutrality bill on 7 June, which later received wide international recognition.[56]

Dulles seemed to be pleased. He would have preferred to see Austria aligned with the West, but he was willing to settle for second best and grant the country its full independence. He said so to the Austrian ambassador in Washington during a diplomatic reception on 19 April. He thought it would be unfair for the Americans to stall the negotiating process now after they had accused the Russians of doing the same for so many years. Also, Dulles was not worried that Austrian neutrality would have negative repercussions on Germany: 'The two countries are different. What suits a small country does not necessarily fit a large country with great power aspirations'. He would be ready to travel to Vienna 'jubilantly' and put his signature to the treaty.[57]

In a press conference on 24 May, Dulles spoke once more on the question of German and Austrian neutrality:

It is all well to talk about neutrality for a country such as Austria, a small country with 7 million people. But I do not believe that anybody realistically believes that the German people, 70-odd million of them, are destined to play the role of a neutral country. Furthermore, as President Eisenhower has pointed out, the kind of neutrality which was discussed in terms of Austria is an armed neutrality, and there is no limit in the Austrian State Treaty upon the size of the Austrian Army. I do not think that the German people or the Soviet people or the Western European people want to see applied to Germany the concept of it being an independent state with an unlimited army.[58]

On 10 June, the Austrian State Treaty was submitted to the Senate for ratification. In his personal introductory statement, Dulles defended the treaty, explaining that Austria's neutrality would be armed and that it had been chosen voluntarily. He expressed the hope that the Senate would ratify the treaty before the forthcoming summit in Geneva, as renewed evidence of the nation's dedication 'to the lofty goals which were proclaimed during World War II and our determination to do all that peacefully lies within our power to achieve these goals.'[59]

Dulles had good reason to be satisfied. Although in a direct sense Austrian neutrality was a Russian initiative, it was the United States that defined the neutralisation process. As Dulles suggested at Berlin, Austria was not to be neutralised by the victors of the Second World War but of its own free will. This had the distinct advantage that there would be no guarantors of Austrian neutrality who, at a later stage, might think of intervening in order to exercise their duties under the State Treaty. Invasions of the Hungarian and Czech type would then have had a basis in international law! Dulles was wise in avoiding this danger.[60]

Dulles was also justified in being slightly optimistic. As he told the Senate, the State Treaty 'may open the way for further cooperation to fulfil other wartime pledges.'[61] He had always seen Austria as a test case for Russian intentions. Of all the outstanding questions in Europe, the Austrian issue could, in his eyes, be settled most easily. The fact that it was indeed settled easily must have raised some hopes in Washington, if only momentarily. As a result of the State Treaty, Eisenhower even managed to convince Dulles to agree to a summit meeting. The Secretary had always cautioned against attending a summit 'merely because of friendly words and plausible promises by the men in the Kremlin.'[62] Now the time seemed ripe even for Dulles.

Dulles must also have realised that the State Treaty had become possible because of a change in the Kremlin power structure: in Berlin, the Molotov line had still prevailed, but, beginning in February 1955, Khrushchev's influence made itself felt.[63] This meant that new ideas flowed into foreign policy. 'Peaceful coexistence' replaced the doctrine of the 'inevitability of war'. Neutrality was one of the 'peaceful' means by which the struggle against capitalism was now to be carried on.[64]

Austria was the first country to feel the consequences of the new policy.[65] Finland was the next. To that uneasy Russian neighbour, Khrushchev returned the Porkkala naval base in 1955, thereby giving a sign of approval of Finnish neutrality.[66] Then came Yugoslavia. Only ten days after the signing of the State Treaty, Khrushchev and Bulganin travelled to Belgrade and ended Stalin's policy of ostracism towards that Communist country. It also implied approval of Tito's pronounced policy of neutralism.[67] India was next on the Kremlin itinerary, and visiting that country meant, of course, also embracing neutralism. In effect, the signing of the Austrian State Treaty proved to be the first step in an entirely new development in Russian foreign policy, mostly directed at the emerging countries of the Third World.[68]

The link between Indian neutralism and the Austrian desire for neutrality was particularly evident. As one of their various strategies to get the stalled State Treaty negotiations going,[69] the Austrians decided in the summer of 1953 to appeal to Molotov with the aid of the Indian government. On 19 and 20 June, Foreign Minister Gruber met Prime Minister Nehru in Switzerland, where he discussed Austria's desire for neutrality in the presence of the Indian ambassador to Moscow, K. P. S. Menon. Nehru showed understanding, and on 30 June, Menon intervened with Molotov. However, the results were inconclusive.[70]

The Indian intervention was part of a wider Austrian strategy to talk to the Russians unilaterally and without Western approval. The three Western governments were unhappy, however, when they learned about the Austrian moves.[71] At a meeting of their foreign ministers in Washington D.C., on 11 July 1953, the issue was discussed, and Dulles in particular seemed anxious. He thought that

> it was of course most undesirable that the Austrians should start negotiations directly with the Russians and we should try to prevent their reaching an arrangement in desperation to end the occupation which would undermine the Western position and set a bad example regarding Germany.[72]

A report by the Office of Intelligence Research of the Department of State, dated 31 August 1953, was more precise. Entitled 'Austria Attempts Independent Foreign Policy', it noted that Austria was aiming for neutrality and that it was doing so in direct contact with the Russians. This 'new approach', said the report, reflected Austrian confidence that they could handle their own relations with the Soviets: 'In pursuing their new Eastern policy, the Austrians have deliberately proceeded without consulting the Western powers.'[73]

The fact that the Austrians did not consult the United States, while they did consult the Indians, did not please the Secretary of State.[74] Given his feelings about Indian foreign policy in general and Nehru's type of neutrality in particular, his anxiety is understandable. However much he had to agree to the specific case of Austrian neutrality, it did not sit well with his overall world view. This showed clearly in one of the answers he gave to Senator Mansfield while testifying before the Senate:

> I think that one can recognize that in the case of small countries, such as Austria and her neighbor, Switzerland, there is a legitimate place for independent neutrality. I do not think the principle is a sound one for general application.[75]

Non-alignment, neutralism, neutrality – whatever the term – were all objectionable to him in principle and justifiable only in rare cases. They meant, to Dulles, a refusal to stand up in the Cold War and to take sides in a struggle that was ultimately moral. This view of the phenomenon was to appear more clearly later on in some of his public utterances, and it was to cause the administration some embarrassment. Its greatest danger was in obscuring the difference between neutrality and neutralism. Against the background of Khrushchev's new strategy, this was likely to happen.

The Eisenhower administration and neutrality

On 16 April 1953, two months after taking office, President Eisenhower delivered a major foreign policy speech. He listed the outstanding problems between the United States and the Soviet Union, and he expressed willingness to settle them through negotiations. Topmost on the agenda was *Korea*, where the Soviets could first demonstrate their willingness to act constructively. Next, Eisenhower mentioned *Indochina, Austria, Germany*, and *Eastern Europe*.[76] In the settlement of all these questions, neutrality could potentially play a role. What was the record of the Eisenhower Administration in this regard? Let us review the Republicans' stance on neutrality and also compare it to the record of the Truman Administration.

In the case of *Korea*, the Republicans were just as willing as the Democrats to accept neutral good offices in order to terminate the conflict. The Truman Administration had agreed to the formation of the NNSC, and the Eisenhower Administration agreed to have India serve as a neutral umpire on the NNRC, despite resistance on Capitol Hill and from South Korea. True, the Eisenhower Administration was not overly happy with the choice of India, either. It would have preferred Sweden or Switzerland in that crucial role, but in order to get the POWs home, it was willing to accept. However, the Republicans were not eager to see a unified and neutralised Korea; this idea became a long-range goal, because to them an allied South Korea was preferable in the short run.

When it came to accepting neutral good offices during the Korean phase of the *Geneva Conference,* Dulles again proved rather flexible. It was his idea to have a Swiss open the conference, and he would not have objected to having India participate in one way or another, if the need arose. If an election supervisory commission had been proposed (along the lines of the NNRC), he might also have approved.

Neutralising the countries of *Indochina,* however, was another matter. As in the case of Korea, Dulles and Eisenhower preferred allies to neutrals. It was one thing to accept the services of existing neutrals but quite another to create new ones, particularly when American security interests were intimately involved.[77] This applied even more to *Germany.* The military potential of the country and its importance for the defence of Western Europe spoke, in the minds of the Republicans, against neutralisation.[78] They were not alone. The Truman Administration had rejected Kennan's 1948 plan (called 'Program A')[79] for neutralisation,[80] and all the Western allies reacted unfavourably to the four Soviet notes of 1952. One wonders whether any of Germany's neighbours was for neutralisation. It is even doubtful whether the Soviets took their own neutralisation proposals seriously. Molotov's arguments never quite convince.

The case of *Austria* was quite different. The Eisenhower Administration decided to agree to neutralisation because the country was of marginal value strategically. This suggests a parallel to the Scandinavian situation under the Truman Administration. At that time, too, the United States, for strategic reasons, was eager to see Norway, Denmark, and even Sweden become allies, whereas it never bothered about including the militarily much less important Finland. The United States never objected to Finnish neutrality. Both administrations, therefore, had a tendency to see the question of neutrality in military and not in political terms. For *Eastern Europe*, the Eisenhower Administration proposed 'rollback' and 'liberation'. This policy was defined more clearly in NSC 174 of 11 December 1953, but the paper never dealt with the question of what political and military order would prevail after the countries had been liberated.[81] Would they become part of NATO, be integrated into a united Europe, or form a neutral buffer zone between the blocs? These were not idle questions. Walter Lippmann raised them as early as 1943 when he wrote about the political shape of Europe after the war. He anticipated problems between Russia and the United States and suggested that a belt of neutral countries in Eastern Europe could possibly lessen tensions.[82] For some time, such ideas remained purely academic, because most of these countries were drawn into the Soviet sphere, but with the break between Stalin and Tito it appeared to some that the neutralist Yugoslav line might suggest a solution for the problems of the other East European countries.

Such ideas even surfaced within the Department of State. In August 1953, the American embassy in Vienna sent a memorandum to Washington in which thoughts were developed about a possible neutralisation of some of the satellite states. In the course of negotiations with the Soviet Union on the Austrian State Treaty, so the recommendation went, 'the possibility of neutralising one or more of Austria's satellite neighbors (e.g. Hungary or Czechoslovakia)'[83] should be proposed. Unfortunately, the idea was not pursued.

When Austria was neutralised in 1955, these speculations took on new life. At a press conference on 24 May 1955, Secretary of State Dulles had to answer questions that went in this direction. One journalist asked him whether the United States would welcome a group of neutral states to the east of Germany. This was his reply:

> Well, we would certainly welcome there a group of independent states playing an independent role. The word 'neutrality' is a very ambiguous word and perhaps needs to be closely defined before you make definite committals to a so-called policy of neutrality.

Asked whether he would favour a series of armed and non-committed states running down from the Baltic to the Adriatic to the east of Germany, Dulles replied: 'Well, I couldn't say we are committed to any such policy; but anything which increases the national independence of the satellite states is along the lines of US policy.'[84] At a news conference held only two weeks later, President Eisenhower sounded much more positive. When asked virtually the same question, his response was this: 'Now, if those people of themselves chose a neutral position instead of the position they now occupy and it were an honest neutrality, it would be a tremendous advance for them.'[85]

What was now the administration's position on the neutrality of Eastern Europe? No one seemed to know for sure, and this in the face of a manifest desire to 'roll back' the Iron Curtain and to 'liberate' the Eastern European countries. A gap existed in the Republican policy towards that part of the world.

For the Truman Administration, the situation had been less difficult. Recently released documents show that the Democrats also aimed for the elimination of Soviet power from Eastern Europe and that their objectives were similar to those of the Republicans.[86] But there was an important difference in strategy and priorities. The Eisenhower Administration wanted to change the Eastern European order profoundly, by actively promoting 'destabilisation' and eventual 'liberation'.[87] The Truman Administration, on the other hand, expected Communist regimes to persist and merely to reject Soviet domination, as Tito had done. NSC 58 spoke of a possible schism in the Communist bloc and anticipated heresy among the faithful.[88] But administration priorities were different too. The Democrats were busy containing Russia in Western Europe and Asia, while the Republicans inherited a 'contained' Russia in those parts of the world. They could therefore concentrate more heavily on such 'forward' areas as Eastern Europe. For all these reasons, the Eisenhower Administration should have been more explicit about the kind of order, national and international, it wanted to see in this region.

However, it never was. NSC 174 of 11 December 1953, a document dealing with American policy towards Eastern Europe, spoke in very broad terms about 'freedom', 'independence', 'governments of their own choice', and 'peaceful members of a free world community'.[89] This was not sufficient. The Eisenhower Administration should have been more precise, and the question of neutrality should have been dealt with as one of the various options. The fact that the Hungarian government of Imre Nagy proclaimed neutrality during the revolution of 1956 goes to show that these were no idle speculations.

At times, however, the Eisenhower Administration's difficulties with neutrality were purely *verbal* and *personal*. While Truman and Acheson could speak clearly and even bluntly, Eisenhower had a gift for verbal imprecision and Dulles for excessive moralising. This sometimes had the unfortunate effect of making their policies appear more muddled than they were. The famous 'neutrality confusion' of early June 1956 was a case in point.

On 6 June 1956, Eisenhower held a press conference at which he spoke rather loosely about neutrality and neutralism. He thought that new nations in particular could not be blamed for refusing to take sides in the Cold War: 'We were a young country once, and our whole policy for the first hundred years was, or more, 150, we were neutral. We constantly asserted we were neutral in the wars of the world and wars in Europe and antagonisms.'[90] Eisenhower added that, at times, it might even be to the disadvantage of a state to be an ally. His utterances were rather incoherent, however, and he ultimately gave up: 'This whole subject is so complicated', he sighed, and he referred the journalists to a speech that Dulles would give in a few days at Ames, Iowa. The Secretary would speak about neutrality and, 'in any event, it will be a definite attempt to bring the thing down to its realities.'[91]

The remarks made front-page news. The *New York Times* ran a headline saying that 'Eisenhower Sees Merit in Attitude of Neutral Lands'. In view of the administration's stern view of neutrality in general, this seemed like a change of policy. But it was not. The White House must have immediately felt uncomfortable with the President's words, especially after it received calls from worried allied embassies. In a press release the following day, the President's words were given 'more exact meaning', but this was not easy and the uncertainty remained.[92]

When Dulles spoke at Ames, Iowa on 9 June, he must have intended to set the record straight. He spoke about the United Nations, collective security and the alliance treaties the United States had signed with forty-two countries. He then referred to neutrality:

These treaties abolish, as between the parties, the principle of neutrality, which pretends that a nation can best gain safety for itself by being indifferent to the fate of others. This has increasingly become an obsolete conception, 'and, except under very exceptional circumstances, it is an immoral and shortsighted conception'.[93]

Unfortunately, these sentences did little to clarify the President's earlier statements. Using words like 'obsolete', 'immoral', and 'shortsighted' confused the public and the world even more, so that now the representatives of a number of neutral and neutralist countries contacted the White House. Still more clarification was needed, if that was possible.[94] Only three days later, Dulles tried again. In a press conference, he answered a good number of questions on the administration's conception of neutrality. To begin with, he said that there were no differences between himself and the President, that words from the Ames speech had been taken out of context. He dodged a question on the 'immorality' of neutrality but answered one about 'exceptional circumstances' under which neutrality was justifiable.

> *Answer:* Well, the outstanding example of neutrality is, of course, Switzerland. Switzerland has declined to join the United Nations because it recognizes that the United Nations Charter is incompatible with strict neutrality.
> *Question:* Well, would you apply that exceptional term to states like India and Indonesia, for example?
> *Answer:* I don't care at this time to get into naming states and passing judgments upon the course of action of other governments.[95]

Of course, nothing was really clarified by these statements.[96] At the very least, an American secretary of state would have had to explain the difference between neutrality (occasional or permanent) and neutralism. He could have cited examples for each and referred to Austria as a case where his own administration had felt that 'exceptional circumstances' did not make permanent neutrality an immoral solution. Had Dulles really tried, he would have been able to make a much stronger defence of his own policies.

It must be remembered that in those days neutralism was a relatively recent phenomenon. Although its origins can be traced back to India's role in the Korean War, the concept only gained widespread acceptance once several countries began to organise themselves into a neutralist movement. A beginning was made at Bandung in 1955, but it was not until the Belgrade meeting of 1961 that the movement gained real momentum and some kind of identity.[97]

Dulles had to adjust to the new phenomenon of neutralism, and he did. His biographer, Michael A. Guhin, comes to the following conclusion:

> In fairness to Dulles during the early years, he had to deal with and adjust to a phenomenon for which there existed no criteria for identification and classification. He assumed office amid the revolution of the 'third world'. Judging from his overall performance, he

neither adhered to nor operated under the burden of any rigid formula on the subject of neutralism.[98]

This is certainly true if one analyses his individual actions and decisions carefully. Like any pragmatic internationalist, he had to live with the tension of adhering to universalist values while having to settle for traditionalist solutions. But in the case of Dulles, this tension was more pronounced because of his excessive moralising. In some speeches, he appeared to be speaking out of both sides of his mouth. Dulles' address in Ames, Iowa is a perfect example. It was basically meant to gain public support for the Mutual Security Programme, which was then running into serious trouble in Congress. Under this programme, military and economic assistance were going to India, Yugoslavia, Indonesia, and even Egypt, the very countries he was accusing, in this same speech, of pursuing an immoral foreign policy![99]

The same applied to his attitude towards the United Nations. There was hardly a speech in which he did not praise the spirit of the Charter and the United States as its most faithful member. On various occasions, he also declared emphatically that neutrality was incompatible with the spirit of collective security. But it was he who agreed with the Russians that Austria should become a member of the United Nations. This was a violation of the interpretation of Articles 5 and 6, as agreed to in San Francisco. The Swiss, who at that time took the interpretation seriously, stayed away from the United Nations. Ironically, Dulles, in his press conference of 12 June 1956, praised the Swiss for doing just that. What makes the case even more ironical is the fact that Austria was explicitly neutralised according to the Swiss model![100]

As indicated, such contradictions in the conception of neutrality of a pragmatic American internationalist were normal, and in this sense the Eisenhower Administration's view of neutrality was not different that of the Truman or Roosevelt Administrations. But the special character of Dulles made the contradiction more blatant. This helped neither the image of the Eisenhower Administration nor the concept of neutrality.

10
The Legal Perspective, 1957

Private opinions

The Korean War stimulated discussion in and out of government about the laws of war, and quite often the question of neutrality was also addressed.[1] It was not a great debate; on the contrary, relatively few people were involved in only a limited number of publications.[2] But the effort had a clear impact that led to new official formulations of the laws of war and of neutrality. By 1957, both the US Army and the US Navy had reworked and restated their positions on the subject.

It will be recalled that as early as 1948 Major William G. Downey Jr, Chief of the International Law Branch of the Judge Advocate General's Office, Department of the Army, had pleaded for some constructive thought in the reformulation of the law of war. At the 1949 Annual Conference of the American Society of International Law, the 'Revision of the Rules of Warfare' was on the agenda. Downey spoke at some length on the subject, clashing vehemently with Professor Fenwick.

When the Korean War broke out, therefore, the military must have already been preoccupied with the matter. It was the business of soldiers to think about the next war, in practical and legal terms, and the Pentagon had done so. It was the civilians, at least some of them, who seemed more taken by surprise. Many scholars considered traditional wars a thing of the past. The discussion among the civilians was carried on within the American Society of International Law, at its annual meeting of 1953 and in a series of articles published in its official organ, the *American Journal of International Law*. The articles began to appear in 1951 and ended in 1956, at the same time that the government published its army and navy handbooks. It is worthwhile to review the chronology of this development.

The articles began with Joseph L. Kunz's contribution on 'The Chaotic Status of the Laws of War and the Urgent Necessity for their Revision.'[3] Kunz was Professor of International Law at Toledo University and a member of the journal's board of editors. He was an Austrian émigré who, sixteen years earlier, while still in Europe, had written a book in which he pleaded for a revision of the laws of war.[4] Now he did the same again.

After criticising certain pacifist scholars of international law for having opposed the revision of the laws of war in the interwar period, he showed that this same opposition was now surfacing under the United Nations. He recalled an exchange between Charles Fenwick and Major Downey at the 1949 annual meeting of the society. Addressing himself to people like Fenwick, Kunz argued that 'to eliminate war is not to replace "force by law", but to replace a primitive by an advanced procedure of law.'[5] He cited the improved Geneva Red Cross Conventions of 1949 as an example. If the United Nations was unwilling or unable to draft new rules, it had to be done outside that organisation. Kunz ended with a hint that the military were already doing this: 'The movement for laws of war, Sumner Maine has stated, owes less to professors, statesmen or moralists than to military commanders. Today, too, the revision of the laws of war is particularly endorsed by military men.'[6]

In the same issue of the journal, Howard J. Taubenfeld of the New York Bar wrote on 'International Armed Forces and the Rules of War'.[7] He compared United Nations enforcement with international police actions of earlier times and concluded that at least some of the classic rules of war seemed to apply. Taubenfeld admitted that it was difficult to delineate the exact scope and content of United Nations obligations under pre-existing rules of war, but he argued that the principle of humanity certainly had to be observed.[8]

The 1953 issue of the journal contained another article by Taubenfeld. It dealt specifically with 'International Actions and Neutrality'.[9] The author first reviewed the status of neutrality under the League of Nations and then turned to the United Nations. He demonstrated that, in San Francisco, permanent neutrality had been declared incompatible with collective security and that, according to Hans Kelsen, this even applied to non-members of the UN. Taubenfeld also showed that the UN's International Law Commission had made efforts that went in the same direction, and that during the Korean War the General Assembly had also passed recommendations that were meant to be applicable to all states, non-members included.

All these efforts, however, merely had the force of non-binding rec-ommendations. In actual fact the organisation had sanctioned neutral-ity in an important way when it approved the formation of two neutral commissions during the Korean War. In light of these facts, Taubenfeld concluded:

> The actual experience of the United Nations indicates, then, that the status of neutrality still exists (for Switzerland, for example), subject to ever increasing pressures and, at least in theory, to a diminution of rights.[10]

The 1953 issue of the journal also contained a brief editorial by Charles G. Fenwick, who commented on the latest revised edition of Oppenheim Lauterpacht's well-known treatise on international law.[11] First written in 1906, the manual contained the classical chapters on the law of war and neutrality. The fact that they had not been elimi-nated bothered Fenwick. To him, it was clear 'that the old law of war and of neutrality must now be written in the past tense.'[12] Given his earlier views on the subject, this statement could hardly come as a sur-prise.[13] The same issue contained a more weighty contribution. Quincy Wright wrote on 'The Outlawry of War and the Law of War'.[14] As in his earlier writings on the subject, he argued that traditional law of war was premised on a contradiction:

> A right means an interest protected by law. For the law to affirm that a person subject to it can help himself to the rights of another subject whenever he has the physical power to do so seems to deny that the interest thus transferred is a right, and, therefore, if all interests may be transferred from one person to another in this way, to deny that there is a law binding them.[15]

Such reasoning, to Wright, made the existence of laws of war logi-cally impossible. To him, this was the scientific basis of the outlawry of war. From here all else followed, and Wright listed seven direct consequences. The fourth related to neutrality in UN enforcement action:

> A state engaged in enforcement action authorized by the United Nations may take measures if specifically authorized by the proper authority of the United Nations to prevent other states from assist-ing the aggressor and to assure the isolation of the aggressor from economic and social intercourse, even though such measures go

beyond the normal right of belligerents in reference to neutrals or enemies.[16]

According to Wright, the United Nations even had the right to encroach upon the sovereignty of non-member neutrals: 'The United Nations includes such a large proportion of the states of the world that its law may be properly regarded as general international law.'[17] Wright's argument was phrased in general terms; he did not refer explicitly to the Korean War or to the fact that all UN action in that war was based on mere recommendations. It was thus impossible to relate his statements to concrete questions of policy. Would the logic, for instance, also apply to non-participating states?

Furthermore, Wright's argument in part simply followed the UN Charter, which, in Art. 2, provides that all members 'shall refrain from giving assistance to any state against which the United Nations is taking preventive or enforcement action.' Provocative, however, was the view that this provision also applied to non-members.[18] This goes to show how strict an internationalist Quincy Wright was. Like Fenwick, he had not changed his views on the subject of neutrality since the early 1930s.

It so happened that at the 1953 Annual Conference of the American Society of International Law, Quincy Wright chaired the meeting that dealt with the law of war. This was the second time since 1945 that the Society discussed the question, and it was not to do so again for some time. In his opening statement, Wright remarked that, to some, it might seem rather out of place to discuss the laws of war, because, some twenty years before, war had been outlawed: 'But we must recognise', he added, 'that those who were outlawing war did not anticipate that it would rapidly end large-scale violence.'[19]

At the meeting, Major Richard R. Baxter of the Judge Advocate General's Corps spoke very generally about the role of law in modern war, and Joseph L. Kunz read a paper on the treatment of prisoners of war, particularly in Korea.[20] As can be expected, both men were of the opinion that most of the traditional rules of war also applied to the conflict in Korea, although the Communist states did not seem to feel bound by those rules.[21] In contrast to the 1949 meeting, the discussion that followed was rather tame and did not deal with the basic issues. Neutrality was mentioned but not in an important context. It seemed that after three years of gruelling war nobody was in a mood to start a debate with two representatives of the military point of view.

For the next two years the Society's journal contained no further articles on the law of war. Only in 1956 did Joseph Kunz once more write about the subject. It was to be the last contribution inspired by the Korean events. Kunz's article was entitled 'The Laws of War' and was as general in its argumentation as the title implied.[22] Presenting the 'realist' point of view, he again opposed Fenwick and Wright. He argued that in the development of the law of war, humanity had come full circle. Before the Enlightenment, barbarism on the battlefield had gone hand in hand with the just war theory. In the twentieth century, man was about to return to similar circumstances: in the UN Charter an updated theory of just war was more proclaimed once more, and on the battlefield the traditional law of war was again disregarded. 'We have arrived where we started, in the sixteenth century, at the threat of total, lawless war.'[23]

There was some hope, however, in Kunz's view. A number of Western governments, including that of the United States, had recently undertaken efforts to update their handbooks on the law of war. The US Army was preparing a new manual on land warfare, and the Navy had just published its new manual on naval warfare. These were meaningful steps towards a revision of the laws of war.

Kunz's paper addressed that very problem – the revision of the laws of war. He envisaged that revision would embrace all cases of conflict, even civil war. It would deal with the conduct of war of legal and illegal belligerents, with 'aggressors' and United Nations troops; it would not only regulate humanitarian questions, but also actual fighting, methods, and weapons. Kunz also wondered whether the law of war could be revised without including the law of neutrality and came to the conclusion that this was undesirable. Since 1907, he argued, the law of neutrality had been

> so intricately linked with the laws of war, it seems difficult to revise the latter without at the same time giving some attention to the law of neutrality, especially since that law is actually in an even more chaotic condition than the laws of war... . As the law of neutrality remains of great importance, a clear statement and revision of the law are also important.[24]

Although Kunz assumes a traditionalist point of view in this article and would, as a European émigré, certainly regard himself as a proponent of the classical tradition in international law, he nowhere pleads for a full return to the Hague Conventions and to integral neutrality. Kunz is very much preoccupied with the military aspect of neutrality and does not speak out in favour of liberal trading rights in war, freedom of the sea, or the classical 'peace through free trade' theory. As a result, Kunz cannot be seen as a direct successor of men like John Bassett Moore, Edwin Borchard, or Manley O. Hudson. By this time, this classical school of thought had vanished for good.

The official position

In 1955, the US Naval War College released an important study on 'The Law of War and Neutrality at Sea', and one year later, the United States Army published its field manual on 'The Law of Land Warfare'. The Navy's publication was a 400-page scholarly treatise written by Robert W. Tucker of Johns Hopkins University. The Army's handbook was half the size and, in contrast to that of the Navy, was a sober enumeration of what the Judge Advocate General's Office regarded as the relevant laws of war and of neutrality. Let us look at the Army's document first and then turn to the more demanding study of the Navy.

The Army's field manual on the law of land warfare contains nine chapters, eight of which are dedicated to topics such as the conduct of hostilities, prisoners of war, wounded and sick, civilians, occupation, non-hostile relations, and war crimes. The ninth, and last, chapter deals with neutrality. It is subdivided into six sections concerned with general rights and duties, recruiting, supplies and services, internment of belligerent forces, tending of wounded and sick, neutral persons, and railway material.[25]

The overall organisation of the manual, and especially of the chapter on neutrality, almost totally resembles an earlier version published in 1917. The content, too, has not changed materially. With two or three exceptions, the treatment of neutrality is virtually identical.[26] Both manuals are based on the Hague Conventions of 1907. One of the changes occurs at the very beginning of the neutrality chapter. After defining neutrality, the old manual continues with a paragraph on the necessity of notifying a state of war to neutrals. The new manual also addressed this question, but a passage on 'Neutrality Under the Charter of the United Nations' merits closer attention.

The passage begins by pointing out that, under Articles 39 to 42 of the Charter, the Security Council is authorised 'to call for the employment of measures short of force, or to take forcible measures to maintain or restore international peace and security.' The manual continues:

Although these provisions of the Charter have not made it impossible for a State to remain neutral, the obligations which the Charter imposes have to a certain extent qualified the rights of States in this respect. For example, if a state is called upon, under Articles 42 and 43 of the Charter, to take military action against an aggressor, that state loses its *right* to remain neutral but actually loses its neutrality only to the extent that it complies with the direction of the Security Council.[27]

The distinction seems to be one between *de jure* and *de facto* neutrality. *De jure*, a member[28] of the United Nations loses its right to be neutral once the Security Council has made a decision but, *de facto*, it can remain neutral if it fails to comply with the decision of the Council. Presumably, the distinction is of importance to military commanders, for whose guidance the manual was written. Does it mean that the United States Army would, in such circumstances, respect the neutrality of a country not fully complying with Security Council directions? The following passage seems to imply just that:

A military commander in the field is obliged to respect the neutrality of third States which are not allied with the United States in the conduct of hostilities and are not violating their duty of neutrality toward this country, except to the extent that the State concerned has expressly qualified its neutrality.[29]

Since all these statements are contained under the heading of 'Neutrality Under the Charter of the United Nations', it must be assumed that, in the context of enforcement action, the United States would make a distinction between *de jure* and *de facto* neutrality, and that it would continue to respect the latter although, in the eyes of the UN Charter, the state concerned would have lost its *right* to be neutral.

Besides this passage on the United Nations and a few other modifications regarding the treatment of the wounded and sick (based on treaties signed after 1917), the two manuals of 1917 and 1956 are practically identical. This is most noticeable in respect to the general rights and duties of neutrals, where the Hague Convention is cited verbatim. The right of free private trade in war is also mentioned:

Commercial transactions with belligerents by neutral corporations, companies, citizens, or persons resident in neutral territory are not prohibited. A belligerent may purchase from such persons supplies, munitions, or anything that may be of use to an army or fleet, which can be exported or transported without involving the neutral State.[30]

Does this mean that the United States, at least in its Army manual, was still dedicated to integral neutrality? From a purely legal viewpoint this could indeed be inferred, but the enumeration of a set of international laws in a handbook does not make official policy. It would be a hasty and superficial conclusion to assume that the government as a whole was still bound by all of the Hague Conventions.

The study of the *United States Naval War College* is more than just a handbook. In its appendix it includes a manual similar to the Army manual, but the main body of the book is a 350-page scholarly treatise on the law of war (160 pages) and the law of neutrality (190 pages). It is impossible to do full justice to this massive study in just a few pages. A review of some of the more important points will have to suffice.

In Part I on 'War and the Law of War', Robert W. Tucker introduces some of the basic questions. He begins by drawing a clear distinction between laws regulating the *resort to war* and the actual *conduct of war*. He concludes that, in view of the UN Charter, 'the resort to war can no longer be regarded as an act which states are at liberty to take for whatever reason they may deem proper.'[31] It follows, in Tucker's view, that there is a possibility today for the existence of just and unjust wars, for legal and illegal belligerents. If to this were added the principle that out of illegal acts no rights can arise *(ex injuria jus non oritur)*, then there would be no more room for the traditional laws of war regulating the conduct of hostilities. These laws treat both belligerents as equals and assign rights and duties to both.

Tucker rejects the full force of this logic: 'for humanitarian reasons alone there has been a marked reticence to contend that the full consequences of the principle ex *injuria jus non oritur* must be drawn in the case of a state waging an unlawful war.'[32] It follows, therefore, that in international law certain rights and duties can arise out of illegal wars. These relate to the *conduct of hostilities*. They do not extend to the *gains* arising from such hostilities, however. The territory an aggressor may have conquered and a peace treaty he might have imposed are deprived of any legal validity. Tucker sums up his argument as follows:

> From the fact that the resort to war is, under certain circumstances, illegal, it follows only that the counter-war is, as a sanction, legal. It does not of necessity follow that the duties and rights of belligerents are, as a matter of positive law, different in an unlawful war from

what they have been in a lawful war... . The legal inequality between belligerents with respect to the war itself does not logically preclude their legal equality as concerns the applicability of the rules regulating the conduct of war.[33]

Tucker then turns to the experience in the Second World War and the Charter of the United Nations. He shows that, in theory, the Security Council was indeed empowered to initiate and conduct a just conflict, but that, in view of present realities, such a case had to be regarded as highly improbable – so improbable, in fact, 'that the utility of a careful examination of the possible effect of this situation on the operation of the law of war appears distinctly limited.'[34] In short, for the military faced with the task of preparing for the next war, such questions were so improbable as to be of no interest.

Tucker, therefore, turns to cases of higher probability, such as the Korean experience. He shows that, for reasons well known, the Security Council actions were not binding and that, consequently, the UN forces were not directed as foreseen by the Security Council but had to be regarded as national forces (acting on behalf of the United Nations). Under such circumstances, it was quite evident that the traditional laws of war applied.[35] Tucker concludes that, in the postwar years, the applicability of the laws of war had actually expanded and not contracted, mainly because the ICRC Geneva Conventions now also applied to all kinds of international armed conflict, and not only to declared wars among sovereign states.[36]

In Part II, Tucker turns to 'Neutrality and the Legal Position of War'. A very thorough treatment of the subject is divided into eight sections dealing with the general legal position of war, the two world wars, the relations between neutral and belligerent states, contraband, blockade, unneutral service, visit and search, and, finally, seizure and destruction of neutral vessels. After reviewing the traditional relationship between war and neutrality, Tucker turns again to the Charter of the United Nations and investigates the question of neutrality first under the highly improbable assumption that the Security Council functions. He concludes that, at least for non-members, there would still be a possibility to declare neutrality. This would only become illegal if the United Nations Charter were regarded as constituting general international law. At the time Tucker was writing, this seemed unlikely.[37]

Tucker concludes that the situation for members was different. They could remain neutral only if the Security Council, under Art. 48, decided to release them from participation in military sanctions, but, even then, the duty not to assist an aggressor under Art. 2 would remain.[38] As a result, such a state would lose its right to trade freely with the belligerent and might lose its impartiality. It would be tantamount to participating in economic sanctions, a duty from which the Security Council could not release a neutral anyway. Such a state would, therefore, at best enjoy qualified or differential neutrality.[39]

More probable, however, are cases where the Security Council does not function. In such instances 'the position of Member states not immediately involved in hostilities will be substantially the same as the position of third states – not immediately involved in the war – under general international law.'[40] This, of course, was the position that prevailed in Korea. As noted earlier, this was a situation where, according to Tucker, forces acted not under the control of the Security Council, but under that of individual nations acting 'on behalf of the United Nations'. In such cases, the traditional law of war applied in its entirety, including the law of neutrality. Members were then in the same position as non-members.

Tucker and the US Navy seemed to be preparing for cases such as this or, worse, for cases in which the Security Council could not even agree on recommendations, and a traditional war, therefore, was being fought. This was a distinctly 'realist' philosophy of international politics typical of the men at the Pentagon. They had been strong supporters of the traditional law of war throughout the Second World War and the years following. As will be recalled, the military were keen on revising the Geneva Conventions.

What was different now was that respected academics like Tucker and Kunz spoke out openly and forcefully for the armed forces' point of view. In the years immediately after the war, there were no big names in America in international law publicly supporting this line of thought. Only in Europe did some well-known scholars think about the possible failure of the United Nations at a time when the signatures were hardly dry on the San Francisco document.[41]

This is not to say that people like Tucker and Kunz were espousing traditional neutrality. I have shown earlier that Kunz remained silent on economic rights, and Tucker, too, pointed out that, in two world wars, neutral rights had suffered badly: 'Where neutrals do not possess an equality of power with belligerents their interests, and hence their legal rights, will suffer accordingly.'[42] The performance of the greatest neutral in the First World War, the United States, did nothing to help that trend.

Tucker shows that, historically, the major disputes between neutrals and belligerents had been over trading rights and that these had suffered mainly in great wars. In small and limited wars, there might be a better chance for preserving them, but the distinction between the private and public economic spheres, on which these rights were premissed, was slowly disappearing:

> It is difficult to discern what possible effect – if indeed there would be any effect – limited wars could have upon this growing obsolescence of rules dependent for their operation upon the possibility of preserving a clear distinction between neutral state and neutral trader.[43]

This is clear language, and it follows that the Navy's standpoint on the question of neutral trading rights had been in line with general policy since 1941. It is also apparent that the Navy's point of view is more clearly defined than that of the Army. Given the fact that the former branch of the armed forces would have to organise a blockade, this should be understandable.

It can also be assumed that Tucker's opinion was practically identical with official thinking. Although it is true that, in the preface to the Navy's handbook, Rear Admiral Thomas H. Robbins Jr, President of the Naval War College, emphasised the fact that the opinions contained in the volume were not necessarily those of the US Navy, it can none the less be assumed that they are very similar.[44] It must also be remembered that in the United States it is difficult at any one moment to get an authoritative statement on such issues. For all practical purposes, Tucker expressed the official point of view.

Legal dualism

The foregoing analysis of private and public positions illustrates once more the division between two opposing viewpoints, between legal 'realism' and 'idealism'. It will be recalled that a debate between the two philosophies was carried on in the interwar period, although then under very different circumstances. At that time the United States was still committed to a policy of isolation and was unsure whether it should return to traditional neutrality or go forward to greater involvement. Now it had become a Great Power and was irrevocably involved in world affairs.

In the meantime, the 'idealist' point of view had scored a success: a universal international organisation had been set up with the ability to make authoritative decisions in matters of war and peace. War as a means of conflict resolution was outlawed, and, in principle, it was now possible to distinguish just from unjust conflicts, 'aggression' from 'enforcement'. It followed that from now on there would no longer be belligerents with equal rights to wage war or bystanders with special rights to remain uninvolved.

But, as the Korean conflict showed, this new legal order was difficult to implement. As a result, the 'idealist' philosophy came under pressure, and the 'realists' scored a comeback. We have shown that at the end of the Second World War the realists tried to suggest a comprehensive revision of the classical rules of war, but when the question was raised in journals and at meetings of international lawyers, the 'idealists' had the upper hand. For a few years the revision of the laws of war was no longer discussed; only with the Korean War did the issue emerge once more. 'Realism' was on the rise.

However, the debates were no longer as heated as they once had been. Viewpoints within the American Society of International Law were as divided as ever, but somehow both sides must have come to the conclusion that neither system of law would dominate and that coexistence had become a fact of life. Almost everyone seemed willing to live with legal dualism.

This viewpoint also prevails in official publications. Tucker admits that with the existence of the United Nations, the recourse to war is no longer legal. To him, only the conduct of war remains subject to conventional rules and regulations, which is an interesting compromise between the two opposing philosophies. The army adopts a similar perspective when it argues that under the United Nations Charter a neutral loses its *de jure* neutrality while keeping it in fact. Instructions to field commanders are then defined in such a way as to embrace the entire Hague Conventions of 1907. In the actual conduct of war, therefore, the United States is *in principle* ready to abide by most of the traditional rules of war, including those of neutrality.

Kunz, Baxter, and Tucker also make it abundantly clear that even in the Korean War the traditional laws of war should have applied. We have shown earlier that this was almost impossible because the Americans, too, often preferred to avoid taking a clear stand on international law. This was particularly true in the case of neutrality. There was, consequently, a wide gap between principles and practice. It showed most vividly in the continued American refusal to respect neutral trading rights.

Still, the United States never denounced the Hague Conventions and, as far as the government is concerned, they are in full force. So, of course, is the Charter of the United Nations. As noted earlier, the result is a legal dilemma. Which set of laws should apply when? The American answer is a pragmatic one, neither purely in the traditionalist nor entirely in the internationalist tradition. Moderate internationalism prevails, with all its inherent contradictions. Sadly enough, the result is that quite often neither of the two legal systems is applied. More than ever, conflicts among nations are settled with no reference to international law, thereby literally creating a state of 'lawlessness'. Politics is on the rise; law on the decline. It should, therefore, not be a surprise that neutrality, too, is increasingly a political and not a legal notion.

11
Southeast Asia, 1960–1970

Neutralism and Southeast Asia

In Europe, the United States had to handle existing and traditional neutrals like Sweden and Switzerland or, as in the case of Austria, it was faced with the question of neutralising a country that was domestically at peace. In Southeast Asia the situation was different. Most countries had only recently obtained their independence, traditional neutrals did not exist, and those aiming at neutralisation were domestically fragile or in a state of war. Furthermore, the concept of *neutralism* was on the rise and did much to confuse matters – as the United States was soon to discover.

Neutralism was a product of the Cold War and of decolonisation. Many of the newly independent countries had no desire to align with either the former colonial power or with the Soviet Union. They preferred an intermediate status, which became known as neutralism or non-alignment. Its chief protagonists in those early years were the leaders of India, Indonesia, Egypt, and Yugoslavia – Nehru, Sukarno, Nasser, and Tito.[1]

The first large neutralist gathering took place at Bandung, Indonesia in 1955. Twenty-nine countries, most of them Asian, participated. It was a heterogeneous group including, among others, Maoist China, neutral Cambodia, and American allies like Pakistan, the Philippines, and Thailand. The rhetoric was stridently anti-colonial and anti-capitalist, which suited the Soviets because at that very time Khrushchev was making efforts to intensify relations with what became known as the Third World. Later on that policy included military support for 'wars of national liberation'.[2] Small wonder that Dulles perceived neutralism as a movement working to the advantage of Moscow and to the disadvantage of the United States, especially in Asia.

At the 1954 Geneva Conference, Dulles made sure that the issue of neutrality did not appear on the agenda. As shown earlier, he preferred allies to neutrals, and he had plans for an alliance system in Southeast Asia. Only two months after the Geneva conference, the South East Asia Treaty Organization (SEATO) was set up in Manila. Its members included the United States, Great Britain, France, Australia, New Zealand, Thailand, the Philippines, and Pakistan. The alliance was part of the American containment policy euphemistically identified with 'collective security', a term generally reserved for the United Nations. At heart SEATO was an anti-Communist alliance, but it was also meant to contain neutralism.[3]

In a supplementary protocol the SEATO members pledged to protect three non-signatory states: South Vietnam, Cambodia, and Laos. Before 1954, all three had been part of French Indochina, but from an American perspective *South Vietnam* was the most important. Once the French withdrew, the United States began to support the new regime politically, economically, and militarily. Given the attempt by the National Liberation Front (NLF), supported by North Vietnam, to unite the country by force the American commitment became steadily more important. As the Cold War intensified, successive American administrations regarded South Vietnam as the place where the spread of communism had to be stopped. There were those in Saigon and in Washington who disagreed and suggested that Vietnam should be neutralised – which in effect meant American withdrawal. Such voices were squashed, however, and the United States began to fight a war that could not be won and that traumatised an entire generation of Americans.

Laos was a troubled country, too. From the very beginning it was divided three ways. When Kennedy came to power, the pro-Western faction was headed by General Phoumi, whose troops had been supported secretly for years by the Eisenhower Administration. The pro-North Vietnamese Pathet Lao faction was led by Prince Souvannavong. Prince Souvanna Phouma tried to steer a middle course between the other two and called himself a neutralist. His attempts at forming coalition governments were adamantly opposed by Dulles.[4] That changed during the Kennedy years. Kennedy agreed to the neutralisation of Laos early in his administration, but the scheme did not work. Laos, too, was drawn into the Vietnam War.

Of the three countries *Cambodia* was initially the most robust. Its president, Prince Norodom Sihanouk, was the first Indochinese leader to call himself both a neutral and a neutralist. He was a fervent nationalist with a quixotic personality, but he managed to keep the country out of overt war until the late 1960s. His neutralism did not endear him to Dulles, however, and as a result Cambodian relations with the Eisenhower Administration were strained. The Kennedy years saw some improvement, but as the Vietnam War escalated under President Johnson, relations deteriorated. Animated by the Laos neutralisation, Prince Sihanouk made various attempts to set up an international conference guaranteeing Cambodia neutrality. His efforts failed, however, and in May 1965 Cambodia severed its relations with the United States. When relations were restored in 1969 Sihanouk had already lost his grip on the country, and at the same time, the Nixon administration began its secret Cambodian bombing campaign. From that moment on, events took a tragic turn ending, after 1975, in the barbaric rule of Pol Pot's Khmer Rouge.[5]

This short summary shows that the fates of Cambodia, Laos, and South Vietnam were closely intertwined – as was the question of neutrality. When Laos was neutralised in 1962, Norodom Sihanouk immediately wanted a similar solution for Cambodia. Later on, as the war in South Vietnam became bogged down, many South Vietnamese, but also some of the ruling generals, searched for a negotiated (or neutralist) solution with the NLF. French President Charles de Gaulle was a constant supporter of neutralism, and some top advisers in the Kennedy and Johnson Administrations also favoured neutralist solutions for Cambodia, Laos, and Vietnam.

Ultimately, however, the opponents of neutrality had the upper hand. The worst enemies of neutrality sat in Hanoi. The regime in North Vietnam had no intention of making the classical concept work or of guaranteeing the non-aligned independence of Laos, Cambodia, and South Vietnam. Ho Chi Minh and his successors aimed at dominating former Indochina, under the guise of 'neutralism' if necessary. Most decision-makers in Washington were unwilling to let that happen, because they thought in ideological terms and equated the 'loss' of Indochina with global defeat. The true reason for the failure of neutrality (or of neutralism) in Southeast Asia lay, therefore, not primarily in a false understanding of the concept itself but in clashing interests and security perceptions.

These perceptions and interests turned out to be mistaken, on the part of both the North Vietnamese and the Americans. Eventually North Vietnam realised it could not dominate all of Indochina, and the United States finally learnt that 'losing' Indochina did not undermine its global security position. At present no North Vietnamese documents are available that would allow evaluation of the factors underlying their miscalculations, but it is evident that the 'China factor' played an important role in American calculations. Washington was right in expecting a 'second Korea' or a massive Chinese intervention should the United States make an attempt to conquer North Vietnam, but it was wrong in perceiving China as a global threat. While it was true that Mao (and Khrushchev) supported 'wars of national liberation', these contests did not affect the core areas of American security, which lay in Europe, the North Atlantic, and in the 'blue waters' of the Pacific.

Laos neutralised

Originally the conflict in Laos was anti-colonial in character, but by the end of the 1950s and the early 1960s it had also become part of the Cold War and the struggle between ideologies. It was seen as one more 'war of national liberation' fought by the anti-imperialist (or socialist) forces against the capitalist West. On 6 January 1961, just two weeks before Kennedy's inauguration, Khrushchev announced that henceforth the Soviet Union would actively support such wars.[6] In his campaign Kennedy had criticised the Eisenhower Administration for not paying enough attention to the emerging Third World. It was no surprise, therefore, when in his first State of the Union Message of 30 January 1961 Kennedy promised to broaden US foreign policy and to pay particular attention to the economic and military needs of developing countries.[7] His administration was willing to meet the new challenge, in Cuba, the Congo – and in Laos.

When Kennedy took office Laos was topmost on the foreign policy agenda. For years the war in Laos had been shifting back and forth, but beginning in December of 1960, the situation was taking a dramatic turn. Pro-American General Phoumi had scored a short-lived military victory – with unfortunate consequences. Phoumi's success drove neutralist Souvanna Phouma into the countryside, where he joined Souvannavong.[8] It also gave the Soviets a pretext to start a massive airlift on 13 December.

The Eisenhower Administration was alarmed but remained largely inactive. It was unsure about the wisdom of military intervention, but it was also unwilling to abandon Phoumi and to back a neutralist government in Vientiane. When the foreign policy teams of the incoming and the outgoing administrations met on 19 January, the dilemma was plainly visible. Although accounts vary on the details discussed and the opinions voiced, it is clear that while Eisenhower was unprepared to abandon Laos, he was equally unwilling to commit regular American forces.[9] The neutralisation option was not mentioned at all.[10]

As it turned out, Kennedy was equally unwilling to significantly increase the American military presence but, and this was the major difference between the two administrations, he was ready to back neutralist Souvanna Phouma and to give neutralisation a try.[11] Although Laos was not a major campaign issue and Kennedy had not committed himself in any way, he had been advised by some members of his entourage to aim at an internationally negotiated neutralisation. At this early stage, the chief advocates of such a policy were Chester Bowles, Ambassador at Large, and Senate Majority Leader Mike Mansfield.[12] They proposed neutrality not only for Laos, but also for all of Indochina. When it came to Vietnam later on, they were joined by Under Secretary of State George W. Ball. All three were known as Euro-centred experts who did not think that Southeast Asia should be given top priority.

Laos was mentioned in Kennedy's first news conference, held five days after coming to office, but he avoided the term neutrality. Instead he used words like 'uncommitted' and expressed the wish that Laos would become an 'independent country not dominated by either side'.[13] Within a month Kennedy's language changed. In a short opening statement given at a press conference held on 23 February, he made a dozen references to neutrality! No American president had in recent memory publicly referred to neutrality so often and so favourably. He announced a willingness to support a neutralist government in Vientiane and was also ready to back a British proposal for an internationally negotiated settlement, which implied the readiness to accept neutralisation.[14]

He embellished history by claiming that 'it was the clear premise of the 1954 settlement that this new country would be neutral.... No such premise existed at the Geneva Conference, at least not on the part of the American government and, as indicated, in the years that followed, the Eisenhower Administration backed the anti-neutralist forces.'[15] Kennedy therefore felt the need to emphasise that 'if in the past there has been any possible ground for misunderstanding of our desire for a truly neutral Laos, there should be none now.'[16]

The decision to opt for a new policy must have been made in early February, perhaps in conjunction with the NSC meeting of 8 February.[17] Whatever the exact date, it was Dean Rusk himself who on 10 February sent a lengthy telegram to the embassy in Laos explaining the new policy and adding that the United States was also ready to envisage the creation of a 'neutral nations commission centering around Cambodia and Burma' to monitor military compliance. The commission was meant to replace the ineffective International Control Commission (ICC) created in Geneva in 1954, but it never came about.[18]

Several factors favoured the new policy. As mentioned in Kennedy's press conference, the United Kingdom welcomed an international conference on Laos, thereby supporting an idea originally launched by Norodom Sihanouk in January. Later on, the Soviets also backed the proposal, which meant that both co-chairmen of the 1954 Geneva Conference approved the idea.[19] The Indians, in their capacity as Chairman of the ICC, had called for a revival of that body as early as December.[20]

Chester Bowles was a strong advocate of neutralisation. On 21 March he wrote a memorandum to Dean Rusk in support of a neutral solution,[21] and two days later the secretary of state received a second, more detailed paper containing some of the arguments Bowles was to advance in the months (and years) to come. The paper started out with a reference to Korea. In that war, Bowles argued, the United States had fought under the authority of the United Nations, while in Laos 'it will be operating under the authority of SEATO, an organisation which is mistrusted by most Asians.' But there were geopolitical differences as well. Bowles was of the opinion that from a logistical point of view, the United States 'would be operating under the worst conceivable conditions', that it could be 'vastly outnumbered' on the ground, and that it could 'become caught up in an escalating dilemma which can easily get out of control'. He added that the Soviets might see an advantage 'in embroiling the United States with the Chinese in a relatively untenable military position nine thousand miles from our shores', and that 'the decision to stake America's power and influence on a wobbly situation nearly as close to the Chinese border as Cuba is to the United States... will appear strange indeed in the history of our time.'[22]

When Kennedy opted for neutralisation he did not put all of his eggs into one basket, however. Upon the recommendation of Dean Rusk he pursued a two-track strategy, by including a careful analysis of all possible military options in Laos.[23] This gave people a chance to become active who had no use for neutrality at all. Two stood out among them: Walt W. Rostow and Roswell Gilpatric. Rostow was Counselor of the Department of State and Chairman of the Policy Planning Council and, as it turned out, a driving force behind efforts to get America into Vietnam.[24] Gilpatric was Deputy Secretary of Defense and, as of April, head of Kennedy's Vietnam Task Force. He, too, was a hard-liner.[25]

Given the two-track approach pursued in Washington and the confusing developments within Laos, the period between Kennedy's press conference on 23 February and the beginning of actual negotiations at the Geneva Conference on 25 July was rather turbulent.[26] At times it appeared as if the administration might opt for military action after all, especially when in April General Phoumi lost further ground and Soviet airdrops continued.[27] However, from 14 April on, the White House was temporarily preoccupied with the Bay of Pigs disaster. For a few weeks that incident quelled the taste for military action.

But the military option was put aside when on 3 May negotiations between the various Laotian factions began at Ban Namone.[28] At about the same time the administration's position paper for the forthcoming 14-Nation Conference on Laos was finalised.[29] Although Laotian neutralisation is envisaged therein, much of the language used is quite traditional and reminiscent of the policy pursued by the Eisenhower Administration. Accordingly, the United States aimed to turn the neutrals into staunch anti-Communists:

> We should seek to make this Conference a turning point for Asian neutralists. In this Conference the three participating Asian neutralists will be faced with the choice of joining a diplomatic effort to *hold the line* against the Communist threat to Southeast Asia or of resigning themselves to ineffectual appeasement of a relentless Communist advance.[30] [emphasis added]

The conception of neutrality in this passage hardly differs from that held by the preceding administration. Neutrals were acceptable when they pursued an anti-Communist line, and the goal of Laotian neutralisation was, therefore, not only to extricate the United States from a political and military commitment of questionable value, but also to 'hold the line'. In the case of Austria that expectation was realistic. Whether the same would be true in Southeast Asia was questionable from the start.[31]

As the Laotian question shows, three different *neutrality conceptions* prevailed in the Kennedy Administration. Chester Bowles opted for neutrality as a means to release the United States from a hopeless commitment and as a chance to redefine the line. For John F. Kennedy and some of his advisers, the line had to be held, and – under certain circumstances – neutrality offered an opportunity to do so more flexibly. But the majority of advisers were totally opposed to neutrality and ready to hold the line at almost any price. Foremost among them were Rostow and Gilpatric. They thought Laotian neutrality would not work, which proved to be correct, and they thought the United States could take a stand almost anywhere in Southeast Asia, which proved to be wrong.

For the time being at least, the President's intermediate position carried the day, as was evident during the Vienna summit of 3 and 4 June 1961. Kennedy met Khrushchev several times, and Laos was an important topic, on an equal footing with Cuba and nuclear weapons. The two agreed that for neither the Soviet Union nor the United States was Laos strategically important, that a negotiated settlement was in both of their interests, and that a unified, independent, and neutralised Laos should emerge.[32] They also discussed neutrality, and Kennedy explained that Yugoslavia, India, and Burma were extremely satisfactory situations as far as the United States was concerned. The problem, he added, 'is if the Communist cause were to win in certain areas and if those areas were to associate themselves closely with the Soviet Union, that would create strategic problems for the United States.'[33] Once again Kennedy indicated his willingness to hold the line.

No neutrality for Vietnam

The question of how to extricate the United States from Vietnam was raised throughout the entire ten-year war, and a number of different ideas were floated, including 'vietnamisation' and 'peace with honour'.[34] Neutralisation was another of these strategies, and it was proposed in 1961 mainly by members inside the administration and only occasionally by the South Vietnamese themselves. That changed beginning in 1963, as American involvement in Vietnam intensified. There were still a few voices in Washington advocating neutralisation, but the issue was now mainly raised in South Vietnam itself. However, it was also taken up by the French and a few leading American journalists.

Before looking at the two periods in detail, it is important to summarise the situation in Vietnam prior to Kennedy's first major decision. In contrast to Laos, where the Geneva Accords of 1954 did not permit the stationing of foreign military advisers, South Vietnam was allowed a contingent of 685 men. Originally these were French troops, but by 1956 the American military had replaced them. From then on, a regular US Military Assistance Advisory Group (MAAG) was stationed in the country. When the Kennedy Administration came to office there were exactly 685 advisers in place. In May of the same year, Kennedy secretly added 500 Special Forces, and in doing so he broke the Geneva Accords.[35]

During the summer, the South Vietnamese army lost further ground, and by the autumn the President was advised to send a large number of additional troops. In preparation for this decision Kennedy sent General Maxwell Taylor, his personal military adviser, to Vietnam to study the situation. Taylor, accompanied by Walt Rostow, left Washington on 15 October and returned on 25 October. Kennedy received the report on 3 November, and on 22 November decided to commit up to 8000 additional troops to Vietnam.[36] This decision, it must be remembered, was made while the United States was negotiating the neutralisation of Laos at the Geneva Conference.

It was before, during, and after the Taylor Mission that neutrality was debated. The administration divided once more along lines familiar from the Laos discussion. The chief advocate of neutrality was again Chester Bowles. Several others voiced similar opinions, including Averell Harriman, who headed the Laos negotiating team in Geneva, Kenneth Galbraith, American ambassador to India,[37] George W. Ball, and Senator Mike Mansfield. Each had his own argument, but they agreed that the Vietnam commitment was ill-conceived and untenable, and that the United States was headed for disaster.

Let us now look at some of the details. Two weeks before the Taylor Mission departed, Chester Bowles sent a memorandum to Dean Rusk, his superior. This time he did not insist upon comparing the situation to Korea. Instead he outlined an alternative, arguing in favour of expanding the concept of a neutral and independent Laos to embrace an entire 'neutral Southeast Asian belt'. The area would include Laos, Burma, Thailand, South Vietnam, Cambodia, and Malaya, and the arrangement would have to be guaranteed by the USSR, China, India, Japan, and the SEATO powers.[38]

The sticking point was Thailand, because the country was a SEATO member, and the hard-liners were absolutely unwilling to let that 'domino' fall. Bowles disagreed, however, and because his argument went to the core of several contested issues, it is worth examining:

> For centuries successive generations of Thais have prided themselves on their ability to assure their security by skilled negotiation. Each powerful new Chinese dynasty in its turn has brought pressure to bear on Thailand, and on each occasion the Thais have managed to preserve their sovereignty by paying some form of political tribute. In the last part of the 19th century and the early part of this one, the Thais played the French against the British. When the Japanese

attacked Pearl Harbor, the Thai response was promptly to declare war on the United States the following day.[39]

Bowles saw the war in Southeast Asia as another manifestation of Chinese dynastic expansion limited to its traditional sphere of influence. His opponents disagreed. For them the conflict was not traditional and limited but modern, ideological, and universal. The disagreement between Bowles and most top advisers was, therefore, profound.

In order to discuss these serious differences, Bowles asked Rusk to arrange a meeting with George Ball, Averell Harriman, and Under Secretary of State Alexis Johnson, but there is no record that it took place or that the memorandum was ever answered.[40] Bowles claims in his memoirs that his recommendations were 'vigorously debated' in the Department and the White House.[41] Perhaps, but there is no record of a meeting among top decision-makers at which neutrality was seriously discussed. The debates must have been informal.

On 2 November, a week after Taylor and Rostow had returned from Vietnam, Senator Mansfield sent the President a lengthy letter. The mission report had not yet been transmitted to the President, but the more essential recommendations had come to Mansfield's attention. Although he did not mention neutrality, the Senator questioned the wisdom of an increased American commitment. Like Bowles, he warned of a second Korea. 'In present circumstances', he argued, 'it seems to me we must exercise every caution to avoid another Korean-type involvement on the Asian mainland.' Alluding to the tensions between Moscow and China, Mansfield argued that 'such an involvement would appear to me to play completely into the hands of the Soviet Union, since it will get them off their present Chinese ideological hook... '. As Bowles continued to argue, the United States should keep out of the traditional Chinese sphere of influence, and its overall strategy should, therefore, resemble that of the second World War 'to minimise our involvement, particularly military, on the Asian mainland, not to maximise it.'[42]

After Mansfield it was Bowles' turn again. On 5 November, Prime Minister Jawaharlal Nehru visited Washington. A folder prepared for the occasion by the Department of State contained a memorandum addressed to President Kennedy in which Bowles again argued in favour of a neutral Southeast Asia.[43] This time Bowles also received the support of Kenneth Galbraith, the American ambassador to India.[44] George Ball was active at the same time. He spoke to the President on 7 November, and his words proved to be prophetic:

Within five years we'll have three hundred thousand men in the paddies and jungles and never find them again. That was the French experience. Vietnam is the worst possible terrain both from a physical and a political point of view.[45]

To Ball's chagrin Kennedy was unwilling to discuss the matter. Lyndon Baines Johnson would be different. As President he at least pretended to listen to Ball.

Taylor's final mission report covered 50 pages and was sent to the President on 3 November, two days before the Nehru visit.[46] In anticipation of the pending decision, the Secretaries of State and of Defense, together with the Joint Chiefs of Staff, sent a memorandum to the President on 8 November. In it they urged Kennedy to 'take the decision to commit ourselves to the objective of preventing the fall of South Vietnam to Communism and the willingness to commit whatever United States combat forces may be necessary to achieve this objective.'[47] As indicated, the President decided to commit on 22 November and, among other things, agreed to raise the number of American troops from 1100 to a maximum of 8000.[48]

Dean Rusk was not surprised. As he comments in his memoirs, 'John Kennedy never questioned that Southeast Asia was vital to American security. His only question: where should we fight if we had to fight? His decision: South Vietnam.'[49] Laos was the wrong place but, as Rusk confided privately to French Ambassador Hervé Alphand two days after the decision was taken, Laos was to him also a 'bad precedent'.[50]

If Kennedy wanted to consider the option of neutralising Vietnam he had an opportunity to do so – but he did nothing to encourage a serious and formal discussion.[51] He was willing to test neutrality in Laos but had no intention of applying it to Vietnam or, more cogently, it was because of his flexibility in Laos that Kennedy felt impelled to be inflexible in Vietnam.[52] The military leg of Rusk's two-track, therefore, extended to Vietnam; while negotiating at the Geneva Conference the President intended to demonstrate determination and strength in Vietnam. This showed in the fact that Kennedy wanted the Laotian Task Force to be run by the State Department, while he assigned the Vietnam Task Force to the Department of Defense. Choosing hardliners like Taylor and Rostow to visit Vietnam was further evidence of the President's desire to differentiate between the two cases.[53]

Kennedy's desire to take a hard line in Vietnam was most certainly related to the otherwise meagre foreign policy performance during his first year in office. The Bay of Pigs invasion was a disaster, the Vienna

meeting with Khrushchev in June was a disappointment, and the con-
struction of the Berlin Wall in August caught Washington by surprise.
It seemed time to take a strong stand and to follow Taylor's
recommendations.

Chester Bowles did not give up. On 30 November, he sent the
President another memo,[54] and on 18 July 1962, just a few days before
the closing of the Geneva Conference, Bowles made a last-ditch effort.
He drafted a 'Peace Charter for Southeast Asia' and wanted to tour the
Far Eastern US embassies to muster support for his idea. At first Rusk
and the President approved the mission, but upon the resistance of the
Far Eastern Bureau it was stopped.[55] In early March 1963, Bowles was
appointed ambassador to India, and immediately thereafter he sent
one more memo to the President – without ever getting an answer.[56]
This cold-shouldering combined with Bowles' transfer was a clear
signal that neutralist New Delhi was a better place for an American
proponent of neutralism than Washington D.C.

The year 1961 had been an important one. Kennedy arrived quickly
at two decisions affecting Southeast Asia and neutrality. They were
largely his initiatives, and there were as yet few neutralisation pressures
from outside the administration. As we have seen, however, that did
not last. As the United States became more deeply involved in South
Vietnam, the pressures from within that country increased. Others also
joined in the demand for neutralisation, especially the French and
some members of the American press. To the extent that Kennedy
increased the American presence in South Vietnam, the neutrality pressures to come were partly of his own making. A vicious circle had been
set in motion.

Neutralist Diem?

Symbolic of the mounting internal problems in South Vietnam was
Diem's assassination in early November 1963, only a few weeks before
Kennedy himself was shot in Dallas. The story of Diem's removal is
well documented, and it is clear that the United States was heavily
involved. There were many reasons why Washington had become
unhappy with his rule, but two stand out as the most important: one
had to do with Diem's domestic political problems, the other with his
secret contacts to the North.[57]

In May and August of 1963, there were two violent clashes between
Diem's troops and Buddhists in Saigon. In the first incident eight civil-

ians were killed, whereupon a monk immolated himself publicly, a picture that sent shock waves around the world. In the second incident forces commanded by Diem's brother Nhu sacked pagodas and arrested 1400 monks.[58] The clashes were only the most obvious expression of great domestic difficulties and of the fact that the war was not going well. In Washington there was a growing consensus that Diem himself was becoming part of the problem.

There was particular unhappiness with his younger brother Nhu, who was reported to be involved in various questionable schemes. Most disturbingly, however, there was clear evidence that Nhu and Diem were exploring a deal with the North and possibly opting for a neutralist solution. Washington was alarmed, and so were some South Vietnamese generals. By August 1963, there were plans to oust Diem, of which John F. Kennedy himself was fully informed. On 24 August, he personally gave the generals the go-ahead, but the coup did not come off at this time.[59]

France got wind of Diem's contacts with the North and of the plans for a coup,[60] and on 29 August Charles de Gaulle reacted. He issued a brief, four-paragraph statement on Vietnam. The words were part of a message to the French Council of Ministers and appeared in the press two days later.[61] De Gaulle stated that France wished to see the people of Vietnam regain their national unity and independence. And he added: 'Naturally it is up to this people, and to them alone, to choose the means of achieving it, but any national effort that would be carried out in Vietnam would find France ready ... to establish cordial co-operation with this country.'[62] The press interpreted the statement as encouraging the South Vietnamese to seek a settlement with the North – with French help and without American interference.

Predictably, Washington was irritated.[63] Even though de Gaulle did not mention neutrality, it seemed to be implied. This was confirmed when on 30 August Alphand was received by Dean Rusk. The French ambassador thought that a neutral solution for Vietnam was possible, because of disagreement between Moscow, Peking, and Hanoi. Mao, Alphand argued, was for a continuation of the war, while Ho and the Soviets had their doubts about Chinese intentions.[64]

De Gaulle's brief statement launched a new debate on neutralisation inside the US government but also in public. On 2 September Walter Cronkite of CBS interviewed the President at Hyannis Port. When asked how he assessed de Gaulle's remarks, Kennedy could not hide his displeasure:

What, of course, makes Americans somewhat impatient is that after carrying this load for 18 years, we are glad to get counsel, but we would like a little more assistance, real assistance. But we are going to meet our responsibility anyway. It doesn't do any good to say, 'Well, why don't we all just go home and leave the world to those who are our enemies.' General de Gaulle is not our enemy. He is our friend and candid friend – and, there, sometimes difficult – but he is not the object of our hostility.[65]

The next day Walter Lippmann wrote a column in which he supported de Gaulle's position and explicitly mentioned neutrality. Lippmann added, 'if there is no settlement such as General de Gaulle proposes, then a protracted and indecisive war of attrition is all that is left.'[66] Kennedy learned about the column, and in a conference held the same day with some of his top decision-makers, he wondered why Walter Lippmann had suggested that the Laotian case provided an illustration of what should be done in Vietnam.[67] By the autumn of 1963, it was obvious that Laotian neutralisation did not work.[68]

The situation in Vietnam became increasingly worrisome, and toward the end of September Kennedy sent General Taylor on another mission, this time in the company of Secretary McNamara. On 2 October, the two submitted a report in which they concluded that despite a deteriorating political situation there was much progress on the military front. They anticipated completing the major part of the task by 1965 and completely withdrawing all US forces by early 1966![69]

This optimistic appraisal motivated Henry Cabot Lodge, the American ambassador in Saigon, to submit to Washington a plan for the possible neutralisation of North Vietnam(!) once the Americans had left the South. Lodge looked for 'a militantly anti-Communist SVN with a Yugoslavia-like neutralist nation to the north'. He also added, 'the neutralisation of NVN might be attractive to the Soviet Union, as counterbalancing the ChiCom influence in Albania. Our reputation among Communists for impatience and impulsiveness might make our proposal plausible to a North Viet-Nam official who is looking for something with which to counter ChiCom hegemony.'[70] Here was a neutralisation plan proposing not to abandon Southeast Asia, not even to 'hold the line' – but to move the line *forward*. Lodge explicitly stated that the plan 'aims at a ChiCom rollback'.

While Lodge was developing this rather absurd scenario, a handful of South Vietnamese generals once more plotted Diem's ouster, again with the full knowledge of the highest levels in Washington. On

2 November, Diem was assassinated. The United States could only hope
that the putschists would in the future handle the Buddhists more intel-
ligently, be more amenable to American demands, and stay away from
negotiating with the NLF. As it turned out, that was but a hopeful wish.
On 22 November, Kennedy himself was killed, and his successor
inherited a difficult situation. In Laos neutralisation had been
attempted and had failed. For Vietnam neutralisation was ruled out
from the beginning, but the military and political results were no
better than in Laos. Given these setbacks, should Kennedy not have listened seriously to those who recommended 'redrawing the line'
through neutralisation? In his memoirs Robert McNamara thinks that
opportunities to do so were missed:

> In retrospect, we erred seriously in not even exploring the neutral-
> ization option. If a sophisticated statesman like de Gaulle thought it
> desirable, it at least deserved close attention.... If France – a charter
> member of SEATO and a prime beneficiary of America's security
> guarantee to NATO – thought a neutralized Vietnam would not seri-
> ously weaken NATO or Western security, then we should, at a
> minimum, have fully debated the issue. We did not.[71]

Kennedy could not fully consider neutralisation as long as he saw it as
just another instrument to contain Communism. That expectation was
realistic in the case of Austria but illusory in Southeast Asia. As Dulles
had argued in 1956, the reasons were domestic: Austrian neutralisation
built on a stable pro-Western government and not on a shaky neutralist coalition or worse, a civil war. Given the domestic instability of Laos
and Vietnam, neutralisation could only mean 'redrawing the line', and
that Kennedy was unwilling to consider. When there were signs that
Diem and Nhu might be willing to negotiate 'the line', Kennedy ruth-
lessly eliminated them. In such an atmosphere it was unthinkable that
neutralisation proposals, whether they emanated from his advisers or
from de Gaulle, would be seriously debated.

Whether Kennedy would have reconsidered his policy after a successful re-election in 1964 remains an open question. According to
some sources he planned to do so, but we will never know for sure.[72]
We do know, however, that the assassination of Diem was a watershed
in the American Vietnam involvement. Highest-level approval of
Diem's elimination in order to achieve American goals created an
atmosphere that was not conducive to a fundamental reorientation of
policy. If Kennedy indeed intended to pull out of Vietnam, he sent the

wrong messages to the generals in Saigon, to his senior advisers at home and, as I will show later on, to Norodom Sihanouk in Cambodia. As McNamara concedes in his memoirs, 'before authorizing the coup against Diem, we failed to confront the basic issues in Vietnam that ultimately led to his overthrow, and we continued to ignore them after his removal.'[73]

Neutralist generals?

It was now Lyndon Baines Johnson who faced an election in 1964. In order to optimise his chances he decided to operate quietly. Dramatic Vietnam decisions were to be avoided at all cost. When he came to office there were 16,000 troops in Vietnam, and over the next year LBJ almost imperceptibly sent another 7000.[74] Domestic politics had priority, and foreign policy was not meant to interfere. Given this atmosphere, few top aides wanted to raise the topic of neutralisation and, as became evident between 1964 and 1965, the neutralisation idea now had its origins mostly within South Vietnam.

Generals Minh and Khanh, who each headed the government for a time during those two years, were suspected of harbouring neutralist sympathies. The reasons were domestic since, like Diem, they walked a political tightrope. The Americans had clear expectations as to how they should run the government and the war, but at the same time the generals were not supposed to be unduly authoritarian and were expected to somehow get along with the Buddhists. The latter chiefly wanted peace and democratic representation, and officially the United States also stood for both. Yet a freely elected government would have been under great pressure to end the fighting by negotiating a political settlement with the NLF. As Emmet John Hughes of *Newsweek* is said to have commented: 'If any elected assembly sits in Saigon, it will be on the phone negotiating with Hanoi within one week.'[75]

There was no elected assembly under General Minh, and yet within less than two months senior Washington policymakers were disappointed with his performance. When it came to running the war, Minh immediately encountered a number of difficulties with the United States. There were disagreements over the strategic hamlet programme, the role and number of American military advisers, and, most importantly, the possible bombing of North Vietnam. But more alarming 'was the possibility that they might negotiate a "neutralist" solution involving an end to the fighting and a compromise agreement with the National Liberation Front.'[76] Contact with the NLF was not difficult.

Minh and other top generals came from Buddhist families, and Minh's brother belonged to the NLF.

On 26 November 1963, only three weeks after Minh had removed Diem, Norodom Sihanouk called publicly for the convening of a 14-Nation Conference to neutralise Cambodia. The Johnson Administration was divided on the issue and, as will be seen in more detail below, remained undecided for two entire years. Opponents worried that a favourable reaction would rekindle talk about Vietnamese neutralisation. But the very fact that Washington was arguing back and forth gave the Vietnamese generals the impression that Washington itself might harbour neutralist plans!

It was a veritable dilemma, and some administration members once more suspected the French of standing behind the Cambodian move. Rumour also had it that de Gaulle intended to establish diplomatic relations with China. That seemed to confirm the worst of suspicions. The problem was compounded when on 10 December Walter Lippmann supported the Cambodian proposal and James Reston of the *New York Times* voiced similar ideas.[77] Rusk reacted immediately. In order to reassure the generals, Rusk cabled to Lodge in Saigon, instructing him to denounce the ideas launched by 'powerful voices' in the press.[78]

In an end-of-the-year report sent to Washington by the embassy, the confusion in Saigon was described in vivid terms:

> Talk of neutralism has spread like wildfire through the Vietnamese community. The *N.Y. Times* editorial and Reston and Lippmann columns on the subject were a body blow to morale in Saigon. The equivocal U.S. stand regarding a conference on Cambodian neutrality took on ominous meaning for many Vietnamese. Even high officials asked: are we next? Rumors of French recognition of the Peiping regime added fuel to the flames. The withdrawal of some forces this month and the suggestion we might pull most of our troops out by the end of 1965 were read by some, however mistakenly, as forerunners of a sharp reduction in our commitment.[79]

Senator Mansfield was active, too. He was scheduled for a talk with the President in early January 1964, and in preparation for the encounter Secretary McNamara sent Johnson a memorandum containing a list of five anti-neutralist arguments. It is uncertain whether the President conveyed McNamara's ideas to the Majority Leader, but if he did, Mansfield heard nothing new. According to the Secretary of Defense, the war was principally a South Vietnamese responsibility (point 1); it could still be won (point 2); neutralising the country would mean a Communist-dominated government in Saigon (point 3); the consequences would be dire for Cambodia, Thailand, Malaysia, and Burma, a truly neutral Southeast Asia would not emerge, and the US capacity to deal with wars of national liberation would be in doubt (point 4); the stakes in preserving an anti-Communist South Vietnam were so high that the United States had to extend every effort to win (point 5).[80]

On 25 January, France announced that it would establish diplomatic relations with China. In commenting on the decision, de Gaulle argued that no issue of war or peace in Asia could be settled without China. He added that 'it would be absolutely impossible to envision, without China, a possible neutrality agreement relating to the Southeast Asian States.'[81] In Washington this set off another wave of neutrality worries that lasted for several months. And in what had become the normal course, much of the trouble originated in South Vietnam itself.

Four days after de Gaulle's announcement, and after just two months in power, Minh was ousted by fellow officers. The new strongman was General Khanh, and he justified the coup, among other things, by claiming that Minh and his friends were pro-French and pro-neutralist.[82] The Johnson Administration immediately accepted the displacement of Minh, and until late summer Washington was generally pleased with Khanh's performance.

In early July, General Maxwell Taylor replaced Henry Cabot Lodge as ambassador. This was a sure sign that more military action was in store. Another signal pointing in the same direction was the retaliatory air strike following the Tonkin Gulf 'incident'. As we know today, Johnson used the minor naval clash to obtain a congressional resolution permitting the executive to pursue the Vietnam War as it saw fit.[83] But the Tonkin Gulf Resolution also served two short-term purposes. At home it undercut Goldwater's claim that Johnson was 'soft on Communism', and in South Vietnam it helped to shore up Khanh's government. But Khanh increasingly came to face the same dilemma as his predecessor. In order to step up the war he had to broaden his political base, but that meant negotiating Buddhist demands. This in turn made him vulnerable to neutralist charges and also worried the Americans, who wanted to step up the war. This was the vicious circle all over again.[84]

George Ball was disappointed with Congress. He had expected that the legislative would insert qualifying language into the Tonkin Gulf

Resolution and feared that now things might really get out of hand. He began to draft a voluminous memorandum that he finished in early October. One of the options he outlined dealt with air warfare:

> We could mount an air offensive against the North to improve our bargaining position for negotiation. But though preferable to a ground force commitment, that would lead to the same result by provoking the North Vietnamese to send ground forces to the South that could be effectively countered only by United States ground forces.[85]

Once again, his prognostics were correct. The top advisers were indeed planning a massive air assault on North Vietnam and were working hard to get the President's approval.[86] In October, with Johnson's landslide victory over Goldwater in sight, Ball submitted the paper to Robert McNamara, McGeorge Bundy, and Dean Rusk and requested a meeting. They met on 7 November, but disagreement was total. There was no point-by-point discussion that Ball had hoped to provoke. The greatest worry was the prevention of a possible leak. Ball's paper never reached the President.[87]

Johnson won the largest electoral mandate in recent history and could have taken new initiatives in foreign policy had he so desired. Various polls showed that up to 75 per cent of the American public favoured negotiations to settle the war in Vietnam.[88] Why not let a neutralist government come to power in South Vietnam and politely bow out? Why not let the neutralists in Saigon get onto the Sihanouk bandwagon and blame the local politicians? This was the last chance to extricate the United States from the war, but Johnson's senior advisers wanted to stay in. They stepped up their efforts to obtain the President's approval for air warfare. Johnson set conditions, however, and the most important was the existence of a stable government in Saigon. Yet Khanh still faced the same dilemma, and now it was becoming more pronounced as the Americans seriously considered the bombing of the North. There were even reports that Khanh, too, was contemplating a neutralist solution!

On 7 February, the Viet Cong attacked a poorly guarded US helicopter base and advisers' barracks at Pleiku. Eight Americans were killed, 126 wounded, and 10 planes destroyed. The incident provided the administration with the opportunity to start the first phase of its bombing programme (Flaming Dart), and on 23 February the second phase was unleashed (Rolling Thunder).[89]

However, there was still no stable government in Saigon, and there was now conclusive evidence that Khanh, like Minh before him, was negotiating seriously with the Buddhists and testing a neutralist arrangement. In order to meet the President's demand, General Westmoreland and Ambassador Taylor decided the time was ripe for a new government. Luckily they managed to convince Khanh that his situation was hopeless and that he should quit unceremoniously. On 24 February, Khan left South Vietnam as Saigon's 'roving ambassador'. The new government was headed by generals Ky and Thieu.[90] On 8 March, the first Marines landed in South Vietnam and were quickly followed by 40,000 additional troops. All told there were now 75,000 American troops in the country, and there were more to come. On 28 July the Administration announced the dispatching of another 50,000 men and a massive stepping up of the military draft. As NSC records reveal, the President was in fact ready to send 100,000 troops.[91] It was now most definitely an American war.

The Vietnamese population began to accept the inevitable and accommodated itself to the massive American presence. As a consequence, the middle ground that the Buddhists had attempted to occupy between the South Vietnamese military and the NLF was eroding. The vicious circle was broken, and from now on the generals in Saigon and the decision-makers in Washington had fewer worries about South Vietnamese neutralism.

Cambodian 'sideshow'

Like Laos, Cambodia was not central to the conduct of the Vietnam War, but as William Shawcross puts it, it was an important sideshow. Seen from an American perspective, relations with Cambodia at that time went through three different phases. From 1954 to 1965, when Sihanouk broke with the United States, the sideshow was mostly peaceful, but that changed with the massive introduction of American forces into Vietnam in 1965. From then on the sideshow assumed an increasingly military and warlike dimension, culminating in Nixon's secret bombardment of 1969, Sihanouk's ouster in 1970, and the massive 'incursion' of the same year. That initiated the third and truly tragic phase, in the course of which Pol Pot fought his way to Phnom Penh and installed a regime that committed genocide on its own people.

The story of the Cambodian tragedy has been told by several authors.[92] In order to gain an understanding of the American conception of Cambodian neutrality it is sufficient to cover the years from 1962 to 1965, when Sihanouk lobbied for the convening of an international conference guaranteeing Cambodian neutrality and territorial integrity. That effort failed definitively when the Johnson Administration decided to commit massive American forces to South Vietnam. As already indicated, this meant the end of an American interest in neutralisation – if such an interest had existed at all.

War was not new to the Cambodian people. Their experience with neighbouring Thailand and Vietnam had long been unhappy. Norodom Sihanouk, like most Cambodians, suspected the Thais and Vietnamese of wanting to further divide and subjugate Cambodia. This was evident in the fact that many of Cambodia's frontiers were being disputed. Since Cambodia was too weak to confront its neighbours directly and alone, the country had a vital interest in influencing them indirectly via the larger world powers. In the 1960s this meant that the Chinese and Soviets should have used their influence to hold back the North Vietnamese, whereas the United States should have applied its weight to rein in the Thais and the South Vietnamese.

This assumed a degree of moderation among the great powers themselves, but in the Cold War the opposite was true. Instead of restraining their local allies, the great powers used them as proxies to promote their own interests – and in Southeast Asia these were antagonistic. Sihanouk could only hope that despite their profound ideological enmity, the Soviets, China, and the United States would show some understanding for Cambodia's desperate situation, but little was forthcoming. Peking and Moscow showed only verbal sympathy for his neutral balancing act, and Washington found it difficult to do even that. US Ambassador William Trimble summed up the situation neatly in a report to the Department of State dated 3 May 1961:

> Cambodian neutrality predicated on balance between major world camps. Without such equilibrium, Cambodians believe neutrality impossible, implying accommodation in that case necessary with winning side. Sihanouk, who formulates Cambodian policy, has expressed conviction that eventual Communist hegemony over world inevitable and in particular that ChiComs 'wave of future' in SEA. However so long as free world power counterbalances bloc, neutrality a viable policy.[93]

Trimble had a working relation with Sihanouk, but he left Phnom Penh in the fall of 1962. After that no influential member of the

American administration showed much understanding for Cambodia's dilemma.[94]

As the war in Vietnam escalated, Sihanouk turned increasingly to the Soviet Union and China but, as it turned out, with little or no success. In the end he and his country were sacrificed by all the major powers. Sihanouk's desperation was revealed clearly in his three attempts to organise an international conference guaranteeing Cambodia's neutrality and territorial integrity. He failed, because none of the great powers was truly behind the idea, but the effort illustrates the specifically American attitude toward Cambodia and toward neutrality.

The first attempt lasted for about a year, from August 1962 to July 1963. Sihanouk announced his plans on 20 August 1962, barely a month after the successful conclusion of the Geneva Conference guaranteeing Laotian neutrality.[95] He stated explicitly that he wanted a similar arrangement, a guarantee of Cambodian neutrality and of its frontiers. Dean Rusk, worried about Thai reactions, immediately sent a cable to the embassy in Bangkok stating unambiguously that he was opposed to the conference mainly because it was likely to 'encourage extension of conference concept to South Viet-Nam'.[96] In a conversation with French Ambassador Alphand in November, Rusk became more specific. He left no doubt about his dislike for guaranteeing neutrality and for discussing disputed frontiers, but what displeased him most was the fact that the plan was aimed against the Thais and the South Vietnamese. This made it difficult for the United States, since 'we are allied with the former under SEATO and heavily engaged with the latter in their struggle for survival'.[97] Members of the NSC staff expressed identical views.[98]

Also in November, the new US ambassador in Phnom Penh, Philip Sprouse, sent three long telegrams to Washington explaining the Cambodian situation, but he stopped short of endorsing the neutralisation plan. He recommended that the United States should co-ordinate its reaction with that of its Western Allies, avoid outright rejection, and consider possible alternatives.[99] This recommendation led to the drafting of a proposal by the office of the Assistant Secretary of State for Far Eastern Affairs, headed by Averell Harriman. It was sent to Dean Rusk on 23 January 1963 in the hope that it would not only meet American requirements 'but be acceptable to the Thai and Vietnamese and hopefully also to Sihanouk'.[100]

Although Kennedy had promised Sihanouk in writing that the American government would give the matter 'urgent attention',[101] nothing came of Harriman's draft proposal. When for months

Washington did not respond, Ambassador Sprouse sent another lengthy message to the Department in May 1963 in which he politely pointed out that except for a Christmas card, no presidential message had been sent to Sihanouk in almost half a year.[102] But other governments also procrastinated, and on 1 July Sihanouk announced that his neutrality proposal had been shelved indefinitely.

The second attempt to launch the plan began in November of the same year and was accompanied by some rather dramatic circumstances. On 2 November, Diem was assassinated, and given Norodom Sihanouk's problematic experience with the CIA, he was frantic that the United States had similar plans in store for him. After all, he, too, was surrounded by generals with American sympathies.[103] To demonstrate his anti-Americanism he embarked on the nationalisation of banks and trading companies, thereby drastically curtailing business with the United States. Furthermore, Sihanouk threatened suspension of US commercial and military aid as well as the severing of diplomatic relations.[104] On 26 November, four days after the assassination of Kennedy, the United States received official notice that Cambodia intended to reconvene the 14-Nation Geneva Conference.[105]

The American reaction was almost identical: once again the administration was split, and procrastination resulted.[106] Dean Rusk, however, had changed his mind. He now told the American embassy in Thailand that he favoured the conference for a number of reasons. He worried that if left alone, Cambodia's internal situation might deteriorate, that a failure to obtain some international statute might be followed by increased Cambodian reliance on the Eastern Bloc, and that there 'are considerable advantages in going to a conference and seeking to mould the result, rather than becoming isolated by refusing [to] participate and removing all restraint on Sihanouk.'[107] Apparently, Sihanouk's pressure tactics had produced some results.

It was now Henry Cabot Lodge in Saigon who opposed the plan most strenuously. He argued that the conference would be disastrous to the war effort in Vietnam, because it encouraged neutralism, promoted talk about unification with the North, and allowed the French to interfere.[108] In the face of such opposition Rusk decided to wait, and once again the US administration was incapable of reacting quickly and favourably.

By mid-February Sihanouk announced that if a conference were not called by May he would break off diplomatic relations with the United States and all of its allies.[109] In March demonstrators attacked the

American embassy in Phnom Penh, and US–Cambodian relations took another turn for the worse.[110] Washington still could not decide on the conference, and in the months to come, relations deteriorated further. In the wake of the Tonkin Gulf incident military activity in South Vietnam was stepped up, and Cambodian border violations became more frequent.

Having failed twice to get a conference by directly appealing to the 14 nations composing the Geneva group, Sihanouk decided to try the indirect route. He organised unilaterally a Conference of Indochinese Peoples in Phnom Penh. The gathering took place in mid-March of 1965 and issued a call for a larger, truly international conference on Cambodian neutrality.[111] As a result, Britain and the Soviet Union, the two co-chairs of the 14-Nation Geneva Conference, once more contacted the United States, but the administration was still divided.[112]

Events then came to a head both in Phnom Penh and in Washington. On 23 April, Sihanouk accused the United States publicly of indecision and added that as matters now stood the idea of a conference was 'outdated'. This prompted Rusk to act, and on 25 April he finally announced American readiness to participate, together with Thailand and South Vietnam. The following day the US embassy in Phnom Penh was attacked for a second time within a year. Officially Sihanouk apologised, but he used the incident to announce on 3 May the suspension of diplomatic relations. By the end of the month all US personnel had left Cambodia.[113]

The quick moves of both Rusk and Sihanouk require some explanation. It was suspected at the time, and documentary evidence confirms it today, that Sihanouk was under Chinese pressure to call off his project. Apparently it was Zhou Enlai personally who asked him to shelve the idea. As long as Washington stalled, the Chinese must have regarded the conference as a useful propaganda weapon, but once the United States responded favourably, Peking feared that the conference might increase Soviet influence over Hanoi and over the war in Vietnam.[114]

The reasons for the sudden American decision also had to do with the conduct of the war in Vietnam. By April 1965, the bombing of North Vietnam had been stepped up dramatically, and US troops were being committed in large numbers. The escalation was part of a carrot-and-stick strategy, or what experts also referred to as coercive diplomacy: while raising the ante, Hanoi would be told that the United States was ready to negotiate.

As a result Washington constantly reiterated its willingness for talks, but for a long time a multilateral neutralisation conference seemed to be the wrong instrument because of its negative effects on Thailand and South Vietnam. However, as the war escalated and the American commitment grew, the two Cambodian neighbours had fewer reasons to suspect the United States of seeking a neutralist solution, and they finally assented. Washington was pleased, because after the massive war efforts the conference would now provide an opportunity to sound out the North.

This idea was suggested by McGeorge Bundy, Johnson's Special Assistant for National Security Affairs. In a memorandum summarising his conversation held with the President on 22 April he stated, 'we should accept the Cambodia Conference and transmit to Hanoi privately the word that we come prepared to discuss larger issues. The latter, of course, should not be said publicly. We do feel it important to let Hanoi know we are serious.'[115] It also explains why Washington, after dragging its feet for nearly three years, held fast to the conference idea for months after diplomatic relations had been broken off, and Sihanouk, together with the Chinese, had abandoned it. In secret direct contacts with the North the conference was mentioned as late as August and September.[116]

For years the United States had cared little about Cambodian neutrality. When it finally agreed to hold the conference it was not to reinforce Cambodian neutrality but to instrumentalise it for 'larger issues', as Bundy told the President. The Cambodian sideshow had left its diplomatic and predominantly peaceful phase; from now on it became progressively military and tragic. The North Vietnamese were increasingly using Cambodian territory as a staging area, and border incidents became frequent. As Senator Mansfield told Johnson in December, the war was on the verge of involving Cambodia.[117]

Cambodia was spared direct and full involvement while Lyndon Baines Johnson was in office, but nevertheless the situation became increasingly desperate, internationally as well as nationally. The economic measures taken in November 1963 sent the economy into a tailspin, alienated the urban rich, and stimulated corruption. Domestic strife increased, and Sihanouk's position began to weaken. Against this background de Gaulle's four-day state visit in August 1966 was a spectacular but ineffective effort to improve Sihanouk's national and international standing.[118] The elections held in September of that year were an expression of the Prince's declining fortunes. Sihanouk could not prevent his antagonists from entering Parliament, and to shore up his position he made General Lon Nol the new Prime Minister. This was one more indication of the increasing militarisation of politics.[119]

The evolving story is summed up well by David Chandler:

> For the next three years Sihanouk, the urban élite, and the Cambodian left were engaged in mortal combat. Broadly, this period can be seen in terms of the left's ascendancy, the urban élite's increasing restlessness, and Sihanouk's decline.[120]

By late 1967 there were indications that in his desperation Sihanouk was trying to mend his fences with the United States. Jackie Kennedy visited the country, and in January 1968, Chester Bowles was sent from his post in New Delhi to see Sihanouk in Phnom Penh. The discussions led to the resumption of diplomatic relations in June of 1969, but Bowles' visit was important for yet another reason. At one point Sihanouk and Bowles discussed the fact that the Vietcong were operating from Cambodian soil and, according to notes taken by members of the American delegation, the Prince, in a reversal of earlier pronouncements, indicated that he would not object to American hot pursuit in unpopulated areas. Years later, this remark was used by Henry Kissinger to justify the large-scale secret bombing of Cambodia that he and Nixon decided on in 1969. It was a desperate attempt at justification, and a twisting of facts. There is no doubt whatsoever that Sihanouk and Bowles had not mentioned massive and prolonged bombing but had spoken of small-scale ground operations.[121]

In 1968 Pol Pot launched the struggle in northwestern Cambodia that led to his conquest in 1975. Furthermore, another successful Tet offensive shattered Washington's expectations that 'the end of the tunnel' was in sight. As a result, Johnson decided in the spring not to run for a second term. In November, Richard Nixon won the elections, and Henry Kissinger became his personal national security adviser. As one of their first foreign policy acts, the two decided to secretly bomb the border areas of Cambodia.[122]

In June, while the bombing was taking its course, Cambodia re-established diplomatic relations with the United States, but the bombing encouraged pro-American Cambodians to further undermine Sihanouk's position. He left the country in January 1970, and, before his planned return in March, he was ousted by his cousin Prince Sirik Matak, in co-operation with General Lon Nol. Whether the United States played an instrumental role in the coup, as was the case in Vietnam when Diem was deposed, is still uncertain.[123] Whatever the exact link, it was only shortly afterwards that Nixon decided to invade Cambodia on the ground. The country's sovereignty and neutrality was now violated massively by both sides of the Vietnam War.[124] It took the Khmer Rouge another five years to reach their goal but, as Kenton J. Clymer remarks, 'had the United States and Cambodia been able to resolve their differences constructively, Cambodia might have been spared the holocaust it endured.'[125]

The fates of all three countries of former French Indochina were tragic, but that of Cambodia surpassed them all. Norodom Sihanouk was correct in his view that neutrality was the only conceivable alternative, but given the confrontation between Washington and Hanoi, neutrality had no chance. This was true for Laos and South Vietnam. As I argued above, the reasons for this failure did not lie primarily in a false understanding of neutrality, but rather in overall foreign policy conceptions that, as we know today, turned out to be mistaken both on the North Vietnamese and the American sides.

The situation in Europe had been very different. In ideological terms the Cold War was as bitter in Europe as it was in Asia, but the two sides, however precariously, managed to stabilise the confrontation by respecting their respective zones of influence. The two Berlin crises and the Hungarian Revolution are evidence of this fact. In Southeast Asia such an arrangement was lacking, and the situation was more complex. In Europe the clash was bipolar. The NATO countries confronted those of the Warsaw Pact or, more precisely, the United States faced the Soviet Union. In Southeast Asia the constellation was multipolar: besides the Soviet Union and the United States, China was a factor as well, and that complicated matters.

Tripolarity meant less discipline, and this showed in the fact that neither Moscow nor Peking had real control over the North Vietnamese. In fact, for many years Hanoi managed to play the two Communist powers off against each other while obtaining the necessary assistance to carry on the war. Much more so than the Americans calculated, Hanoi had its own foreign policy agenda and was in fact a 'loose gun'. Equally troublesome, however, was the difficulty that all the powers had in figuring out China. No one seemed to be quite sure what Mao's foreign policy aims were and how they related to the ongoing Cultural Revolution. The inscrutability of China was an additional factor complicating multipolarity, and for the United States this turned out to be decisive. A different assessment of China would have entailed a different definition of American security interests in the area, and it might also have led to another conception of neutrality.

The China factor

After de Gaulle recognised China in 1964, the impact of that country on the war was a regular topic in Washington and, as documents show, the American Vietnam policy was heavily influenced by the 'China factor'. The administration's attitude toward China also explains a number of issues related to neutralisation. It indicates why Vietnam was considered vital for American security, why so much value was placed on honouring the SEATO commitment, and, finally, why world-wide credibility was supposed to be at stake.

China debates were not new in Washington. They had occurred several times before, and from a military perspective they often revolved around the question of whether the United States should fight on the 'Asian mainland'. The issue had a geopolitical dimension that went back to the nineteenth century when Admiral Mahan, in the spirit of Halford Mackinder, conceived of American security in largely naval terms. He saw the United States as a large 'island' flanked by immense oceans. Control of these waters was considered 'vital', and it was in the interest of the United States to maintain a strong navy and to occupy strategically important points. Mahan meant Hawaii and the Philippines, but as a result of the Second World War and the communist takeover in China, Japan and Taiwan were also added to the list.

In naval terms, therefore, American security interests ended in the 'blue waters of the Pacific' and did not extend to the Asian mainland. If the United States had interests at all on the mainland, they were of a secondary nature and would not warrant massive intervention. The contrast with Europe was obvious. After the Second World War and especially with the coming of the Cold War, Western Europe – although in naval terms also located on the Eurasian mainland – was considered vital for American security, as evidenced in the creation of NATO.

While there was general agreement on the European commitment, there was much disagreement over where to draw the line in Asia. This was evident with respect to Korea. As a result of the Second World War, the United States had troops stationed south of the 38th Parallel, but the Truman Administration was ill at ease with this commitment and ready to leave the mainland as soon as possible. When the Korean War broke out that became impossible, and when the American troops were thrown back to the 38th Parallel by the intervening Chinese, a furious debate erupted over the wisdom of fighting on the Asian mainland.

The division ran mainly along party lines. For the Republicans, but also for General MacArthur, America had clear security interests on the mainland; the Democrats denied this and stuck by the traditional concept. The issue was never clearly settled, but when the Republicans came to office they not only aimed at the isolation of China but also tried to roll back the 'bamboo curtain', as it was called. The creation of SEATO and the commitment to South Vietnam were part of this strategy.

Although Kennedy was a Democrat, he did not return to the Roosevelt–Truman line but, as shown, carried on in the Dulles tradition. In his and Johnson's administrations Dean Rusk was the most explicit exponent of this continuity. As a former State Department 'Asia hand' he had survived the McCarthy era unscarred and in his memoirs admits having supported the Roosevelt–Truman doctrine. As a result he originally disapproved of the Eisenhower Administration's Asia policy:

> Although I was out of government and watching only from the side-lines, I thought that the SEATO Treaty was a mistake. Of course, we in the Kennedy and Johnson administration made our own decisions on Vietnam, and events of the 1960s remain our responsibility, but I think the die for American commitment to Southeast Asia was cast in 1955. When the United States signed that treaty, SEATO became the law of the land and linked South Vietnam to the general structure of collective security.[126]

It is true, of course, that SEATO was a turning point, but it linked Vietnam only tenuously to the American alliance system, or 'the general structure of collective security', as Rusk preferred. His interpretation seems exceedingly legalistic and can only be understood if 'ChiCom' is brought into the picture. SEATO was meant to contain Chinese expansion in Southeast Asia and, as Lodge showed in his neutralisation plan, it was intended to promote roll-back! A number of officials in Washington had never quite overcome the 'loss' of China in 1949.

As indicated earlier, the Department of State was right in anticipating Chinese intervention in case the United States massively invaded North Vietnam on the ground, thereby provoking another Korean situation. Some Chinese evidence now available points in the same direction.[127] But the American administration miscalculated the global dimensions of the Chinese threat, and in this it deviated from the perceptions of its European allies.

The difference between the American and the European standpoints shows neatly in two discussions Dean Rusk held in 1964. Both involved French diplomats and dealt with China – and neutralisation. On 12 April, Rusk met French Foreign Minister Couve de Murville at the American Embassy in Manila. The conversation centred on the French understanding of neutrality and quickly turned to the role of China. In the eyes of Couve de Murville China was 'an expansionist, imperialist country', and Southeast Asia had always been a target of China's expansionism. 'All Southeast Asian countries are terrified at the thought of Chinese expansion', Couve added, but he thought it was in China's own interest to reach an accommodation with the West:

> ... in order to concentrate on internal development and to reduce the threat to it, China would renounce its expansionist drive in Southeast Asia on the understanding that Southeast Asia would not be hostile. The Hanoi government would have to follow suit.[128]

China was also the topic of a second conversation held in July between Rusk and French Ambassador Alphand. Alphand felt that it was necessary to talk to the Chinese, upon which Rusk replied that the United States had talked with them more seriously than any other Western nation: 'We have not ignored China but we haven't liked what we have heard in these talks.'[129] The difference between the French and Rusk was obvious: France was willing to live with Chinese expansion and thought it could somehow be accommodated, but Dean Rusk saw no such possibility. To him the Chinese threat was global rather than regional.

Walter Lippmann, when at the White House on 31 May, also discussed China. Present were Secretary McNamara, National Security Adviser McGeorge Bundy, and George Ball. The President sat in on part of the discussion. According to a summary written by George Ball, Lippmann stated that the course of action he proposed 'was based on the assumption that all of Southeast Asia was destined inevitably to become a zone of Chinese Communist control', that the United States 'could not halt Chinese expansionism in that area', and that the best hope 'was to seek by political means to slow that expansionism down and make it less brutal'.[130]

The three conversations reveal that the proponents of neutralisation had a view of China that was rejected by most officials in Washington. While everyone agreed that China was an expansionist and even imperialist power, the administration thought that accommodation was out of the question. In the administration's view, this was no longer the Imperial China of former centuries, as Chester Bowles would have it, and neither was it the China of the Second World War, as Mansfield claimed. As the recent border incidents with India and the unleashing of the Cultural Revolution showed, Mao's China had become an intensely ideological power with universal ambitions unwilling to coexist with its capitalist enemies. In tandem with the Soviet Union it was spreading revolution around the globe, often under the mantle of neutralism. It was an illusion to argue, as Alphand and Mansfield did, that there were serious differences between Moscow and 'Peiping' over influence in Southeast Asia. There was more to unite the two Communist powers than to separate them.

Given the world-wide dimension of the challenge, American security interests reached beyond the Pacific Ocean and included the Asian mainland. As Rusk told Ambassador Alphand in an earlier conversation, he and Kennedy saw Southeast Asia and Vietnam as vital to American security.[131] And as he emphasised in his memoirs, this region was every bit as vital as Cuba or Berlin.[132] On this last point the French disagreed completely, and so did Ball, Bowles, Mansfield, and Lippmann. In their eyes an American withdrawal from Southeast Asia would not affect European security; on the contrary, it would enhance it. Should the United States get lost in the paddies and jungles of Vietnam, as Ball liked to say, it would damage rather than help NATO and 'collective security'. They all agreed that Europe was more important than Southeast Asia. Redrawing the line through neutralisation would in effect increase American credibility in Europe.

12
Summary and Conclusions

Conceptions before 1941

As I stated at the outset of this study, the United States was intimately involved in both the rise and the demise of neutrality. America contributed in an important way to the shaping of classical neutrality in the eighteenth and nineteenth centuries, but it was equally instrumental in weakening neutrality in the twentieth century. The decisive turning point was the year 1941, when the United States once and for all changed from isolationism to international involvement. Before 1941 the country had regularly been neutral, afterwards no more. The reversal altered the American conception of neutrality and contributed to neutrality's general decline. The origins of the reversal lie before 1941, however, and any attempt to appreciate its significance must begin with a look at the past. The purpose of this final chapter is to summarise the American experience with neutrality and to draw general conclusions.

From 1776 to 1914, the United States adhered to a classical neutrality conception. It embraced a number of rules laid down in international law that regulated neutral conduct in times of war. The rules pertained mainly to military matters but also included the right of free trade with all belligerents. This broad and comprehensive conception was also called integral neutrality. It stood in contrast to qualified neutrality, a term implying the voluntary or forced abandonment of the right to trade freely. Integral neutrality coincided for many years with American military and economic interests.

It is not surprising that *militarily* the United States wanted to abstain from international conflict. America was a weak and vulnerable nation in the early years of its existence and could only lose by getting involved in great power rivalries. It was natural, therefore, that George Washington, faced with the possibility of siding with France against Great Britain in 1793, decided to remain uninvolved and impartial. This was the first instance of American neutrality, and there were more to come. As time went on, the United States contributed in an important way to the definition of neutral military duties at sea. At that time military abstention governed by rules of international law gave America more security than military power or alliances. Of course, this presupposed that other nations would honour the laws of neutrality. In the nineteenth century, this was by and large the case.

Economic interests were also helped. America carried on trade with many parts of the world, even in times of war. As one of the first American foreign policy acts, therefore, the 'Plan of 1776' was worked out. It contained a long list of neutral trading rights in times of war. If free trade represented an American commercial interest, it also squared with the liberal philosophy of economics. As propagated by Adam Smith and as practised by Americans, the free trade philosophy was staunchly *universalist* in character, and its *multilateralist* features were bound to clash with the *unilateralist* conception of military noninvolvement and of neutrality. This is what happened during the Wars of the French Revolution but most dramatically in the First World War. During most of the nineteenth century, however, the tensions did not show. Given the limited nature of the various wars, it was possible for neutrals to carry on trade while conflicts were taking place. Had the international system been more polarised and the conduct of war less limited, the tensions would have become apparent much earlier.

When the moderate nineteenth-century system disappeared and the First World War broke out, the contradictions became apparent. In the face of what quickly became a total war, the United States abandoned a number of neutral duties and, most importantly, almost all its neutral trading rights. This hurt, since few Americans were willing to forego rights for which they had struggled so long.

International law permitted the neutral to *enforce* his rights, yet military enforcement meant different things to different people. When the traditionalists called for military action, they meant measures to defend the classical conception of neutrality. When Woodrow Wilson called for military action, he thought of something very different. He, too, wanted to fight for the maintenance of free trade but in his eyes power politics had to be transcended. Wilson was ready to make the world a safer place both for liberal trade *and* for democracy. In so doing he ended the contradiction inherent in neutrality, the tensions between a multilateral conception of trade and a unilateral conception of security. From now on, American economic *and* security interests would be global; collective commerce would be matched by collective security. It meant abandoning neutrality once and for all, a step that proved to be too sudden. After the experience of the First World War and the wrangling over the merits of the League of Nations, America returned to isolation.

It was not a return to classical neutrality, however. Classical neutrality continued to have its adherents, but they were gradually losing influence. A new form of neutrality gained popularity: neo-isolationist neutrality. Its logic was simple and appealing – America should match military withdrawal with economic withdrawal and try to stay out of war for good. The result of this argument was the embargo legislation of 1935, 1936, and 1937, called Neutrality Acts. In the 1930s, the neo-isolationists had the upper hand. The internationalists, like the traditionalists, could not sway the country. But they attempted to steer American foreign policy in an internationalist direction whenever they could. Internationalist neutrals also tried to influence the various Neutrality Acts by turning embargoes into sanctionist instruments against possible aggressors, thereby allowing the United States indirectly to become a 'supporting state' of the League. The Neutrality Acts ultimately passed were a combination of various ideas and contained components of all three schools of neutrality. Overwhelmingly, however, they were neo-isolationist in nature.

This uneasy situation prevailed when war broke out again in Europe, but it did not last for long. Roosevelt systematically drove the neo-isolationists out of Congress, and the traditionalists, for some time now a dwindling group, disappeared quietly. The internationalists now had the upper hand. Henceforth the United States would adhere to a predominantly (but not exclusively) universalist worldview comprising a multilateralist component. It remained to be seen, however, whether the *moderate* or the *radical* internationalists would be more influential. Moderate internationalists were willing to accept military abstention but expected co-operation in economic warfare; radical internationalists were unwilling to tolerate any kind of neutrality, because for them the total transformation of international politics was at stake. As part of their universalist conception they were going to abandon 'balance of power politics', outlaw war, and practice collective security. Which group would be more influential, the radicals or the moderates? Now that the United States itself had foresworn neutrality – how tolerant would it be of the neutrality of others and how greatly would this affect the existence of neutrality in general? That is the question at the heart of this study.

The Second World War

In the conduct of war, the moderately internationalist conception of neutrality prevailed: America expected the remaining neutrals to pursue the kind of neutrality that many internationalist neutrals had wanted to practise before the war. This meant that during the war, the United States respected military neutrality but demanded co-operation in economic warfare. Compensations for bombing damages to neutrals, for instance, were paid according to established international custom, but the neutral right of free trade was not respected. As a result, America, in the conduct of hostilities, adhered not to an integral form of neutrality but rather to a qualified one.

There were good reasons for tolerating *military neutrality*. In the early years of the war, the American military position was so weak that every neutral, especially those having some military strength and located close to Germany, was regarded as an asset to the Allied cause. Better to have a neutral than another ally of Germany. Impartiality and non-involvement, too, could be of help. Sweden and Switzerland extended their good offices, and these could benefit American citizens, properties, POWs, and communications with the enemy. America discovered that neutrals could share the same humanitarian values and could be ideological allies.

All this seemed irrelevant, however, when it came to *economic warfare*. Particularly towards the end of the war, Sweden and Switzerland came under considerable pressure to become 'supporting states' and to participate in economic sanctions against Germany. Some of these measures were carried on in the name of the wartime alliance or, to be precise, on behalf of the nascent United Nations. As far as the two neutrals were concerned, they were forced into a position similar to the one advocated for the United States by the moderate internationalists before the war.

This showed most clearly with respect to 'Safehaven', a programme of economic coercion elaborated by the American government and sanctioned by the Allies at Bretton Woods. Under this programme, Switzerland, in particular, came under pressure, because it had acquired Germany monetary gold as well as German assets of Nazi and of Jewish origin. Efforts to enforce the programme were carried on into the postwar years; American economic warfare did not stop when military warfare ended.

The spirit of *radical internationalism* prevailed in the drafting of the United Nations Charter. The document is strongly universalist in matters of politics, security, and economics. The new world organisation was to be a true 'community of power', thereby replacing the old 'balance of power' system. From now on, the management of international conflict would be every nation's business, and isolation, indifference and impartiality would no longer be tolerated. For the Americans, UN membership meant overcoming the isolationist and essentially unilateralist past once and for all.

At heart it was a renewal of Wilsonian internationalism. Yet the United Nations Charter was more universalist and anti-neutral in spirit than the League Covenant. Under the latter peace became the business of all states, yet war as such was not outlawed, and the conduct of hostilities was left up to each individual state. The UN Charter went further. It explicitly outlawed the unleashing of war and made the conduct of hostilities the organisation's business. Enforcement measures would no longer be carried on along traditional lines. International command structures were planned, and new rules of warfare (actually of police action) were meant to be written. This was one of the main reasons why the United Nations International Law Commission would not even discuss the traditional laws of war and neutrality in its deliberations. It goes to show the strength with which radical internationalism prevailed in the spirit of the Charter.

Hostility towards neutrality also prevailed at the founding conference in San Francisco. Not only were the neutrals excluded from participation but neutrality was condemned explicitly, first in the opening address of the American Secretary of State and then in a French–American agreement on the question of admission. A passage was written into the official protocol that UN membership was incompatible with neutrality.

In Paris, in 1919, there was no anti-neutral sentiment. It is true that the representatives of neutral countries were not present at the negotiating table either, but they were tolerated in the wings, and they expressed their countries' points of view. The Swiss even managed to influence Wilson's decisions. For one, they obtained a promise that their neutrality would be compatible with the Covenant (this was later formally acknowledged by the League members), and Wilson could also be convinced that the new organisation should be located on neutral territory. In Wilson's eyes neutrality could be helpful to collective security.

Radical internationalism did not prevail for very long after 1945. At Potsdam, America agreed to admitting neutrals to the United Nations if they were 'willing and able' to fulfil the obligations of the Charter, and one year later the United States approved the admission of Sweden. In the following years, the United States co-operated constructively in the revision of the Geneva Red Cross Conventions, a document that is part of the traditional law of war and also mentions neutrality. As the Cold War approached and the United Nations became increasingly inoperable, conflict had to be settled outside the organisation and with more traditional methods. In this context neutrality surfaced regularly as an issue in American foreign policy. This was the case in the founding of NATO, the conduct and the termination of the Korean War, the settling of the German and Austrian questions, and the conduct of the Vietnam War.

Still, radical internationalism had a lasting impact on postwar politics. International law was never to be the same again. There were now two systems of law, one traditional and one modern, one fitting the classical state system and another tailored to the needs of collective security. In actual conflict situations this meant uncertainty as to the applicability of one system of law or the other. Often it ended in the application of no law at all. A growing state of 'lawlessness' was the result. This also affected neutrality. Since the Second World War, there have been very few formal declarations of neutrality, and neutral law has hardly been cited in legal proceedings. This further promoted the decline of that body of law, a development that had begun as early as the outbreak of the First World War.

Cold War and Korea

With the outbreak of the Cold War the international system polarised for the third time within half a century. Given the centrality of atomic weapons, war became more total than ever before, if only in the shape of nuclear deterrence. Quite obviously, this was not a propitious context for the practice of classical neutrality. Neutrality, therefore, continued its decline, a development that had begun with the American reversal in 1917. As I will show, its legal core was almost entirely lost. Neutrality became a purely political notion with contours that were increasingly difficult to define.

When NATO was founded, the United States adopted the same qualified conception of neutrality it had practised in the Second World War. Although there were attempts to turn Sweden into an American ally, the United States ended up respecting Swedish and Swiss military independence. However, pressure was put on both countries to co-operate in the implementation of the Cocom embargo against NATO's communist enemies. The idea of the 'supporting state', originating as it did in the interwar period, continued to have its validity, although circumstances had changed profoundly.

While the United States was organising NATO, Sweden made efforts to set up a Neutral Nordic Bloc meant to separate the Eastern and the Western alliance systems. It would have meant the extension of Swedish neutrality to most of Scandinavia. The scheme failed not only because Norway preferred to join NATO, but also because the United States did not want to see an expansion of Swedish neutrality. Some State Department officials even pressured Sweden to abandon its own neutrality and to join NATO, but the effort failed. Strategic considerations played a part; the Pentagon was convinced that Sweden would not be able to withstand a Russian advance through Scandinavia.

At first glance neutrality experienced a revival during the *Korean War*, because it played a part both in the conduct of hostilities and in the termination of the conflict. On closer scrutiny, however, the concept was much abused, and its meaning became fuzzy. In the conduct of hostilities, the United States tried to avoid the issue of neutrality whenever possible. At times this was facilitated by the inconsistent behaviour of the Russians and the Chinese. Both could have drawn the United States into awkward questions of neutral law but chose not to do so.

In the termination of hostilities, neutrality surfaced prominently. Two neutral commissions were set up to deal with the supervision of the truce and the repatriation of POWs. Every side at Panmunjom had the right to appoint two neutrals, so that in the end there were, in American parlance, two 'aggressor neutrals' (Poland and Czechoslovakia) and two 'UNC neutrals' (Sweden and Switzerland). The neutrals were in a curious position. Those on the American side were the agents of the United Nations, the very organisation that only a few years earlier had declared that neutrality was incompatible with the Charter. Now the United Nations possessed its own neutrals. The neutrals on the Communist side were in a strange position, because their governments had supplied the aggressors with arms and were, by traditional standards, anything but neutral. They could be regarded as such only because the definition of neutrality was based on the concept of 'non-participation', a term referring to those nations whose combatant forces did not participate in the hostilities. By those minimal standards almost any country was neutral. Needless to say, a commission made up of such 'neutrals' could not function. The fronts of the Cold War ran through the very centre of such a body, and if there was any chance of making it operable a fifth member would have to be found. This was the case with the Neutral Nations Repatriation Commission. Each side seemed eager to bring its captured soldiers home, and so India was selected as a chairman, executive agent, and umpire of the commission. India, therefore, was the only truly impartial neutral in the sense that it had obtained the trust of both sides. The irony was, however, that India did not claim to be neutral in the traditional sense but neutralist or non-aligned. The emergence of these concepts did not help matters. The uncertainty as to the exact meaning of neutrality was only heightened.

During the Korean War *economic sanctions* were stepped up. The Cocom lists were expanded and also applied to China. The European neutrals came under special pressure to conform. For Sweden and Switzerland it was a repetition of their experience in the Second World War: there was no tolerance of 'courant normal'. The British were more generous in the eighteenth and nineteenth centuries: they did not permit the United States to carry on free trade, but they did allow 'courant normal'. The concept, like neutrality itself, lost much of its former clarity.

Neutralism and neutrality

During the Cold War the polarisation of the international system was not total. There was a group of non-aligned states consisting mostly of former colonies that had just gained their independence. Headed by Nehru, Tito, Sukarno, and Nasser, the movement called itself 'neutralist', but their neutrality was not of the traditional kind and had little or nothing to do with that of permanent neutrals such as Sweden and Switzerland. Neutralist states were not wedded to a policy of absolute military abstention and peace. Several of them fought wars when it suited their purpose. Also, neutralism was not grounded in international law but merely in the tensions of the Cold War. It was the intention of these countries to belong neither to the Eastern nor to the Western bloc. The appearance of neutralist countries on the international scene did not help to clarify the concept of neutrality. To the contrary, its meaning continued to suffer.

John Foster Dulles exhibited difficulty in dealing with neutralist countries, and he had trouble distinguishing between them and the traditional neutrals. Although Dulles could be entirely pragmatic at times, he had a tendency to see things in strongly moral and even religious terms. The neutrals and neutralists did not fit well into this frame of mind. In the famous 'neutrality muddle' of 1956, he and Eisenhower managed to confuse public opinion completely about the meaning of neutrality and neutralism.

At other times, the Eisenhower Administration had a more lucid and constructive view of the subject. This was the case when *Austria* was neutralised. Basically it was a Russian idea, but Dulles quickly agreed and made a valuable contribution: at his behest Austria was not neutralised by an international treaty but by its own unilateral action. It gave the Russians no legal pretext for future interventions. In view of what happened later on in Hungary and Czechoslovakia, this was a wise decision. The case of Austria showed that America was not disinclined to use neutralisation as a means for settling Cold War conflicts and for promoting international peace and security. The neutralisation of Austria was a positive event in the development of the American conception of neutrality after 1941, but some questions remained.

 The neutralisation of Austria was a political move that in no way implied renewed respect for the traditional law of neutrality. Actually, from a legal standpoint, the status of neutrality was now more confused than ever, because the Big Four, when neutralising Austria, also decided to admit the country to the United Nations. By so doing they showed great pragmatism, but they did not in any way deal with the legal questions involved. In the case of Security Council sanctions, what system of law would Austria have to follow, that of the United Nations (which would rob it of its neutrality) or that of traditional international law (which would permit its maintenance)? Presumably such questions would be left up to the Austrians to answer when the occasions arose.

The issue was further complicated by the fact that upon Russian insistence Austria was supposed to practise perpetual neutrality 'as handled by Switzerland'. The irony was that because of their adherence to classical and integral neutrality, the Swiss at that time regarded UN membership as problematic and refused to join the organisation. But Austria, meant to be neutral like Switzerland, was asked to join! Quite evidently, a number of legal questions about neutrality remained unsettled.

However, the Eisenhower Administration was unwilling to envisage neutralisation for countries located behind the Iron Curtain. The position papers on 'roll-back' do not mention neutralisation as one of the options. Given the massive Russian military presence in Eastern Europe, neutralisation was an unlikely alternative, but not an entirely unrealistic one, as the example of Hungary went to show. Tito, too, had managed to become non-aligned. The Eisenhower Administration was simply not willing to embrace neutrality and neutralism in a general way. Austria remained an exception.

The same reasoning applied to *Germany*, although in this case questions of military strength were topmost in Dulles' mind. On more than one occasion he made it perfectly clear that Germany was too large and important a country for neutralisation, especially if that should imply armed neutrality, as it did in the case of Austria and the other European neutrals. The neutralisation of Germany would have overturned the Eisenhower Administration's entire defence strategy, which, partly for budgetary reasons, aimed at increasing American nuclear strength while decreasing its conventional presence in Asia and Europe. Allies were to assume some of the conventional burden, and a rearmed Western Germany was vital for this reason. Rearmament could be tied to membership in the European Defence Community or, as eventually happened, to NATO membership. Germany was to be part of a strong and multilateral security community.

The same attitudes prevailed half a century later when German unification became a reality. Even though the Russians mentioned neutralisation they had no interest in seeing a militarily independent Germany. Virtually everyone agreed that German neutralisation was not in the interest of European stability. Fortunately, the Germans themselves were opposed to neutralisation. When the Cold War ended it had become clear that – in Europe at least – history was not on the side of neutrality but of multilateral security and supranational integration. In the North–Atlantic area classical 'balance of power politics' had come to an end. Woodrow Wilson would not have been overly surprised, one would assume.

During the Cold War, neutrality was also an issue in *Southeast Asia*. However, it never assumed the importance it did in Europe. The 1954 Geneva Conference provided the French with an opportunity to withdraw from that part of the world, but the agreement settled very little. In contrast to Europe there were no stable Cold War frontiers, no Iron Curtain. Internally, too, the countries lacked stability. Laos, Cambodia, and South Vietnam were politically torn and in danger of succumbing to the regional hegemony of Ho Chi Minh's North Vietnam. As US administration officials liked to say, somewhere they had to 'hold the line'. Yet, as in Korea, there was disagreement as to where the line should be drawn: In the 'blue waters of the Pacific' or on the Asian mainland? Judging Laos to be of only secondary strategic importance, Kennedy decided to give neutralisation a try. He also showed some understanding for the type of neutralism practised by Norodom Sihanouk in Cambodia. However, developments indicated unmistakenly that neutralisation did not stabilise either country and that it worked to the advantage of North Vietnam. J. F. Kennedy was unwilling to witness similar tendencies in Vietnam and decided to oppose forcefully the country's neutralisation. It was a policy also followed by Lyndon B. Johnson. Richard Nixon and Henry Kissinger went further, however, and terminated what was left of Cambodian neutralism.

It took Kennedy and Johnson a while to find South Vietnamese generals willing to form a truly anti-neutralist government and to fight the North. However, the American effort failed; North Vietnam eventually conquered the South. Given Ho Chi Minh's hegemonic ambitions, neutrality had no place in Southeast Asia. At best neutralisation could have served the United States as a pretext to extricate itself from a mistaken military adventure on the Asian mainland. Some of Johnson's advisers toyed with the idea after the landslide victory against Barry Goldwater in 1965. Instead, Johnson decided to drastically increase the American military commitment.

The 'American century' and the decline of neutrality

Let me now summarise the American conception of neutrality after 1941. The eighteenth and nineteenth centuries saw the rise of neutrality; the twentieth century witnessed its gradual decline. Neutrality was an integral part of the multipolar European 'balance of power', a system in which war was considered normal and rational, but where conflicts remained short and their conduct was restrained. By modern standards it was a moderate type of international politics. Neutrality flourished under these circumstances but declined when the structure of the system changed and conflicts became long, ideological and total. During the twentieth century the system vacillated regularly between extreme polarisation on the one hand and attempts at multilateral pacification on the other. Wars, in turn, became increasingly immoderate, long, and ideological. Neutrality suffered from both developments, from the *changing nature of war* and from the extreme *shifts in structure*.[1]

The American experience with neutrality runs parallel to this development. In the eighteenth and nineteenth centuries the United States was a minor player in international affairs profiting from the European balance and from neutrality. In the twentieth century the country became a major power participating in total wars and developing a highly qualified conception of neutrality. America contributed actively to the rise and the fall of neutrality. As a neutral it promoted the growth of the classical law of war and of neutrality; as a large power it fought ideological wars, participated in polarising alliance systems, and undertook efforts to pacify the system through multilateralism. The United States was anything but a passive bystander.

The present study focuses on America's contribution to the *demise of neutrality* after 1941. In this period the United States made major attempts to restructure the international system and to change the nature of war. The story is complex, has many dimensions and cannot be subsumed easily under one heading. Various American presidents having different conceptions of world politics were involved, and they confronted a motley group of opponents: autocratic monarchs, fascist tyrants and Bolshevik dictators. One fact stands out clearly, however: the United States assumed world leadership, put its stamp on world politics and turned the era into what some have called an 'American century'. For better or worse, it was the United States that dominated twentieth-century world affairs.

There is no coherent US doctrine of international politics, no single ideology giving substance to the 'American century'. The United States is too pluralistic and diverse to produce a systematic world view. Contradictions are inherent in US foreign policy. Moments of narrow national self-interest alternate with moments of generous solidarity; the pursuit of universal peace can go hand in hand with a complete disregard for human rights. America has promoted theories of unilateral and of multilateral war and of limited and of total conflict. In some parts of the world the United States encouraged co-operation and integration; in other parts it promoted nationalism and conflict. Still, American foreign policy is not a mere conglomerate of pragmatic decisions and actions. Some themes are fairly clear.

To begin with, the United States – once it assumed world leadership – did not subscribe to a systematic continuation of European 'balance of power politics'. Although there were 'realist' moments in American foreign policy when some of the practices advocated by Metternich, Bismarck, or Churchill dominated, the United States never really subscribed to Realpolitik. Liberalism is too deeply engrained in American political culture for a systematic pursuit of conservative values. There is a strong Wilsonian streak in the American tradition, often identified as 'idealist'. It is based on two major convictions: first, that war is not to be considered as a normal, natural, and neutral occurrence that man must suffer fatalistically and, second, that unilateralism (or bilateralism) should whenever possible give way to multilateralism. The two principles imply a transformation of nineteenth-century European politics and undermine the classical (and conservative) conception of war and of diplomacy. To implement these principles the United States at times engaged in radical internationalism. More often, however, it practised a moderate type of internationalism that, among other things, spelled the decline of classical neutrality.

At the global level the impact showed in the founding of the United Nations. Although the organisation is too weak to guarantee universal peace and to implement the rule of law, it has undertaken first steps in that direction and thereby undermined the classical conception of neutrality and its practice in actual conflict situations. At the regional level, the American impact is most clearly visible in Europe. When initiating economic reconstruction after the Second World War the United States insisted upon the creation of a multilateral body, the OEEC. When the United States entered into a military alliance with the Europeans, it suggested the establishment of NATO. Finally, when the Europeans untertook first steps to integrate by setting up the EEC, they could count on American backing.

The supranational EEC has evolved to become the European Union (EU), and NATO has been converted into a Euro-Atlantic security partnership extending to Eastern Europe. Together the two organisations have changed the rules of European politics and undermined neutrality. Three permanent neutrals, Austria, Sweden, and Finland, have joined the EU and are co-operating closely with NATO. Nominally they still adhere to neutrality, but their decision to integrate signals the beginning of the final phase in the decline of classical neutrality. Switzerland is more reluctant to integrate but will join the Union in due course. The trend is irreversible.

Neutrality might very much be alive if American leadership had been more unilateralist and traditionally conservative. If the United States had withdrawn from Europe after the end of the Cold War, NATO could have become a mere paper alliance. The re-nationalisation of European security policy would have ensued, European integration might have stagnated, and balancing could have been resumed.[2] Under such circumstances many of the Eastern European countries might have opted for a position of neutrality. Such scenarios were in the minds of some politicians, and there were experts predicting that neutrality would get a new lease on life.[3] They were wrong. In Europe, the birthplace of classical neutrality, the concept is gradually fading away.

Notes and References

Introduction

1. United States Department of State, *Foreign Relations of the United States* (Washington D.C.: US Government Printing Office), Vol. I, II, IV, V, XXIII, XXIV (1961–63), Vol. I, II, III, IV, XXVIII (1964–68).
2. United States Department of State, *U.S. and Allied Efforts To Recover and Restore Gold and Other Assets Stolen or Hidden by Germany During World War II*, co-ordinated by Stuart E. Eizenstat, Undersecretary of Commerce for International Trade (Washington D.C.: US Government Printing Office, May 1997 – *Eizenstat Report*); Unabhängige Expertenkommission Schweiz-Zweiter Weltkrieg, *Die Schweiz und die Goldtransaktionen im Zweiten Weltkrieg*, Zwischenbericht (Bern: EDMZ, 1998 – *Bergier Report*).
3. Jürg Martin Gabriel, 'The Price of Political Uniqueness', in Jürg Martin Gabriel and Thomas Fischer (eds), *Swiss Foreign Policy in a Changing World: 1945–2000* (forthcoming).
4. *FRUS*, Vol. V (1955–57), pp. 11–115.
5. *Dokumente zur Deutschlandpolitik*, Deutsche Einheit, Sonderedition aus den Akten des Bundeskanzleramtes 1989/90 (eds) Hanns Jürgen Küsters and Daniel Hofmann, (München: Oldenbourg, 1998).
6. Jürg Martin Gabriel, 'La neutralidad de Suiza y de Costa Rica', in *Relaciones Internacionales* Vol. 28, Heredia, Costa Rica, tercer trimestre de 1989, pp. 59–65; Jürg Martin Gabriel, 'La neutralidad en el mundo contemporaneo' in *Beiträge und Berichte*, Institute for Political Science, University of St Gallen, Nr. 191/1992.
7. Jürg Martin Gabriel, 'Das amerikanische Exportkontrollsystem', in *Aussenwirtschaft*, Vol. 44 (1989), pp. 59–74.
8. Jürg Martin Gabriel (ed.), *Schweizerische Aussenpolitik im Kosovo-Krieg* (Zürich: Orell Füssli, 2000); see also Jürg Martin Gabriel, *Sackgasse Neutralität* (Zürich: vdf Hochschulverlag an der ETH, 1997).
9. Alexander Gallus, *Die Neutralisten, Verfechter eines vereinten Deutschland zwischen Ost und West 1945–1990* (Düsseldorf: Droste, 2001), p. 15. See also Gallus' article in Neue Zürcher Zeitung, 25 May 2001, p. 7.
10. *Dokumente zur Deutschlandpolitik*, p. 300.
11. Ibid., p. 754, 784.
12. Ibid., pp. 1161–2, 1178–80.
13. Ibid., p. 604, 641, 784, 794, 827.
14. Ibid., pp. 860–77.
15. Ibid., p. 467, 574, 588, 634, 735, 771, 775, 921, 973, 1022, 1066, 1163. See also Hans-Dietrich Genscher, *Erinnerungen* (Berlin: Siedler Verlag, 1995), pp. 710–4; Gallus, *Die Neutralisten*, pp. 13–16.
16. *Dokumente zur Deutschlandpolitik*, p. 604, 641, 784–785, 794, 827, 953, 1195, 1373.
17. Ibid., pp. 795–804.

18. Ibid., p. 685, 758, 844–6, 911.
19. Ibid., p. 998.
20. Any general history of American diplomacy deals with the subject. The following are some of the best known: Thomas A. Bailey, *A Diplomatic History of the American People* (New York: Appleton-Century-Crofts, 1969); Samuel F. Bemis, *A Diplomatic History of the United States* (New York: Henry Holt, 1936); Richard W. Leopold, *The Growth of American Foreign Policy: A History* (New York: Alfred A. Knopf, 1962); Thomas G. Paterson *et al.*, *American Foreign Policy: A History* (Lexington: D. C. Heath, 1977); Julius W. Pratt *et al.*, *A History of United States Foreign Policy* (Englewood Cliffs, NJ, Prentice-Hall, 1980); Armin Rappaport, *A History of American Diplomacy* (New York: Macmillan, 1975). The following works are among the most important on the Second World War and the interwar period: Charles Seymour, *American Neutrality: 1914–1917* (New Haven, Conn.: Yale University Press, 1935); John W. Coogan, *The End of Neutrality* (Ithaca, NY: Cornell University Press, 1981); Edwin Borchard and William Potter Lage, *Neutrality for the United States* (New Haven, Conn.: Yale University Press, 1937); Robert A. Divine, *The Illusion of Neutrality* (Chicago: University of Chicago Press, 1962); Charles G. Fenwick, *American Neutrality, Trial and Failure* (New York: Oxford University Press, 1940); Philip C. Jessup *et al.*, *Neutrality: Its History, Economics and Law* (New York: Columbia University Press, 1936); Quincy Wright, 'The Present Status of Neutrality', *American Journal of International Law*, Vol. 34 (1940) pp. 391–415; Quincy Wright, 'The Future of Neutrality', *International Conciliation* (1928) pp. 353–72.
21. Charles S. Hyneman, 'The First American Neutrality: A Study of the American Understanding of Neutral Obligations During the Years 1972 to 1815', *University of Illinois Bulletin*, Vol. 32 (1934) pp. 7–29; Carlton Savage, *Policy of the US Toward Maritime Commerce in War* (Washington D.C.: US Government Printing Office, 1934–36); Robert G. Albion and Jennie B. Pope, *Sea Lanes in Wartime* (New York: W. W. Norton, 1942); Thomas A. Bailey, *The Policy of the United States Toward the Neutrals: 1917–1918* (Baltimore: Johns Hopkins University Press, 1942); Nils Ørvik, *The Decline of Neutrality 1914–1941* (Oslo: J. Grundt Tanum, 1953).
22. There are a number of publications, however, that deal with some aspects of the question: Cordell Hull, *The Memoirs of Cordell Hull* (New York: Macmillan Company, 1948); Ruth B. Russell, *A History of the United Nations Charter: The Role of the United States, 1940–45* (Washington D.C.: The Brookings Institution, 1958); Dean Acheson, *Present at the Creation: My Years in the State Department* (New York: New American Library, 1970); D. G. Gordon and R. Dangerfield, *The Hidden Weapon: The Story of Economic Warfare* (New York: Harper, 1976); these four books permit a partial assessment of the American attitude towards neutrality during the Second World War. The following four deal with the Cold War period: George F. Kennan, *Memoirs 1925–1950* (New York: Pantheon Books, 1967); George F. Kennan, *Memoirs 1950–1963* (New York: Pantheon Books, 1972); Michael A. Guhin, *John Foster Dulles: A Statesman and his Times* (New York: Columbia University Press, 1972); Hamilton Fish Armstrong, 'Neutrality: Varying Tunes', *Foreign Affairs*, Vol. 35 (1956), pp. 57–71. The next two publications are virtually the only ones dedicated

exclusively to neutrality from a political point of view: Cyril E. Black, Richard A. Falk, Klaus Knorr and Oran R. Young, *Neutralization and World Politics* (Princeton, NJ: Princeton University Press, 1968); Fred Greene, 'Neutralization and the Balance of Power', *The American Political Science Review*, Vol. 47 (1953) pp. 1041–57. The rest are legal studies. Patrick M. Norton, 'Between the Ideology and the Reality: The Shadow of the Law of Neutrality', *Harvard International Law Journal*, Vol. 17 (1976), pp. 249–311; Joseph L. Cans, 'The Chaotic Status of the Laws of War and the Urgent Necessity of their Revision', *AJIL*, Vol. 45 (1961) pp. 37–61; Howard J. Taubenfeld, 'International Actions and Neutrality', *AJIL*, Vol. 47 (1953), pp. 377–96; Quincy Wright, 'The Outlawry of War and the Law of War', *AJIL*, Vol. 47 (1953), pp. 365–76; Robert W. Tucker, *The Law of War and Neutrality at Sea* (Washington D.C.: US Government Printing Office, 1957); Morris Greenspan, *The Modern Law of Land Warfare* (Berkeley: University of California Press, 1959).

23. This is the reason why, outside the United States, the question of neutrality has continued to receive a great deal of attention since 1941. The most prolific analysts of the topic, of course, are scholars in permanently neutral countries like Sweden and Switzerland. The following are some of their publications that shed light on the American attitude towards neutrality: Gunnar Adler-Karlsson, *Western Economic Warfare 1947–1967* (Stockholm: Almquist & Wiksell, 1968); Geir Lundestad, *America, Scandinavia, and the Cold War 1945–49* (New York: Columbia University Press, 1980); Grethe Vaerno, 'The United States, Norway, and the Atlantic Pact, 1948–49', *Scandinavian Studies*, Vol. 50 (1978), pp. 150–76; Constantin Guise, *Die Neutralität der Vereinigten Staaten* (Bern: Gustav Grunau & Cie, 1946); Heinz K. Meier, *Friendship Under Stress: US-Swiss Relations 1900–1950* (Bern: Herbert Lang, 1970); Marco Durrer, *Die schweizerisch-amerikanischen Finanzbeziehungen im Zweiten Weltkrieg* (Bern: Paul Haupt, 1984); Daniel Frei, 'Das Washington Abkommen von 1946', *Revue suisse d'histoire*, Vol. 19 (1969), pp. 567–619.

24. United States Department of State, *Foreign Relations of the United States* (Washington D.C.: US Government Printing Office). Of the sixteen volumes planned for the period 1952–54, ten have now been published.

25. The Vietnam War had a similar effect in that it prompted a number of publications on the law of war. Neutrality was not very important in that context. For one example, see John N. Moore, *Law and the Indochina War* (Princeton, NJ: Princeton University Press, 1972). Central American troubles have recently led to discussion of the relevance of American domestic neutrality legislation to that conflict. The central question raised is whether the President is not violating US (neutrality) laws in outfitting mercenaries to fight on foreign soil. For one example, see Jules Lobel, 'The Rise and Decline of the Neutrality Act: Sovereignty and Congressional War Powers in US Foreign Policy', *Harvard International Law Journal*, Vol. 24 (1983), pp. 1–71.

26. Raymond Aron, *Peace and War: A Theory of International Relations* (Garden City, NY: Doubleday, 1966), pp. 5–6.

27. Daniel Frei, *Dimensionen neutraler Politik: Ein Beitrag zur Theorie der internationalen Beziehungen* (Geneva: Institut universitaire des hautes études internationales, 1969), pp. 103–47.

28. Ibid., pp. 21–91.

29. Peace-keeping missions of the United Nations represent an interesting combination of impartiality and indifference. The fact that the organisation intervenes at all in a conflict shows that it is not indifferent, but the fact that it merely tries to interpose itself between the two belligerents and to mediate shows that it wants to remain impartial and to preserve careful symmetry. This is in contrast to the intentions of the Charter, which, in the spirit of collective enforcement action, demand active partiality. For a more detailed analysis, see Larry L. Fabian. *Soldiers Without Enemies* (Washington D.C.: The Brookings Institution, 1971).

30. D. Frei, *Dimensionen neutraler Politik*, pp. 151–201.

31. For a comprehensive treatment of permanent neutrality, see Dietrich Schindler, 'Dauernde Neutralität', in Alois Riklin, Hans Haug and Hans Christoph Binswanger (eds), *Handbuch der schweizerischen Aussenpolitik* (Bern: Paul Haupt, 1976), pp. 159–80. See also Alois Riklin, 'Neutralität', in Wichard Woyke (ed.), *Handwörterbuch Internationale Politik* (München: Francke Verlag, 1980), pp. 270–8; Rudolf L. Bindschedler, 'Die Neutralität im modernen Völkerrecht', *Zeitschrift für ausländisches, öffentliches Recht und Völkerrecht*, Vol. 17 (1956), pp. 1–37; Erik Castrén, *The Present Law of War and Neutrality* (Helsinki: Suomalainen, 1954), pp. 448–9.

32. For an excellent study of legal neutrality, see Stephen C. Neff, *The rights and duties of neutrals, A general history* (Manchester : Manchester University Press, 2000). For a detailed listing and interpretation of neutral rights and duties, see Marjorie M. Whiteman, *Digest of International Law* (Washington D.C.: US Government Printing Office, 1968) Vol. 11. This is the official Department of State publication on the subject. See also Bindschedler, 'Die Neutralität im modernen Völkerrecht', pp. 1–7; Schindler, 'Dauernde Neutralität, pp. 169–75; Castrén, *The Present-Law of War and Neutrality,* pp. 439–44.

33. In German it is common to speak of *Neutralitätsrecht* and *Neutralitätspolitik*. While it poses no problem to refer in English to 'neutral law' or 'the law of neutrality', it is somewhat problematic to speak of 'neutral politics' or 'the politics of neutrality'. Still, the attempt is made here, and it will be carried on in Chapter 6.

34. For a more detailed discussion of armed neutrality, see Bindschedler, 'Die Neutralität im modernen Völkerrecht', pp. 2, 35–7.

35. As will be shown later on, American isolationism was in a number of ways similar to what today is called 'neutralism' or 'non-alignment'.

36. For a more detailed discussion of the phenomenon of neutralisation, see Cyril E. Black, Richard A. Falk, Klaus Knorr and Oran R. Young, *Neutralization and World Politics* (Princeton, NJ: Princeton University Press, 1968). See also Riklin, 'Neutralität', pp. 270–1, 273–5; Schindler, 'Dauernde Neutralität', pp. 163–4.

37. For more details see Riklin, 'Neutralität', p. 270; Schindler, 'Dauernde Neutralität', p. 164.

38. See Riklin, 'Neutralität', p. 270; Schindler, 'Dauernde Neutralität', p. 164.

39. Dietrich Schindler, 'Aspects contemporains de la neutralité', *Hague: Recueil des Cours*, Vol. 121 (1967), pp. 263–7; Castrén, *The Present-Law of War and Neutrality*, pp. 449–52; Riklin, 'Neutralität', p. 270.
40. Schindler, 'Dauernde Neutralität', pp. 165–6; Daniel Frei, 'Neutrality and Nonalignment: Convergences and Contrasts', *Korea and World Affairs*, Vol. 3 (1979), pp. 275–86.

1   Neutrality before 1941

1. For a clear discussion of the three groups, see Edwin M. Borchard, 'Neutrality', *Yale Law Journal*, Vol. 48 (1938), pp. 37–53. The best general studies on the Neutrality Acts are: Robert A. Divine, *The Illusion of Neutrality* (Chicago: University of Chicago Press, 1962); Wayne S. Cole, *Roosevelt and the Isolationists, 1934–45* (Lincoln: University of Nebraska Press, 1983).
2. Cole, *Roosevelt and the Isolationists, 1934–45*, pp. 409–555. Cole describes in some detail how Roosevelt eliminated the isolationists politically. For a more general account, see also Thomas A. Bailey, *A Diplomatic History of the American People* (New York: Appleton-Century-Crofts, 1969), pp. 711–56, and Armin Rappaport, *A History of American Diplomacy* (New York: Macmillan, 1975), pp. 329–43.
3. For a good general account of the traditionalist position, see Samuel F. Bernis, *A Diplomatic History of the United States* (New York: Henry Holt, 1936), pp. 584–809; Edwin Borchard and William Potter Lage, *Neutrality for the United States* (New Haven: Yale University Press, 1937), pp. 59–239.
4. Bemis, *A Diplomatic History of the United State*, pp. 95–9; Julius W. Pratt *et al.*, *A History of United States Foreign Policy* (Englewood Cliffs, NJ: Prentice Hall, 1980), pp. 28–30. See also Charles M. Thomas, *American Neutrality in 1793* (New York: Columbia University Press, 1931), p. 294.
5. For a detailed study of the first American Neutrality Act, see Charles S. Hyneman, 'The First American Neutrality: A Study of the American Understanding of Neutral Obligations During the Years 1792 to 1815', *University of Illinois Bulletin*, Vol. 32 (1934), pp. 11–165; a more recent analysis has been undertaken by Jules Lobel, 'The Rise and Decline of the Neutrality Act: Sovereignty and Congressional War Powers in US Foreign Policy', *Harvard International Law Journal*, Vol. 24 (1983), pp. 11–15.
6. For a more detailed account, see Dietrich Schindler, 'Aspects contemporains de la neutralité', *Hague, Recueil des Cours*, Vol. 121 (1967), pp. 228–30. The influence of Vattel on American thinking is well documented by Charles M. Wiltse, 'Thomas Jefferson on the Law of Nations', *AJIL*, Vol. 29 (1935), p. 75. See also Charles G. Fenwick, *American Neutrality, Trial and Failure* (New York: New York University Press, 1940), pp. 9–11.
7. *14 June 1797* 'An Act to prevent Citizens of the United States from Privateering against Nations in Amity with, or against Citizens of, the United States'; *3 March 1817* 'An act more effectually to preserve the Neutral Relations of the United States'; *20 April 1818* 'An Act in addition to the "Act for the Punishment of Certain Crimes against the United States", and to repeal the Acts therein mentioned'.

8. *22 June 1860* 'An Act to carry into effect Provisions of the Treaties between the United States, China, Japan, Siam, Persia, and other countries'; *1874*, 'Revised Statutes of 1874'; *22 April 1898* 'Joint Resolution to prohibit the Export of Coal or Other Material Used in War from any Seaport of the United States'; *4 March 1909* 'An Act to codify, revise, and amend the Penal Laws of the United States'; *14 March 1912* 'Joint Resolution to amend the joint Resolution to prohibit the Export of Coal or Other Materials Used in War from any Seaport of the United States'.

9. For a complete listing of all Neutrality Acts, see Francis Deàk and Philip C. Jessup (eds), *A Collection of Neutrality Laws, Regulations and Treaties of Various Countries* (Washington D.C.: Carnegie Endowment for International Peace, 1939).

10. Bailey, *A Diplomatic History of the American People*, p. 20. For the pre-1776 experience, see Bailey, ibid., pp. 19–25.

11. Quincy Wright, 'The Future of Neutrality', *International Conciliation* (1928) p. 357. See also Bemis, *A Diplomatic History of the United States*, p. 12; Philip Jessup, *Neutrality: Its History, Economics and Law* (New York: Columbia University Press, 1936) p. 4.

12. The importance of the United States as a promoter of the international law of neutrality in the eighteenth and nineteenth centuries is generally recognized, also by non-American scholars. See Schindler, *Aspects contemporains de la neutralité*, pp. 233–4; Erik Castrén, *The Present Law of War and Neutrality* (Helsinki: Suomalainen, 1954) pp. 19–20; Titus Komarnicki, 'The Place of Neutrality in the Modern System of International Law', *Hague, Recueil des Cours* (1952), pp. 415–16.

13. For more details on the 'Plan of 1776,' see Carlton Savage, *Policy of the United States Toward Maritime Commerce in War* (Washington D.C.: US Government Printing Office, 1934–36), pp. 114–21; Samuel Flagg Bemis, *The Diplomacy of the American Revolution* (Bloomington: Indiana University Press, 1957), pp. 45–63, 130–3; Richard W. Leopold, *The Growth of American Foreign Policy* (New York: Alfred A. Knopf, 1962), pp. 30–1; Borchard and Lage, *Neutrality for the United States*, pp. 21–32.

14. The old rule went back to the late Middle Ages and was part of the so-called 'Consolato del Mare', a body of naval laws originally regulating Mediterranean trade. However, the nascent European trading nations of the Northern Atlantic preferred a reversal of this rule so as to favour their extensive carrying trade. For a discussion of the nature and the origins of sea neutrality, see Castrén, *The Present Law of War and Neutrality*, pp. 492–600; also Richard Pares, *Colonial Blockade and Neutral Rights, 1739–1763* (Philadelphia: Porcupine Press, 1975); Max Savelle, *The Origins of American Diplomacy: The International History of Angloamerica* (New York: Macmillan, 1967).

15. The 'Rule of 1756' was also related to the concept of 'broken voyage', whereby the British (originally) allowed the Americans to load French goods in the West Indies, to reload them in American ports, subject to a phoney tax that was reimbursed, and to carry them on to France as 'American' products representing 'normal' trade. In the famous 'Essex Ruling' of 1805, the British reversed themselves, a decision that angered Americans and contributed to the eventual American declaration of war in

1812. For more details, see Bemis, *A Diplomatic History*, pp. 138–44; Robert G. Albion and J. B. Pope, *Sea Lanes in Wartime* (New York: W. W. Norton, 1942), pp. 65–73; Armin Rappaport, *A History of American Diplomacy*, pp. 58–9.

16. 'Absolute' contraband included goods that were clearly strategic; 'conditional' contraband, goods that were quasi-strategic in nature. The distinction helped to ease the problem on contraband in the nineteenth century, but in 1776 there was no such agreement. Of course, the issue arises again today, particularly in the context of Cocom.

17. For more details on the 'Plan of 1784', see Carlton Savage, *Policy of the United States Toward Maritime Commerce in War*, pp. 8–9; Leopold, *The Growth of American Foreign Policy*, p. 31.

18. At the close of the Crimean War, the major European powers met in Paris and agreed to the abolition of privateering (Declaration of Paris of 1856). For the curious American reaction, see Bemis, *A Diplomatic History*, p. 336; Savage, *Policy of the United States Toward Maritime Commerce in War*, pp. 38, 17; Castrén, *The Present Law of War and Neutrality*, pp. 19–20.

19. Savage, *Policy of the United States Toward Maritime Commerce in War*, p. 46.

20. See Bemis, *A Diplomatic History*, pp. 123–5; Bailey, *A Diplomatic History of the American People*, pp. 97–9.

21. See Bemis, *A Diplomatic History*, pp. 101–3; Bailey, *A Diplomatic History of the American People*, pp. 75–80; Savage, *Policy of the United States Toward Maritime Commerce in War*, pp. 14–15.

22. The 'Essex' ruling was mentioned earlier. For more details on the general problem, see Albion and Pope, *Sea Lanes in Wartime*, pp. 65–94; Bemis, *A Diplomatic History*, pp. 138–44.

23. For an excellent discussion of the divergent British and American interests, see John W. Coogan, *The End of Neutrality: The United States, Britain, and Maritime Rights, 1899–1915* (Ithaca, NY: Cornell University Press, 1981), pp. 17–29; Nils Ørvik, *The Decline of Neutrality, 1914–1941* (Oslo: J. Grundt Tanum, 1935), pp. 29–37.

24. See Bemis, *A Diplomatic History*, pp. 26, 374–5.

25. Ibid., p. 109. Washington's Farewell Address has been interpreted variously, of course. Isolationists, for instance, see Washington as firmly advocating non-intervention in European affairs, and by this they mean keeping *militarily* out of any conflict. In the light of the American neutrality conception prevailing at that time, however, this view seems questionable. As Reginald C. Stuart shows in a recent study, the generation of the Founding Fathers had a fairly traditional or 'realist' philosophy of war, this is in contrast to later generations. This is not to say that the American conception of war and power was in the European tradition or even Clausewitzian, but it certainly was a good deal less 'idealist' than isolationists often assume. The important break in American military thinking occurred *after* the Napoleonic Wars. See Reginald C. Stuart, *War and American Thought, From the Revolution to the Monroe Doctrine* (Kent, Ohio: Kent State University Press, 1982), pp. 245

26. Only during the 'undeclared war' with France, from 1797 to 1800, did the United States possess the power to enforce its neutrality conception upon a third state. On the one hand, the US navy was built up to an amazingly

effective force in a short time, and, on the other hand, it helped that the British navy stood by and practically supported the Americans. Under such circumstances, the United States managed to confront the French navy successfully. See Bemis, *A Diplomatic History*, pp. 111–25; Bailey, *A Diplomatic History of the American People*, pp. 83–99.

27. It is true, of course, that British opposition to American neutral trading rights stemmed to a large extent from the desire of its trading companies to conquer markets during times of war. See Jessup, *Neutrality: Its History, Economics and Law*, pp. 26, 40–1.

28. John Quincy Adams' 'Project of 1823' was very explicitly anti-mercantilist and anti-colonial. The project aimed at convincing the British to become neutrals in future wars, to join the liberal and peace-loving cause, and thereby to initiate what Adams called 'the downfall of the colonial system'. In his instructions to the American Minister in Great Britain, Adams explicitly stated that his objective was to abolish private war at sea. See Savage, *Policy of the United States Toward Maritime Commerce in War*, pp. 46–7, 307.

29. For an excellent discussion of American commercial interests at that time, see Albion and Pope, *Sea Lanes in Wartime*, pp. 65–94. For a general discussion of the economic aspects of American neutrality, see Jessup, *Neutrality: Its History, Economics and Law*, pp. 20–34.

30. More will have to be said about the Swedish and Swiss cases later on. The details are somewhat more complicated.

31. One of the rare discussions of this problem is to be found in Geoffrey Best, *Humanity in Warfare* (London: Weidenfeld & Nicolson, 1980), p. 69.

32. For more details on Jefferson's embargo, see L. M. Sears, *Jefferson and the Embargo* (New York: Octagon Books, 1978); W. W. Jennings, *The American Embargo, 1907–1909* (Iowa City: University of Iowa Studies, 1938); Albion and Pope, *Sea Lanes in Wartime*, pp. 96–111; Bemis, *A Diplomatic History*, pp. 147–53. For details on Washington's attempted embargo in 1794, see Bailey, *A Diplomatic History of the American People*, pp. 74–5; Bemis, *A Diplomatic History*, pp. 100–1.

33. Bailey, *A Diplomatic History of the American People*, p. 593 For more details, see Bailey, ibid., pp. 582–95 and Bemis, *A Diplomatic History*, pp. 584–610. For a most thorough and recent study on the subject, see Coogan, *The End of Neutrality*, pp. 193–256. Coogan is extremely critical of Wilson and accuses him of having destroyed the entire traditional legal structure.

34. The authors most critical of Wilson include Bemis, Bailey, Borchard, Lage, Coogan and Orvil. They accuse Wilson of not having been truly neutral from 1914 to 1917 and for engaging in a veritable anti-neutral crusade afterwards. On the latter point Bailey disagrees. In a separate study he shows that during the war the United States did not violate neutral rights any more than the British had done before; see Thomas A. Bailey, *The Policy of the United States Toward the Neutrals: 1917–1918* (Baltimore: Johns Hopkins Press, 1942). The best known defenders of Wilson are Arthur S. Link, his biographer, and Charles Seymour. They maintain that Wilson was highly impartial before he entered the war and was perceived as such by the public. He did not violate neutral customs any more than was

absolutely necessary under very difficult circumstances: see Charles Seymour, *American Neutrality 1914–1917* (New Haven: Yale University Press, 1935): Charles Seymour, *American Diplomacy During the World War* Baltimore: Johns Hopkins University Press, 1934); Arthur S. Link, *Wilson* (Princeton: Princeton University Press, 1965); another very interesting account of Wilson is that by Robert E. Osgood, *Ideals and Self-Interest in Americas Foreign Relations* (Chicago: University of Chicago Press, 1953) pp. 172–94, 223–63.

35. For some Americans, the era of transition had begun earlier. Alfred T. Mahan, admiral, naval strategist and geopolitician, had had first-hand experience with great power rivalries during the Spanish–American War and developed a hard-nosed theory of international politics. He perceived in the world a constant struggle for national power, and he saw the need for America to participate actively. He advocated a large navy and expected that the two Anglo-Saxon powers would in the future fight side by side, a prediction that proved to be entirely correct. Mahan was a member of the American delegation to the Hague Conferences of 1899 and 1907. In preparation for the second conference he tried to convince President Roosevelt that in the long run a strengthening of the international law of neutrality might not be in the best American interest. He gained the support of Admiral Dewey but in the end failed to convince both the President and Secretary of State Elihu Root. Mahan's view was not typical of the US government at that time; he remained an outsider. The fact that he did question traditionalist neutrality, however, goes to show that some elements in America were ready to abandon a long tradition as early as the turn of the century. See Coogan, *The End of Neutrality,* pp. 55–69. In his own publications, Mahan avoided taking a direct stand against neutrality, but his main line of argument certainly left little doubt about his view. See Alfred T. Mahan, *The Interest of America in Sea Power* (Boston: Little, Brown, 1918) pp. 144–71. See also Osgood, *Ideals and Self-Interest in America's Foreign Relations,* pp. 29–41.

36. Bemis, *A Diplomatic History,* p. 809. The neo-isolationists were not a homogeneous group, of course. For a description of the various people, interests and ideas that made up the movement, see Manfred Jonas, *Isolationism in America, 1935–41* (Ithaca, NY: Cornell University Press, 1966), pp. 1–31; Cole, *Roosevelt and the Isolationists, 1934–45,* pp. 6–9.

37. Borchard and Lage, *Neutrality for the United States,* pp. 281–311.

38. Borchard and Lage, ibid., pp. 304–13.

39. At about the same time, a book was published that received wide attention. It dealt with America's entry into the First World War, and the main argument was that Big Business, Big Money, and Big Profits had been the chief causes. It must be remembered that this was in the middle of the great Depression. See Walter Millis, *Road to War: America, 1914–1917* (Boston: Houghton Mifflin, 1935).

40. Charles Warren, 'Troubles of a Neutral', *Foreign Affairs,* Vol. 12 (1935), pp. 377–94.

41. Warren, ibid., pp. 386, 389

42. Borchard and Lage, *Neutrality for the United States,* p. 314.

43. For more details, see Robert A. Divine, *The Illusion of Neutrality* (Chicago: University of Chicago Press, 1962), pp. 81–120; also Leopold, *The Growth of American Foreign Policy,* pp. 504–6; Borchard and Lage, *Neutrality for the United States,* pp. 313–17

44. Borchard and Lage, ibid.

45. Ibid., pp. 324–31.

46. See also Nils Ørvik, *The Decline of Neutrality, 1914–1941* (Oslo: J. Grundt Tanum, 1953), pp. 157–67; Bailey, *A Diplomatic History,* pp. 700–3.

47. Borchard and Lage, *Neutrality for the United States,* pp. 337–43.

48. Ørvik speaks of 'neutrality without rights'. See Ørvik, *The Decline of Neutrality, 1914–1941,* p. 157.

49 Bemis, *A Diplomatic History,* p. 806.

50. Cole, *Roosevelt and the Isolationists,* p. 310.

51. For a more detailed account see Bailey, *A Diplomatic History,* pp. 711–56; Cole, *Roosevelt and the Isolationists,* pp. 409–555; Leopold, *The Growth of American Foreign Policy,* pp. 557–67.

52. Stimson was a typical 'cooperationist'. In 1932, he published an article in *Foreign Affairs* in which he reviewed the Kellogg–Briand Pact. His argument was that the Pact established a link between its members and those of the League of Nations in the sense that there now existed a moral duty to consult in case of aggression: 'It is a policy which combines the readiness to *cooperate for Peace* [emphasis added] and justice in the world, which Americans have always manifested, while at the same time it preserves the independence of judgement and the flexibility of action upon which we have always insisted.' Henry L. Stimson, 'The Pact of Paris: Three Years of Development', *Foreign Affairs* (Special Supplement), Vol. 11, (October 1932), pp. i–ix. Stimson, of course, was also the author of the 'Stimson Doctrine', which, in connection with the Japanese invasion of Manchuria, established the principle that America would not recognize territorial acquisitions based on conquest. This, too, was an 'internationalist' step. Other internationalists published in *Foreign Affairs,* such as Allen W. Dulles, brother of John Foster Dulles and future head of the CIA: Allen W. Dulles, 'The Cost of Peace', *Foreign Affairs,* Vol. 12, July (1934), pp. 567–78.

53. Cole, *Roosevelt and the Isolationists,* pp. 1–6. For an excellent discussion of Roosevelt's sometimes wavering attitude towards internationalism, see Whittle Johnston, 'Franklin D. Roosevelt and the Wartime Strategy for Peace', in Norman Graebner (ed.), *Traditions and Values: American Diplomacy 1865–1945* (New York: University Press of America, 1985), pp. 161–98.

54. Borchard and Lage, *Neutrality for the United States,* p. 281.

55. Wright, 'The Future of Neutrality', p. 369.

56. Clyde Eagleton, 'Neutrality and Neutral Rights Following the Pact of Paris for the Renunciation of War', *Proceedings of the ASIL* (1930), p. 92.

57. The discussion over the meaning of the Pact for the international law of war and neutrality was also carried on in Europe. Various points of view emerged. For a more contemporary perspective, see Schindler, 'Aspects contemporains de la neutralité', pp. 268–72; Komarnicki, 'The Place of Neutrality', pp. 433–7; Ørvik, *The Decline of Neutrality,* pp. 142–44.

58. Divine, *The Illusion of Neutrality*, pp. 13–15.
59. For more details see Cole, *Roosevelt and the Isolationists*, pp. 239–62.
60. Borchard and Lage, *Neutrality for the United States*, pp. 317–22.
61. For greater detail see Divine, *The Illusion of Neutrality*, pp. 122–34; Leopold, *The Growth of American Foreign Policy*, pp. 505–6; Schindler, 'Aspects contemporains de la Neutralité', pp. 257–8.
62. A thorough discussion of the 1937 Act is contained in Cole, *Roosevelt and the Isolationists*, pp. 223–38 and Divine, *The Illusion of Neutrality*, pp. 162–99. It was also in 1937, on 5 October, that FDR held his famous 'Quarantine Speech'. For greater detail, see Roland N. Stromberg, *Collective Security and American Foreign Policy: From the League of Nations to NATO* (New York Praeger, 1963), pp. 117–18; also Robert Dallek, *Franklin D. Roosevelt and American Foreign Policy 1932–1945* (New York: Oxford University Press, 1979), pp. 148–50.
63. The two differing philosophies of law can also be expressed in terms of jus *ad bellum* and jus *in bello*. As Geoffrey Best explains, the former governs 'your going to war in the first place', and the latter governs 'what you do when you get there'. Since jus *ad bellum* governs the recourse to war, it automatically distinguishes between just and unjust causes of war and is, therefore, part of the just war philosophy. As a rule, the traditional law of war and neutrality was considered to be part of jus *in bello*, while the modern law of the United Nations is part of jus *ad bellum*. See Best, *Humanity in Wartime*, pp. 8–9.
64. Universalist values and universalist power combine to form what Whittle Johnston calls a 'community of power'. This is in contrast to a mere 'balance of power'. As Johnston shows, Woodrow Wilson (and all the true internationalists) wanted to convert the prevailing balance-of-power system into a community-of-power system. See Whittle Johnston, 'Reflections on Wilson and the Problems of World Peace', in Arthur S. Link (ed.), *Woodrow Wilson and a Revolutionary World, 1913–21* (Chapel Hill, NC: The University of North Carolina Press, 1982), pp. 197, 202.
65. For a more detailed discussion, see Quincy Wright, 'Changes in the Conception of War', *AJIL*, Vol. 18 (1924), pp. 755–67; Quincy Wright, 'The Concept of Aggression in International Law', *AJIL*, Vol. 29 (1935), pp. 373–95.
66. Edwin Borchard, 'Neutrality', *Yale Law Journal* (1938), p. 41. See also Borchard and Lage, *Neutrality for the United States*, pp. v–viii.
67. Quincy Wright, 'The Present Status of Neutrality', *AJIL*, Vol. 34 (1940), pp. 399–400.
68. The Swiss have learned to live with this contradiction and have even institutionalised it. One of the various states of national emergency is called *Neutralitätsschutz*. It implies defending the borders on land and in the air short of general war. It is a grey zone, of course, that entails a number of legal, strategic, and especially political problems.
69. Fenwick, *American Neutrality, Trial and Failure*, pp. 3, 4.
70. Philip C. Jessup, 'The Birth, Death and Reincarnation of Neutrality', *AJIL*, Vol. 26 (1932), p. 789.
71. Ibid., p. 792.

72. Philip C. Jessup, 'The Saavedra Lamas Anti-War Draft Treaty', *AJIL*, Vol. 27 (1933), pp. 109–14; Philip C. Jessup, 'The Argentine Anti-War Pact', *AJIL*, Vol. 28 (1934), pp. 538–41.

73. For more information about neutral leagues, see Carl J. Kulsrud, 'Armed Neutralities to 1780', *AJIL*, Vol. 29 (1935), pp. 423–47; Bemis, *A Diplomatic History*, pp. 39–41; Ørvik, *The Decline of Neutrality, 1914–1941*, pp. 89–118.

74. Ørvik, ibid., p. 149; see also Fenwick, *American Neutrality, Trial and Failure*, pp. 21–2.

75. Jessup, 'The Saavedra Lamas Anti-War Draft Treaty', p. 111.

76. Jessup, *Neutrality, Its History, Economics and Law*, pp. 207–13.

77. Ibid., p. 162.

78. Ibid., p. 181.

79. This may be the reason why Borchard spoke favourably of Jessup's ideas. See Borchard, 'Neutrality', p. 53.

80. Jessup, *Neutrality: Its History, Economics and Law*, p. 182.

81. Harvard Research in International Law, Draft Convention on Rights and Duties of States in Case of Aggression, *AJIL*, Vol. 33 (1939), p. 823.

82. The two conventions are contained in the supplement edition of the *American Journal of International Law*, Vol. 33 (1937), pp. 167–203, 820–80.

83. Draft Convention, p. 827. The two Harvard Draft Conventions are also discussed by Komarnicki in 'The Place of Neutrality', pp. 440–2. Philip Jessup, besides chairing the group that drafted the two conventions, also wrote the foreword to a book about neutrality written by a Danish author, Georg Cohn. It was published the same year in which the conventions were written, and there are some parallels between its conception of neutrality, that of Jessup, and the idea of 'supporting state'. See Georg Cohn, *Neo-Neutrality* (New York: Columbia University Press, 1939).

84. Draft Convention, p. 829.

85. There was much neutral co-operation, however, between the United States and Latin America. Washington was interested in obtaining Latin American co-operation in the defence of the hemisphere. In September 1939, a consultative conference was held in Panama that resulted in a general declaration of neutrality and the establishment of a 'neutrality zone' of some 300 miles in width around the entire hemisphere. An Inter-American Neutrality Committee was set up to study and formulate further common steps. When violations of the zone occurred, joint protests were dispatched to Europe *(DSB, 24 February 1940, pp. 199–201)*. After the capitulation of France, America feared a fascist take-over of French possessions in the Caribbean. Hull called for a hemispheric foreign ministers' conference and managed to get Latin support for the establishment of an Inter-American Commission for Territorial Administration that, if the need arose, would preventively take over French colonies and administer them temporarily *(DSB, 24 August 1940, pp. 127–48)*. The internationalist neutrals welcomed these steps, most of all Charles G. Fenwick, a specialist not only in international law but also in Latin American affairs. It was quite obvious to him that neutral co-operation in the hemisphere was merely a 'side-door' to full involvement in international politics; see Charles G. Fenwick, 'A New Symbol of Pan American Unity', *DSB*,

4 May 1940, p. 472. For further details on neutral co-operation in the hemisphere, see Ruth B. Russell, *A History of the United Nations Charter* (Washington D.C.: The Brookings Institution, 1958), pp. 16–27; *FRUS,* 1940, Vol. I, pp. 727–39.

86. *FRUS,* 1940, Vol. I, p. 117. See also *DSB,* 24 February 1940, p. 153.

87. For a general account of the situation, see Cordell Hull, *The Memoirs of Cordell Hull* (New York: Macmillan, 1948), Vol. I, pp. 1625–33; also William L. Langer and S. Everett Gleason, *The Challenge to Isolation, 1937–1940* (New York: Harper, 1952), pp. 250–4. Interestingly enough, Sumner Welles, the person appointed with the task of gaining neutral co-operation in February 1940 was later assigned to set up the committee that drafted the United Nations Charter.

88. For greater detail see Bailey, *A Diplomatic History,* pp. 711–56; Leopold, *The Growth of American Foreign Policy,* pp. 557–80; Cole, *Roosevelt and the Isolationists,* pp. 409–555.

89. For legal opinions on this subject, see Edwin Borchard, 'War, Neutrality and Non-Belligerency', *AJIL,* Vol. 35 (1941), pp. 618–25; Schindler, 'Aspects contemporains de la neutralité', pp. 264–7.

90. It is interesting that the United States did not want to abandon the status of neutrality officially. It had an opportunity to do so when, in April 1940, the State Department was approached by Argentina with a proposal that all the American republics abandon traditional neutrality and become non-belligerents (or benevolent neutrals). The proposal was a thorough challenge to the United States, since America was soon to be impartially neutral in name only. Supporting the Argentine proposal would, therefore, not have conflicted with actual behaviour. But it would, apparently, have conflicted with Secretary Hull's desire to remain verbally consistent. He and Sumner Welles became two of the most ardent defenders of traditional neutrality in their reply to Argentina! In a conversation with the Argentine ambassador, Welles thought that 'the American Republics constituted the one remaining portion of the civilised world which stood for, which upheld and which practiced the standards of international law which were being openly violated in every other part of the world' (*FRUS,* 1940, Vol. I, pp. 743–4). Did the United States really have an interest in upholding the traditional law of neutrality in 1940? Did the FDR, too, intend to violate it flagrantly? Welles must have meant a different type of international law, possibly that of the coming United Nations, of which he became one of the main promoters.

91. See Russell, *A History of the United Nations Charter,* pp. 34–42.

2   Second World War, 1941–1945

1. John Lewis Gaddis, *The United States and the Origins of the Cold War, 1941–47* (New York: Columbia University Press, 1972), pp. 25–6.

2. The United States made extensive use of neutral good offices. Switzerland, in particular, was asked to assume American representation in enemy capitals and to take over the traditional mandate services. This included care of buildings, repatriation of diplomatic personnel, protection of stranded citizens and their property. Swedish and Swiss services were also used to

communicate with the enemy where that proved to be necessary. The most famous instance was the transmission via Switzerland of the Japanese message of surrender in August 1945. Neutral services were also valuable for remaining in touch with American prisoners of war. In this respect the International Committee of the Red Cross (ICRC) played a crucial role. Although nominally an independent organisation established in connection with the various Geneva Red Cross Conventions, the organ is made up totally of Swiss citizens and functions very much like a neutral body. Since the Swiss government often assumed the role of Protecting Power in regard to prisoners of war, the functions of the ICRC and the Swiss government became intimately intertwined. The United States appreciated their services and respected the international law underlying them both. For more details, see Heinz K. Meier, *Friendship Under Stress: US–Swiss Relations, 1900–1950* (Bern: Herbert Lang, 1970), pp. 297–312.

3. For more details on the general American policy towards the neutrals, see Cordell Hull, *The Memoirs of Cordell Hull* (New York: Macmillan, 1984), pp. 1324–76.

4. Ibid., p. 1322.

5. George F. Kennan, *Memoirs, 1925–1950* (New York: Pantheon Books, 1967), p. 161. For greater detail, see also *FRUS*, 1943, Vol. II, pp. 527–6.

6. *NARS*, Legislative and Diplomatic Branch; US Department of State, George C. Marshall, Secretary of State, to Joseph W. Martin, Jr, Speaker of the House of Representatives, 2 July 1947.

7. Meier, *Friendship Under Stress*, pp. 313–15. See also Jonathan E. Helmreich, 'The Diplomacy of Apology: US Bombings of Switzerland during the Second World War', *Air University Review* (May–June 1977), pp. 19–37.

8. United States Senate, *Providing for the Payment of Neutral Claims*, Report No. 805, 18 December 1947.

9. *NARS*, Legislative and Diplomatic Branch; US Department of State, Office of the Legal Adviser, 'Duty of Belligerent to Provide Compensation for Damage Caused by the Dropping of Bombs or the Crash–Landing of its Military Aircraft on Neutral Territory', 18 December 1947. See also C. C. Hyde, *International Law, Chiefly as Interpreted and Applied by the United States* (Boston: Little, Brown, 1945), p. 2344.

10. See also Spaight, *Air Power and War Rights* (London: Longmans, Green, 1947), pp. 420–78.

11. US Department of State, Office of the Legal Adviser, 'Duty of Belligerent', p. 3.

12. Livingston Merchant, 'Certain Aspects of Our Economic Policy Toward the European Neutrals', *DSB*, 27 May 1944, p. 493.

13. David L. Gordon and Royden Dangerfield, *The Hidden Weapon: The Story of Economic Warfare* (New York, Da Capo Press, 1976), pp. 33–40.

14. Herbert E. Duttwyler, *Der Seekrieg und die Wirtschaftspolitik des neutralen Staates* (Zurich: Polyraphischer Verlag, 1945), pp. 243; Edgar Bonjour, *Geschichte der schweizerischen Neutralität* (Basel: Helbing & Lichtenhahn, 1970) Vol. VI (1939–1945), pp. 289–302.

15. For a general discussion of the blockade, see Gordon and Dangerfield, *The Hidden Weapon*, pp. 33–42; also H. Ritchie, *The 'Navicert' System During the*

World War (Washington D.C.: Carnegie Endowment for International Peace, 1938). This study describes the navicert system of the First World War but was also written in anticipation of another application. For a neutral viewpoint of the blockade, see Duttwyler, *Der Seekrieg und die, Wirtschaftspolitik des neutralen Staates*, pp. 63–111.

16. W. N. Medlicott, *The Economic Blockade* (London: Longmans, Green, 1952), pp. 44–62.
17. W. N. Medlicott, 'Economic Warfare', in A. and V. Toynbee, *The War and the Neutrals* (London: Oxford University Press, 1956), p. 65; see also Medlicott, *The Economic Blockade*, p. 46; Hull, *Memoirs*, p. 1325; Gordon and Dangerfield, *The Hidden Weapon*, pp. 181–5.
18. Medlicott, *The Economic Blockade*, p. 53. For a discussion of inter–allied co-ordination, see Gordon and Dangerfield, pp. 42–52.
19. Gordon and Dangerfield, Ibid., pp. 57–8.
20. For a discussion of non–belligerence in the Second World War, see Dietrich Schindler, 'Aspects contemporains de la neutralité', *Recueil des Cours*, Académie de Droit International, Le Haye (1967), pp. 263–4.
21. For a representative characterisation of the European neutrals, see Gordon and Dangerfield, *The Hidden Weapon*, pp. 3-6. Cordell Hull deals in some detail with American relations to each one of the neutrals; see Hull, *Memoirs*, pp. 1324-75. For an account of Swedish–Finnish relations, see W. M. Carlgren, *Swedish Foreign Policy During the Second World War* (London: Ernest Benn, 1977), pp. 28–53.
22. *FRUS*, The Conferences at Cairo and Teheran 1943, p. 226.
23. Hull, *Memoirs*, p. 1321.
24. Dean Acheson, *Present at the Creation* (New York: New American Library, 1969), pp. 89–90.
25. *DSB*, 15 April 1944, pp. 335–42.
26. Hull, *Memoirs*, p. 1322.
27. Merchant, 'Certain Aspects of Our Economic Policy Toward the European Neutrals', pp. 493–5; John V. Lovitt, 'The Allied Blockade', *DSB*, 19 November 1944, pp. 597–615.
28. Merchant, 'Certain Aspects of Our Economic Policy Toward the European Neutrals', pp. 493–4.
29. See Hull, *Memoirs*, pp. 1324–44, 1365–76.
30. Acheson, *Present at the Creation*, p. 85.
31. For more details see H. Gunnar Hägglöf, 'A Test of Neutrality: Sweden in the Second World War', *International Affairs* (April 1960), pp. 162–4.
32. Hägglöf, 'A Test of Neutrality', p. 165.
33. For a more detailed account of the negotiations of the year, see Carlgren, *Swedish Foreign Policy During the Second World War*, pp. 157–68. See also Hull, *Memoirs*, pp. 1345–8; and Bruce Hopper, 'Sweden, A Case Study in Neutrality', *Foreign Affairs*, Vol. 23 (1945), pp. 435–49.
34. *FRUS*, Vol. V (1945), p. 732.
35. Ibid., p. 733.
36. Ibid., p. 738.
37. Ibid., p. 740.
38. Ibid., p. 742.
39. Ibid., p. 746.

40. For a general view of the economic situation of Switzerland and of American strategy, see Hull, *Memoirs*, pp. 1348–51. For the Swiss point of view, see Heinrich Homberger, *Schweizerische Handelspolitik im Zweiten Weltkrieg* (Erlenbach: Eugen Rentsch, 1970); also Duttwyler, *Der Seekrieg und die Wirtschaftspolitik des neutralen Staates*, pp. 112–224.
41. Hull, *Memoirs*, p. 1349.
42. *FRUS*, Vol. IV (1944), pp. 760–1.
43. Ibid., p. 761.
44. For more details about the various pressures brought to bear on the Swiss, see Bonjour, *Geschichte der schweizerischen Neutralität*, pp. 347–56; Marco Durrer, 'Les négotiations économiques entre Alliés et Suisses à la veille de la défaite du Troisième Reich: à propos du point de vue anglo–américain', *Relations Internationales*, Vol. 30 (1982), p. 196. The establishment of 'blacklists' proved to be a particularly successful weapon of economic warfare. For details, see Medlicott, *Economic Warfare*, p. 79; and Meier, *Friendship Under Stress*, p. 324.
45. *FRUS*, Vol. IV (1944), p. 782.
46. In his memoirs Dean Acheson also attests to the fact that the blockade served the purposes of the Department of State: 'Negotiations with the Swiss moved at their glacial rate. We took advantage of the uncertainty the military situation had created in communication with Switzerland to suspend shipments.' Acheson, *Present at the Creation*, p. 92.
47. *FRUS*, Vol. V (1945), p. 767.
48. Meier, *Friendship Under Stress*, p. 331.
49. *FRUS*, Vol. IV (1944), p. 791.
50. *FRUS*, Vol. V (1945), p. 771.
51. Ibid., p. 770.
52. Ibid., p. 782.
53. *DSB*, 8 April 1945, p. 601. For a more detailed evaluation of the Currie Mission, see Bonjour, *Geschichte der schweizerischen Neutralität*, pp. 357–84, Durrer, 'Les négotiations économiques', pp. 202–5; Daniel Frei, 'Das Washington Abkommen von 1946', *revue Suisse d'histoire*, Vol. 19 (1969), p. 575.
54. For the Swiss point of view, see Homberger, *Schweizerische Handelspolitik*, pp. 117–31.
55. Gordon and Dangerfield, *The Hidden Weapon*, p. 2.
56. Ibid., p. 171.
57. Daniel Frei, *Dimensionen neutraler Politik: Ein Beitrag zur Theorie der internationalen Beziehungen* (Geneva: Institut Universitaire de Hautes Etudes Internationales, 1969), p. 571.
58. *FRUS*, Vol. II (1944), pp. 213–14. For a general discussion of the origins of US policy in this regard, see US Department of State, *U.S. and Allied Efforts To Recover and Restore Gold and Other Assets Stolen or Hidden by Germany During World War II*, co–ordinated by Stuart E. Eizenstat, Undersecretary of Commerce for International Trade, Washington D.C., May 1997, pp. 46–9 (Eizenstat Report I).
59. Eizenstat Report I, pp. 53–4; see also US Senate, *Elimination of German Resources for War*, part 2: Testimony of State Department; Hearings before

a Subcommittee of the Committee on Military Affairs, 79th Congress, 1st Session, 1945. See also Gordon and Dangerfield, *The Hidden Weapon*, pp. 164–80; Marco Durrer, *Die schweizerisch–amerikanischen Finanzbeziehungen im Zweiten Weltkrieg* (Bern: Paul Haupt, 1984), pp. 132–40.

60. *FRUS*, Vol. II (1944), pp. 218–22; Eizenstat Report I, p. 27, 54–6.
61. Durrer, *Die schweizerisch–amerikanischen Finanzbeziehungen*, pp. 148–84 (Safehaven and Switzerland), pp. 184–214 (Safehaven and Currie mission).
62. *FRUS*, Vol. V (1945), p. 783.
63. Ibid., pp. 782–3; Eizenstat Report I, p. 28, 64–5.
64. Eizenstat Report I, pp. 4, 64, 67–72; Unabhängige Expertenkommission Schweiz–Zweiter Weltkrieg, *Die Schweiz und die Goldtransaktionen im Zweiten Weltkrieg*, Zwischenbericht (Bergier Report), pp. 122–31, 204–5.
65. Durrer, *Die schweizerisch–amerikanischen Finanzbeziehungen*, pp. 218–24.
66. Gordon and Dangerfield, *The Hidden Weapon*, p. 177; Eizenstat Report I, pp. 28, 73–4.
67. Eizenstat Report I, pp. 74–6.
68. Ibid., p. 29, 76–82.
69. Ibid., p. 84.
70. Medlicott discusses in some detail the domestic and legal aspects of this question. See Medlicott, *The Economic Blockade*, pp. 47–50.
71. Eizenstat Report I, p. 27.
72. William Clayton, 'Security Against Renewed German Aggression', in *DSB*, 1 July 1945, p. 27.
73. John V. Lovitt, 'Survey of Economic Policy Toward the European Neutrals', in *DSB*, 18 November 1945, p. 779.
74. Frei, *Dimensionen neutraler Politik*, pp. 586–9.
75. Durrer, *Die schweizerisch–amerikanischen Finanzbeziehungen*, pp. 251–85.
76. Eizenstat Report I, p. 4.
77. Ibid., pp. 83–96.
78. Gordon and Dangerfield, *The Hidden Weapon*, p. 180. The American position was weakened by a split within the administration; see Eizenstat Report I, p. 6, 29, 96.
79. Eizenstat Report I, p. 83–4.
80. US Department of State, *U.S. and Allied Wartime and Postwar Relations and Negotiations With Argentina, Portugal, Spain, Sweden, and Turkey on Looted Gold and German External Assets and U.S. Concerns About the Fate of the Wartime Ustasha Treasury*, co–ordinated by Stuart E. Eizenstat, Under Secretary of State for Economic, Business, and Agricultural Affairs, Washington D.C., June 1998, pp. 37, 128–44 (Eizenstat Report II).
81. Eizenstat Report II, pp. 81–106, 107–27.
82. Eizenstat Report I, pp. 108–22.
83. Eizenstat Report II, p. 5.
84. Eizenstat Report I, p, 88.
85. Bergier Report, pp. 25–63, 69; Eizenstat Report II, p. 2.
86. Eizenstat Report I, p. 97.
87. Meier, *Friendship Under Stress*, pp. 363–7.
88. Frei, *Dimensionen neutraler Politik*, pp. 602–8.
89. Meier, *Friendship Under Stress*, p. 105.

90. An effort was made in 1962, but it lacked credibility; see Eizenstat Report I, p. 5.
91. Roland N. Stromberg, *Collective Security and American Foreign Policy* (New York: Praeger, 1963), pp. 117–20.
92. Eizenstat Report II, p. 36.
93. Medlicott, *The War and the Neutrals*, pp. 97–101.
94. Willard Range, *Franklin D. Roosevelt's World Order* (Athens, Georgia.: University of Georgia Press, 1959), p. 219.
95. *FRUS*, Vol. II (1944), p. 243.
96. Gordon and Dangerfield, *The Hidden Weapon*, p. ix.
97. *Neue Zürcher Zeitung*, 9 May 1997, 'Kein Verständnis für die Neutralität'; Eizenstat Report II, p. 7.
98. Jürg Martin Gabriel, *Worldviews and Theories of International Relations* (London: Macmillan, 1994).
99. *Bericht über die Aussenpolitik der Schweiz in den 90er Jahren*, Berne, 29 November 1993.

3   United Nations, 1945–1946

1. Robert A. Divine, *Roosevelt and World War II* (Baltimore: Johns Hopkins University Press, 1969), pp. 49–58.
2. J. F. Lalive, 'International Organizations and Neutrality', *British Yearbook of International Law*, Vol. 24 (1947), pp. 78–9. Lalive mentions the two dimensions of hierarchisation and centralisation as the most essential differences.
3. A number of legal scholars, therefore, openly attacked the UN Charter as institutionalising great power hegemony and legal inequality. See Edwin Borchard, 'Flaws in the Post-war Peace Plans', *AJIL*, Vol. 38, p. 288; Edwin Borchard, *American Foreign Policy* (Indianapolis: National Foundation Press, 1946), p. 61; William Rappard, 'Dumbarton Oaks et nous', *Die Schweiz*, Vol. 16, pp. 7–25; Paul Guggenheim, *Völkerbund, Dumbarton Oaks und die schweizerische Neutralität* (Zürich: Europa Verlag, 1945), pp. 112.
4. Cordell Hull, *The Memoirs of Cordell Hull* (New York: Macmillan, 1948), p. 1642. Hull also gives a general account of the President's ideas. Ibid., pp. 1634–48.
5. *FRUS*, Vol. III (1942), p. 569.
6. *FRUS*, 'The Conferences at Cairo and Teheran' (1948), pp. 530–1.
7. Sumner Welles, *Where Are We Heading?* (New York: Harper, 1946), p. 4. See also Willard Range, *Franklin D. Roosevelt's World Order* (Athens, Ga.: University of Georgia Press, 1959), pp. 173–89; John Lewis Gaddis, *The United States and the Origins of the Cold War 1941–47* (New York: Columbia University Press, 1972), pp. 24–31; Divine, *Roosevelt and World War II*, p. 58.
8. Ruth B. Russell, *A History of the United Nations Charter* (Washington D.C.: The Brookings Institution, 1958), p. 96.
9. Sumner Welles, *Seven Decisions That Shaped History* (New York: Harper, 1951), p. 178. See also Divine, *Roosevelt and World War II*, pp. 61–2, 66.
10. Hull, *Memoirs*, pp. 1662–3.

11. For more details, see Lalive, 'International Organizations and Neutrality', p. 88; Dietrich Schindler, 'Aspects contemporains de la neutralité', *Recueil des Cours*, Académie de Droit International, La Haye (1967), pp. 248–9; Josef Köpfer, *Die Neutralität im Wandel der Erscheinungsformen militärischer Auseinandersetzungen* (München: Bernard & Graefe, 1975), p. 135; Titus Komarnicki, 'The Place of Neutrality in the Modern System of International Law', *Recueil des Cours*, Académie der Droit International, La Haye (1952), pp. 479–80.

12. Non-participation was to play an important role in the Korean War. See Chapter 7.

13. See Köpfer, *Die Neutralität*, p. 135.

14. See Lalive, 'International Organizations and Neutrality', pp. 74–7; Charles M. Chaumont, 'Nations Unies et neutralité', *Hague, Recueil des Cours*, Académie de Droit International, La Haye (1956), pp. 24–6.

15. This became particularly evident when in 1949 the United Nations International Law Commission refused to deal with the laws of war and neutrality because, as the British representative stated, such action 'might be interpreted as a lack of confidence in the United Nations and the work of peace which the latter was called upon to carry out' *Yearbook of the International Law Commission* (New York: United Nations, 1956) p. 52. Quite obviously, the 'idealist' philosophy of the strict internationalists prevailed not only in some quarters of the United States but also in Great Britain.

16. About 200 scholars and specialists of international law from the United States and Canada published, on 1 January 1944, a list of *Postulates Principles and Proposals*, in which they spelled out their ideas about the international law of the future. As it was a highly heterogeneous group, consensus could only be reached on very general statements that did not touch the problems dividing the proponents of traditional and modern law. Still, the terms 'war' and 'neutrality' were nowhere mentioned; 'The International Law of the Future: Postulates, Principles and Proposals', 1 January 1944, *AJIL* (Supplement) (1944), pp. 41–62.

17. *Documents of the United Nations Conference on International Organization, San Francisco 1945* (New York: United Nations Information Organization, 1945), Vol. I, p. 126.

18. There was anti-neutral hostility in the public and the media; see Heinz K. Meier, *Friendship Under Stress: US–Swiss Relations 1900–1950* (Bern: Herbert Lang, 1970), pp. 347–9. It was rather exceptional that a strongly pro-neutral article was published in those days; Bruce Hopper, 'Sweden: A Case Study in Neutrality', *Foreign Affairs*, Vol. 23 (1945), pp. 435–49.

19. *Documents of the United Nations Conference on International Organization*, p. 124.

20. For more details, see H. Gunnar Hägglöf, 'A Test of Neutrality: Sweden in the Second World War', *International Affairs* (April 1960), pp. 156–9; W. M. Carlgren, *Swedish Foreign Policy During the Second World War* (London: Ernest Benn, 1977), pp. 28–53.

21. Meier, *Friendship Under Stress*, pp. 319–21

22. The Americans received some very clear signals that the Russians wanted to isolate the Swiss diplomatically. In January 1945, the Russian represen-

tative to UNRRA raised the question of the organisation's relations with neutral nations. The British felt that UNRRA should co-ordinate its efforts with similar relief measures by the neutral countries and that neutral personnel possibly should serve with UNRRA. The Russians objected. They spoke of 'the reactionary and pro-fascist views of the Swiss ruling classes' and argued that 'if raw materials were given to Switzerland for the purpose of manufacturing relief goods, it is probable that Germany would profit' *FRUS*, Vol. II (1945), p. 960.

As American diplomatic documents also show, the Swiss were keenly aware of Soviet hostility. In Washington, the Swiss ambassador, on 15 May, talked to Acting Assistant Secretary of State Joseph C. Grew. They discussed the new international organisation, and the ambassador wondered 'what the position of Switzerland would be in relation to the eventual world organization.' Grew expressed the hope that 'all "peace-loving" countries would eventually become members.' The ambassador then once more raised the point of obtaining the special status of a differential neutral, but added himself 'that Soviet Russia, which does not like Switzerland, might refuse to permit such an exception' *FRUS*, Vol. 1 (1945), p. 749.

23. Reinhart Ehni, *Die Schweiz und die Vereinten Nationen, 1944–47* (Tübingen: Mohr, 1967), pp. 33–4. See also Hans Kelsen, *The Law of the United Nations* (London: Stevens, 1950), pp. 94,107; Howard J. Taubenfeld, 'International Actions and Neutrality', *AJIL*, Vol. 47 (1953), p. 385; Lalive, 'International Organizations and Neutrality', pp. 77–8; Anton Greber, *Die Dauernde Neutralität und das Kollektive Sicherheitssystem der Vereinten Nationen* (Fribourg: Dissertation, 1967), pp. 85–8.

24. It seems that what the French aimed at behind the scenes was a condemnation of Switzerland because, like Stalin, they had an axe to grind. Among other things, they could not easily forgive the Swiss for having, very much like the Americans, snubbed the French under de Gaulle and, additionally, for carrying on diplomatic relations with Vichy France. For more details, see Ehni, *Die Schweiz und die Vereinten Nationen, 1944–47*, pp. 32–4. For a detailed discussion of FDR's decision to keep up relations with Vichy France, see Sumner Welles, *Seven Decisions That Shaped History*, pp. 31–65. For more details on Swiss–French relations, see Gérard Lévèque, *La Suisse et la France Gaulliste, 1943–1945* (Geneva: Studer, 1979), pp. 194–230; Schindler, 'Aspects contemporains de la neutralité', pp. 244–5.

25. *FRUS*, Vol. I (1945), p. 811.

26. Ibid., p. 941.

27. Ehni, *Die Schweiz und die Vereinten Nationen, 1944–47*, pp. 102–10.

28. At the beginning of the conference, the American delegation even discussed the possibility of inviting the neutrals to participate in the final stages. John Foster Dulles, one of the delegation members, said that 'he personally would not oppose having the Conference at the end become more universal in its membership.' Secretary Stettinius objected: 'it would be difficult to do that because if Switzerland and Portugal were invited, for example, the U.S.S.R. would object strongly' *FRUS*, Vol. I (1945), p. 417.

29. Some legal scholars question that limit, as they believe that the United Nations Charter is part of general international law applying equally to all states whether members or not. Hans Kelsen is one of these experts. See Taubenfeld, 'International Actions and Neutrality', p. 386.
30. Meier, *Friendship Under Stress*, p. 119.
31. Ibid., p. 115. This goes to show that Wilson could be entirely flexible and pragmatic and was by no means as rigid and dogmatic as he is sometimes made out to be by some of his critics.
32. A dissertation written in Switzerland at that time reflects the negative mood. It deals with American conception of neutrality in the eighteenth and nineteenth centuries and comes to the conclusion that the United States never appreciated the problems of a land neutral like Switzerland, because it had always been a sea neutral with primarily commercial inter- ests. While there is much truth to this argument, the author goes over- board in characterising American pressures against the Swiss as dictated by business interests alone. In his eyes America became a neo-mercantilist state out to conquer markets in times of war. That is a fairly simplistic view of American foreign policy, but it is reflective of the mood that pre- vailed in 1945; Constantin Guise, *Die Neutralität der Vereinigten Staaten* (Bern: Gustav Grunau, 1946), pp. 112.
33. *FRUS*, The Conference of Berlin (The Potsdam Conference) Vol. II (1945), p. 1510. Also *DSB*, 5 August 1945, pp. 159–60.
34. *FRUS*, 1945, The Conference of Berlin (The Potsdam Conference) Vol. II (1945), pp. 147–8.
35. Ibid., pp. 326–7.
36. Ehni, *Die Schweiz und die Vereinten Nationen, 1944–47*, pp. 30, 98.
37. *DSB*, 15 September 1946, pp. 487–90.
38. United Nations, Security Council, 57th Meeting, Thursday 29 August 1946, pp. 111–12.
39. Borchard, 'Flaws in Post-War Peace Plans', p. 284.
40. Ibid., p. 288.
41. Borchard, *American Foreign Policy*, p. 65.
42. Russell, *A History of the United Nations Charter*, p. 96.
43. Ibid., p. 98.
44. Scholars have since argued about the effect that the event had on the general decline of the law of neutrality. There is agreement that the abandonment of neutrality by the greatest neutral was an important factor in the decline of the law, but just how important was it? Ørvik feels that the United States 'wrecked' the law of neutrality, and Coogan even argues that 'Wilson perverted the very concept of neutrality and thereby undermined the entire system of international relations which had dominated Western civilization since the rise of the nation-state.' Schindler and Riklin disagree. Both authors show that a number of dif- ferent factors created a climate favourable to the development of the law of neutrality in the nineteenth century and that these turned against it in the twentieth century: (i) a rough balance of power; (ii) an international law regulating war; (iii) limited warfare; (iv) economic liberalism; (v) humanitarian and pacifist movements; and, last but not least, (vi) the existence of a large neutral, the United States.

See Nils Ørvik, *The Decline of Neutrality 1914–1941* (Oslo: J. Grundt Tanum, 1953), pp. 189–215; John W. Coogan, *The End of Neutrality* (Ithaca, NY: Cornell University Press, 1981), p. 254; Schindler, 'Aspects contemporains de la neutralité', pp. 230–4; Alois Riklin, 'Neutrality', in Wichard Woyke (ed.) *Handwörterbuch Internationale Politik* (Opladen, Leske & Budrich, 1980), pp. 270–8. See also Titus Komarnicki, 'The Place of Neutrality in the Modern System of International Law', *Recueil des Cours*, Académie de Droit International, La Haye (1952), pp. 415–18.

4   UN law versus Geneva law, 1946–1949

1. See Edwin Borchard and William Potter Lage, *Neutrality for the United States* (New Haven: Yale University Press, 1937), p. 24; Armin Rappaport, *A History of American Diplomacy* (New York: Macmillan, 1975), p. 60.
2. United States Senate, *Geneva Conventions for the Protection of War Victims*, Message from the President of the United States, 82nd Congress, 1st Session, 26 April 1951, p. A3.
3. Dietrich Schindler, 'Das Internationale Komitee vom Roten Kreuz und die Menschenrechte', *Revue internationale de la Croix-Rouge* (1979), p. 5.
4. *FRUS*, Vol. III (1950), p. 1586.
5. The Interparliamentarian Union meeting at Copenhagen in April 1946 offered a first opportunity, after San Francisco, to discuss neutrality in an international setting. As the Swiss delegation had to discover, the mood was also strongly anti-neutral; see Reinhart Ehni, *Die Schweiz und die Vereinten Nationen, 1944–47* (Tübingen: Mohr, 1967), pp. 95-6.
6. The International Law Association, *Report of the Forty-First Conference* held in Cambridge (London 1948), p. 45.
7. Ibid., p. 46.
8. At the 1955 meeting of the Association, the tenor was different. With the experience of the Korean War, neutrality had become more respectable again. The president of the Association, Lord Normand, had this to say: 'The existence of neutrality forms an oasis of international alleviation, independence and sanity ... neither the Korean nor the Indo-China wars would have ended without neutrality'; The International Law Association, *Report of the Fort-Sixth Conference* (held at Edinburgh) (London 1955), p. 20.
9. The International Law Association, *Report of the Forty-First Conference*, p. 50.
10. Manley Hudson of Harvard University was present at the conference. He did not speak on this issue, but he must have disagreed with the prevailing mood. He was a traditionalist neutral in the interwar period and remained so for the rest of his life. As a former judge of the Permanent Court of International justice, he was known for his espousal of the traditional law of war and of neutrality. Hudson got a chance to praise the Geneva Conventions once they were submitted to the Senate for ratification: *AJIL*, 45 (1951), pp. 776.
11. *Proceedings of the American Society of International Law*, 42nd Annual Meeting, 22–24 April 1948, p. 32.

12. *Proceedings of the American Society of International Law,* 43rd Annual Meeting, 28–30 April 1949, pp. 102–9.
13. Ibid., p. 109.
14. Ibid., pp. 110–11.
15. Ibid., pp. 111–12.
16. Disagreement over the traditional law of war and neutrality also surfaced in the discussions of the legal foundations of the Nuremberg Trials. Count 2 of the charges brought against the Nazi defendants referred to crimes against peace, and the Kellogg–Briand Pact was cited as a legal premiss. But, as some experts argued, if Hitler's invasions were a crime under the Pact, so was American neutrality from 1939 to 1941! George A. Finch, editor-in-chief of the *American Journal of International Law,* argued the point most cogently: 'To maintain retroactively that these invasions were international criminal acts involving personal responsibility is to suggest that the United States officially compounded international crime with international criminals. The United States continued to recognize the Government of Germany as legitimate, to receive its diplomatic representatives at Washington, and to accredit American diplomatic representatives to Berlin', George A. Finch, 'The Nuremberg Trial and International Law', *AJIL,* Vol. 41 (1947), p. 28. For an answer to these arguments, see Quincy Wright, 'The Law of the Nuremberg Trial', *AJIL,* Vol. 41 (1947), pp. 38–72; Quincy Wright, 'Legal Positivism and the Nuremberg Judgment', *AJIL,* Vol. 42 (1948), pp. 405–14.
17. Such close co-operation did not exist in Great Britain, for example; see Geoffrey Best, 'Making the Geneva Conventions of 1949: The View from Whitehall', in Christophe Swinarski (ed.), *Studies and Essays on International Humanitarian Law and Red Cross Principles in Honor of Jean Pictet* (The Hague: Martinus Nijhoff, 1984).
18. For more details, see Jean S. Pictet, 'The New Geneva Conventions for the Protection of War Victims', *AJIL,* Vol. 45 (1951), pp. 464–7. At the 1946 conference in particular, the United States played a leading role, since the president of the American Red Cross, Basil O'Connor, also attended in his capacity as president of the Governing Council of the League of National Red Cross Societies; see *Conférence Préliminaries des Sociétés Nationales de la Croix-Rouge,* Genève 26 July–3 August 1946, procès-verbaux, p. 910.
19. As was one of the last traditionalists of the interwar period, Manley O. Hudson, in a short commentary he praised the Geneva Conventions: 'The remarkable achievement of the Conference on Protection of Victims of War, which sat at Geneva from 21 April to 12 August, 1949, stands out as a landmark in the history of international legislation' Manley O. Hudson, 'Progress of the Geneva Conventions of 1949', *AJIL,* Vol. 45 (1951), p. 776.
20. United States Senate, Geneva Conventions for the Protection of War Victims, pp. A3–A4.
21. Raymund T. Yingling and Robert W. Ginnane, 'The Geneva Conventions of 1949', *AJIL,* Vol. 46 (1952), pp. 393–8.
22. International Committee of the Red Cross, *The Geneva Conventions of August 12 1949* (Geneva: ICRC reprint, 1983), pp. 23–7.

23. Short editorial comments in the *American Journal of International Law* accompanied the death of each of the three major traditionalists. References to their espousal of neutrality were the rule. Borchard wrote of Moore that he 'did his level best to keep Woodrow Wilson straight on neutrality problems ... but it was too difficult for him to debate with President Wilson, and most of his advice was not taken', *AJIL*, Vol. 42 (1948), p. 99. Briggs wrote of Borchard that he had become so imbued 'with the idea that the United States had taken the wrong path in the two World Wars and their aftermath that he tended to become polemical against the participation of the United States in efforts at collective security', *AJIL*, Vol. 45 (1951), p. 709.
24. The Swiss government had such expectations until 1975. Only in that year did it admit publicly that a formal recognition by the UN was impossible; see *Bericht der beratenden Kommission für die Beziehungen der Schweiz zur UNO an den Bundesrat* vom 20. August 1975, pp. 95–6.
25. Charter of the United Nations and Statute of the International Court of Justice (New York: United Nations), p. 1. Jean Pictet, *The Fundamental Principles of the Red Cross* (Geneva: Henry Dunant Institute, 1979), p. 5.
26. For many years Fenwick carried on with his campaign against the traditional law of war and neutrality. His final effort came at the age of 89, when he reviewed Majorie Whiteman's *Digest of International Law,* written for the Department of State. He chided Whiteman for treating neutrality at all: 'She presents the law of war almost as if there had been no Charter ... . The terms of the Charter in respect to neutrality are clear and explicit ... . The rights and duties of the old law of neutrality have terminated with the Charter', *AJIL*, Vol. 63 (1969), pp. 100–2. The International Law Commission of the UN also discussed the question of whether the law of war and of neutrality should be considered as part of its task. As is well known, the Commission decided against it; *Yearbook of the International Law Commission,* 1949, pp. 52–3.
27. *Proceedings of the American Society of International Law*, 43rd Annual Meeting, p. 111.

5 Alliance building, 1948–1949

1. For a general account of Swedish foreign policy after the Second World War, see Samuel Abrahamsen, *Sweden's Foreign Policy* (Washington D.C.: Public Affairs Press, 1957).
2. For an exhaustive discussion of the revisionist viewpoint, see Geir Lundestad, *America, Scandinavia, and the Cold War, 1945–49* (New York: Columbia University Press, 1980), pp. 7–84.
3. F. Herbert Capps, Bureau of Intelligence Research (INR/WEA), US Department of State; Interview October 1983.
4. Ibid., p. 353.
5. Grethe Vaerno, 'The United States, Norway, and the Atlantic Pact, 1948–49', *Scandinavian Studies*, Vol. 50 (1978), p. 174.
6. Barbara G. Haskel, *The Scandinavian Option* (Oslo: Universitetsforlaget, 1976), pp. 49–59. Richard P. Joyce, *Swedish Neutrality and the North*

Atlantic Pact (Washington D.C.: Georgetown University, 1951), dissertation. Escott M. Reid, *Time of Fear and Hope: The Making of the North Atlantic Treaty, 1947–49* (Toronto: McClelland & Steward, 1977), pp. 195–8.

7. Haskel, *The Scandinavian Option*, p. 61.
8. Walter Lippmann, *US Foreign Policy: Shield of the Republic* (London: Hamish Hamilton, 1943), pp. 92–3.
9. George F. Kennan, *Memoirs, 1925–1950* (New York: Pantheon Books, 1967), pp. 463–4.
10. *FRUS*, Vol. III (1948), p. 244.
11. Ibid., pp. 268–70.
12. Lundestad, *America, Scandinavia, and the Cold War, 1945–49*, pp. 246–51. See also *FRUS*, Vol. IV (1949), p. 13.
13. Ibid., pp. 239–40.
14. Ibid., p. 242.
15. For more background on the Matthews appointment, see Lundestad, *America, Scandinavia, and the Cold War, 1945–49*, p. 102.
16. Ibid., p. 221.
17. *FRUS*, Vol. III (1948), p. 24.
18. Ibid., p. 23.
19. The American Ambassador to Norway, Bay, shared Matthews' views. Actually, Bay had an outright conspiratorial perception of the Swedish neutrality plans – he was convinced that their origin lay in Moscow! See *FRUS*, Vol. IV (1949), p. 35.
20. *FRUS*, Vol. III (1948), pp. 97–8. See also *FRUS*, Vol. IV (1949), p. 5.
21. Ibid., p. 120.
22. Lundestad, *America, Scandinavia, and the Cold War, 1945–49*, pp. 222–34.
23. *FRUS*, Vol. III (1950), pp. 15–16.
24. Ibid., pp. 19–20.
25. *FRUS*, Vol. III (1948), p. 233.
26. *FRUS*, Vol. IV (1949), p. 775.
27. Kennan, *Memoirs, 1925–1950*, p. 400.
28. Ibid., pp. 407–8.
29. Reid, *Time of Fear and Hope*, p. 106.
30. Robert E. Osgood, *NATO, The Entangling Alliance* (Chicago: University of Chicago Press, 1962), p. 34. Reid interprets the Vandenberg Resolution as a defeat for Kennan; see Reid, *Time of Fear and Hope*, p. 109.
31. Lundestad, *America, Scandinavia, and the Cold War, 1945–49*, p. 257.
32. Kennan, *Memoirs, 1925–1950*, p. 412.
33. The precarious nature of Finnish independence was highly visible in 1948. During the height of the Czech coup, on 22 February 1948, Stalin sent a note inviting the Finnish government to come to Moscow to negotiate a mutual security pact. Would Stalin demand bases, territory, 'association'? As Secretary Marshall cabled the American minister in Helsinki, the United States had an interest in maintaining full Finnish independence, but not much could be done except to bring the case before the UN, if necessary (*FRUS*, Vol. IV (1948), p. 767). Once the Finnish–Soviet Pact was signed, there was general relief, however. Its rather benign content (consultation should Germany or any of its allies attack) came as a surprise,

and the United States wondered whether there were no secret protocols (ibid., p. 776). American policy had been characterised by caution; in contrast to Sweden, no pressure was ever exerted. Even Matthews warned against any kind of interference (ibid., p. 769). In the long run, too, the pact had no bearing on mutual relations. In the spring of 1949, Hickerson told the Finns that the pact had not affected Finnish–American relations, and that NATO would not have any influence either *(FRUS,* Vol. V (1949), pp. 434–8). In short, American–Finnish relations took place *outside* the alliance framework of the Cold War. This was confirmed by the Department of State Policy Statement of 1 December 1949 (ibid., pp. 443–50) in which mutual relations were termed satisfactory. Once more caution prevailed, because Finnish participation in European economic co-operation would have to be considered with regard to its effects on Finnish–Soviet relations, and the United States was not going to disturb those relations. It is also of some interest that neither the Finns nor the Americans ever spoke of *neutrality.* Finland was seen to occupy a special position between the East and the West, but it was not (yet) seen as a neutral. For more details on Finnish neutrality, see Ulrich H. E. Wagner, *Finnlands Neutralität: Eine Neutralitätspolitik mit Defensiv-Allianz* (Kiel: Dissertation, 1974), pp. 35–9. See also Max Jakobson, *Finnish Neutrality: A Study of Finnish Foreign Policy Since the Second World War* (New York: Praeger, 1969), p. 116; Raimo Väyrynen, 'Finland's Role in Western Policy Since the Second World War', *Cooperation and Conflict,* Vol. 12 (1977), pp. 87–108.

34. Lundestad, *America, Scandinavia, and the Cold War, 1945–49,* pp. 258–9.
35. John Foster Dulles, *War or Peace* (New York: Macmillan, 1950), p. 97.
36. Lundestad, *America, Scandinavia, and the Cold War, 1945–49,* pp. 260–1.
37. Ibid., p. 269.
38. *FRUS,* Vol. III (1948), pp. 256–7.
39. Lundestad, *America, Scandinavia, and the Cold War, 1945–49,* p. 266.
40. *FRUS,* Vol. III (1948), pp. 279–80.
41. Ibid., p. 134.
42. Lundestad, *America, Scandinavia, and the Cold War, 1945–49,* pp. 263–4.
43. *FRUS,* Vol. III (1948), pp. 264–6.
44. *FRUS,* Vol. VI (1949), p. 67.
45. Ibid., p. 71.
46. Ibid., p. 82.
47. Ibid., p. 89.
48. Lundestad, *America, Scandinavia, and the Cold War, 1945–49,* p. 298.
49. *FRUS,* Vol. IV (1949), pp. 95–101.
50. Mauro Mantovani, *Schweizerische Sicherheitspolitik im Kalten Krieg 1947–1963* (Bern: Paul Haupt Verlag, 1999), pp. 40–2.
51. *FRUS,* Vol. III (1948), pp. 264–6.
52. Ibid., p. 265.
53. Ibid., p. 281.
54. The same opinion is contained in a Department of State Policy Statement about Finland dated 1 December 1949; see *FRUS,* Vol. V (1949), p. 445. Joyce shares the view; see Joyce, *Swedish Neutrality and the North Atlantic Pact,* p. 89.

55. Lundestad also discusses the difference; see Lundestad, *America, Scandinavia,and the Cold War, 1945–49*, p. 107.
56. *FRUS*, Vol. III (1950), p. 1584. See also NSC 119, A Report to the National Security Council by the Executive Secretary on the Position of the United States with Respect to Switzerland, 20 November 1951. The same favourable assessment of Swiss military strength was given by the Department of State two years later, in August 1951. At that time the Swiss made an effort to purchase American military hardware but met with opposition by the Department of the Army. In an effort to support the Swiss cause, the Department of State argued that 'unquestionably the defensive strength of Switzerland constitutes a potential contribution to the collective defense of Western Europe, and indirectly to the security of the United States.' In the same letter the Department of State also suggests that 'the possibility of thereby establishing closer and more cooperative relations with the Swiss General Staff should not be overlooked.' The suggestion was to 'talk turkey' to the Swiss, whatever that meant. At any rate, Colonel Von Wattenwyl, Chief of the Swiss Army Technical Staff, had assured the Department of State 'that the Swiss Airforce would be willing to supply the appropriate US authorities with all relevant information regarding the precise location and use to which radar equipment obtained from the United States would be put.' If this is true, the Swiss were ready to violate neutrality in a political if not legal sense in order to obtain military equipment. *NARS*, Records of the Office of the Secretary of Defense; Department of State to Office of the Secretary of Defense, 13 August 1951.
57. *FRUS*, Vol. III (1950) pp. 1586–7.
58. Ibid., p. 1587.
59. As Mantovani shows, economic considerations did at times surface in the discussions. Some American officials argued that putting pressure on the Swiss might jeopardise their participation in European reconstruction. The point is not very convincing, however, because throughout the Cold War the Swiss made a clear distinction between economics and security. For more details, see Mantovani, *Schweizerische Sicherheitspolitik im Kalten Krieg 1947–1963*, pp. 43–4; Kurt R. Spillmann, Andreas Wenger, Christoph Breitenmoser and Marcel Gerber, *Schweizer Sicherheitspolitik seit 1945* (Zürich: Verlag Neue Zürcher Zeitung), pp. 15–25.
60. Haskel, *The Scandinavian Option*, p. 67.
61. Kennan, *Memoirs, 1925–1950*, pp. 462, 463.
62. *FRUS*, Vol. VI (1950), pp. 1111, 1167.
63. Ibid., pp. 1110–11. See also *FRUS*, Vol. VII (1949), pp. 806, 891.
64. *FRUS*, Vol. VII (1949), p. 928. For Dulles' opinion on Japanese neutrality, see *FRUS*, Vol. VI (1950), pp. 1161–2.
65. *FRUS*, Vol. VI (1950), pp. 1213–21.

6 Cold War economic warfare, 1949–1951

1. *FRUS*, Vol. IV (1948), p. 492.

2. Ibid., p. 512.
3. Gunnar Adler-Karlsson, *Western Economic Warfare, 1947–67* (Stockholm: Almquist & Wiskell, 1968), p. 23.
4. William Diebold, Jr. 'East–West Trade and the Marshall Plan', *Foreign Affairs*, Vol. 26 (1948), p. 719.
5. Ibid., pp. 717–19.
6. *FRUS*, Vol. IV (1948), pp. 565–7.
7. The act was supplemented in 1951 by the Mutual Defense Assistance Control Act (Battle Act) and in 1969 and 1979 by the Export Administration Acts.
8. *FRUS*, Vol. V (1949), pp. 130–1.
9. *FRUS*, Vol. IV (1950), p. 67.
10. Congress of the United States, Office of Technology Assessment, *Technology and East–West Trade* (Washington D.C.: US Government Printing Office, 1984), p. 155.
11. Ibid., pp. 155–7. For more details see also *FRUS*, Vol. IV (1950), pp. 146–8.
12. For exact figures see *Technology and East–West Trade*, p. 156. See also Adler-Karlsson, *Western Economic Warfare, 1947–67*, p. 30. For a useful general account of the general question of technology transfer to the East, see Angela E. Stent, *Technology Transfer to the Soviet Union* (Bonn: Europa Union Verlag, 1983), p. 125.
13. For a general discussion of the American approach to the neutrals, see Adler-Karlsson, *Western Economic Warfare, 1947–67*, pp. 75–8.
14. *FRUS*, Vol. V (1949), pp. 63–4.
15. Ibid., p. 68.
16. United States Congress, *Progress in the Control of Strategic Exports to the Soviet* Bloc, Report by Hon. Laurie C. Battle (Washington D.C.: US Government Printing Office), 29 January 1953, p. 2. In his report, Representative Battle characterises neutrality in the Cold War as unrealistic: 'The neutrality of non-Communist European nations is possible, in a world threatened by Communist aggression, only because of the cooperative effort of the NATO countries and others willing to take a positive stand' (ibid., p. 24).
17. See also Adler-Karlsson, *Western Economic Warfare, 1947–67*, p. 58.
18. *FRUS*, Vol. V (1950), pp. 137–8, 211.
19. *FRUS*, Vol. I (1949), p. 625; also pp. 431–4, 565–8.
20. *FRUS*, Vol. IV (1950), pp. 137–8.
21. Ibid., p. 138.
22. Ibid., p. 256.
23. Ibid., p. 180.
24. Ibid., p. 198.
25. Ibid.
26. Ibid., p. 200.
27. Ibid., pp. 210–11.
28. Ibid., p. 211.
29. Ibid., pp. 257–8.
30. *FRUS*, Vol. I (1950), pp. 1015–16.
31. Ibid., p. 1021.

32. Ibid., pp. 1077–8. There is some evidence that the US secured SKF co-operation through direct contacts between the Stockholm embassy and the company, as in the Second World War. See Adler-Karlsson, *Western Economic Warfare, 1947–67*, p. 77.
33. *FRUS*, Vol. I (1951), pp. 1103–4.
34. For a detailed discussion and analysis of the bilateral Swiss-American negotiations that followed, see André Schaller, *Schweizer Neutralität im West-Ost-Handel* (Bern: Paul Haupt Verlag, 1987).
35. *FRUS*, Vol. I (1951), pp. 1128–9.
36. The Swiss had even contacted Belgium on their own initiative to get more information! *FRUS*, Vol. IV (1950), p. 131.
37. *FRUS*, Vol. I (1950), p. 1138.
38. Ibid., p. 1157.
39. Ibid., p. 1160.
40. The fact that the Swiss had made some concessions in American eyes was also mentioned by Ambassador Richard C. Patterson Jr in a letter to the Department of State. He felt that the Swiss had 'stretched' their neutrality a good deal to the advantage of the United States and that they were severely reducing exports to the Soviet bloc at US request. *NARS*, Records of the Office of the Secretary of Defense; Richard C. Patterson Jr to Mr Perkins, Assistant Secretary of State, 5 October 1961.
41. For a detailed discussion of the problems arising from this situation of neither peace nor war, see Dietrich Schindler, 'Aspects contemporains de la neutralité', *Recueil des Cours*, Académie de Droit International, La Haye (1967), pp. 239–40, 295–9.
42. See Dietrich Schindler, 'Dauernde Neutralität', in Alois Riklin *et al., Handbuch der schweizerischen Aussenpolitik* (Bern: Paul Haupt, 1975), p. 241. See also Alois Riklin, 'Neutralität', in Wichard Woyke (ed.) *Handwörterbuch Internationale Politik* (Opladen: Leske und Budrich, 1980), p. 272.
43. See Schindler, 'Dauernde Neutralität', pp. 174–5. Also Schindler, 'Aspects contemporains', pp. 299–310.
44. See Dietrich Schindler, 'Dauernde Neutralität', pp. 171–2.
45. Since 1948, the Finnish have had an alliance of sorts with the Soviet Union. It does not bind either party, however, to come to the aid of the other. It is at best an obligation to consult in times of danger, more precisely if Russia should be attacked by Germany or any of its allies.
46. See Schaller, *Schweizer Neutralität im West–Ost Handel*, pp. 177–216.
47. To rationalise the contradiction a convenient solution was found. Art. 52 of the UN Charter permits the existence of regional arrangements for the maintenance of international peace and security, and Art. 51 specifies that such mechanisms are allowed to function 'until' the Security Council has taken action. NATO was seen to be such an arrangement functioning 'until' the Security Council intervened! To interpret the term 'until' in this manner, however, was to stretch the meaning of the Charter considerably. It was a purely legalistic justification.
48. For a more detailed discussion of the relation of 'collective security' to NATO, see Roland N. Stromberg, *Collective Security and American Foreign Policy: From the League of Nations to NATO* (New York: Praeger, 1963),

pp. 192–5; John Lewis Gaddis, *Strategies of Containment* (New York: Oxford University Press, 1982), pp. 56–7.
49. *FRUS*, Vol. IV (1948), p. 512.
50. Some experts suggested this. William Diebold Jr published an article in 1948 in which he proposed to weigh costs and benefits of such a policy carefully: 'Recognising the risk of war and our continuing rivalry with Russia, we may still run a reasonable risk of strengthening somewhat the war potential of a possible enemy if that improves the chances of reaching one of our important goals: an independent and self-sustaining Western Europe.' William Diebold Jr, 'East–West Trade and the Marshall Plan', *Foreign Affairs* (1948), p. 719.

7 Korean War, 1950–1953

1. Leland M. Goodrich, 'Korea: Collective Measures against Aggression', *International Conciliation*, No. 494 (October 1953), p. 131.
2. Dietrich Schindler, 'Aspects contemporains de la neutrality', *Recueil des Cours*, Académie de Droit International, La Haye (1967), p. 238; Günter Steinaecker, *Das Problem der Neutralität im Korea Konflikt* (Würzburg: Dissertation, 1966), p. 168.
3. Julian G. Verplaetse, 'The ius *in bello* and Military Operations in Korea 1950–53', *Zeitschrift für ausländisches öffentliches Recht und Völkerrecht*, Vol. 23 (1963), p. 712.
4. The idea of non-participation also appears in the Panmunjom Agreements, where a neutral is defined as one 'whose combatant forces have not participated in the hostilities in Korea'. See Friedrich Berber, *Völkerrecht, Dokumentensammlung* (München: C. H. Beck, 1967) Band 11, p. 2190.
5. For more details, see Edwin C. Hoyt, 'The United States Reaction to the Korean Attack', *AJIL*, Vol. 55 (1961), pp. 52–5.
6. Ibid., pp. 49–50.
7. Goodrich, 'Korea', pp. 141–2.
8. Hoyt, 'The United States Reaction to the Korean Attack', p. 51.
9. Josef L. Kunz, 'Legality of the Security Council Resolutions of June 25 and 27, 1950', *AJIL*, Vol. 45 (1951), p. 140; Robert W. Tucker, *The Law of War and Neutrality at Sea* (Washington D.C.: Government Printing Office, 1957), pp. 16–17; Titus Komarnicki, 'The Place of Neutrality in the Modern System of International Law', *Recueil des Cours*, Académie de Droit International, La Haye (1952), pp. 490–4; Steinaecker, *Das Problem der Neutralität im Korea Konflikt*, pp. 144–6; Schindler, 'Aspects contemporains', p. 247.
10. A parallel to the Ethiopian case under the League of Nations is suggested by Julius Stone, *Legal Controls of International Conflict* (London: Stevens, 1954), p. 236.
11. The 'Uniting for Peace' Resolution has been interpreted variously. Fenwick and Wright feel that it is binding upon members, most other experts disagree. See Charles G. Fenwick, 'The Legal Aspects of "Neutralism"', *AJIL*, Vol. 51 (1957), p. 73; Quincy Wright, 'Collective Security in the Light of the Korean Experience', *Proceedings of the American Society of International Law* (1951), p. 171.

12. Steinaecker, *Das Problem der Neutralität im Korea Konflikt*, p. 146.
13. For a discussion of the relation between neutrality and non-participation, see Steinaecker, ibid., pp. 152–4.
14. Fenwick discusses the link between the two in the context of the 'Uniting for Peace' Resolution. He argues that it is typical of neutralist states to abstain from voting and then to feel that they are not bound by General Assembly resolutions. See Fenwick, 'The Legal Aspects of "Neutralism"', p. 73.
15. *Yearbook of the United Nations* (1952), pp. 214–31.
16. Steinaecker, *Das Problem der Neutralität im Korea Konflikt*, pp. 155–6.
17. Patrick M. Norton, 'Between the Ideology and the Reality: The Shadow of the Law of Neutrality', *Harvard International Law Journal*, Vol. 17 (1976), pp. 302–3.
18. Ibid., p. 303.
19. Pitman B. Potter, Professor of Law at the American University and a member of the board of editors of the *American Journal of International Law*, was emphatic in his support of the traditional law of blockades: 'This is a second or third case of the necessity for the application to organized international police action of the old laws of war ... . It does not appear that any articles of the United Nations Charter or any special agreements of recent date modify the historic provisions of the international law or war or pacific blockade very greatly'. *AJIL*, Vol. 47 (1953), p. 274.
20. *FRUS*, Vol. VII (1951), pp. 1923–9, 1991–2. Chief opponent was Great Britain, which questioned its feasibility in view of broad opposition by Asian countries.
21. For a more detailed discussion of the legal viewpoint, see Verplaetse, 'The *ius in bello*', pp. 697–701.
22. *FRUS*, Vol. VII (1950), pp. 699, 703–4.
23. Ibid., p. 699. In December 1951 the opposite happened; the Soviets downed an American bomber. This time the Legal Adviser's Office gave the question careful consideration. On the basis of earlier precedents (discussed above), it ruled out direct American–Russian protests and claims, but it also argued that the United States had no right to act directly on behalf of the UNC. Only the UNC could act, and that would lead to no result. The United States was in a real quandary, legally and politically. For details, see *FRUS*, Vol. VII (1951), pp. 1245–6, 1308–9, 1353–4.
24. *FRUS*, Vol. VII (1950), pp. 917, 922, 941. The US documents do not refer to neutrality either.
25. *Yearbook of the United Nations* (1950), p. 287.
26. Ibid.
27. Ibid.
28. *FRUS*, Vol. VII (1950), p. 798.
29. *Yearbook of the United Nations* (1950), p. 262.
30. For a general account of the situation, see Goodrich, 'Korea', pp. 147–52.
31. United Nations, General Assembly, Fifth Session, Wednesday 6 December 1950, Official Record, p. 592.
32. Ibid., p. 592. For a more detailed discussion, see Verplaetse, 'The *ius in bello*', pp. 716–20.

33. United Nations, General Assembly, First Committee, Friday 8 December, Saturday 9 December, Monday 11 December 1950, pp. 405–29.
34. Cordell Hull, *The Memoirs of Cordell Hull* (New York: Macmillan, 1948), pp. 1662–4.
35. United Nations, General Assembly, First Committee, Saturday 9 December 1950, p. 417.
36. *Yearbook of the International Law Commission* (1949), p. 53.
37. For details, see *FRUS*, Vol. VII (1951), pp. 861–1107. Legal aspects of the question are discussed by Norton, 'Between the Ideology and the Reality', p. 266, and Verplaetse, 'The *ius in bello*', pp. 707–11.
38. For details, see *FRUS*, Vol. VII (1951), pp. 491–913. Legal aspects are discussed by Verplaetse, *op. cit.*, pp. 703–6.
39. As far as the Soviet Union is concerned, its neutrality conception was almost wholly negative until 1952 or, more precisely, the death of Stalin. As Fiedler shows, all Soviet commentaries and positions regarding neutrality were until then at best 'episodic'. This opportunistic attitude must have prevented the Russians from systematically taking advantage of neutrality. That changed under Khrushchev, of course. See Heinz Fiedler, *Der sowjetische Neutralitätsbegriff in Theorie und Praxis* (Köln: Verlag für Politik und Wirtschaft, 1959), pp. 218–19.
40. For a general account of the negotiations, see William H. Vatcher, *Panmunjom: The Story of the Korean Military Armistice Negotiations* (New York: Praeger, 1958).
41. *FRUS*, Vol. VII (1951), p. 599.
42. Ibid., p. 624.
43. Ridgway had already mentioned neutrality in his message of 30 June, when he proposed meeting on a Danish hospital ship in 'a completely neutral atmosphere' (ibid., p. 671).
44. *DSB*, 3 September 1951, pp. 389–93.
45. Ibid., pp. 671–3, 682–7, 900–3.
46. *FRUS*, Vol. VII (1951), p. 1235. The first documentary evidence that can be found at the National Archives is dated 3 December and relates to a discussion between U. Alexis Johnson, at that time Deputy Assistant Secretary for Far Eastern Affairs, and Pierre Millet, Counsellor, French Embassy. See *NARS*, Legislative and Diplomatic Branch, Department of State, Memorandum of Conversation, 3 December 1951.
47. *FRUS*, Vol. VII (1951), pp. 1242, 1250, 1279–80.
48. Ibid., p. 1250. See also *NARS*, Legislative and Diplomatic Branch; Memorandum for Mr Hickerson, Korean Briefing Meeting, 2 December, 1951.
49. *FRUS*, Vol. VII (1951), p. 1307.
50. Ibid. See also *NARS*, Legislative and Diplomatic Branch; Department of State, Memorandum of Conversation between Representatives of the JCS and DoSt, 12 December 1951. In all the above documents 'neutral' is usually written in quotation marks to indicate the prevailing uncertainty.
51. *NARS*, Legislative and Diplomatic Branch; Department of State, Memorandum of Conversation, Subject: Neutral Inspection in Korea, 13 December 1951.

52. *NARS*, Legislative and Diplomatic Branch; Department of State, Memorandum of Conversation, Subject: Possible Swedish Membership on Non-Combatant Commission in Korea, 14 December 1951.
53. *NARS*, Legislative and Diplomatic Branch; Department of State, Memorandum of Conversation, Subject: Possible Norwegian membership on Non-Combatant Inspection Commission in Korea, 13 December 1951.
54. Vatcher, *Panmunjom*, p. 247.
55. *FRUS*, Vol. VII (1951), p. 1284.
56. *FRUS*, Vol. XV (1952–54) p. 71.
57. Ibid., p. 90.
58. Ibid., p. 96.
59. Ibid., p. 167.
60. Ibid., p. 107.
61. The term 'non-participation', as mentioned earlier, was also contained in the Panmunjom Agreements, where a neutral nation was defined as one 'whose combatant forces have not participated in the hostilities in Korea'. This, of course, is not the definition used by the United Nations.
62. Verplaetse, 'The *ius in bello*', pp. 720–1.
63. Charles H. Heimsath and Surjit Mansingh, *A Diplomatic History of Modern India* (Bombay: Allied Publishers, 1971), pp. 70–2. See also Charles H. Heimsath, *India's Role in the Korean War* (New Haven: Yale University Press, 1956).
64. *DSB*, 22 June 1953, pp. 866–8.
65. Ibid., p. 866.
66. *FRUS*, Vol. XV (1952-54), pp. 566–8.
67. Ibid., p. 585.
68. Ibid., pp. 595–6.
69. *NARS*, Legislative and Diplomatic Branch; Department of State, Memorandum of Conversation, 1 April 1953.
70. Other 'neutrals' mentioned were Pakistan, Norway, Mexico, and Burma.
71. *FRUS*, Vol. XV (1952–54), p. 956. Congressional opposition continued until May. Ibid., p. 1058.
72. Goodrich, 'Korea', p. 185.
73. *FRUS*, Vol. XV (1952–54), pp. 830, 917, 920.
74. Ibid., p. 924n.
75. Ibid.
76. Ibid., p. 984.
77. Ibid., p. 994.
78. *NARS*, Legislative and Diplomatic Branch; Department of State, Memorandum of Conversation, 28 April 1953.
79. *NARS*, Legislative and Diplomatic Branch; Department of State, Korean Briefing Meeting, 1 May 1953.
80. *NARS*, Legislative and Diplomatic Branch; Department of State, Memorandum of Conversation, 1 May 1953.
81. For a critical assessment of India's role, see James F. Chancel and Robert J. Watson, *History of the Joint Chiefs of Staff, The Korean War*, Vol. III, Part 2. Under the heading 'India Complicates matters' the authors argue that in the matter of POWs India interfered with better proposals of the United States (p. 917). A defender of Indian motives was the American ambassador to India, Chester Bowles. He served in India from 1951 to 1953, and

upon his return published a book in which he defended Indian foreign policy. He compared Indian non-alignment to American neutrality from 1783 to 1941, a policy typical for young nations with a colonial past. See Chester Bowles, *Ambassador's Report* (London: Gollancz, 1954), p. 243.

82. The Swiss government pretended not to be a 'UNC neutral' but a mandatory of both 'sides'. It said so in its acceptance note to the American government, and it also questioned (naively) the role of India as an umpire above the 'neutrals'; NARS, Legislative and Diplomatic Branch, US Department of State, Legation of Switzerland (translation), 9 June 1953. Denise Bindschedler-Robert criticised the Swiss government for being inconsistent: 'Il apparaissait contradictoire d'accepter de faire figure de représentant d'une des parties au conflit en admettant qu'un autre pays ... sans vraie tradition de neutralité, fût traitée comme le neutre par excellence' Denise Bindschedler-Robert, 'Les commissions neutres instituées par l'armistice de Corée', *Schweizerisches Jahrbuch für Internationales Recht*, Vol. 10 (1953), p. 127. For a more general account of the Swiss point of view, see Klaus Urner, 'Das Mandat und seine Problematik', *Dreissig Jahre Schweizerische Korea-Mission 1953–1983* (Zürich: Archiv für Zeitgeschichte, 1983), pp. 7–17.

83. See Titus Komarnicki, 'The Problem of Neutrality under the United Nations Charter', *Transactions of the Grotius Society* (1952), p. 89.

84. The term 'super-neutral' is used by Bindschedler-Robert. See Denise Bindschedler-Robert, 'Les commissions neutres instituées par l'armistice de Corée', p. 113.

85. The confusion surrounding neutrality was matched by the uncertainty regarding the concept of 'war'. As Verplaetse puts it, 'never before was there so much discussion on that concept. Never before have such a wide variety of legal figures, old and new, been considered in order to find the legal definition and the proper hallmark of the operations', Verplaetse, 'The *ius in bello*', p. 681. See also Norton, 'Between the Ideology and the Reality', pp. 263–5. An effort will be made to follow the private and official debate in the United States towards the end of this study in Chapter 10.

86. Howard J. Taubenfeld, 'International Armed Forces and the Rules of War', *AJIL*, Vol. 45 (1951), p. 676.

87. This may have been the reason why, in the case of the accidental bombing of China in 1950, the United States proposed the setting up of a neutral investigative group. It also applies to General Ridgway's proposal for a neutral zone at Kaesong. Both are in no way related to the Hague Conventions.

88. According to Steinaecker, Sweden thereby followed a policy of qualified neutrality. See Steinaecker, *Das Problem der Neutralität im Korea Konflikt*, p. 166.

89. See Bindschedler-Robert, 'Les commissions neutres instituées par l'armistice de Corée', pp. 108, 113.

90. For details, see Heimsath and Mansingh, *A Diplomatic History of Modern India*, pp. 60, 74.

91. See Gunnar Adler-Karlsson, *Western Economic Warfare, 1947–1967* (Stockholm: Almquist & Wiksell, 1968), p. 30. Also Steinaecker, *Das Problem der Neutralität im Korea Konflikt*, p. 160.

92. For details, see Howard J. Taubenfeld, 'International Actions and Neutrality', *AJIL*, Vol. 47 (1953), p. 393; *DSB*, 28 May 1951, pp. 848–51; *DSB*, 9 July 1951.

8   Geneva Conference, 1954

1. *FRUS*, Vol. XV (1952–54), p. 1492.
2. Ibid., p. 1494.
3. Ibid.
4. Ibid., p. 1503.
5. Ibid., pp. 1531–4.
6. Ibid., pp. 1540–1.
7. Ibid., p. 1587.
8. Ibid., p. 1155.
9. Ibid., p. 1722.
10. *FRUS*, Vol. XVI (1952–54), p. 23.
11. *FRUS*, Vol. XV (1952–54), p. 1750.
12. *FRUS*, Vol. XVI (1952–54), p. 16.
13. Ibid., p. 79.
14. *FRUS*, Vol. XVI (1952–54), pp. 129,139.
15. Ibid., p. 129.
16. Ibid.
17. Ibid., pp. 139–40.
18. Ibid., pp. 144–5.
19. Ibid., p. 310.
20. Ibid., pp. 312, 353.
21. Ibid., p. 350.
22. Ibid., p. 318. More evidence of this strategy is contained in *FRUS*, Vol. XV (1952–54), pp. 1947–56.
23. *FRUS*, Vol. VII (1950), p. 720.
24. Ibid., p. 983.
25. Ibid., pp. 983–4.
26. Ibid., p. 1003.
27. *FRUS*, Vol. XV (1952–54), pp. 1446–90.
28. See also In K. Hwang, *The Neutralized Unification of Korea in Perspective* (Cambridge, Mass.: Schenkman, 1980), p. 107.
29. *FRUS*, Vol. XV (1952–54), pp. 1600–4.
30. Ibid., pp. 1620–4.
31. Ibid., p. 1623.
32. Ibid., p. 1950.
33. In a position paper intended for the forthcoming political conference, the Department of State mentioned not only neutralisation but also the possible creation of a neutral buffer zone along the Yalu river. None of these proposals can be found, however, in the instructions sent to Geneva. See *NARS*, Legislative and Diplomatic Branch, Department of State, 'US Position Regarding a Political Conference on Korea Following an Armistice', 8 June 1953.

34. *FRUS*, Vol. XVI (1952–54), pp. 131–9.
35. *FRUS*, Vol. XIII (1952–54), p. 1864.
36. *FRUS*, Vol. XVI (1952–54), pp. 995–1001. This is a good example of one of the many discussions of this topic.
37. Ibid., p. 1516.
38. Ibid., p. 422.
39. *FRUS*, Vol. XIII (1952–54), p. 1865.
40. *FRUS*, Vol. XVI (1952–54), pp. 1363–4.
41. Ibid., pp. 778, 1389–90.
42. Ibid., p. 1169.
43. Ibid., p. 1225.
44. Ibid., p. 1338; also *FRUS*, Vol. XIII (1952–54), p. 1405.
45. *FRUS*, Vol. XVI (1952–54), pp. 1552–5. This was the opinion of the State Department's Legal Adviser. In an opinion dated 27 July 1954 he concluded that both Cambodia and Laos would be permitted to participate as members of a Southeast Asia collective security arrangement.
46. Ibid., p. 1555.
47. As various NSC Reports show, the importance of Southeast Asia for the security of the United States had increased in the meantime, at least in American eyes. NSC 51 of July 1949 characterised the area as 'at best of secondary strategic significance'. Five years later, NSC 5405 contained more dramatic language: 'Communist domination of all Southeast Asia would seriously endanger in the short term, and critically endanger in the long term, United States security interests'. Under those circumstances it was but natural that allies should be perceived as more desirable than neutrals. See *NARS*, Judicial, Fiscal and Social Branch, NSC 51, 'A Report to the National Security Council by the Secretary of State on US Policy toward Southeast Asia', 1 July 1949; also NSC 5405, 'A Report to the National Security Council by the Executive Secretary of US Objectives and Courses of Action with Respect to Southeast Asia', 16 January 1954.

9 Germany and Austria, 1953–1955

1. For a discussion of the general Russian strategy in this matter, see Heinz Fiedler, *Der sowjetische Neutralitätsbegriff in Theorie und Praxis* (Köln: Verlag für Politik und Wirtschaft, 1959), pp. 233–4.
2. *FRUS*, Vol. VII (1952–54), pp. 169–327. See also Heinrich von Siegler (ed.), *Wiedervereinigung und Sicherheit* (Bonn: Siegler, 1967), pp. 41–2.
3. At the Department of State, officials had few illusions about the purpose of these notes. They were seen as aiming clearly at the 'contractual negotiations' and the European Defence Community. See *FRUS*, Vol. VII (1952–54), p. 172.
4. *FRUS*, Vol. VII (1952–54), p. 171.
5. Ibid., p. 204.
6. Ibid., p. 243.
7. Interestingly enough, the focus on free elections led to neutrality once more, because in one of their notes the Americans suggested the formation of an 'impartial' commission to supervise free elections. The Russians,

in their answer, spoke of a 'neutral' commission but rejected the idea; *(FRUS,* Vol. VII (1952–54), pp. 288–9, 620). This leads us to some interesting reflections about language: the term 'neutral' was used by Americans and Russians when they disliked a proposal, other terms (such as 'impartial' or 'not part of any coalition or alliance') were used when they liked a proposal. It appears that the term 'neutrality' had certain pejorative connotations on both sides of the Iron Curtain.

8. *FRUS,* Vol. V (1952–54), p. 518.
9. Ibid., pp. 517–18.
10. Ibid., pp. 1181, 1184.
11. Ibid., p. 897.
12. Ibid., p. 899.
13. Ibid., p. 985.
14. Ibid., p. 1030.
15. Ibid., p. 1032.
16. Ibid., p. 1120.
17. Ibid., p. 1145.
18. Ibid., p. 1205.
19. Ibid., p. 1266.
20. Ibid., pp. 1268–71.
21. Ibid., p. 1269.
22. Ibid., p. 1271.
23. Ibid., p. 1270.
24. Fiedler, *Der sowjetische Neutralitätsbegriff,* p. 235.
25. For a comprehensive discussion of the various targets in Western Germany, see Rainer Dohse, *Der Dritte Weg, Neutralitätsbestrebungen in Westdeutschland zwischen 1945 und 1955* (Hamburg: Holsten Verlag, 1974). An investigation of French neutralism is contained in Marina Salvin, 'Neutralism in France', *International Conciliation,* Carnegie Endowment for International Peace (June 1951), pp. 283–318.
26. *FRUS,* Vol. V (1952–54), pp. 1384–5, 1490.
27. *Public Papers of the Presidents of the United States, Dwight D. Eisenhower* (Washington D.C.: US Government Printing Office, 1955), p. 601.
28. Fiedler, *Der sowjetische Neutralitätsbegriff,* p. 236.
29. For details, see Gerald Stourzh, 'Zur Entstehungsgeschichte des Staatsvertrags und der Neutralität Oesterreichs 1945–1955', *Oesterreichische Zeitschrift für Aussenpolitik,* Vol. 5 (1965), pp. 301–36.
30. Bruno Kreisky, 'Der Weg Oesterreichs zu Staatsvertrag und Neutralität', *Oesterreichische Zeitschrift für Aussenpolitik,* Vol. 5 (1965), pp. 67–70; Felix Ermacora, *20 Jahre Oesterreichische Neutralität* (Frankfurt a.M.: Metzner, 1975), p. 265; Alfons Schilcher, *Oesterreich und die Grossmächte* (Wien: Geyer Verlag, 1980) p. 359; Stourzh, 'Zur Entstehungsgeschichte', pp. 315–23; Gerald Stourzh, *Kleine Geschichte des österreichischen Staatsvertrags* (Graz: Styira, 1975), p. 255.
31. The Russian strategy is described by various of the Austrian authors cited above but also by the Danish diplomat, Sven Allard; see Sven Allard, *Russia and the Austrian State Treaty: A Case Study of Soviet Diplomacy in Europe* (University Park: Pennsylvania State University, 1970), p. 248.

32. *FRUS*, Vol. III (1949), p. 1288. In a memo to the American legation in Austria, Acheson indicates that the Department was aware of Austrian wishes to become neutral since 1947, and then added: 'We need not stress political seriousness such writing-off of country before the event, if it shld become common knowledge or viewed as certainty by Aust Govt.' In other words, he was ready to 'write off' Austria, but it should not become public knowledge for reasons of bargaining with Austria and the Russians. During the same month (November 1949) the American High Commissioner for Austria, Keyes, reported that *de facto* Austria was already pursuing a policy of neutrality *(FRUS*, Vol. III (1949), pp. 1288–90). And in the context of elaborating NSC 68 (January 1950) Kennan wrote that the 'Austrians are impatient, to a serious degree, with foreign occupation, and many would prefer to risk attempt at "neutralized status" if foreign troops could be gotten out' *(FRUS*, Vol. I (1950), p. 129).

33. During two state visits in 1952 neutrality was not mentioned. In May 1952, Leopold Figl (Austrian Chancellor) visited Washington, but neutrality was not a topic. One month later, in June, Dean Acheson visited Vienna, and again neutrality was not discussed *FRUS*, Vol. VII (1952–54), pp. 1748–66. This was not yet the year 1953!

34. *FRUS*, Vol. III (1949), pp. 1190–7.

35. *FRUS*, Vol. VII (1952–54), p. 1918.

36. Ibid., pp. 1910–11.

37. Ibid.

38. Ibid., pp. 1901–2.

39. Ibid., p. 1015.

40. Ibid., p. 1194. See also Hans Mayrzedt and Waldemar Hummer, *20 Jahre Oesterreichische Neutralitäts- und Europapolitik (1955–75)* (Wien: Braumüller, 1976), p. 68.

41. *FRUS*, Vol. VII (1952–54), pp. 1193–4, 1201–2.

42. Ibid., p. 1088. See also Ermacora, *20 Jahre Oesterreichische Neutralität*, p. 33; Mayrzedt and Hummer, *20 Jahre Oesterreichische Neutralitäts-*, p. 70.

43. *FRUS*, Vol. VII (1952–54), p. 1195. See also William L. Stearman, *The Soviet Union and the Occupation of Austria* (Bonn: Siegler Verlag, 1962), p. 170; Stourzh, 'Zur Entstehungsgeschichte', pp. 325–6.

44. Kreisky, 'Der Weg Oesterreichs', pp. 67–70. See also Alfred Puhan in *Protokolle des wissenschaftlichen Symposiums vom 16. und 17. Mai 1980, 25 Jahre Staatsvertrag* (Wien: Bundesministerium für Wissenschaft und Forschung und Institut für Zeitgeschichte der Universität Wien, 1980), p. 35. Puhan is a former American ambassador and was intimately involved in the Austria question at that time.

45. This feeling of hopelessness was expressed well by Foster Dulles in his report to the National Security Council of 26 February 1954. See *FRUS*, Vol. VII (1952–54), pp. 1221–2.

46. Chancellor Raab visited Washington between 22 and 26 November 1954 but, as documents show, neutrality was not a topic.

47. For more details on the Russian strategy, see Stearman, *The Soviet Union and the Occupation of Austria*, p. 188, and Stourzh, 'Zur Entstehungsgeschichte', p. 329.

48. An excellent account of Kremlin politics at that time is contained in Vojtech Mastny, 'Kremlin Politics and the Austrian Settlement', *Problems of Communism*, Vol. 31 (July–August 1982), pp. 37–51.

49. Mayrzedt and Hummer, *20 Jahre Oesterreichische Neutralitäts-*, p. 71. See also William B. Bader, *Austria Between East and West, 1945–1955* (Stanford, Ca.: Stanford University Press, 1966), p. 202.

50. *FRUS*, Vol. V (1955–57), p. 27.

51. Ermacora, *20 Jahre Oesterreichische Neutralität*, p. 46.

52. Kreisky, 'Der Weg Oesterreichs', p. 70; Ermacora, ibid., pp. 45–6.

53. *FRUS*, Vol. V (1955–57), p. 35.

54. Ibid., p. 62–5.

55. Ibid., p. 114.

56. For a comprehensive interpretation of the treaty, see Joseph L. Kunz, 'The State Treaty with Austria', *AJIL*, Vol. 49 (1955), pp. 535–42.

57. Schilcher, *Oesterreich und die Grossmächte*, pp. 292–3.

58. *DSB*, 6 June 1955, p. 932. Anthony Eden, British Foreign Secretary at that time, expresses the same view. See Anthony Eden, *The Memoirs of Anthony Eden: Full Circle* (London: Cassell, 1960), p. 75. See also McGeorge Bundy, 'Isolationists and Neutralists: A Sketch in Similarities', *Confluence*, Vol. I (1952), p. 75. One of the rare scholarly discussions of neutralisation appeared in *The American Political Science Review of 1953*. In it, Fred Greene of Williams College deals very comprehensively with the European situation at that time and the possibility of promoting peace through neutralisation. He, too, clearly distinguishes between the cases of Germany and Austria. While he maintains that Austria (and Korea) offer a fruitful soil for consideration, he feels that 'it does not appear that a great power like Germany can be effectively neutralized', Fred Greene, 'Neutralization and the Balance of Power', *The American Political Science Review*, Vol. 47 (1953), pp. 1052–3.

59. United States Congress, Senate; *The Austrian State Treaty, Hearing before the Committee on Foreign Relations, United States Senate*, 10 June 1955, p. 5.

60. The term 'neutralization' is, therefore, not entirely correct in the case of Austria. Neutrality was never imposed on either Austria or Switzerland, as it was on Belgium and Luxemburg in the early nineteenth century. For details, see Dietrich Schindler, 'Dauernde Neutralität', Alois Riklin, Hans Haug and Hans Christoph Binswanger (eds), *Handbuch der schweizerischen Aussenpolitik* (Bern: Paul Haupt, 1975), pp. 163–4.

61. US Congress, Hearings, *The Austrian State Treaty*, p. 5.

62. Bader, *Austria Between East and West*, p. 203.

63. Allard, *Russia and the Austrian State Treaty*, p. 215. See also Mastny, 'Kremlin Politics and the Austrian Settlement', pp. 37–51.

64. Allard, *Russia and the Austrian State Treaty*, p. 211. Fiedler, op. cit., pp. 221–5.

65. Bader, *Austria Between East and West*, p. 200.

66. Fiedler, *Der sowjetische Neutralitätsbegriff*, pp. 231–2.

67. Stourzh, 'Zur Entstehungsgeschichte', p. 330. Fiedler, *Der sowjetische Neutralitätsbegriff*, pp. 248–52. For a general account of the new direction in Russian foreign policy see Allard, *Russia and the Austrian State Treaty*, pp. 204–14.

68. 1955 was, of course, also the year of the Bandung Conference.
69. The Department of State was aware of such a move as early as 1952. See *FRUS*, Vol. VII (1952–54), p. 1767.
70. Kreisky, 'Der Weg Oesterreichs', p. 30. Schilcher, *Oesterreich und die Grossmächte*, p. 178.
71. Gruber informed the US High Commissioner in Austria on 23 June, who in turn reported to Washington. *FRUS*, Vol. VII (1952–54), pp. 1867–8.
72. *FRUS*, Vol. V (1952–54), p. 1620. At about the same time, the Austrian representative in Moscow made an attempt to invite some neutral diplomats to a dinner in honour of the newly appointed Russian ambassador to Vienna. When the American Ambassador, Charles Bohlen, heard of the idea he was not pleased at all and tried to talk the Austrians into some other arrangement! Did he want to discourage Austrian ties to India? See Schilcher, *Oesterreich und die Grossmächte*, p. 177.
73. NARS, US Department of State, Office of Intelligence Research, Report No. 6403, 31 August 1953.
74. *FRUS*, Vol. VII (1952–54), p. 1869–70.
75. US Congress, Hearings, *The Austrian State Treaty*, pp. 7–8.
76. *FRUS*, Vol. V (1952–54), p. 391. Also *DSB*, 27 April 1953.
77. NSC 5405 of 16 January 1954 reflects the high security priority attached to Southeast Asia. The paper opens with the following sentence: 'Communist domination, by whatever means, of all Southeast Asia, would seriously endanger in the short term, and critically endanger in the longer term, United States security interests.' NSC 51, drafted in 1949, stated that Southeast Asia was 'at best of secondary strategic significance'. Against this background, it becomes evident that, as the strategic significance of the area increased, the desirability of neutrals decreased. *(NARS,* Judicial, Fiscal and Social Brauch, NSC 51, 'A Report to the National Security Council by the Secretary of State on US Policy toward Southeast Asia', 1 July 1949; NSC 5405, 'A Report to the National Security Council by the Executive Secretary on United States Objectives and Courses of Action with Respect to Southeast Asia', 16 January 1954.
78. Dulles was very consistent on this point. As early as 1950, he argued that the neutralisation of Germany (and of Japan) made no military sense *(FRUS,* Vol. VI (1950), pp. 1161–2). Five years later, in a letter to Foreign Secretary Macmillan, he voiced the same opinion *(FRUS,* Vol. IV (1955–57), pp. 362–3).
79. *FRUS*, Vol. II (1948), pp. 1320–31. 'Program A' was a policy paper drafted by Kennan's Policy Planning Staff and outlined one of many options to be pursued at a possible future meeting of the Council of Foreign Ministers. Against the background of the Berlin Blockade, the paper had little chance of becoming official policy. Such option papers are common practice in the Department of State and must be interpreted with caution. The same holds for reports of all kinds; a single document does not yet make American foreign policy. This is why the recent publication of 'Intelligence Report No. 6993' by Alfred Schickel does not prove at all that the United States was interested in German neutralisation, as he claims. (Alfred Schickel, 'Washington war nicht dagegen', *Deutschland Archiv*, Vol. 17 (1984), pp. 590–3). Such reports

are freely accessible at the National Archives precisely because they are not very important.

80. 'Program A' does not explicitly call for neutralisation but for demilitarised reunification.
81. Ernst-Otto Czempiel and Carl-Christoph Schweitzer, *Weltpolitik der USA nach 1945* (Leverkusen: Leske and Budrich, 1984), pp. 135–43.
82. Walter Lippmann, *US Foreign Policy: Shield* of *the Republic* (London: Hamish Hamilton, 1943), pp. 90–4.
83. *FRUS*, Vol. VII (1952–54), pp. 1895–6.
84. *DSB*, 6 June 1955, p. 932.
85. *Public Papers of the Presidents of the United States*, p. 589.
86. NSC 58, 14 September 1949; 'United States Policy Toward the Soviet Satellite States in Eastern Europe', in Thomas H. Etzold and John Lewis Gaddis (eds), *Containment: Documents on American Policy and Strategy, 1945–1950* (New York: Columbia University Press, 1978), pp. 211–23.
87. NSC 174, 11 December 1953; Entwurf einer Politikrichtlinie des NSC zur Politik gegenüber den sowjetischen Satelliten in Osteuropa; Ernst-Otto Czempiel and Carl-Christoph Schweitzer (eds), *Weltpolitik der USA nach 1945, Einführung und Dokumente* (Leverkusen: Leske und Budrich Verlag, 1984), pp. 135–43.
88. NSC 58 uses clear language: 'Democracy in the western sense is alien to their culture and tradition .... If, however, we are willing that, as a first step, schismatic Communist regimes supplant the present Stalinist governments, we stand a much better chance of success .... Such a development could conceivably grow to the point where there would be two opposing blocs in the Communist world – a Stalinist group and a non-conformist faction, either loosely allied or federated under Tito's leadership.' (NSC 58, pp. 219–20)
89. NSC 174, pp. 137–9.
90. *New York Times*, 7 June 1956, p. 10.
91. Ibid.
92. *DSB*, 18 June 1956, pp. 1004–5. Also *New York Times*, 8 June 1956, p. 1.
93. *DSB*, 18 June 1956, pp. 999–1000. Also *New York Times*, 10 June 1956, pp. 1, 24. In October 1955, nine months earlier, Dulles had spoken about neutrality in Miami. Although the language was fairly similar, it did not create a stir. It took Eisenhower's bungling introduction to make the words so important! In Miami, Dulles said this: 'The United States does not believe in practising neutrality. Barring exceptional cases, neutrality today is an obsolete conception. It is like asking each community to forego a police force and to leave it to each citizen to defend his own home with his own gun.' *(DSB*, 24 October 1955, p. 642)
94. *New York Times*, 11 June 1956, p. 1. In the 12 June issue of the *Washington Post*, Walter Lippmann commented on the confusion: 'What has brought about the Eisenhower–Dulles muddle is that apparently uncontrollable itch in high quarters to utter resounding generalizations' *(Washington Post*, 12 June 1956, p. 12). This was indeed part of the problem. If Dulles had made specific reference to neutrals like Switzerland or Austria, he might have made more sense.
95. *DSB*, 25 June 1956, pp. 1064–5. Also *New York Times*, 13 June 1956, pp. 1, 4.

96. On 17 June the *New York Times* ran two cartoons on the Eisenhower–Dulles neutrality muddle. One depicts Dulles and Eisenhower back to back on one bicycle pedalling in opposite directions. The other shows Ike welcoming a neutral with a bunch of flowers while Dulles throws a bomb at him (*New York Times*, 17 June 1956, p. 3).
97. Laurence W. Martin, 'The Emergence of the New States', in Laurence W. Martin (ed.), *Neutralism and Nonalignment: The New States in World Affairs* (New York: Praeger, 1962), pp. xi–xxi.
98. Michael A. Guhin, *John Foster Dulles: A Statesman and his Times* (New York: Columbia University Press, 1972), p. 264. Only a year later, another biography was published on Dulles that hardly deals with the issue of neutrality and neutralism at all. See Townsend Hoopes, *The Devil and John Foster Dulles* (Boston, Mass.: Little, Brown, 1973), p. 562.
99. Guhlin, *John Foster Dulles*, pp. 258–9.
100. During the Senate hearings on the Austrian State Treaty, Senator Humphrey sensed the contradiction inherent in Dulles' position. He wondered why the Great Powers had agreed to neutralise Austria 'along Swiss lines' and to urge it to enter the United Nations if Switzerland thought that its neutrality was incompatible with the spirit of the UN Charter. Dulles did not answer Humphrey correctly and clearly, so the matter remained unsettled. It definitely appears that Dulles never took the trouble to think through his position on neutrality clearly or, if he did, he never took the trouble to explain it publicly (United States Congress, Hearings, *The Austrian State Treaty*, pp. 14–15).

10 The legal perspective, 1957

1. Between 1945 and 1950, the major topics discussed in the *American Journal of International Law* related to collective security and the Nuremberg Trials.
2. At the Hague Academy of International Law, too, the Korean War stimulated discussion of the laws of war and neutrality. Here the topic had also been excluded from the agenda since 1945, but, in 1952, Titus Komarnicki, former Polish ambassador to Switzerland and expert on the law of neutrality, held five lectures on the subject; see Titus Komarnicki, 'The Place of Neutrality in the Modern System of International Law', *Hague, Recueil des Cours* (1952), pp. 399–510.
3. Joseph L. Kunz, 'The Chaotic Status of the Laws of War and the Urgent Necessity for their Revision', *AJIL*, Vol. 45 (1951), pp. 37–61.
4. Joseph L. Kunz, *Kriegsrecht und Neutralitätsrecht* (Wien: Julius Springer, 1935).
5. Ibid., p. 44.
6. Ibid., p. 61.
7. Howard J. Taubenfeld, 'International Armed Forces and the Rules of War', *AJIL*, Vol. 45 (1951), pp. 671–9.
8. Ibid., pp. 676–7.
9. Howard J. Taubenfeld, 'International Actions and Neutrality', *AJIL*, Vol. 47 (1953), pp. 377–96.
10. Ibid., p. 395.

11. Charles G. Fenwick, 'Editorial Comment', *AJIL*, Vol. 47 (1953), pp. 84–7.
12. Ibid., p. 86.
13. Fenwick was invited to lecture at the Hague Academy in 1951. He spoke on 'The Progress of International Law during the past 40 Years'. Obviously, for Fenwick progress meant the demise of the traditional law of war and neutrality and the advent of the law of the United Nations. Lecturing in the city where the Hague Conventions of 1907 had been signed and where, in 1923, an attempt was made to update the classical laws of war, he could not help making negative reference to those events: 'Gone, and it is to be hoped, gone forever is the naive belief that it is possible to draft new laws of war for new wars, as in the case of the Commission which sat at The Hague in 1923' (Charles G. Fenwick, 'The Progress of International Law during the past 40 Years', *(Hague, Recueil des Cours*, Vol. 79 (1951), pp. 170).
14. Quincy Wright, 'The Outlawry of War and the Law of War', *AJIL*, Vol. 47 (1953), pp. 365–76. At about the same time, Quincy Wright published an article in which he dealt very generally with the basic question of 'realism' and 'idealism' in international law. He did not mention neutrality but, as usual, it was excellent scholarship; see Quincy Wright, 'Realism and Idealism in International Politics', *World Politics*, Vol. 5 (1952-3), pp. 116–28. In 1951, Quincy Wright lectured at the Annual Meeting of the American Society of International Law. He spoke about the Korean War and the problem of collective security but, once more, did not mention neutrality; see Quincy Wright, 'Collective Security in the Light of the Korean Experience', *Proceedings, AJIL* (1951), pp. 165–82.
15. Quincy Wright, 'The Outlawry of War', p. 366.
16. Ibid., p. 371.
17. Ibid., p. 372.
18. According to Taubenfeld, Hans Kelsen, specialist on the law of the United Nations, shares this view; see Howard J. Taubenfeld, 'International Actions and Neutrality', *AJIL*, Vol. 47 (1953), p. 386.
19. *Proceedings, AJIL* (1953), p. 90.
20. Ibid., pp. 90–8, 99–111.
21. At the 1952 Annual Meeting of the American Society of International Law, a report was submitted that had been drafted by a work group headed by Clyde Eagleton. It dealt with the question of whether the traditional laws of war should apply to UN enforcement action. Unfortunately, it did not deal with neutrality; see 'Should the Laws of War Apply to United Nations Enforcement Action?', *Proceedings, AJIL* (1952), pp. 216–20.
22. Joseph L. Kunz, 'The Laws of War', *AJIL*, Vol. 50 (1956), 313–37.
23. Ibid., p. 313.
24. Ibid., pp. 326, 328.
25. Department of the Army, *The Law of Land Warfare*, Washington D.C. July 1956.
26. War Department, *Rules of Land Warfare*, Washington D.C. 1917.
27. Department of the Army, *The Law of Land Warfare*, p. 184.
28. By 'State' the manual seems to mean UN members.
29. Department of the Army, *The Law of Land Warfare*, p. 184.
30. Ibid., p. 187.

31. Robert W. Tucker, *The Law of War and Neutrality at Sea* (Naval War College, Newport, RI; US Government Printing Office, 1957), p. 4.
32. Ibid., p. 6.
33. Ibid., pp. 9–10.
34. Ibid., p. 15.
35. Ibid., p. 26, p. 22.
36. Ibid., p. 23.
37. Ibid., pp. 176-7.
38. Ibid., p. 173.
39. Ibid., p. 174.
40. Ibid., p. 177.
41. Paul Guggenheim, Professor of Law at the Geneva Graduate Institute of International Studies, was one of them. When, in 1945, he wrote about the new UN Charter and the problem of neutrality, he expected that the veto would be used regularly in the Security Council and that, consequently, neutrality would again become possible: 'L'existence de nombreuses divergences entre les grandes puissances permet de prévoir que Faction commune ne sera pas la règle dans les situations où leur intérêt majeur sera en jeu ... . Le recours au droit de veto dans ce domaine central de la sécurité collective a pour conséquence de faire revivre le statut de neutralité en faveur des Etats tiers'. See Paul Guggenheim, 'La sécurité collective et le problème de la neutralité', *Annuaire Suisse de Droit International*, Vol. 2 (1945), pp. 30–2. Two years later, J. F. Lalive published an article in Great Britain in which he enumerated the various possibilities for neutrality to re-emerge under the UN Charter; see J. F. Lalive, 'International Organization and Neutrality', *The British Yearbook of International Law*, Vol. 24 (1947), pp. 72–89.
42. Tucker, *The Law of War and Neutrality at Sea*, p. 181.
43. Ibid., p. 194.
44. Ibid., p. vii.

11 Southeast Asia, 1960–1970

1. Richard L. Jackson, *The Non-Aligned, the UN and the Superpowers* (New York: Praeger, 1983), pp. 11–36.
2. George C. Herring, *America's Longest War, The United States and Vietnam 1950–1975* (New York: John Wiley & Sons, 1979), pp. 73–6.
3. When it was set up Rusk thought SEATO was unnecessary, but once Secretary of State he was heavily committed to defend the principle of 'collective security'; see Dean Rusk, *As I Saw It* (New York: W.W. Norton Company, 1990), p. 426; see also George W. Ball, *The Past Has Another Pattern* (New York: W.W. Norton Company, 1982), p. 361.
4. For a discussion of American policy during these years, see Arthur J. Dommen, *Conflict in Laos, The Politics of Neutralization* (New York: Praeger, 1971), pp. 51–7, 78–87, 94–199; see also Ball, *The Past Has Another Pattern*, pp. 361–2.
5. William Shawcross, *Sideshow, Kissinger, Nixon and the Destruction of Cambodia* (New York: Simon and Schuster, 1979).

6. Khrushchev Report on Moscow Conference of Representatives of Communist and Workers Parties, 6 January 1961, John F. Kennedy Library, POF Box 126a, USSR, Khrushchev Reports, 1961, pp. 23–4.

7. *Public Papers, 1961, John F. Kennedy*; Annual Message to the Congress on the State of the Union, 30 January 1961, pp. 19–28.

8. For an assessment of the situation, see Chester Bowles, *Promises to Keep, My Years in Public Life 1941–1969* (New York: Harper & Row, 1971), pp. 334–5; for a general background discussion, see Dommen, *Conflict in Laos*, pp. 94–118, 142–70.

9. *FRUS*, Vol. XXIV (1961–63), pp. 1–25; Fred I. Greenstein and Richard H. Immerman, 'What Did Eisenhower Tell Kennedy about Indochina? The Politics of Misperception', in *Journal of American History*, Vol. 79/2 (September 1992), pp. 568–87; Rusk, *As I Saw It*, p. 428; Charles A. Stevenson, *The End of Nowhere, American Policy Toward Laos Since 1954* (Boston: Beacon Press, 1972), pp. 123–8.

10. As far as can be derived from FRUS documents the Eisenhower Administration never seriously considered neutralisation as an option. The term 'neutral' appears at times but is used in a very general way. See, for instance, a statement by Secretary of State Herter in *FRUS*, Vol. XVI (1958–60), pp. 641–4. The vagueness also shows in a report prepared and submitted 23 January 1961, by the Eisenhower Inter-Agency Task Force on Laos; the report mentions 'neutralisation' but is very vague about what this means; see *FRUS*, Vol. XXIV (1961–63), pp. 28–40.

11. Ball, *The Past Has Another Pattern*, pp. 362–3.

12. As early as 21 and 23 January 1961, Kennedy received two neutrality-related memos from Senator Mansfield; see Harald Biermann, *John F. Kennedy und der Kalte Krieg, Die Aussenpolitik der USA und die Grenzen der Glaubwürdigkeit* (Paderborn: Ferdinand Schöningh, 1997), p. 91; see also Bowles, *Promises to Keep*, p. 334.

13. Biermann, *John F. Kennedy*, p. 91; Stevenson, *The End of Nowhere*, p. 133.

14. Public Papers of the Presidents of the United States (PPP), *John F. Kennedy*, 1961 (20 January to 31 December, 1961), pp. 213–14.

15. Ball, *The Past Has Another Pattern*, p. 362.

16. PPP, p. 214.

17. Unfortunately, the summary record of the NSC meeting held on that day is rather sketchy; see *FRUS*, Vol. XXIV (1961–63), pp. 48–50.

18. *FRUS*, Vol. XXIV (1961–63), pp. 50–4.

19. Bowles, *Promises to Keep*, p. 339.

20. Stevenson, *The End of Nowhere*, p. 122.

21. Bowles, *Promises to Keep*, p. 337.

22. Ibid., pp. 337–8.

23. Biermann, *John F. Kennedy*, p. 92.

24. See for instance *FRUS*, Vol. XXIV (1961–63), pp. 315–17.

25. For a personal comment on Rostow, see Ball, *The Past Has Another Pattern*, p. 365. In May 1961 Gilpatric's Task Force submitted to the President a memorandum entitled 'A Program of Action to Prevent Communist Domination of South Vietnam', which was an early expression of his views, see *FRUS*, Vol. I (1961–63), pp. 92–115; also pp. 115–23.

26. An indication of this was the discussion held at a NSC meeting of 20 April, 1961; see *FRUS*, Vol. XXIV (1961–63), pp. 976–80.
27. Stevenson, *The End of Nowhere*, p. 142; Ball, *The Past Has Another Pattern*, p. 363.
28. Biermann, *John F. Kennedy*, p. 97; Dommen, *Conflict in Laos*, pp. 200–22.
29. *FRUS*, Vol. XXIV (1961–63), pp. 176–83.
30. Ibid., p. 177.
31. Dulles had questioned such a possibility and explicitly ruled out any parallels between Austria and Southeast Asia; see *FRUS*, Vol. XXI (1961–63), pp. 826–7.
32. *FRUS*, Vol. V (1961–63), pp. 182–97; 206–11.
33. Ibid., p. 194.
34. Herring, *Longest War*, pp. 225–51.
35. Rusk, *As I Saw It*, p. 431; Biermann, *John F. Kennedy*, pp. 217–18; Herring, *Longest War*, pp. 78–9; *The Pentagon Papers*, as published by The New York Times (New York: Bantam Books, 1971), pp. 79–86.
36. For personal commentaries, see Ball, *The Past Has Another Pattern*, pp. 365–8; Walt W. Rostow, *The Diffusion of Power, An Essay in Recent History* (New York: The Macmillan Company, 1972), pp. 274–6. For a telegram sent to the Department of State on 25 October containing a summary of the report to come, see *FRUS*, Vol. I (1961–63), pp. 427–9.
37. *FRUS*, Vol. I (1961–63), pp. 474–6.
38. According to Bowles, it was not the first time Rusk heard of the idea. Bowles hat presented it to him in February and had also talked to Kennedy about it right after the election; see Bowles, *Promises to Keep*, p. 407–9.
39. *FRUS*, Vol. I (1961–63), p. 323.
40. Ibid., p. 325 (note by the editors); Herring, *Longest War*, pp. 81–2.
41. Bowles, *Promises to Keep*, p. 409.
42. *FRUS*, Vol. I (1961–63), pp. 468–70.
43. Ibid., pp. 540–1.
44. Ibid., pp. 474–6. See also Biermann, *John F. Kennedy*, p. 227.
45. Ball, *The Past Has Another Pattern*, p. 366.
46. *FRUS*, Vol. I (1961–63), pp. 477–532.
47. Ibid., p. 564.
48. Ibid., p. 591–4; see also Biermann, *John F. Kennedy*, p. 234.
49. Rusk, *As I Saw It*, p. 430.
50. *FRUS*, Vol. I (1961–63), p. 585.
51. Next to Bowles, Galbraith, and Ball, Senator Mansfield was also active; see *FRUS*, Vol. I (1961–63), pp. 467–70.
52. *Pentagon Papers*, p. 87; Herring, *Longest War*, p. 77.
53. Frederick Nolting, *From Trust to Tragedy* (New York: Praeger, 1988), pp. 12, 15–16.
54. *FRUS*, Vol. I (1961–63), pp. 700–1.
55. Bowles, *Promises to Keep*, pp. 410–7.
56. Ibid., p. 415.
57. *Pentagon Papers*, pp. 158–90; Herring, *Longest War*, pp. 94–8, 101.
58. Biermann, *John F. Kennedy*, p. 249–52; Ball, *The Past Has Another Pattern*, p. 370.

59. McNamara, *In Retrospect, The Tragedy and Lessons of Vietnam* (New York: Random House, 1985), pp. 51–62; Rusk, *As I Saw It*, pp. 436–41; Ball, *The Past Has Another Pattern*, pp. 371–4.
60. McNamara, *In Retrospect*, p. 51; for CIA information on this point see *FRUS*, Vol. IV (1961–63), p. 89.
61. *Le Monde*, 31 August 1963, p. 2.
62. *FRUS*, Vol. IV (1961–63), p. 55.
63. *Le Monde*, 1–2 September 1963, p. 2.
64. *FRUS*, Vol. IV (1961–63), pp. 60–1.
65. Ibid., p. 94. For background material relating to the interview, see *FRUS*, Vol. IV (1961–63), pp. 81–8.
66. *The Washington Post*, 3 September 1963 (Column: 'Today and Tomorrow...').
67. *FRUS*, Vol. IV (1961–63), p. 100.
68. Rusk, *As I Saw It*, p. 434.
69. Biermann, *John F. Kennedy*, pp. 256–7.
70. *FRUS*, Vol. IV (1961–63), pp. 656-8.
71. McNamara, *In Retrospect*, p. 62; Pentagon Papers, p. 158; Herring, *Longest War*, p. 101.
72. According to Dean Rusk, both Kenneth O. Donnel and Mike Mansfield claimed that Kennedy spoke to them about planning to withdraw following the election of 1964; see Rusk, *As I Saw It*, p. 441; see also Ball, *The Past Has Another Pattern*, pp. 441–2.
73. McNamara, *In Retrospect*, p. 70.
74. *Pentagon Papers*, p. 83; Herring, *Longest War*, p. 116.
75. Cited in George McT. Kahin, *Intervention, How America Became Involved in Vietnam* (New York: Alfred A. Knopf, 1986), p. 416.
76. Kahin, *Intervention*, p. 182; Herring, *Longest War*, p. 111.
77. Reston had recently begun questioning US policy in Vietnam; see *New York Times*, 6 November 1963, p. 40, 8 November 1963, p. 8.
78. *FRUS*, Vol. IV (1961–63), p. 695.
79. Ibid., p. 754.
80. Ibid., pp. 12–13; see also Kahin, *Intervention*, pp. 190–1; Herring, *Longest War*, p. 115.
81. Ibid., p. 49.
82. Kahin, *Intervention*, pp. 197–8.
83. *Pentagon Papers*, pp. 234–70; Herring, *Longest War*, pp. 118–23.
84. Kahin, *Intervention*, pp. 234–6, 238.
85. Ibid., p. 381.
86. Herring, *Longest War*, pp. 126–8.
87. Kahin, *Intervention*, pp. 241–3.
88. Ibid., pp. 289–90.
89. Herring, *Longest War*, pp. 128–44.
90. Kahin, *Intervention*, pp. 294, 303–4.
91. The National Security Council met three times in one week, on 21, 22 and 27 July; see *FRUS*, Vol. III (1964–68), pp. 189–204, 209–20, 260–3.
92. David P. Chandler, *The Tragedy of Cambodian History, Politics, War, and Revolution since 1945* (New Haven CT: Yale University Press, 1991); William Shawcross, *Sideshow, Kissinger, Nixon and the Destruction of*

Cambodia (New York: Simon and Schuster, 1979); Arnold R. Isaacs, *Without Honor, Defeat in Vietnam and Cambodia* (Baltimore MD: The Johns Hopkins University Press, 1983); Milton Osborne, *Sihanouk, Prince of Light, Prince of Darkness* (Honolulu: University of Hawaii Press, 1994).

93. *FRUS*, Vol. XXIII (1961–63), p. 148.
94. For a general discussion of Sihanouk's relations with the United States from 1954 to 1962, see Kenton J. Clymer, 'The Perils of Neutrality: The Break in U.S.–Cambodian Relations, 1965', in *Diplomatic History*, Vol. 23/4, Fall 1999, pp. 613–15.
95. For the complete text of Sihanouk's letter to JFK, see American Foreign Policy, Current Documents, 1962, Parts 8–14, pp. 1002–3; see also Clymer, 'The Perils of Neutrality', p. 617.
96. *FRUS*, Vol. XXIII (1961–63), p. 199.
97. Ibid., p. 222.
98. Ibid., pp. 225–6.
99. Ibid., pp. 218–19.
100. Ibid., p. 227.
101. Ibid., p. 224; see also American Foreign Policy, Current Documents, 1962, Parts 8–14, pp. 1003–4.
102. *FRUS*, Vol. XXIII (1961–63), p. 234.
103. Clymer, 'The Perils of Neutrality', p. 614; Chandler, *The Tragedy of Cambodian History*, p. 130; Shawcross, *Sideshow*, p. 60.
104. Chandler, *The Tragedy of Cambodian History*, p. 130.
105. *FRUS*, Vol. IV (1961–63), p. 641.
106. Chandler, *The Tragedy of Cambodian History*, p. 135; Clymer, 'The Perils of Neutrality', p. 617.
107. *FRUS*, Vol. XXIII (1961-63), p. 272; *FRUS*, Vol. IV (1961–63), pp. 695–6; Clymer, 'The Perils of Neutrality', p. 617.
108. *FRUS*, Vol. XXIII (1961–63), p. 277; *FRUS*, Vol. IV (1961–63) p. 697, 713.
109. It was at about the same time that Sihanouk cut a secret deal with the North Vietnamese. He allowed them to use the Port of Sihanoukville to ship Chinese weapons to the NLF. As a quid pro quo the Cambodian army skimmed off 10 per cent of the supplies: Chandler, *The Tragedy of Cambodian History*, p. 140; Shawcross, *Sideshow*, p. 64.
110. Clymer, 'The Perils of Neutrality', p. 617.
111. Ibid., p. 622; Chandler, *The Tragedy of Cambodian History*, p. 145; Osborne, *Sihanouk*, p. 171.
112. *FRUS*, Vol. II (1964–68), p. 572.
113. Clymer, 'The Perils of Neutrality', p. 609, 625–6.
114. Ibid., p. 627; Osborne, *Sihanouk*, p. 171; *FRUS*, Vol. II (1964–68), p. 639.
115. *FRUS*, Vol. II (1964–68), p. 604; Clymer, 'The Perils of Neutrality', p. 625.
116. *FRUS*, Vol. III (1964–68), pp. 328–32; Clymer, 'The Perils of Neutrality', pp. 626–7.
117. Ibid., p. 649.
118. Chandler, *The Tragedy of Cambodian History*, pp. 150–3.
119. Ibid., pp. 153–8.
120. Ibid., p. 159.
121. Shawcross, *Sideshow*, pp. 68–71; Chandler, *The Tragedy of Cambodian History*, pp. 172–3.

122. Ibid., pp. 80–4.
123. Ibid., pp. 112–23; Chandler, *The Tragedy of Cambodian History*, pp. 192–9.
124. Ibid., pp. 128–49.
125. Clymer, 'The Perils of Neutrality', p. 631.
126. Rusk, *As I Saw It*, p. 427.
127. Quing Zhai, 'Beijing and the Vietnam Conflict, 1964-1965: New Chinese Evidence', in *Cold War International History Project*, Woodrow Wilson International Center for Scholars, Washington D.C., Winter 1995/1996, Issues 6–7, pp. 233–50.
128. *FRUS*, Vol. I (1961–63), p. 235.
129. Ibid., p. 535.
130. Ibid., p. 400.
131. Ibid., p. 585.
132. Rusk, *As I Saw It*, p. 435.

12   Summary and conclusions

1. Jürg Martin Gabriel, *Sackgasse Neutralität* (Zürich: Hochschulverlag AG an der ETH Zürich, 1997), pp. 75–91.
2. John J. Mearshheimer, 'Back to the Future; Instability in Europe after the Cold War', *International Security*, No. 15, 1990, pp. 5–56.
3. Alois Riklin, 'Die Neutralität der Schweiz', in Alois Riklin, Hans Haug and Raymond Probst (eds), *Neues Handbuch der schweizerischen Aussenpolitik* (Bern: Paul Haupt Verlag, 1992), pp. 206–7.

Bibliography

1. Bibliographies, handbooks, and guides

Behrmann, Lilly-Ralon, Peter Proché and Wolfgang Strasser, *Bibliographie zur Aussenpolitik der Republik Oesterreich seit 1945*. Vienna: W. Braumüller, 1974.

Berber, Friedrick, *Völkerrecht, Dokumentensammlung*. Vol. 11, Konfliktrecht. Munich: C. H. Beck, 1967.

Blanchard, Carrol H., *Korean War Bibliography*. Albany, NY: State University of New York, 1964.

Burns, Richard Dean, *Guide to American Foreign Relations Since 1700*. Santa Barbara, CA: ABC-CLIO, 1983.

Dexter, Byron, *The Foreign Affairs 50-Year Bibliography, 1920–1970*. New York: R. R. Bowker, 1972.

Gordon, Colin, *The Atlantic Alliance: A Bibliography*. London: Frances Pinter, 1978.

Gustafson, Milton O. *The National Archives and Foreign Relations Research*. Athens, Ohio: Ohio University Press, 1974.

Haines, Gerald K. and J. Samuel Walker, *American Foreign Relations: A Historiographical Review*. London: Frances Pinter, 1981.

Kreslins, Janis A., *Foreign Affairs Bibliography, 1962–1972*. London: R. R. Bowker, 1976.

Langer, William L. (ed.), *An Encyclopedia of World History*. Boston, Mass.: Houghton Mifflin, 1952.

Langer, William L. and Hamilton F. Armstrong, *Foreign Affairs Bibliography, 1919–1932*. New York: Harper, 1933.

Roberts, Henry L., *Foreign Affairs Bibliography 1942–1952*. New York: Harper, 1955.

Roberts, Henry L., *Foreign Affairs Bibliography, 1952–1962*. New York: Harper, 1964.

Woolbert, Robert G., *Foreign Affairs Bibliography, 1932–1942*. New York: Harper, 1943.

2. Official sources, records, and publications

Austrian Government, *25 Jahre Staatsvertrag, Protokolle des wissenschaftlichen Symposiums vom 16–17. Mai 1980*. Vienna: Bundesministerium für Wissenschaft und Forschung, 1980.

German Government, Bundesministerium des Innern, *Dokumente zur Deutschlandpolitik, Deutsche Einheit, Sonderedition aus den Akten des Bundeskanzleramtes 1989/90*. München: Oldenbourg 1998.

International Committee of the Red Cross, *Commission d'experts gouvernementaux pour l'étude des conventions protégeant les victimes de la guerre*. Rapport sur les travaux. Geneva, 1947.

International Committee of the Red Cross, *Final Record of the Diplomatic Conference of Geneva of 1949*. Bern: Federal Political Department, 1949.

International Committee of the Red Cross, *The Geneva Conventions of 12 August, 1949*. Geneva: ICRC, 1983.

National Archives, Washington D.C., Modern Military Headquarters Branch. *The History of the Joint Chiefs of Staff: The Korean War* (vol. III, Part 2), by James F. Schnabel and R. J. Watson. Washington D.C.: US Government Printing Office, 1979.

National Archives, Washington D.C., Modern Military Headquarters Branch. *JCS Records*.

National Archives, Washington D.C., Modern Military Headquarters Branch. *OSD Records 1947–1953*.

National Archives, Washington D.C.,Modern Military Headquarters Branch. *Records of the Army Staff*.

National Archives, Washington D.C., Modern Military Headquarters Branch. *American-British Conversations 1942–47* (ABC Files),

National Archives, Washington D.C., Legislative and Diplomatic Branch. Central Decimal Files of Department of State. *Korea: Internal Political Affairs*.

National Archives, Washington D.C., Legislative and Diplomatic Branch. *Department of State: Office of Intelligence Research* (R & A Reports).

National Archives, Washington D.C., Legislative and Diplomatie Branch. *Department of State: Office of the Legal Adviser*.

National Archives, Washington D.C., Judicial, Fiscal and Social Branch. *NSC Policy Papers*.

Pentagon Papers (The), as published by the *New York Times*. New York: Bantam Books, 1971.

Public Papers of the Presidents of the United States, John F. Kennedy, 1961. Washington D.C., US Government Printing Office, 1961.

Swiss Government, *Bericht der beratenden Kommission für die Beziehungen der Schweiz zur UNO an den Bundesrat vom 20. August 1975*. Bern: EDMZ, 1975.

Swiss Government, Unabhängige Expertenkommission Schweiz-Zweiter Weltkrieg. *Die Schweiz und die Goldtransaktionen im Zweiten Weltkrieg, Zwischenbericht*. Bern: EDMZ, 1998.

United Nations, *Documents on the United Nations Conference on International Organization, San Francisco 1945*. New York: United Nations Information Organizations, 1945. Vol. I.

United Nations, *Yearbook of the International Law Commission*. New York: United Nations, 1956.

United Nations, *Yearbook of the United Nations, 1950*. New York: Department of Public Information, United Nations.

United Nations, *Security Council, Official Records (5th Year)*. 501st Meeting, Lake Success, New York, 12 September 1950.

United Nations, *General Assembly, Official Records (5th Session)*. 319th Plenary Meeting, 6 December 1950.

United Nations *General Assembly, Official Records (5th Session)*. First Committee, 9 November 1950; 10 November, 1950; 8 December 1950; 9 December 1950; 11 December 1950.

United States Congress, House of Representatives, *Progress in the Control of Strategic Exports to the Soviet Bloc*. Report submitted to the House Committee on Foreign Affairs by Hon. Laurie C. Battle, 23 January 1953. Washington D.C.: US Government Printing Office, 1953.

United States Congress, Senate, *The Austrian State Treay*, Hearing before the Committee on Foreign Relations, 84th Congress, 10 June 1955. Washington D.C.: US Government Printing Office, 1955.

United States Congress, Office of Technology Assessment, *Technology and East–West Trade*. Washington D.C.: US Government Printing Office, 1979.

United States Department of State, *Foreign Relations of the United States*. Washington D.C.: US Government Printing Office.

United States Department Of State, *Department of State Bulletin*. Washington D.C.: US Government Printing Office.

United States Department of State, *American Foreign Policy, Basic Documents*. Washington D.C.: US Government Printing Office.

United States Department of State, *Public Papers of the Presidents of the United States; Dwight D. Eisenhower, 1955*. Washington D.C.: US Government Printing Office, 1956.

United States Department of State, Office of The Legal Adviser, *Treaties in Force*. Washington D.C.: US Government Printing Office, 1976.

United States Department of State, *Digest of International Law* by Marjorie M. Whiteman, Assistant Legal Adviser. Washington D.C.: US Government Printing Office, Vol. 11, 1968.

United States Department of State, Office Of The Legal Adviser, *Treaties and Other International Agreements of the United States of America, 1766–1949*. Washington D.C.: US Government Printing Office.

United States Department of State, *Mutual Defense Assistance Control Act, Annual Reports to Congress*. Washington D.C.: US Government Printing Office, 1952, 1953, 1955.

United States Department of State, *U.S. and Allied Efforts To Recover and Restore Gold and Other Assets Stolen or Hidden by Germany During World War II*, co-ordinated by Stuart E. Eizenstat, Undersecretary of Commerce for International Trade. Washington D.C.: US Government Printing Office, May 1997.

United States Department of The Air Force, *International Law – The Conduct of Armed Conflict and Air Operations*. Washington D.C.: US Government Printing Office, 1976.

United States Department of The Army, *Field Manual on the Law of Land Warfare*. Washington D.C.: US Government Printing Office, 1956.

United States Department of The Navy, *Laws of Naval Warfare*. Washington D.C.: US Government Printing Office, 1955.

United States Department of War, *Rules of Land Warfare*. Washington D.C.: US Government Printing Office, 1917.

United States Naval War College, *The Law of War and Neutrality at Sea* by Robert W. Tucker. Washington D.C.: US Government Printing Office, 1957.

3. Journals, reports, newspapers

American Journal of International Law
American Political Science Review
American University International Law Review
Aussenwirtschaft (St. Gallen)
British Yearbook on International Law

Confluence
Cooperation and Conflict (Stockholm)
Deutschland Archiv
Foreign Affairs
Harvard International Law Journal
International Affairs (Oslo)
International Conciliation
Le Monde
Neue Zürcher Zeitung
New York Times
Oesterreichische Zeitschrift für Aussenpolitik
Problems of Communism
Proceedings of the American Society of International Law
Recueil des Cours (Hague)
Relations Internationales (Paris)
Reports of the International Law Association
Revue internationale de la Croix Rouge (Geneva)
Revue suisse d'histoire
Scandinavian Studies
Schweizerisches Jahrbuch für Internationals Recht
Transactions of the Grotius Society
University of Illinois Bulletin
Washington Post (The)
World Politics
Yale Law Journal
Zeitschrift für ausländisches, öffentliches Recht und Völkerrecht

4. Books and articles

(a) The period before 1941

Adler, Selig, *The Isolationist Impulse*. New York: Abelard-Schumann, 1957.
Adler, Selig, *The Uncertain Giant: 1921–1941*. New York: Macmillan, 1965.
Albion, Robert G. and Jennie B. Pope, *Sea Lanes in Wartime*. New York: Norton, 1942.
Bailey, Thomas A., *The Policy of the United States Toward the Neutrals: 1917–1918*. Baltimore, Md.: Johns Hopkins University Press, 1942.
Bailey, Thomas A., *A Diplomatic History of the American People*. New York: Appleton Century Crofts, 1969.
Beard, Charles A. *President Roosevelt and the Coming of the War, 1941*. New Haven, Conn.: Archon Books, 1948.
Bemis, Samuel F., *A Diplomatic History of the United States*. New York: Henry Holt, 1936.
Bemis, Samuel F., *The Diplomacy of the American Revolution*. Edinburgh: Oliver Boyd, 1957.
Berber, Friedrich, *Die Amerikanische Neutralität im Kriege, 1939–41*. Essen: Essener Verlags-Anstalt, 1943.
Bernard, Montague, *A Historical Account of the Neutrality of Great Britain During the American Civil War*. New York: B. Franklin, 1971.

Borchard, Edwin M., 'Neutrality', *Yale Law Journal*, Vol. 48 (1938), pp. 37–53.

Borchard, Edwin M. 'War, Neutrality and Non-Belligerency', *AJIL*, Vol. 35 (1941), p. 618.

Borchard, Edwin M. and Lage W. Potter, *Neutrality for the United States*. New Haven, Conn.: Yale University Press, 1937.

Chaumont, Marie C., *La Conception Americaine de la Neutralité*. Paris: A. Rousseau, 1936.

Cohn, Georg, *Neo-Neutrality*. New York: Columbia University Press, 1939.

Cole, Wayne S., *Roosevelt and the Isolationists, 1932–45*. Lincoln, Nebr.: University of Nebraska Press, 1983.

Coogan, John W. *The End of Neutrality*. Ithaca, NY: Cornell University Press, 1981.

Current, Richard. *Secretary Stimson: A Study in Statecraft*. New Brunswick, NJ: Rutgers University Press, 1954.

Dallek, Robert, *Franklin D. Roosevelt and American Foreign Policy, 1934–45*. New York: Oxford University Press, 1979.

Divine, Robert A., *The Illusion of Neutrality*. Chicago, Ill.: University of Chicago Press, 1962.

Divine, Robert A., *The Reluctant Belligerent: American Entry into World War II*. New York: Wiley, 1965.

Drummond, Donald F., *The Passing of American Neutrality, 1937–1941*. New York: Greenwood Press, 1968.

Dulles, Allen W., 'The Cost of Peace', *Foreign Affairs*, Vol. 12 (1934), pp. 567–78.

Dulles, Allen W. and Hamilton F. Armstrong, *Can We Be Neutral?* New York: Harper, 1936.

Eagleton, Clyde, 'Neutrality and Neutral Rights Following the Pact of Paris for the Renunciation of War', *Proceedings of the American Society of International Law*, (1930), pp. 87–114.

Fenwick, Charles G., *The Neutrality Laws of the United States*. Washington D.C.: Carnegie Endowment for International Peace, 1913.

Fenwick, Charles G., *International Law*. New York: Appleton Century Crofts, 1924.

Fenwick, Charles G., *American Neutrality: Trial and Failure*. New York: Oxford University Press, 1940.

Fenwick, Charles G., 'The Declaration of Panama', *AJIL*, Vol, 34 (1940), pp. 116–19.

Fenwick, Charles G., 'Neutrality on the Defensive', *AJIL*, Vol. 34 (1940), pp. 697–9.

Fenwick, Charles G., 'The Inter-American Neutrality Committee', *AJIL*, Vol. 35 (1941), pp. 12–40.

Graebner, Norman A. (ed.), *Ideas and Diplomacy: Readings in the Intellectual Tradition of American Foreign Policy*. New York: Oxford University Press, 1964.

Guinsburg, Thomas N., *The Pursuit of Isolationism in the United States Senate from Versailles to Pearl Harbor*. New York: Garland, 1982.

Guttmann, Allen, *American Neutrality and the Spanish Civil War*. Boston, Mass.: D. C. Heath, 1963.

Harris, Brice, *The United States and the Italo-Ethiopian Crisis*. Stanford, Calif.: Stanford University Press, 1964.

Harvard Research In International Law, 'Draft Convention on Rights and Duties of Neutral States in Naval and Aerial War', *AJIL*, Supplement 33 (1939), pp. 167–754.

Harvard Research In International Law, 'Draft Convention on Rights and Duties of States in Case of Aggression', *AJIL*, Supplement 33 (1939), pp. 819–909.

Hyneman, Charles S., 'The First American Neutrality', *University of Illionois Bulletin*, Vol. 32 (1934), pp. 1–178.

Jennings, W. W., *The American Embargo, 1807–1809*. Iowa City, Iowa: University of Iowa Studies, 1938.

Jessup, Philip C., *Neutrality: Its History, Economics and Law*. New York: Columbia University Press, 1935–6.

Jessup, Philip C., *International Security: The American Role in Collective Action*. Westport, Conn.: Greenwood Press, 1935.

Jessup, Philip C., 'The Birth, Death and Reincarnation of Neutrality', *AJIL*, Vol. 26 (1932), pp. 789–93.

Jessup, Philip C., 'The Saavedra Lamas Anti-War-Treaty', *AJIL*, Vol. 27 (1933), pp. 109–14.

Jessup, Philip C., 'The Argentine Anti-War Pact', *AJIL*, Vol. 28 (1934), pp. 538–41.

Jessup, Philip C., 'The Neutrality Act of 1939', *AJIL* Vol. 34 (1940), pp. 96–9.

Johnston, Whittle, 'Franklin D. Roosevelt and the Wartime Strategy for Peace', in Norman Graebner (ed.), *Traditions and Values: American Diplomacy, 1865–1945*. New York: University Press of America, 1985, pp. 16–198.

Johnston, Whittle, 'Reflections on Wilson and the Problems of World Peace', in Arthur S. Link (ed.), *Woodrow Wilson and a Revolutionary World, 1913–21*. Chapel Hill, NC: The University of North Carolina Press, 1938, pp. 190–231.

Jonas, Manfred, *Isolationism in America, 1935–41*. Ithaca, NY: Cornell University Press, 1966.

Kulsrud, Carl J., 'Armed Neutralities to 1780', *AJIL*, Vol. 29 (1935), pp. 423–47.

Langer, W. L. and Everett Gleason, *The Challenge to Isolation, 1937–1940*. New York: Harper, 1952.

Langer, W. L. and Everett Gleason, *The Undeclared War, 1940–41*. New York: Harper, 1953.

Leopold, Richard W., *The Growth of American Foreign Policy: A History*. New York: Alfred A. Knopf, 1962.

Link, Arthur S., *Wilson*. Princeton, NJ: Princeton University Press, 1947, 1956, 1960, 1964, 1965.

Link, Arthur S. (ed.), *Woodrow Wilson and a Revolutionary World, 1913–21*. Chapel Hill, NC: University of North Carolina, 1982.

Lippmann, Walter, 'The Intimate Papers of Col. House', *Foreign Affairs*, Vol. 4 (1926), pp. 383–93.

Mahan, Alfred T., *Retrospect and Prospect: Studies in International Relations Naval and Political*. Boston, Mass.: Little, Brown, 1903.

Mahan, Alfred T., *The Problem of Asia and Its Effect upon International Policies*. Boston; Mass.: Little, Brown, 1905.

Mahan, Alfred T., *The Interest of America in Sea Power, Present and Future*. Boston, Mass.: Little, Brown, 1918.

Mahan, Alfred T., *The Lessons of the War with Spain*. Boston, Mass.: Little, Brown, 1918.

Mahan, Alfred T., *The Influence of Sea Power upon History*. Boston, Mass.: Little, Brown 1918.

May, Ernest R., *The World War and American Isolation*. Cambridge, Mass.: Harvard University Press, 1959.

Millis, Walter, *Road to War: America, 1914–1917*. Boston, Mass.: Houghton Mifflin, 1935.

Morison, Elting, *Turmoil and Tradition: A Study of the Life and Times of Henry L. Stimson*. Boston, Mass.: Houghton Mifflin, 1960.

Morrissey, Alice M., 'The US and the Rights of Neutrals, 1917–1918', *AJIL*, Vol. 31 (1937), pp. 17–30.

Neff, Stephen C., *The Rights and Duties of Neutrals, A General History*. Manchester: Manchester University Press, 2000.

Nevins, Allan, *The New Deal and World Affairs, 1933–45*. New Haven, Conn.: Yale University Press, 1950.

Nixon, Edgar B. (ed), *Franklin D. Roosevelt and Foreign Affairs*. Cambridge, Mass.: Harvard University Press, 1969.

Ørvik, Nils, *The Decline of Neutrality, 1914–1941*. Oslo: J. Grundt Tanum, 1953.

Osgood, Robert E., *Ideals and Self-Interest in Americas Foreign Relations*. Chicago, Ill.: The University of Chicago Press, 1953.

Pares, Richard, *Colonial Blockade und Neutral Rights, 1739–1763*. Philadelphia, Pa.; Porcupine Press, 1975.

Parmelee, Maurice, *Blockade and Sea Power: The Blockade, 1914–1919 and Its Significance for a World State*. London: Hutchinson, 1924.

Paterson, Thomas G. *et al.*, *American Foreign Policy: A History*. Lexington, Mass.: D. C.Heath, 1977.

Petrie, John N., *American Neutrality in the 20th Century: The Impossible Dream*. Washington D.C.: National Defense University, 1995.

Pratt, Julius W. *et al.*, *A History of United States Foreign Policy*. Englewood Cliffs NJ: Prentice-Hall, 1980.

Rappaport, Armin, *A History of American Diplomacy*. New York: Macmillan, 1975.

Ritchie, Hugh, *The 'Navicert' System during the World War*. Washington D.C.: Carnegie Endowment for International Peace 1938.

Savage, Carlton, *Policy of the US Toward Maritime Commerce in War*. Washington D.C.: US Government Printing Office, 1934–36.

Savelle, Max, *The Origins of American Diplomacy: The International History of Angloamerica, 1492–1763*. New York: Macmillan, 1967.

Scott, James B., *The Controversy over Neutral Rights Between the US and France, 1797–1800*. New York: Oxford University Press, 1917.

Schlesinger, Arthur M. Jr, *The Age of Roosevelt*. London: Heinemann, 1957–61.

Seager, Robert and Doris Maguire (eds), *Letters and Papers of Alfred Thayer Mahan*. Annapolis, MD: Naval Institute Press, 1975.

Sears, Louis Martin, *Jefferson and the Embargo*. New York: Octagon Books, 1978.

Seymour, Charles, *Woodrow Wilson und the World War*. New Haven, Conn.: Yale University Press, 1921.

Seymour, Charles, *American Diplomacy during the World War*. Baltimore, Md.: Johns Hopkins Press, 1934.

Seymour, Charles, *American Neutrality: 1914–1917*. New Haven, Conn.: Yale University Press, 1935.

Seymour, Charles, 'American Neutrality, the Experience of 1914–17', *Foreign Affairs*, Vol. 14 (1935).

Stimson, Henry L., 'The Pact of Paris: Three Years of Development', *Foreign Affairs* (Special Supplement) 11 (1932) pp. i–ix.

Stimson, Henry L., 'Neutrality and War Prevention', *American Society of International Law, Proceedings* (1935), pp. 123–6.

Stimson, Henry L. and McGeorge Bundy, *On Active Service in Peace and War*. New York: Harper, 1947.

Stuart, Reginald C. *War and American Thought from the Revolution to the Monroe Doctrine*. Kent, Ohio: Kent State University Press, 1982.

Thomas, Charles M. *American Neutrality in 1793*. New York: Columbia University Press, 1931.

Warren, Charles, 'Troubles of a Neutral', *Foreign Affairs*, Vol. 12 (1934), pp. 377–94.

Wiltse, Charles M., 'Thomas Jefferson and the Law of Nations', *AJIL*, Vol. 29 (1935), pp. 66–81.

Wright, Quincy, *The United States and Neutrality*. Chicago, Ill.: The University of Chicago Press, 1935.

Wright, Quincy, 'Changes in the Conception of War', *AJIL*, Vol. 18 (1924), pp. 755–67.

Wright, Quincy, 'The Future of Neutrality', *International Conciliation* (1928), pp. 353–72.

Wright, Quincy, 'The Concept of Aggression in International Law', *AJIL*, Vol. 29 (1935), pp. 373–95.

Wright, Quincy, 'The Present Status of Neutrality', *AJIL*, Vol. 34 (1940), pp. 391–415.

Wright, Quincy, 'Repeal of the Neutrality Act', *AJIL*, Vol. 36 (1942), pp. 8–23.

(b) The period after 1941

Abrahamsen, Samuel. *Sweden's Foreign Policy*. Washington D.C.: Public Affairs Press, 1957.

Acheson, Dean G., *The Pattern of Responsibility*. Boston, Mass.: Houghton Mifflin, 1952.

Acheson, Dean G., *Present at the Creation: My Years in the State Department*. New York: New American Library, 1970.

Acheson, Dean G., *The Korean War*. New York: Norton, 1971.

Adler-Karlsson, Gunnar. *Western Economic Warfare, 1947–1967*. Stockholm: Almquist & Wiksell, 1968.

Allard, Sven. *Russia and the Austrian State Treaty: A Case Study of Soviet Policy in Europe*. University Park, Pa.: Pennsylvania State University, 1970.

Armstrong, Hamilton F., 'Neutrality: Varying Tunes', *Foreign Affairs*, Vol. 35 (1956), pp. 57–71.

Aron, Raymond, *Peace and War: A Theory of International Relations*. Garden City, NY: Doubleday, 1966.

Bader, William B., *Austria Between East and West, 1945–1955*. Stanford, Ca.: Stanford University Press, 1966.

Bailey, Sydney D., 'Cease-fires, Truces, and Armistices in the Practice of the Security Council', *AJIL*, Vol. 71 (1977), pp. 461–73.

Ball, George, *The Past Has Another Pattern*. New York: W. W. Norton Company, 1982.

Baxter, Richard R.,'The Role of Law in Modern War', *ASIL Proceedings*, 1953, pp. 90–8.

Baxter, Richard R., 'Humanitarian Law or Humanitarian Politics? The 1974 Diplomatic Conference of Humanitarian Law', *Harvard International Law Journal*, Vol. 16 (1975), pp. 1–26.

Best, Geoffrey, *Humanity in Warfare*. New York: Columbia University Press 1980.

Biermann, Harald, *John F. Kennedy und der Kalte Krieg: Die Aussenpolitik der USA und die Grenzen der Glaubwürdigkeit*. Paderborn: Ferdinand Schöningh, 1997.

Bischoff, Gunter, *Austria in the First Cold War, 1945–55: The Leverage of the Weak*. New York: Palgrave, 1999.

Bill, James, *George Ball: Behind the Scenes in U.S. Foreign Policy*. New Haven CT: Yale University Press, 1997.

Bindschedler, Rudolf F., 'Die Neutralität im modernen Völkerrecht', *Zeitschrift für ausländisches, öffentliches Recht und Völkerrecht*, Vol. 17 (1956), pp. 1–37.

Bindschedler-Robert, DENISE, 'Les Commissions neutres instituées par l'armistice de Corée', *Schweizerisches Jahrbuch für Internationales Recht*, Bd. X (1953), pp. 89–130.

Black, Cyril E., Richard A. Falk, Klaus, Knorr and Oran R. Young, *Neutralization and World Politics*. Princeton, NJ: Princeton University Press, 1968.

Boczek, Boleslaw Adam, 'Law of Warfare at Sea and Neutrality: Lessons from the Gulf War', *Ocean Development and International Law*, Vol. 20, (1989), pp. 239–71.

Bohlen, Charles E., *The Transformation of American Foreign Policy*. New York: Norton, 1969.

Bonjour, Edgar, *Geschichte der Schweizerischen Neutralität*. Basel: Helbing & Lichtenhahn, 1976 (Vols V, VI, IX).

Borchard, Edwin M., *American Foreign Policy*. Indianapolis, Ind.: National Foundation Press, 1946.

Borchard, Edwin M., 'Flaws in Post-war Peace Plans', *AJIL*, Vol. 38 (1944), pp. 284–9.

Borchard, Edwin M., 'International Law and International Organization', *AJIL*, Vol. 41 (1947), pp. 106–8.

Bochard, Edwin M., 'Intervention: The Truman Doctrine and the Marshall Plan', *AJIL*, Vol. 41 (1947), pp. 885–8.

Borchard, Edwin M., 'United States Foreign Policy', *AJIL*, Vol. 43 (1949), pp. 333–5.

Borel, Eugène, 'Mémoire du groupe Suisse de l'International Law Association sur la neutralité hélvétique', *Schweizerisches Jahrbuch für Internationales Recht*, Vol. 2 (1946), pp. 103–9.

Bowett, D. W., *United Nations Forces: A Legal Study*. New York: Praeger, 1964.

Bowie, Robert R. and Richard H. Immerman, *Waging Peace: How Eisenhower Shaped an Enduring Cold War Strategy*. New York: Oxford University Press, 1998.

Bowles, Chester, *Ambassador's Report*. London: Gollancz, 1954.

Bowles, Chester, *The Conscience of a Liberal: Selected Writings and Speeches*. New York: Harper, 1962.

Bowles, Chester, *Promises to Keep, My Years in Public Life 1941–1969*. New York: Harper & Row, 1971.

Brands, Henry William, *The Specter of Neutralism: The United States and the Emergence of the Third World, 1947–1960*. New York: Columbia University Press, 1989.

Brodin, K., C. Lange, and K. Goldmann, 'The Policy of Neutrality: Official Doctrines of Finland and Sweden', *Conflict and Cooperation*, Vol. 3 (No. 1, 1968), pp. 18–51.

Brown, Seyom, *The Faces of Power, Constancy and Change in United States Foreign Policy from Truman to Clinton*. New York: Columbia University Press, 1994.

Brownlie, I., 'Volunteers and the Law of War and Neutrality', *International and Comparative Law Quarterly*, Vol. 5 (1956), pp. 570–80.

Bundy, McGeorge, 'Isolationists and Neutralists: A Sketch in Similarities', *Confluence,* Vol. 1 (1952), pp. 70–8.

Byrnes, James F., *Speaking Frankly.* New York: Harper & Row, 1947.

Carlgren, W. M., *Swedish Foreign Policy During the Second World War.* London: Ernest Benn, 1977.

Castle, Timothy N., *At War in the Shadow of Vietnam, U.S. Military Aid to the Royal Lao Government 1955–1975.* New York: Columbia University Press, 1993.

Castrén, Erik, *The Present Law of War and Neutrality.* Helsinki: Suornalainen, 1954.

Chamling, Dhiraj R., *India and the United Nations.* New Delhi: Associated Publishing House, 1978.

Chandler, David P., *The Tragedy of Cambodian History: Politics, War, and Revolution since 1945.* New Haven CT: Yale University Press, 1991.

Chaumont, Charles M., 'Nations Unies et neutralité', *Hague, Recueil des Cours,* Vol. 89 (1956), pp. 9–58.

Childs, Marquis W., *The Ragged Edge: The Diary of a Crisis.* Garden City, NY: Doubleday, 1955.

Childs, Marquis W., *Sweden: The Middle Way on Trial.* New Haven, Conn.: Yale University Press, 1980.

Clark, Mark W., *From the Danube to the Yalu.* New York: Harper Row, 1954.

Clymer, Kenton J., 'The Perils of Neutrality: the Break in U.S.– Cambodian Relations, 1965', *Diplomatic History,* Vol. 23/4 (1999), pp. 613–15.

Codevilla, Angelo M., *Between the Alps and a Hard Place: Switzerland in World War II and the Rewriting of History.* Washington D.C.: Regnery Publishing, 2000.

Conboy, Kenneth, *Shadow War: The CIA's Secret War in Laos.* Boulder, Col.: Paladin Press, 1995.

Copeland, William R., *The Uneasy Alliance.* Helsinki: Suomalainen, 1973.

Crabb, Cecil V. M., *The Elephants and the Grass: A Study of Nonalignment.* New York: Praeger, 1965.

Cronin, Audrey Kurth, *Great Power Politics and the Struggle over Austria, 1945–1955.* Ithaca NY: Cornell University Press, 1986.

Cummings, Edward R., 'The Evolution of the Notion of Neutrality in Modern Armed Conflicts', *Revue de droit pénal, militaire et de droit de la guerre.* Brussels, Vol. 17 (1978), pp. 37–69.

Czempiel, Ernst-Otto and Carl-Christoph Schweitzer, *Weltpolitik der USA nach 1945.* Leverkusen: Leske Budrich, 1984.

Deàk, Francis, *Neutrality Revisited.* New York: Columbia University Press, 1972.

Deàk, Francis and Philip Jessup, *A Collection of Neutrality Laws, Regulations and Treaties of Various Countries.* Washington D.C.: Carnegie Endowment for International Peace, 1939.

Dehn, G. C., 'The Effect of the UN Charter in the Development of International Law with Reference to the Status of Neutrality and the Hague and Geneva Conventions', *Proceedings, International Law Association,* 1946.

Dehn, G. C., 'The Problem of Neutrality', *Transactions of the Grotius Society,* Vol. 31 (1946), pp. 139–49.

Diebold, William, Jr, 'East–West Trade and the Marshall Plan', *Foreign Affairs,* Vol. 26 (No. 4, 1948), pp. 709–22.

Divine, Robert A., *Second Chance: The Triumph of Internationalism in America during World War II.* New York: Atheneum, 1967.

Divine, Robert A., *Roosevelt and World War II*. Baltimore, Md.: Johns Hopkins University Press, 1969.

Doenecke, Justus D., *The Battle Against Intervention, 1939–1941*. Malabar FL: Krieger Publishing, 1997.

Dohse, Rainer, *Der Dritte Weg: Neutralitätsbestrebungen in Westdeutschland zwischen 1945–1955*. Hamburg: Holsten, 1974.

Dommen, Arthur J., *Conflict in Laos, The Politics of Neutralization*. New York: Praeger, 1971.

Downey, William G., Jr,'Training in the Geneva Conventions of 1949', *AJIL*, Vol. 46 (1952), pp. 143–4.

Doxey, Margaret P., *Economic Sanctions and International Enforcement*. New York: Oxford University Press, 1971.

Duft, Peter, *Das Mandat der Neutralen Ueberwachungskommission in Korea*. Zurich: Polygraphischer, 1969.

Dulles, John Foster, *War or Peace*. New York: MacMillan, 1950.

Durrer, Marco, *Die schweizerisch-amerikanischen Finanzbeziehungen im Zweiten Weltkrieg*. Bern: Paul Haupt, 1984.

Durrer, Marco, 'Les negotiations économiques entre Alliés et Suisses à la veille de la défaite du Troisième Reich: à propos du point de vue anglo-américain', *Relations Internationales*, Vol. 30 (1982), pp. 193–207.

Duttwyler, Herbert, *Der Seekrieg und die Wirtschaftspolitik des Neutralen Staates*. Zurich: Polygraphischer Verlag, 1945.

Eden, Anthony, *The Memoirs of Anthony Eden: Full Circle*. London: Cassell, 1960.

Ehni, Reinhart, *Die Schweiz und die Vereinten Nationen, 1944–47*. Tübingen: Mohr, 1967.

Eisenhower, Dwight D., *The White House Years*. London: Heinemann, 1963–1965.

Erdman, Paul, *Swiss–American Economic Relations: Their Evolution in an Era of Crisis*. Basel: Kyklos, 1959.

Ermacora, Felix, *20 Jahre österreichische Neutralität*. Frankfurt a/Main: Metzner, 1975.

Etzold, Thomas H. and John Lewis Gaddis, (eds), *Containment: Documents on American Policy and Strategy, 1945–1950*. New York: Columbia University Press, 1978.

Ewing, Blair G., *Peace Through Negotiation: The Austrian Experience*. Washington D.C.: Public Affairs Press, 1966.

Fabian, Larry L., *Soldiers Without Enemies*. Washington D.C.: The Brookings Institution, 1971.

Fellner, Fritz, 'Teilung oder Neutralisierung?' *Oesterreichische Zeitschrift für Aussenpolitik*, Heft 4, (14. Jg. 1974), pp. 199–216.

Fenwick, Charles G., *The Inter-American Regional System*. New York: McMullen, 1949.

Fenwick, Charles G., 'The Progress of International Law During the Past 40 Years', *Hague, Recueil des Cours*, Vol. 79 (1951), pp. 1–70.

Fenwick, Charles G., 'The Old Order Changeth, Yielding Place to New', *AJIL*, Vol. 47 (1953), pp. 84–7.

Fenwick, Charles G., 'Legal Aspects of "Neutralism" ', *AJIL*, Vol. 51 (1957), pp. 71–4.

Fenwick, Charles G., 'Is Neutrality Still a Term of Present Law?', *AJIL*, Vol. 63 (1969), pp. 100–2.

Fiedler, Heinz, *Der sowjetische Neutralitätsbegriff in Theorie und Praxis*. Köln: Verlag für Politik und Wirtschaft, 1959.

Finch, George A., 'The Nuremberg Trial and International Law', *AJIL*, Vol. 41 (1947), pp. 20–37.

Freedman, Lawrence, *Kennedy's Wars: Berlin, Cuba, Laos, and Vietnam*. New York: Oxford University Press, 2000.

Frei, Daniel, *Dimensionen neutraler Politik*. Geneva: Institut Universitaire de Hautes Etudes Internationales, 1969.

Frei, Daniel, 'Das Washington Abkommen von 1946', *Revue Suisse d'histoire*, vol. 19 (No. 3, 1969), pp. 567–619.

Frei, Daniel, 'Neutrality and Non-alignment: Convergencies and Contrasts'. *Korea and World Affairs*, Vol. 3 (1979), pp. 275–86.

Freidel, Frank, *Franklin D. Roosevelt: A Rendezvous with Destiny*. Boston MA: Little, Brown, 1990.

Friedman, Leon (ed.), *The Law of War: A Documentary History*. New York: Random House, 1972.

Fulbright, J. William, *The Arrogance of Power*. New York: Random House, 1966.

Gabriel, Jürg Martin, 'Die schweizerische Neutralität in einem veränderten Umfeld', *Aussenwirtschaft*, Vol. IV (1990) pp. 495–515.

Gabriel, Jürg Martin, *Schweizer Neutralität im Wandel – Hin zur EG*. Frauenfeld: Huber, 1990.

Gabriel, Jürg Martin, 'Switzerland and Economic Sanctions – The Dilemma of a Neutral', in Marko Milivojevic and Pierre Maurer (eds), *Swiss Neutrality and Security, Armed Forces, National Defense and Foreign Policy*. Oxford: Berg, 1990, pp. 232–45.

Gabriel, Jürg Martin, 'Die Stellung der Schweiz zu Wirtschaftssanktionen', in Alois Riklin, Hans Haug and Raymond Probst (eds), *Neues Handbuch der schweizerischen Aussenpolitik*. Bern: Haupt, 1992, pp. 919–28.

Gabriel, Jürg Martin, *Sackgasse Neutralität*. Zürich: vdf Hochschulverlag AG an der ETH, 1996.

Gabriel, Jürg Martin (ed.), *Schweizerische Aussenpolitik im Kosovo-Krieg*. Zürich: Orell Füssli Verlag, 2000.

Gaddis, John L., *We Now Know: Rethinking Cold War History*. New York: Oxford University Press, 1997.

Gallus, Alexander, *Die Neutralisten: Verfechter eines vereinten Deutschland zwischen Ost und West 1945–1990*. Düsseldorf: Droste Verlag, 2001.

Garfinkle, Adam M., *Finlandization: A Map to a Metaphor*. Philadelphia, PA: Foreign Research Institute, 1978.

Ginsburgs, George, 'The Soviet Union, the Neutrals and International Law in World War II', *International and Comparative Law Quarterly*, Vol. 11 (1962), pp. 171–230.

Ginther, Konrad, *Neutralität und Neutralitätspolitik*. Vienna: Springer, 1975.

Goodrich, Leland M., *Korea, A Study of US Policy in the United Nations*. New York: Council on Foreign Relations, 1956.

Goodrich, Leland M., 'Korea, Collective Measures against Aggression', *International Conciliation*, No. 494 (October 1953), pp. 131–2.

Gordon, D. G. and R. Dangerfield., *The Hidden Weapon: The Story of Economic Warfare*. New York: Harper, 1976.

Graebner, Norman A., *The New Isolationism: A Study in Politics and Foreign Policy since 1950*. New York: Ronald Press, 1956.

Greber, Anton, *Die Dauernde Neutralität und das Kollektive Sicherheitssystem der Vereinten Nationen*. Fribourg: Dissertation, 1967.

Greene, Fred, 'Neutralization and the Balance of Power', *APSR*, Vol. 47 (1953), pp. 1041–57.

Greenspan, Morris, *The Modern Law of Land Warfare*. Berkeley, Cal.: University of California Press, 1959.

Greenspan, Morris, *The Soldier's Guide to the Laws of War*. Washington D.C.: Public Affairs Press, 1969.

Greenstein Fred I. and Richard H, Immerman., 'What Did Eisenhower Tell Kennedy about Indochina? The Politics of Misperception', *Journal of American History*, Vol. 79, (No. 2, 1992), pp. 568–87.

Grob, Fritz, *The Relativity of War and Peace*. New Haven, Conn.: Yale University Press, 1949.

Gröndal, Benedikt, *Iceland from Neutrality to NATO Membership*. Olso: Universitets forlaget, 1971.

Gruber, Karl, *Between Liberation and Liberty: Austria in the Post-War World*. New York: Praeger, 1955.

Gruchmann, Lothar, 'Schweden im Zweiten Weltkrieg', *Vierteljahreshefte für Zeitgeschichte*, Vol. 25 (1977), pp. 591–657.

Guggenheim, Paul, *Völkerbund, Dumbarton Oaks und die schweizerische Neutralität*. Zurich: Europa, 1945.

Guggenheim, Paul, 'La sécurité collective et le problème de la neutralité', *Schweizerisches Jahrbuch für Internationales Recht*, Vol. 2 (1945), pp. 9–47.

Guggenheim, Paul, *Der Neutralitätsbegriff im Allgemeinen Völkerrecht und in der Internationalen Organisation*. Munich: Wilhelm Fink, 1971.

Guhin, Michael A., *John Foster Dulles: A Statesman and his Times*. New York: Columbia University Press, 1972.

Guise, Constantin, *Die Neutralität der Vereinigten Staaten*. Bern: Gustav Grunau, 1946.

Guitard, Odette, *Bandoeng et le Réveil des Peuples Colonisés*. Paris: Presse universitaire de France, 1961.

Gutzwiller, Maxuno, 'Neutralität, Internationales Privatrecht. Bericht von der 41. Konferenz der International Law Association'. *Schweizerische Juristenzeitung*, Vol. 42, No. 23, (December 1946), pp. 355–60.

Hagglof, H. Gunnar, 'A Test of Neutrality: Sweden in the Second World War', *International Affairs* (April 1960), pp. 153–67.

Halbrook, Stephen P., *Target Switzerland: Swiss Armed Neutrality in World War II*. Rockeville Centre NY: Sarpedon, 1998.

Harper, John Lamberton, *American Visions of Europe: Franklin D. Roosevelt, George F. Kennan, and Dean G. Acheson*. Cambridge MA: Cambridge Uniersity Press, 1994.

Harriman, W. A., *America and Russia in a Changing World: A Half Century of Personal Observation*. New York: Doubleday, 1971.

Haskel, Barbara G., *The Scandinavian Option: Opportunities and Opportuniy Costs in Post-war Scandinavian Foreign Policies*. Oslo: Universitets forlaget, 1976.

Haug, Hans, *Neutralität und Völkergemeinschaft*. Zurich: Polygraphischer Verlag, 1962.

Haug, Hans, *Das Verhältnis der Schweiz zu den Vereinten Nationen*. Bern: Paul Haupt, 1972.

Heimsath, Charles H., *India's Role in the Korean War*. New Haven, Conn.: Yale University Press, 1956.

Heimsath, Charles H. and Surjit Mansingh, *A Diplomatic History of Modern India*. Bombay: Allied Publishers, 1971.

Heiskanen, Ilkka *et al.*, *Essays on Finnish Foreign Policy*. Vammala: Finnish Political Science Association, 1969.

Helmreich, Jonathan E., 'The Diplomacy of Apology: US Bombings of Switzerland During World War II', *Air University Review* (May–June 1977), pp. 19–37.

Henderson, Nicholas, *The Birth of NATO*. London: Weidenfeld & Nicolson, 1982.

Henkin, Louis, 'Force, Intervention, and Neutrality in Contemporary International Law', *Proceedings of the American Society of International Law*, 57th Annual Meeting (April 1963), pp. 147–73.

Herring, George C., *America's Longest War, The United States and Vietnam 1950–1975*. New York: John Wiley & Sons, 1979.

Hilderbrand, Robert, *Dumbarton Oaks: The Origins of the United Nations and the Search for Postwar Security*. Chapell Hill NC: University of North Carolina Press, 1990.

Hillgruber, Andreas, *Alliierte Pläne für eine 'Neutralisierung' Deutschlands 1945–1955*. Opladen: Westdeutscher Verlag, 1987.

Homberger, Heinrich, *Schweizerische Handelspolitik im Zweiten Weltkrieg*. Erlenbach: Eugen Rentsch, 1970.

Hoopes, Townsend, *The Devil and John Foster Dulles*. Boston, Mass.: Little, Brown, 1973.

Hoopes, Townsend, *FDR and the Creation of the U.N.* New Haven, Conn.: Yale University Press, 1997.

Hoover, Herbert, *Addresses upon the American Road, 1950–55*. Stanford, Cal.: Stanford University Press, 1955.

Hopper, Bruce, 'Sweden, a Case Study in Neutrality', *Foreign Affairs*, Vol. 23 (1945), pp. 435-49.

Hudson, Manley O., 'Switzerland and the International Court of Justice', *AJIL*, Vol. 41 (1947), pp. 866–71.

Hudson, Manley O., 'Progress of the Geneva Conventions of 1949', *AJIL*, Vol. 45 (1951), pp. 776–7.

Hulkko, Jonko, *Finland, 1917–1967: An Assessment of Independence*. Helsinki: Kirjaythyma, 1967.

Hull, Cordell, *The Memoirs of Cordell Hull*. New York: Macmillan, 1948.

Hwang, In K., *The Neutralized Unification of Korea in Perspective*. Cambridge, Mass.: Schenkman, 1980.

Hyde, C. C., *International Law, Chiefly as Interpreted and Applied by the United States*. Boston, Mass.: Little, Brown, 1945.

Isaacs, Arnold R., *Without Honor, Defeat in Vietnam and Cambodia*. Baltimore MD: The Johns Hopkins University Press, 1983.

Jackson, Richard L., *The Non-Aligned, the UN and the Superpowers*. New York: Praeger, 1983.

Jakobson, Max, *Finnish Neutrality: A Study of Finnish Foreign Policy since the Second World War*. New York: Praeger, 1969.

Jakobson, Max, 'Substance and Appearance: Finland', *Foreign Affairs*, Vol. 58 (1980), pp. 1034-44.

Jansen, Godfrey H., *Nonalignment and the Afro-Asian States*. New York: Praeger, 1966.

Jenny, Christian, *Konsensformel oder Vorbild? Die Entstehung der österreichischen Neutralität und ihr Schweizer Muster*. Bern: Paul Haupt, 1995.

Jessup, Philip, *A Modern Law of Nations*. New York: Macmillan, 1948.

Jessup, Philip, 'Should International Law Recognize an Intermediate Status Between War and Peace?', *AJIL*, Vol. 48 (1954), pp. 98–103.

Joyce, Richard P., *Swedish Neutrality and the North Atlantic Pact*. Washington D.C.: Georgetown University Thesis, 1951.

Kahin, George McT., *Intervention, How America Became Involved in Vietnam*. New York: Alfred A. Knopf, 1986.

Kaushik, Ram pal, *The Crucial Years of Nonalignment: USA, Korean War, India*. New Delhi: Kumar, 1972.

Kekkonen, Urho, *Neutrality, the Finnish Position*. London: Heinemann, 1970.

Kekkonen, Urho, *A President's View*. London: Heinemann, 1982.

Kelsen, Hans, *Law and Peace in International Relations*. Cambridge, Mass.: Harvard University Press, 1942.

Kelsen, Hans, *Peace Through Law*. Chapell Hill, NC: University of North Carolina Press, 1944.

Kelsen, Hans, *The Law of the United Nations*. London: Stevens, 1950.

Kelsen, Hans, *Principles of International Law*. New York: Holt, Rinehart & Winston, 1952.

Kennan, George F., *Russia, the Atom and the West*. New York: Harper, 1958.

Kennan, George F., *Memoirs*. New York: Bantam Books, 1969.

Komarnicki, Titus, 'The Place of Neutrality in the Modern System of International Law', *Hague, Recueil des Cours*, (1952), pp. 395–502.

Komarnicki, Titus, 'The Problem of Neutrality under the United Nations Charter', *Transactions of the Grotius Society*, Vol. 38 (1952), pp. 77–91.

Köpfer, Josef, *Die Neutralität im Wandel der Erscheinungsformen militärischer Auseinandersetzungen*. Munich: Bernard & Graefe, 1975.

Kreis, Georg (ed.), *Switzerland and the Second World War*. London: Frank Cass, 2000.

Kreisky, Bruno, *Neutralität und Koexistenz*. Munich: List, 1975.

Kreisky, Bruno, 'Der Weg Oesterreichs zu Staatsvertrag und Neutralität', *Oesterreichische Zeitschrift für Aussenpolitik*, Vol. 5 (1965), pp. 67–70.

Krosby, H. Peter, 'Perspectives of Finnish Foreign Policy', *Yearbook of Finnish Foreign Policy* (1978), pp. 40–5.

Kundra, Jaydish C., *Indian Foreign Policy, 1947–54*. Groningen: J. B. Wolfers, 1955.

Kunz, Josef L., *Kriegsrecht und Neutralitätsrecht*. Vienna: Julius Springer, 1935.

Kunz, Josef L., *The Changing Law of Nations*. Columbus, Ohio: Ohio State University Press, 1968.

Kunz, Josef L., 'Plus de lois de guerre?' *Revue Générale de Droit International Public* (January–February, 1934), pp. 22–57.

Kunz, Josef L., 'Individual and Collective Self-Defense in Art. 51 of the Charter of the UN', *AJIL*, Vol. 41 (1947), pp. 872–9.

Kunz, Josef L., 'The Chaotic Status of the Laws of War and the Urgent Necessity for Their Revision', *AJIL*, Vol. 45 (1951), pp. 37–61.

Kunz, Josef L., 'Legality of the Security Council Resolutions of June 25 and 27, 1956', *AJIL*, Vol. 45 (1951), pp. 137–42.

Kunz, Josef L., 'Treatment of Prisoners of War', ASIL, *Proceedings of the American Society of International Law*, (1953), pp. 99–121.

Kunz, Josef L., 'The State Treaty with Austria', *AJIL*, Vol. 49 (1955), pp. 535–42.

Kunz, Josef L., 'The Laws of War', *AJIL*, Vol. 50 (1956), pp. 313–37.

Kunz, Josef L., 'Austria's Permanent Neutrality' (edit. comment). *AJIL*, Vol. 50 (1956), pp. 418–25.

Kunz, Josef L., 'The New US Army Field Manual on the Law of Land Warfare', *AJIL*, Vol. 51 (1957), pp. 388–96.

Lalive, J. F., 'International Organizations and Neutrality', *British Yearbook of International law*, Vol. 24 (1947), pp. 72–89.

Lauterpacht, Elihu, 'The Legal Irrelevance of the "State of War"', ASIL, *Proceedings of the American Society of International Law*, (1986), pp. 58–68.

LeBor, Adam, *Hitler's Secret Bankers: The Myth of Swiss Neutrality during the Holocaust*. Secaucus NJ: Carol Publishing Group, 1997.

Leckie, Robert, *Conflict, the History of the Korean War, 1950–1953*. New York: Putnam, 1962.

Leitz, Christian, *Nazi Germany and Neutral Europe during the Second World War: Sympathy for the Devil?* Manchester: Manchester University Press, 2000.

Leonhard, Alan T. (ed.), *Neutrality: Changing Concepts and Practices*. Lanham MD: University Press of America, 1988.

Lévèque, Gérard, *La Suisse et la France gaulliste, 1943–1945: problèmes économiques et diplomatiques*. Geneva: Editons Studer, 1979.

Lippmann, Walter, *US Foreign Policy: Shield of the Republic*. Boston, Mass.: Little, Brown, 1943.

Lippmann, Walter, *The Cold War: A Study in US Foreign Policy*. New York: Harper & Row, 1947.

Lippmann, Walter, *Isolation and Alliances: An American Speaks to the British*. Boston, Mass.: Little, Brown, 1952.

Lobel, Jules, 'The Rise and Decline of the Neutrality Act: Sovereignty and Congressional War Powers in US Foreign Policy', *Harvard International Law Journal*, Vol. 24 (1983), pp. 1–71.

Lundestad, Geir, *The American Non-policy Towards Eastern Europe, 1943–47*. Oslo: Universitets forlaget, 1978.

Lundestad, Geir, *America, Scandinavia, and the Cold War, 1945–49*. New York: Columbia University Press, 1980.

Luciri, Pierre, *Les Sources de la Neutralité économique Suisse*. Geneva: Institut universitaire de Hautes Etudes Internationales, 1976.

Malborg, Mikael, *Neutrality and State-Building in Sweden*. New York: Palgrave, 2001.

Mallik, Dera N., *The Development of Non-alignment in Indias Foreign Policy*. Allahabad: Chaitanya Publishing House, 1967.

Mantovani, Mauro, *Schweizerische Sicherheitspolitik im Kalten Krieg 1947–1963*. Zürich: Orell Füssli Verlag, 1999.

Marcus, John T., *Neutralism and Nationalism in France: A Case Study*. New York: Bookman Associates, 1958.

Martin, Laurence W. (ed.), *Neutralism and Nonalignment: The New States in World Affairs*. New York: Praeger, 1962.

Mastanduno, Michael, *Economic Containment: CoCom and the Politics of East–West Trade*. Ithaca NY: Cornell University Press, 1992.

Mastny, Vojtech J., 'Kremlin Politics and the Austrian Settlement', *Problems of Communism*, Vol. 31 (July–August 1982), pp. 37–51.

Matson, Robert W., *Neutrality and Navicerts: Britain, the United States, and Economic Warfare, 1939–1940*. New York: Garland, 1994.

Maude, George, *The Finnish Dilemma: Neutrality in the Shadow of Power*. London: Oxford University Press, 1976.

Maude, George, 'The Further Shores of Finlandization', *Cooperation and Conflict*, Vol. 17 (l/1982), pp. 3–16.

Mayrzedt, Hans and Waldemar Hummer, *20 Jahre österreichische Neutralitäts- und Europapolitik (1955–1975)*. Vienna: Wilhelm Braumüller, 1975.

McCarthy, Josef R., *Americas Retreat from Victory*. New York: Devin Adair, 1951.

McDougal, Myres S. and F. P. Feliciano, *Law and Minimum World Public Order: The Legal Regulation of International Coercion*, New Haven, Conn.: Yale University Press, 1961.

McDougal, Myres S., 'Peace and War: Factual Continuum with Multiple Legal Consequences', *AJIL*, Vol. 49 (1955), pp. 63–8.

McNamara, Robert, *In Retrospect: The Tragedy and Lessons of Vietnam*. New York: Vintage Press, 1995.

McNamara, Robert, *et al.*, *Argument Without End: In Search of Answers to the Vietnam Tragedy*. Washington D.C. : Office of Public Affairs, 1999.

McPhee, John, *La Place de la Concorde Suisse*. New York: Farrar, 1984.

Mearsheimer, John J., 'Back to the Future; Instability in Europe after the Cold War', *International Security*, (15, 1990), pp. 5–56.

Medlicott, W. N., *The Economic Blockade*. London: Longmans, Green, 1952.

Meier, Heinz K., *Friendship under Stress. US–Swiss Relations, 1900–1950*. Bern: Herbert Lang, 1970.

Milivojevic, Marko and Pierre Maurer (eds), *Swiss Neutrality and Security: Armed Forces, National Defense and Foreign Policy*. New York: Berg, 1990.

Miller, Richard, *The Law of War*. Lexington, Mass.: D.C. Heath, 1975.

Moore, John N., *Law and the Indo-China War*. Princeton, NJ: Princeton University Press, 1972.

Moos, Malcolm, 'Swiss Neutrality', *Yale Review*, Vol. 33 (1943), pp. 12–134.

Nehru, Jawaharlal, *Indias Foreign Policy: Selected Speeches 46-61*. New Delhi: Government of India, 1961.

Neuhold, Hanspeter, 'Permanent Neutrality and Non-Alignment: Similarities and Differences', *Oesterreichische Zeitschrift für Aussenpolitik*, Vol. 19 (1979), pp. 79–99.

Nolting, Frederick, *From Trust to Tragedy*. New York: Praeger, 1988.

Norton, Patrick M., 'Between the Ideology and the Reality: The Shadow of the Law of Neutrality', *Harvard International Law Journal*, Vol. 17 (1976), pp. 249–311.

Nuechterlein, Donald E., *Iceland: Reluctant Ally*. Ithaca, NY: Cornell University Press, 1961.

Ochsenbein, Heinz, *Die verlorene Wirtschaftsfreiheit, 1914–1918*. Bern: Stämpfli, 1971.

Ogley, Roderick (ed.), *The Theory and Practice of Neutrality in the XX Century*. London: Routledge & Kegan Paul, 1970.

Osborne, Milton, *Sihanouk, Prince of Light, Prince of Darkness*. Honolulu: University of Hawaii Press, 1994.

Osgood, Robert E., *NATO – The Entangling Alliance*. Chicago, Ill.: University of Chicago Press, 1962.

Osgood, Robert E., *Alliances and American Foreign Policy*. Baltimore, Md.: Johns Hopkins University Press, 1968.

Packard, Jerrold M., *Neither Friend nor Foe: The European Neutrals in World War II*. New York: Scribner, 1992.

Patterson, James T., *Mr. Republican: A Biography of Robert A. Taft*. Boston, Mass.: Houghton Mifflin, 1972.

Perkins, Dexter, *Foreign Policy and the American Spirit*. Ithaca, NY: Cornell University Press, 1957.

Pictet, Jean, *The Fundamental Principles of the Red Cross*. Geneva: Henry Dunant Institute, 1979.

Pictet, Jean, 'The New Geneva Conventions for the Protection of War Victims', *AJIL*, Vol. 45 (1951), pp. 462-75.

Potter, Pitman B., 'Pacific Blockade or War?' *AJIL*, Vol. 47 (1953), pp. 273-4.

Potter, Pitman B., 'Neutrality 1955' (edit. comment), *AJIL*, Vol. 50 (1956), pp. 101-2.

Power, Paul F., *Neutralism and Disengagement*. New York: Scribner 1964.

Pratt, Julius, *Cordell Hull*. New York: Cooper Square Publ., 1964.

Punasalo, V. I., *The Reality of Finlandization*. London: Institute for the Study of Conflict, 1978.

Randle, Robert F., *Geneva 1954. The Settlement of the Indochinese War*. Princeton, NJ: Princeton University Press, 1969.

Range, Willard, *Franklin D. Roosevelt's World Order*. Athens, Ga.: University of Georgia Press, 1959.

Rappard, William, 'The United Nations and Switzerland', *The Annuals of the American Academy of Political and Social Sciences*, Vol. 246 (1946), pp. 64-71.

Rathkolb, Oliver, *Washington ruft Wien: US-Grossmachtpolitik und Österreich, 1953-1963*. Wien: Böhlau, 1997.

Rees, David, *Korea: The Limited War*. New York: St Martin's Press, 1964.

Reeves, Richard, *President Kennedy: Profile of Power*. New York: Simon & Schuster, 1993.

Reid, Escott M., *Time of Fear and Hope: The Making of the North Atlantic Treaty 1947-49*. Toronto: McClelland & Stewart, 1977.

Reitzel, William, Morton Kaplan and Constance Coblenz et al., *United States Foreign Policy 1945-1955*. Washington D.C.: The Brookings Institution, 1956.

Riklin, Alois, 'Neutralität', in Wichard Woyke (ed.), *Handwörterbuch Internationale Politik*. Munich: Francke, 1980, pp. 270-8.

Riklin, Alois, Hans Haug and Hans C. Binswanger (eds), *Handbuch der schweizerischen Aussenpolitik*. Bern: Paul Haupt, 1975.

Riklin, Alois, Hans Haug and Raymond Probst (eds), *Neues Handbuch der schweizerischen Aussenpolitik*. Bern: Paul Haupt, 1992.

Rosner, Gabriella, *The United Nations Emergency Force*. New York: Columbia University Press, 1963.

Ross, John F. L., *Neutrality and International Sanctions: Sweden, Switzerland and Collective Security*. New York: Praeger, 1989.

Rostow, Walt W., *The Diffusion of Power, An Essay in Recent History*. New York: Macmillan, 1972.

Rubin, Seymour J., 'The Washington Accord Fifty Years Later: Neutrality, Morality, and International Law', *American University International Law Review*, Vol. 14, (No. 1, 1998), pp. 61-82.

Rusk, Dean, *As I Saw It*. New York: W. W. Norton Company, 1990.

Russell, Ruth B., *A History of the United Nations Charter: The Role of the US, 1940–45*. Washington D.C.: The Brookings Institution, 1958.

Russo, Francis V. Jr, 'Neutrality at Sea in Transition: State Practice in the Gulf War as Emerging International Customary Law', *Ocean Development and International Law*, Vol. 19 (1988), pp. 381–99.

Salvin, Marina, 'Neutralism in France', *International Conciliation*. Carnegie Endowment for International Peace (June 1951), pp. 283–318.

Schäfer, Stefan, *Hitler und die Schweiz: deutsche militärische Planungen 1939–1943 und die 'Raubgold'-Frage*. Berlin: Edition Q, 1998.

Schaller, Andre, *Schweizer Neutralität im West-Ost-Handel: Das Hotz-Linder-Agreement vom 23. Juli 1951*. Bern: Paul Haupt Verlag, 1987.

Scheuner, Ulrich, *Die Neutralität im heutigen Völkerrecht*. Köln: Westdeutscher Verlag, 1969.

Schiemann, Catherine, *Neutralität in Krieg und Frieden: Die Aussenpolitik der Vereinigten Staaten gegenüber der Schweiz 1941–1949*. Zürich: Rüegger, 1991.

Schilcher, Alfons, *Oesterreich und die Grossmächte*. Vienna: Geyer, 1980.

Schindler, Dietrich (ed.), 'Aspects contemporains de la neutralité', *Hague, Recueil des Cours*, Vol. 121 (1967), pp. 220–321.

Schindler, Dietrich, 'Dauernde Neutralität', in A. Riklin, H. Hang and H. C. Binswanger (eds), *Handbuch der schweizerischen Aussenpolitik*. Bern: Paul Haupt, 1975, pp. 159–80.

Schindler, Dietrich, 'Das Internationale Komitee vom Roten Kreuz und die Menschenrechte', in *Revue internationale de la Croix-Rouge* (November–December, 1979), pp. 3–16.

Schindler, Dietrich (ed.), *Dokumente zur schweizerischen Neutralität seit 1945*. Bern: Paul Haupt, 1984.

Schindler, Dietrich, 'Changing Conceptions of Neutrality in Switzerland', *Austrian Journal of Public International Law*, Vol. 44 (1992), pp. 105–16.

Schlesinger, Thomas O., *Austrian Neutrality in Postwar Europe*. Vienna: Braumüller, 1972.

Schlesinger, Thomas O., *The United States and the European Neutrals*. Vienna: Braumüller, 1991.

Schmid, Georg, *Die rechtliche Stellung von Mitgliedern der Schweizer Delegation in einer neutralen Waffenstillstandskommission*. Zürich: Juris Druck, 1974.

Schmidt, Peter H., *Der Wirtschaftskrieg und die Neutralen*. Zürich: Schulthess, 1918.

Serfaty, Simon, *The Elusive Enemy: American Foreign Policy Since World War II*. Boston, Mass.: Little, Brown, 1972.

Seyerstedt, F., *United Nations Forces in the Law of Peace and War*. Leyden: Sijthoff, 1966.

Shawcross, William, *Sideshow, Kissinger, Nixon and the Destruction of Cambodia*. New York: Simon and Schuster, 1979.

Siegler, Heinrich Von, *Oesterreichs Weg zur Souveränität, Neutralität, Prosperität, 1945–59*. Vienna: Verlag für Zeitarchiv, 1967.

Siegler, Heinrich Von, *Wiedervereinigung und Sicherheit Deutschlands*. Bonn: Siegler, 1967.

Sihanouk, Norodom, *War and Hope: The Case for Cambodia*. New York: Pantheon Books, 1980.

Singleton, Fred, 'The Myth of Finlandization', *International Affairs*, Vol. 57 (1981), pp. 270–85.

Spaight, J. M., *Air Power and War Rights*. London: Longmans, Green, 1947.

Spillmann, Kurt R., Andreas Wenger, Christoph Breitenmoser and Marcel Gerber, *Schweizer Sicherheitspolitik seit 1945*. Zürich: Verlag Neue Zürcher Zeitung, 2001.

Stamm, Konrad W., *Die Guten Dienste der Schweiz*. Bern: Herbert Lang, 1974.

Stearman, William L., *The Soviet Union and the Occupation of Austria*. Bonn: Siegler, 1962.

Steinaecker, Günter (Freiherr von), *Das Problem der Neutralität im Korea-Konflikt*. Würzburg: Dissertation, 1966.

Stevenson, Charles A., *The End of Nowhere, American Policy Toward Laos Since 1954*. Boston: Beacon Press, 1971.

Stone, Julius, *Legal Controls of International Conflicts*. London: Stevens, 1954.

Stourzh, Gerald, 'Zur Entstehungsgeschichte des Staatsvertrags und der Neutralität Oesterreichs, 1945–55', *Oesterreichische Zeitschift für Aussenpolitik*, Vol. 5 (1965), pp. 301–36.

Stourzh, Gerald, *Kleine Geschichte des österreischen Staatsvertrags*. Graz: Styria, 1975.

Stourzh, Gerald, *Um Einheit und Freiheit: Staatsvertrag, Neutralität und das Ende der Ost-West-Besetzung Österreichs 1945–1955*. Wien: Böhlau, 1998.

Stromberg, Roland N., *Collective Security and American Foreign Policy: From the League of Nations to NATO*. New York: Prager, 1963.

Strout, Cushing, *The American Image of the Old World*. New York: Harper & Row, 1963.

Sundelius, Bengt (ed.), *Foreign Policies of Northern Europe*. Boulder, Col.: Westview Press, 1982.

Swinarski, Christophe (ed.), *Studies and Essays on International Humanitarian Law and Red Cross Principles in Honor of Jean Pictet*. The Hague: Martinus Nijhoff, 1984.

Taft, Robert A., *A Foreign Policy for Americans*. Garden City, NY: Doubleday, 1951.

Taubenfeld, Howard J., 'International Armed Forces and the Rules of War', *AJIL*, Vol. 45 (1951), pp. 671–9.

Taubenfeld, Howard J., 'International Actions and Neutrality', *AJIL*, Vol. 47 (1953), pp. 377–96.

Törngren, Ralf, 'The Neutrality of Finland', *Foreign Affairs* (July 1961), pp. 601–9.

Toynbee, Arnold and Veronica M. Toynbee (eds), *Survey of International Affairs, 1939–1946: The War and the Neutrals*. London: Oxford University Press, 1956.

Truman, Harry S., *Memoirs: Years of Trial and Hope (1946–52)*. Garden City, NY: Doubleday, 1956.

Tucker, Robert W., 'The Interpretation of War Under Present International Law', *International Law Quarterly*, Vol. 4 (1951), pp. 11–38.

Tucker, Robert W., *The Law of War and Neutrality at Sea*. Washington D.C. : US Government Printing Office, 1957.

Tucker, Robert W., *The Just War: A Study in Contemporary American Doctrine*. Baltimore, Md.: Johns Hopkins University Press, 1960.

Tusell, Javier, *Franco, España y la II Guerra Mundial: Entre el Eje y la neutralidad*. Madrid: Temas de Hoy, 1995.

Urner, Klaus, 'Das Mandat und seine Problematik', in *Dreissig Jahre schweizerische Korea-Mission, 1953-1983*. Zürich: Institut für Geschichte ETHZ, Archiv für Zeitgeschichte, 1983, pp. 7–17.

Urner, Klaus, 'Let's Swallow Switzerland: Hitler's Plans Against the Swiss Confederation'. Lanham MD: Lexington Books, 2001.

Vaerno, Grethe, 'The United States, Norway, and the Atlantic Pact, 1948–49', Scandinavian Studies, Vol. 50 (1978), pp. 150–76.

Vagts, Detlev F., 'The Traditional Legal Concept of Neutrality in a Changing Environment', American University International Law Review, Vol. 14 (No. 1, 1998), pp. 83–102.

Vagts, Detlev, 'Switzerland, International Law and World War II', American Journal of International Law, Vol. 91 (1997), pp. 466–75.

Vandiver, Frank E., Shadows of Vietnam: Lyndon Johnson's Wars. College Station TX: Texas A&M University Press, 1997.

Vatcher, William H., Panmunjom: The Story of the Korean Military Armistice Negotiations. New York: Praeger, 1958.

Vayrynen, Raimo, Conflicts in Finnish-Soviet Relations: Three Comparative Case Studies. Tampere: Tampereen Yliopistio, 1972.

Vayrynen, Mimo, 'Finland's Role in the Western Strategy since World War II', Cooperation and Conflict, Vol. 14 (1977), pp. 87–108.

Verdross, Alfred, Die immerwährende Neutralität der Republik Oesterreich. Vienna: Verlag für Geschichte und Politik, 1977.

Verdross, Alfred, 'Austria's Permanent Neutrality and the United Nations Organization', AJIL, Vol. 50 (1956), pp. 61–8.

Verplaetse, Julian G., 'The ius in bello and Military Operations in Korea, 1950–53', Zeitschrift für ausländisches öffentliches Recht und Völkerrecht, Vol. 23 (1963), pp. 679-738.

Vloyantes, John P., Silk Glove Hegemony: Finnish–Soviet Relations, 1944–74. Kent, Ohio: Kent State University Press, 1975.

Wagner, Ulrich, Finnlands Neutralität. Hamburg: C. von der Ropp, 1974.

Wainhouse, David W. et al., International Peace Observation. Baltimore, Md.: Johns Hopkins University Press, 1966.

Wainhouse, David W., International Peacekeeping at the Cross Roads. Baltimore, Md.: Johns Hopkins University Press, 1973.

Waldheim, Kurt, Der österreichische Weg aus der Isolation zur Neutralität. Vienna: Molden Verlag, 1971.

Welles, Sumner, Where Are We Heading? New York: Harper, 1946.

Welles, Sumner, Seven Decisions That Shaped History. New York: Harper, 1951.

Wettig, Gerhard, Entmilitarisierung und Wiederbewaffnung in Deutschland, 1943–55. Munich: R. Oldenburg, 1967.

Wildhaber, Luzius, 'Die Mitgliedschaft dauernd neutraler Staaten im UNO-Sicherheitsrat', Oesterreichische Zeitschrift für Aussenpolitik, (1971), pp. 130–45.

Williams, Walter L., Jr, 'Neutrality in Modern Armed Conflicts: A Survey of the Developing Law', Military Law Review, Vol. 90 (1980), pp. 9–48.

Wilson, Dick, The Neutralization of Southeast Asia. New York: Praeger, 1975.

Wilson, Hugh R., Switzerland: Neutrality as a Foreign Policy. Philadelphia, Pa.: Dorrance, 1974.

Woker, Daniel, Die skandinavischen Neutralen: Prinzip und Praxis der schwedischen und finnischen Neutralität. Bern: Paul Haupt, 1978.

Woyke, Wichard (ed.), Handwörterbuch Internationale Politik. Munich: Francke, 1988.

Wright, Quincy, A Study of War. Chicago, Ill.: University of Chicago Press, 1942.

Wright, Quincy, 'The Law of the Nuremberg Trial', *AJIL*, Vol. 41 (1947), pp. 38–72.

Wright, Quincy, 'Legal Positivism and the Nuremberg Trial', *AJIL*, Vol. 42 (1948), pp. 405–14.

Wright, Quincy, 'Collective Security in the Light of the Korean Experience', *Proceedings of the American Society of International Law*, (1951), pp. 165–82.

Wright, Quincy, 'Realism and Idealism in International Politics', *World Politics*, Vol. 5 (1952–3), pp. 116–28.

Wright, Quincy, 'The Outlawry of War and the Law of War', *AJIL*, Vol. 47 (1953), pp. 365–76.

Wright, Quincy, 'The Strengthening of International Law', *Hague, Recueil des Cours*, Vol. 98 (1959), pp. 1–295.

Yingling, Raymund T. and Robert W. Ginnane, 'The Geneva Conventions of 1949', *AJIL*, Vol. 46 (1952), pp. 393–411.

Young, Allen, *Swiss Neutrality in the Cold War*. New York: Columbia College, 1962.

Index